Karl Dilgskron

Life of Blessed Gerard Majella

Lay-Brother of the Congregation of the Most Holy Redeemer. Second Edition

Karl Dilgskron

Life of Blessed Gerard Majella
Lay-Brother of the Congregation of the Most Holy Redeemer. Second Edition

ISBN/EAN: 9783337289904

Printed in Europe, USA, Canada, Australia, Japan

Cover: Foto ©Lupo / pixelio.de

More available books at **www.hansebooks.com**

Blessed Gerard Majella.
C. SS. R.

Born 1726; Died 1755;
Beatified 1893; • Feast October 10th.

LIFE
OF BLESSED GERARD MAJELLA,

Lay-brother of the Congregation of the Most Holy Redeemer.

Translated from the German
Of Rev. Charles Dilgskron, C. SS. R.

SECOND EDITION.

By the Redemptorist Fathers, 173 E. 3d. St., New York.
1896.

This book may be had from all leading Publishers

LIFE OF BLESSED BROTHER GERARD,

of the Congregation of the Most Holy Redeemer.

Translated from the German Edition.

NIHIL OBSTAT.
T. L. Kinkead,
Censor Librorum.

IMPRIMATUR.
Michael Augustine,
Archbishop of New York.
May 6th, 1896.

APPROBATION.

By virtue of the authority granted me by the Most Reverend Mathias Raus, Superior General of the Congregation of the Most Holy Redeemer, I hereby sanction this edition of the Life of Blessed Brother Gerard, translated from the German.

It is my ardent desire that this book may spread devotion to Blessed Gerard, and inspire the hearts of the young with love for the religious vocation. May all who feel themselves called resolutely embrace the state of life, which however humble, Blessed Gerard has rendered so illustrious by his virtues.

FERD. A. LITZ, **C. SS. R.**
Provincial.

New York, April 26th, 1896.

Feast of our **Lady of Good Counsel.**

PREFACE TO THE FIRST GERMAN EDITION.

An abundance of **the most extraordinary operations** of divine **grace, set in the** frame of a **very ordinary** human life, **is** what is here presented to the reader.

The atmosphere of miracles, which he **enters who disdains** not to peruse these pages, will in no manner **mislead** the reader, provided he keeps constantly in mind the design of God in raising up souls **similar to the** Venerable Gerard Majella.

God's design does not aim simply at setting in the firmament of the Church, as new stars, those extraordinary beings who shall serve to increase the knowledge of "day and night," and point out the right course through the dangerous sea of this life; that is, God does not wish to raise up only such saints, who **by their efforts** and struggles and the clear manifestation **of their soul's** life in every particular may serve as models for instruction and imitation. God's design is a loftier one, showing forth, in these vessels of grace, in an unmistakable and even palpable manner, His continued presence and working in the Church; and by means of heavenly ornaments, exhibiting this Spouse of **the** Holy Ghost in all her grandeur and majesty.

As our Lord, in the beginning of His Church sought, by the glory of His miracles and those of His Apostles, to attract the attention of men and to make them acknowledge "*Here is the truth because here is omnipotence;*" so He also acts, and shall act, continually to the end of time, for the benefit of future generations.

He permits saints to appear who stand forth like supernatural beings, in whom miracles become in a certain sense personified, and who force us to acknowledge that "*There is the finger of God.*"

These saints are to us arguments for our holy faith rather than models for imitation. They are the visible signs of God's spirit invisibly operating in His Church. They are the fulfilment of the prophecy of the Redeemer: "And these signs shall follow them that believe; in my name, they shall cast out devils, they shall speak with new tongues, they shall take up serpents, and if they drink any deadly thing it shall not hurt them, they shall lay their hands upon the sick and they shall recover." (Mark XVI; 17, 18.)

Such saints are the bridal ornaments of the Church of which only she can boast, and, in which she can not be imitated in the remotest degree by any of the heretical sects.

The appearance of these highly privileged souls has for its first object the awakening of faith, of conviction, of enthusiasm for our holy religion, and of that sentiment which our enemies so fondly and so absurdly call, the fanaticism of the Catholic Church. Besides, by these specially gifted members are often healed the partial injuries done to the Church, which require the services of extraordinary physicians; sometimes, they are needed to enkindle the fire of zeal in a particular part of God's Kingdom, or to put the seal of divine approval on a recently established sacred institution.

Keeping these things in view, the Catholic reader will find in the life of the servant of God, Gerard Majella, nothing strange or repulsive, notwithstanding the superabundance of what is wonderful. To the infidel, as well as to those under the erroneous impression that the Church is merely a human institution, and not a divine organism, vivified by the divine spirit, the history of the life of Brother Gerard will certainly appear to be only a fable and a tissue of lies; to the believer however, it will afford a new argument for truth; a consolation and strength in the exercise of faith. He will meditate with edification on the virtues of the saintly young man, especially the virtues of humility and heroic obedience, and will reflect with salutary astonishment on the great number of wonderful gifts which the Lord designed to bestow upon him.

A touching spectacle will be to him the poor lay-brother, who, with the greatest simplicity and the most childlike innocence accomplished an extraordinary design of God.

Called by the Lord, even in the days of his childhood, Gerard obeys the divine voice with the most astonishing zeal; steadily and rapidly growing in spirit under the pressure of all kinds of sufferings and trials, he manifests himself, under the influence of grace, a worker of miracles, a prophet, a theologian, a director of souls, and a man of God.

Wherever he goes, he revives languishing piety, enkindles ardent faith, enlivens Christian Charity, rescues innumerable souls from destruction. To his country, he is an ornament, and to the recently established Congregation of Saint Alphonsus, a support. After a few years, he is called from the earth leaving behind him the splendor of his miracles. This is truly a life which manifests the power of grace! It is the happy consummation of one of those designs of God which are conceived for the salvation of those who say: "Oh Lord I believe! help my unbelief!" The reader is, however, justified in asking the question, whether the narration of so wonderful a life can lay claim to full credibility? To this we can answer most decidedly in the affirmative. The sources from which is drawn the history contained in these pages, are of such a nature, that there cannot be the least doubt as to their genuineness and authenticity.

In regard to the history of Gerard's life and miracles, very many intelligent and truth-loving persons have given, under oath, their testimony contained in the "Acts relative to the Beatification and Canonization,"— Acts from which the highest ecclesiastical authorities have formed the judgement that the Venerable servant of God practised the Christian Virtues in a heroic degree. These declarations, being pure and genuine sources, must be of the highest value to the historian.

Of not less importance and value are to the reader the two lives of the Servant of God written by Fathers Anthony Tannoja and Joseph Landi. Father Tannoja, the well known, exact, and conscientious biographer of St. Alphonsus, not only lived in the Congregation with the servant of God, but also had opportunities to observe him more closely, and perfectly to discern his spirit. The little book he wrote of him, and in which he recorded with his usual care the most important events of his life, was published in 1804.

Even before Father Tannoja, Father Landi had taken up his pen in behalf of the saintly brother. He, too, could speak from personal observation; still his work, though finished in the year 1870, was never published, and exists only in MSS.

From the following three sources, later biographers have principally drawn their materials, viz: from Father Celestine Berruti; then from the author of the Life of the Servant of God, published in Rome in 1875; (Compendio della vita del V. Gerardo Majella della Congregazione del SS. Redentore e narrazione di molte grazie miracolose operate da Dio ad intercesione del Venerabile,) and, lastly, from the Author of the French Life, published in 1878: "Life of the Venerable Gerard Majella." (Vie du Venerable Gerard Marie Majella Frère servant de la Congregation du Très Saint Rédempteur par, un Pére Rédemptoriste (Fred. Kuntz.) The latter author, by a careful and critical use of the above-mentioned sources, was able to furnish a work which may be regarded complete in every sense, especially as he sought to establish the correct chronological order of events, to which slight attention had been paid by the other authors.

As regards the present history of the life of the Venerable Gerard, it is also taken from the "Acts of Beatification" and the notes of Father Tannoja. **(Father Landi's work was not** so accessible to the author) yet strict regard was paid to the French life above mentioned, from which we have borrowed the order of **events, as well as several other incidents** not elsewhere mentioned, and **from** which we did not depart in any essential point.

The short notices relative to the Congregation of the **Most Holy** Redeemer **and a few of** its prominent members, interwoven **in the narrative** of the Life of Gerard are **taken from the "Croniche** della **Congregazione** del SS. Redentore," written by Father **Alexander de Risio** C.SS.R., now Archbishop of San Severino.

Every **one may now read** this book with the **assurance that what he has before him** has been drawn from **trustworthy sources, which have several** times been **subjected to a rigorous examination.**

Besides, as is required by the Holy See, we here declare, that to the Acts recorded as miracles and as having been performed by the Servant of God, simple human faith should be ascribed, and in regard to them, we do not wish that the judgement of the Church should be anticipated.

The same **remark** must hold good with **respect to the** names *Blessed* and *Saint* used in this book, so far **as they are given to persons who are not yet** honored **by the Church with these titles.**

May this book contribute to the honor of God, and the glory of His Servant Gerard!

May the reader while tasting the sweet kernel not become displeased with the bitter shell that surrounds it.

CHARLES DILGSKRON, C.SS.R.

Vienna, Church of Our Lady of the Strand, Feast of the Sacred Heart of Jesus, 1879.

PREFACE TO THE SECOND GERMAN EDITION.

In concluding the first edition of the life of the Venerable Brother Gerard we expressed the hope that the servant of God would soon be honored on our altars. This hope has been realized; Leo XIII., now gloriously reigning has solemnly numbered Gerard Majella among the Blessed, and sanctioned his public veneration with the usual restrictions. The fulfilment of our hope allows us to publish a new edition of the life of the Blessed Brother. We do this with the consoling conviction that this new edition will be perused with greater interest by the reader, since the subject of this biography now belongs to those whom every faithful Catholic is, not to say bound, but at least disposed to regard with especial sympathy and veneration.

Whilst reminding the reader that the remarks prefixed to the first edition apply equally to the second, we desire to add an observation which is especially called for by this edition. The reader will not only find in it many corrections that explain themselves, but also several material changes, principally in regard to the chronological sequence of events; and the changes demand a satisfactory explanation. In regard to these changes, we make the following observations:

When the first edition **of the life of** Blessed Gerard was **written, the material as** well as the chronological order **of** events **had** to be drawn from the oldest sources then obtainable, namely the writings of Fathers Tannoja **and** Landi. These first biographers **of the** Blessed Brother had made use of the notes of Father Cajone, Gerard's last confessor, which this Father had collected immediately after the Brother's death by the order of St. Alphonsus. They did not make direct use of these notes which were not published at the **time for** good reasons, and were afterwards entirely forgotten. They made use of a more compendious work of Father Cajone, in which he reproduced **the** contents of his original notes, but without strict accuracy regarding the chronological order of facts and many other details. The consequence was that in regard to chronology and several circumstances, errors crept into the works of Fathers Tannoja and Landi. By a happy coincidence the original notes of Father Cajone, so long forgotten, were lately discovered; and it became possible to cor**rect** the inaccuracies of those biographers, and to rectify **the chronological** order of facts. This, therefore, is the reason for the material changes, which the reader finds in this new edition.

May the second edition meet with the same favorable reception as the first, and procure for the Blessed **Brother** many friends, clients and imitators.

Rome, Convent of St. Alphonsus. On the Feast of the **Purification of** Our Blessed Lady, 1893.

FATHER CHARLES DILGSKRON.

PREFACE TO THE ENGLISH TRANSLATION.

Ever since the Church has decreed to Blessed Brother Gerard the honor of her altars, devotion to him has spread widely in this country. This increase is largely due to the confidence in his intercession which the miraculous character of his life cannot fail to inspire. Few saints of the last century were more favored with extraordinary gifts than the humble lay-brother of the Congregation of the Most Holy Redeemer.

Man is always impressed by the marvellous and extraordinary; it is therefore to be expected that he who was so highly favored by God, should also be greatly honored by men. Wherever the virtues of the holy brother are extolled and published, the demand for a complete biography of Brother Gerard becomes universal. It is to comply with this demand that the present edition of Blessed Gerard's life is offered to the public.

We hope that it will increase in the reader's heart the love of Our Lord and of His Blessed Mother, which was the source of Gerard's holiness. May he still extend his tender sympathy and efficacious intercession to those who confidently invoke him.

THE REDEMPTORIST FATHERS.
173 East Third Street,
New York City.

LETTERS APOSTOLIC

In Reference to the Beatification of the Ven. Servant of God Gerard Majella, Lay-Brother of the Congregation of the Most Holy Redeemer.

LEO XIII.

For a Perpetual Remembrance.

Innocence of life, which is so very pleasing to the heavenly Lamb Who feedeth among the lilies, can with truth be called the foundation of all Christian virtues. Wherefore, among the number of the most renowned heroes of God's church, have always been counted those who have preserved untarnished the white robe of innocence received in Baptism; and, strenuously repelling the wily attacks of the common foe, have preserved the first years of their youth in purity and holiness, although subject to so many evil inclinations and surrounded by so many grave dangers. These angelic youths Whom God prevented with the blessings of His sweetness, preserving the prerogatives of divine grace with unshaken fortitude amidst the trials and troubles of this world,—these youths, I say, shine as beautiful lights, and serve in these important times to the Christian people, as models and examples. Among these holy youths may justly be classed the Venerable Servant of God, Gerard Majella, professed lay-brother of the Congregation of the Most Holy Redeemer, who, following the footsteps of St. Aloysius and St. Stanislaus, seems to be an angel from heaven come among men, and who has been to the aforesaid Congregation, already renowned for its merit, a most beautiful example and ornament.

The servant of God was born at Muro, in 1726, of honest and pious parents, and received in Baptism the name of Gerard. From his very youth it was his delight to study piety, integrity of morals, and to practise obedience towards his parents. Therefore he abstained from all frivolous plays and sinful occupations, and employed his time in heavenly things, especially in meditating on the sufferings of Christ, before a crucifix which he had erected in his garden. Next to God he loved the Blessed Virgin Mary, and as soon as he was able to do so, he journeyed through the rough streets to the Holy House of the Mother of God. Not far from the city there was a little chapel erected in honor of the Blessed Virgin Mary, commonly called "Captignagno," and there he would venerate the statue of the Blessed Virgin, holding the Infant Jesus in her arms. Kneeling in the chapel before the altar one day imploring the help of the Infant Jesus and His divine Mother with fervent supplication, wonderful to relate, the Divine Child left the arms of His mother and hastening towards Gerard and embracing him, handed him a beautiful loaf of white bread. Gerard was beside himself with joy, and filled with celestial happiness he remained in the embrace of the Infant Jesus for some time. Having been favored with such great condescension on the part of God, and presented with the wonderful bread by the Holy Child, Gerard now turned his thoughts towards the Most Blessed Sacrament of the altar. Burning with desire to receive this heavenly bread he hastened to the church. It happened that a priest was distributing Holy Communion to some of the faithful. Gerard urged by his ardent desire, pressed foward and joined those who were to receive. The priest, however, noticing the child beckoned him to depart. Overcome with shame, and with tears in his eyes, he left the Holy Table only to beseech God the more fervently to grant his prayer; nor was his petition in vain. That same evening while Gerard was praying in his little room, St. Michael whom he highly venerated, appeared to him surrounded by a most radiant light and coming near administered to **him** the Holy Communion and transported him to the heavenly choirs. The pious youth in the embrace of his beloved Jesus was filled with joy, as **though he** were already in heaven possessing the celestial **vision of God.** Henceforth all his thoughts and cares were directed towards overcoming all obstacles in the acquirement of virtue. By means of penance **and** purity of heart; by watching and fasting and **cruel** scourging, he strove to subdue his flesh. Meanwhile his parents had nothing more at heart than that Gerard should be educated in the liberal arts, to which he also applied himself with such zeal that he was a model and example to all. The **death** of his father, however, which occurred soon after, interrupted his course of studies. Confronted by poverty, his mother was obliged to put Gerard to work. Therefore she **apprenticed him to a** tailor, and here according to the will and permission of God, the pious youth **had** ample opportunity to practise patience.

One of **the** foremen of the tailor-shop, a wicked, unjust man, and prone to anger, who hated the youth on account of his piety, besides overwhelming him with abusive language, often laid hands on him and cruelly beat him. Gerard, however, bore this cruel treatment with a cheerful mind and for the love of God. The cruel and unjust treatment only ceased when the wicked man himself recognized the sanctity of **the** youth. **Gerard** now besought God with fervent prayers and pious supplications, that He might make known to him His Holy Will as to what kind of vocation he should follow. It happened that the Redemptorist Fathers came to Muro **to conduct** the exercises of a mission. Gerard recognizing **their piety** and virtue asked to be received among **their number.** On account of **the** poor health of the **young man, the** superior refused to accede to his wishes, which refusal Gerard bore with patience. But, finally, discarding the prayers and petitions of his mother, and firm in his resolve, he fled from home, and hastening to the Fathers who were just departing after the close of the mission, he overtook them and again overwhelming them with his prayers and petitions to be admitted as a member, the Superior finally, by the inspiration of Divine Providence, received him, and he was placed among the lay-brothers. Freed from all the cares and distractions of the world he now began his novitiate, and strove in the holy house of God, — the cloister, to advance in the way of sanctity. Appointed sacristan, he fulfilled his duties in a most perfect manner and spent whole hours, day and night, in adoration before the Most Blessed Sacrament. As Almoner he visited, on foot, the neighboring villages and environs, everywhere exhibiting the brightest examples of patience and charity. With the greatest patience and zeal for souls he strove to bring back the wicked from their evil ways, and with glowing words to exhort them to the practice of virtue and piety; to the sick and poor he rendered all possible assistance. Nor were his labors in vain, for very many were brought back to the path of virtue and integrity of morals. Filled with the spirit of God, he seemed to be actuated by divine rather than human power, and hence he was commonly called an apostle. His novitiate being now over, he pronounced his religious vows in 1752, on which occasion he returned most fervent thanks to God, promising, with the divine assistance, in the future to make still greater progress on the road to perfection. When appointed janitor he exclaimed with joy on receiving the keys of the convent: "Behold the keys of paradise" — and the virtues which he practised in that position have certainly merited for him the happiness of heaven. As porter, the Servant of God was most solicitous and exact in the observance of the rules and in the practice of fraternal charity. He often shared his own meals with others, imparting to them at the same time some timely advice, and encouraging them to place all their hopes in their heavenly Father, Who giveth to all abundantly. God Who loves the humble heart, was pleased to confirm this admirable charity of Gerard by miracles. On account of the want of grain and the hard times, the inhabitants of that place were eking out a miserable existence. In order to relieve such a want, the pious servant of God opened the store-room of the convent, and gave to the needy the necessary assistance. The Superior of the convent being worried at this, reprimanded him; but wonderful to relate, the store-room was never empty and bread was never wanting in the dining-room. This marvelous event caused the servant of God to be held in high veneration and to be called a saint. Wherever he went the people received him with joy; they looked upon him as one come from heaven, and they desired much to hear him speak. Although not a man of learning he was nevertheless enlightened from on high, and by his simple way of speaking could move the hearts and the minds of men; he could moreover solve even the most difficult questions proposed to him. Already ripe for heaven, the end of his life was drawing near, and he himself foretold that he would soon die. In the month of June 1755 he was seized with a mortal illness; he made his confession, received the Holy Viaticum and Extreme Unction. When about to depart this life, suddenly raising himself he exclaimed: "Behold the Virgin is coming." and seeing the mother of God who came to visit him, he fell into ecstasy, and like a seraph for a little while enjoyed the delights of heaven. Soon after, repeating again the Holy Names of Jesus and Mary, he peacefully rendered up his pure soul to God — at the age of 29 yrs. 7 mos. and 7 days. The fame of his sanctity which was spread far and wide, was much increased by the miracles which God wrought through his intercession. For this reason the Cause of the life and virtues of the Venerable Servant of God was brought before the most eminent Cardinals of the Holy Roman Church of the Sacred Congregation of Rites, and all things having been submitted to a careful examination, Pius IX. of blessed memory, on June 8th, 1877, pronounced the virtues of Gerard heroic. Later on, the miracles wrought through the intercession of the Venerable Servant of God, which confirmed his heroic virtues, were taken into account, and upon thorough examination four of them were declared authentic. We issued a decree as to their authenticity on March 25th of the past year. One thing still remained, namely, that the Most Eminent Cardinals of the aforesaid Sacred Congregation of Rites should be asked whether they thought it proper or opportune, to place the Servant of God among the Beatified, and in a general session held by us on April 26th of the past year, they all unanimously declared that the Process of Beatification could safely be begun. The event however, being of such great importance, we hesitated until with fervent prayers we should ask the divine assistance. This having been done on the 8th day of September of the present year, the day consecrated to the Nativity of the Blessed Virgin Mary, we solemnly decided that the cause of the Beatification of the Servant of God could safely be introduced. Therefore, in accordance with the most fervent petition of the clergy of the Congregation of the Most Holy Redeemer, with the advice and consent of the aforesaid Congregation of Cardinals, by these apostolic letters, we hereby decree that the Venerable Servant of God, Gerard Majella, professed lay-brother of the Congregation of the Most Holy Redeemer should be henceforth numbered among the Beatified, and that his relics may be exposed for veneration to the faithful at large, and that his pictures may be surmounted with rays. We hereby also permit the recitation of the Office of the Venerable Servant and the Celebration of **the** Mass de Commune Confessoris non Pontificis, with the Oration proper as approved by us according to **the** rubrics of the Missal and the Roman Breviary. The recitation of the Office and celebration of **Holy** Mass is however permitted only in the cities and dioceses of Muro and Conza, and in all the chapels and churches of the priests of the Congregation of the Most Holy Redeemer. Furthermore, that Holy Mass may be celebrated in honor of the Beatified by all the clergy secular or regular, who happen to sojourn in a place where the feast of the Beatified is commemorated. Finally, we hereby permit that with the consent of the Ordinary, the Solemnities of the Beatification of the Venerable Servant of God, may be **celebrated** with holy Mass and divine Office of double rite in all the aforesaid churches and chapels of the Congregation of the Most Holy **Redeemer.** This celebration is to take place within the space of one year after the Solemn Beatification of the Servant of God has been celebrated by us in the Vatican Basilica. **We** wish, moreover, that copies of this apostolic brief, if duly signed by the secretary **of the** aforesaid Sacred Congregation of Rites and sealed with the seal of the Prefect of said Congregation, that **such copies should** enjoy the same amount of credence and authority as **the original which** was published by us.

Given at St. Peter's, Rome, under the Fisherman's Ring, December 6th, 1892, the 15th of our Pontificate.

SERAPH CARD. VANUTELLI.

CHAPTER I.

THE HIGHLY FAVORED CHILD.

In Basilicata, a province of the kingdom of Naples, on a slope of the Appennines, in a most charming spot, lies the little town of Muro. A row of hills protects it from the rough storms of the north, while toward the south a vast smiling and fertile plain is stretched out before it. At the time of which we write, it had a population of seven thousand, and it was not only an Episcopal see, but gave shelter to a large number of monks and nuns. In the course of centuries there came forth from this pretty little town many able men, who shed lustre on their native place by the splendor of their piety, their reputation for learning, as well as by the laurels which they had won on the battle-field. Perhaps there was never born in Muro one [1] that was **destined to** become the joy of its native place in so extraordinary a manner as the child whose wonderful life we have undertaken to write. He was born on the 6th of April, 1726,[2] and was baptized on the same day, **in** the cathedral, by the Archpriest Felix Coccicone.

The Blessed Gerard Mary Majella may be said to be one of the grandest phenomena of the Church of the eighteenth century.

He is in fact one of the purest and most **cultivated** flowers in the garden of the Catholic Church, one of those

---

[1] Besides Gerard Maria Majella, we know only the Venerable Dominic Gerardelli, a Conventual, the cause of whose **beatification** has been begun.

[2] **Thus** according to the acts in **the** process of beatification. According to the testimony of the present bishop of Muro, Monsignor Rafaele Capone this date does **not agree** with that given in the statistics. There the 23rd of April is given as the birthday of Blessed Gerard.

great, incomprehensible souls, whose deeds, miracles, and life constitute an uninterrupted intercourse with heaven. He is one of those brilliant stars that appear from time to time in the firmament of the Church, and usually exercise a powerful and salutary influence over men whom the night of infidelity threatens to overtake.

His cradle swayed in a very modest house. Gerard's parents, Dominic Majella, who was a tailor by trade, and Benedicta Galella, were indeed rich in heavenly gifts, and highly esteemed by their townsmen for their virtuous lives; but they were very poor in this world's goods, and were obliged to support four children, Bridget, Anne, Elizabeth and Gerard by the work of their hands.

God provided most lavishly for Gerard, from the beginning of his life. He, as it were, put upon his first steps and movements the mark of His special and extraordinary predilection. His countenance always appeared sweet and calm, so that all persons gazed on him with pleasure. Among the first words that he uttered were the Holy names of Jesus and Mary; and one of his first actions was to make the sign of the Cross on his forehead, mouth, and breast.

When he was six years old, he was so intelligent and zealous in exercises of piety that one could have supposed him to be much older. In spite of his precocity, however, he preserved the tenderness and sweetness of his years. He did not like the amusements of children; his recreation consisted in making little altars, which he adorned with flowers and pictures, in erecting small crosses, and in doing other similar things, by which he wished to imitate the ceremonies of the Church. He took delight in singing hymns while gazing upon the pictures of God's chosen servants. Another enjoyment was to bend the knee, thus proving his constant communion with God. When he succeeded in obtaining fragments of wax from one of his relatives, who was sacristan of the cathedral, he made little candles, which he burned on his altar. Sometimes he would gather children around him, lead them in procession and teach them to pray and sing.

This highly favored child became so fond of prayer, that he was able to devote whole hours to it. He was sometimes discovered in some hiding-place of his father's house, rapt in familiar intercourse with God, quite estranged from this world, like one transported to another sphere. When he was with his mother at church, he knelt so quietly, so modestly, and so devoutly, that he edified everybody and was looked upon by all persons as an angel from paradise. He was scarcely six years old when our Lord manifested Himself to him in a most **loving manner.**

Near the little town of Muro, at a distance of about half a mile, there is a small, solitary church, dedicated **to our** Lady of Capotignagno, which, in spite of the stony and rough road leading to it, was, and is even now a favorite resort of the faithful. In this church is venerated a small wooden statue representing the Blessed Virgin with the Infant Jesus in her arms. Gerard soon became acquainted and familiar with this popular sanctuary, and felt himself powerfully attracted to it. One day he went there alone in order to relieve his glowing heart. Scarcely had he begun to pray, when it seemed to him that the Infant and His Mother on the altar became animated, and that the former stretched out His arms as if longing for his approach. In fact, a moment after, the Infant Jesus stood before him in all His heavenly loveliness, and with a smile invited him to play with **Him. After a** short time of most wondrous play, the **Infant gave Gerard** a loaf of fine, snow-white bread, and **disappeared.** The highly favored boy immediately ran home, and with an **air of triumph** showed the bread to his mother. When asked who had given **it to him, he** answered: "The **dear little son** of a beautiful lady gave it to me."

Such an experience allowed the boy no rest; thenceforth, he often hastened to **the** holy chapel of our Lady of Capotignagno, as if a regular place of meeting had been agreed upon between himself and the wonderful child. In fact, he had the happiness of often seeing him, and of receiving from him presents of the same excellent bread. This strange white bread which Gerard always brought home was so mysterious a gift, that it **excited the curiousity of his** mother and sisters and induced them to investigate the matter. The mother, and **later his sister Anne,** undertook the investigation and **secretly followed** him hurrying to church, where, while **they quietly watched him,** they witnessed a most mysterious as well as a most touching spectacle.

It appears that Gerard sometimes received bread not **from** the child, but from the Blessed Virgin. At least he expressed himself in a way that such a fact may be **supposed.** For when he again visited his favorite church with his mother, he pointed to the statue of our Lady **with the** divine Infant and said: "See, mother, there is the noble lady who sometimes gave me bread, and there is the child with whom I used to play."

A favor similar to that which he had received in the church of our Lady of Capotignagno, was also bestowed **on Gerard in his favorite** resort, the garden of the Archpriest **De Cillis.** He had one day led a number of **children to the garden,** and while engaged in his devotion **before a simple cross,** made of pieces of wood rudely put together and fastened to an almond-tree, there suddenly appeared a brilliant light among the branches. So remarkable was this light that it was seen by many who were outside of the garden, although they saw nothing except the unusual light. Not so Gerard: he saw in the middle of this light the well-known, beautiful child, and **that he was** coming down from the tree and moving towards him. The divine child having reached the ground came to him and gave him a piece of white bread, and Gerard ate it. But his mother who noticed that on his return he did not wish to eat the food which she had kept for him, asked him for an explanation. He innocently said to her, "Mother I have already eaten; the child gave me some bread."

When he attended the Holy Sacrifice of the Mass, he also repeatedly noticed that the priest held in his hands a beautiful child; and it was for him a very strange thing to see the priest after breaking it in pieces put it into his mouth and eat it. On one occasion after witnessing the same spectacle; he said in childlike wonder to the priest who had returned from the altar to the sacristy: "Ah! you have done something beautiful; indeed, you have eaten a little child."

At that time Gerard did not as yet perfectly know who the child was that exercised so powerful an influence over him; but at a subsequent period these heavenly favors were made clear to him. Twenty years after these events he said with his usual simplicity to his sister Bridget, who had come to visit him when he had become a religious in the convent: "Now I know that it was the Infant Jesus Who gave me the bread when I was a child; then I believed that He was a **child** like other children." "Well then," answered his sister jockingly, "come back to Muro some day in order to visit the Madonna of Capotignagno and to find the beautiful child." "No" said Gerard, "**I need not go to Muro to find the** Madonna and her child; now I can see them **everywhere.**"

This unmistakable sign of divine predilection inspired his parents with the desire to bring up, as carefully as possible, the child whom they regarded as a divine treasure which had been confided to them. Benedicta who well knew, as she expressed herself, "that her son was created only for heaven," neglected nothing that might assist in developing in his heart the seeds of virtue. It was also not difficult to direct the education of a child who showed himself docile in all things, and who by nature was desirous to hear others speak of divine things rather than of things of this world.

When Gerard was seven or eight years old, he was sent to a school, over which Donato Spicci, a relative of his family, presided. Here he very soon learned how to read and write, and express himself with facility. In a short time he served as a model to his school-fellows, and became the favorite of his teacher. Spicci called him "the delight of his soul," and loved him with the tenderness of a father. The experienced master detected very soon that the boy possessed the talent of instructing others and of influencing them encouragingly. He therefore took pleasure in employing him to teach the smaller or weaker children the rudiments of knowledge.

Gerard, however, always remained the simple and obedient child who was attentive to every command of his parents, rendering them the most exact obedience. In consequence of his wonderful intercourse with heaven, there were early developed in him an uncommon desire for mortifying his own body, and such a charity towards his poor neighbor that he was always ready to assist him. Hence, he frequently fasted on bread and water, and with this meagre fare was still so abstemious that it was a marvel how he could live at his tender age, when he was so much in need of proper nourishment. Many a day he did not break his fast, and not unfrequently he forgot entirely to take his meals, during three successive days. It often happened that his mother, who usually went out to **work** early in the morning, found, on her return, that the bread which she had left for Gerard's dinner had not been touched. But the food thus saved and the bread which his mother occasionally gave him, he generally distributed among the poor children. Nevertheless, he would not refuse to eat when commanded by his parents; for he was as free from self-will in regard to mortifying himself as he was in regard to all other things. This is the surest sign that he was animated by the right spirit. He had so great a fear of offending his parents, that if against his will and without his fault, offence was given, he did all in his power to make amends for the wrong done. This fear also gave occasion to one of the first miracles that were wrought through him. The object of it was a little lamb which had been intrusted to Gerard's care and which disappeared one morning. After diligent search had been made, it **was** found out that thieves **had** stolen the lamb and slaughtered it. As the lamb was not the property of Gerard's parents and had **only** been confided to their safe-keeping, their grief was doubly great. Gerard was also greatly troubled. As he could not bear to see the grief of his parents, he **consoled them by saying:** "Be sure, dear parents, the lamb will return, the lamb will come back." He then began to pray, and firmly believed that God would aid him in his trouble and grant his petition. Soon after, the same animal that had been carried off and killed **was actually restored to its owner;** no one knew how such a wonderful thing had been accomplished.

That this highly favored child entertained a most **tender** love for the Blessed Virgin can excite no surprise, **if we reflect on** what has just been related. We **have already** heard that the holy name of Mary was **one of the first** words that **were uttered** by Gerard; **thus the love for the** Mother of divine grace was, as it were, born with him. As he grew older, this love increased rapidly and became most ardent, especially since the Madonna of Capotignagno had begun to exercise so charming an influence over his soul. The recital of the Rosary and other acts of devotion in honor of the Queen of heaven was easy and highly pleasing to him; and her festivals, for which he prepared himself by different pious exercises and works of penance, were for him happy days on which the members of his family saw him more joyful than usual, his eyes sparkling with delight. But Mary on her part bestowed on her little client greater marks of her affection. It was during the time of his early youth that Gerard was enabled to see Caposele for the first time, where at a later period, as a religious, he was to receive very many graces, and where he was to end his earthly career. His mother or a relative had taken him to this place to visit the sanctuary of the Blessed Virgin, venerated under the title of "Mater Domini" (Mother of the Lord). While he was praying before the holy image, and when he had offered the first salutation to our Lady, he fell into a very profound ecstasy — a most consoling spectacle to all who were present. Perhaps she permitted him to taste of the joys which are prepared for those who persevere in their devotion to her, or she gave him the assurance of her aid and protection, in which he firmly trusted throughout his earthly career. From Gerard himself we have received no explanation on this matter, as he concealed these mysteries unless obedience obliged him to speak of them, or his simplicity betrayed them.

But if the Blessed Virgin filled the heart of Gerard with the greatest joy and love, it may be imagined that this must have been done in a higher degree as regards the Blessed Sacrament. To the Holy Sacrifice of the Mass the boy hastened as other boys hasten to their

most favorite games. As soon as the priest raised the
consecrated host, he bent his body to the ground and
remained in that posture for a long time; yet the liveliness of his faith, which showed itself in his whole being, as well as in his childlike simplicity, never permitted
any one to discover in this unusual behavior anything
unnatural or affected. When, at the communion of the
priest, the sacred species disappeared, in which, as has
been related, he saw the form of a beautiful child, he
often burst into tears, occasioned by the mere thought
that he was as yet deprived of this heavenly food. He
had an indescribable longing for it, and to be refused
when he asked the priest's permission to gratify this
strong desire, was bitter and painful. But, one day,
Gerard was then about eight years old, — he could no
longer restrain this desire when he was hearing Mass
at the cathedral, and saw the faithful about to receive
Holy Communion. Following, therefore, as it were, a
divine attraction, he advanced to the altar and knelt
with other persons who intended to receive Holy Communion. The priest, however, did not comply with his
desire, and passed him by, as is usually done in the case
of any child that perchance has made its way to the
altar-railing.

Sad, and bathed in tears, Gerard returned home, and
as he could not hide his distress of mind, he expressed
it to several of his intimate friends; among them was
a certain Emanuela Vetromile, a woman who loved him
as her own son, and therefore endeavored, like a mother,
to console him in his sorrows. Meanwhile, our Lord
Himself undertook to bestow upon His faithful child
the most efficacious consolation. The following night
the boy saw an angel, whom he recognized to be his
dearly beloved patron St. Michael, who gave him the
divine food which the priest had refused him the day
before. It is related that the very morning on which

this occurred, Gerard communicated it with all simplicity to his dear friend Vetromile and cried out with great joy: "Yesterday the priest would not give me Holy Communion, and last night St. Michael gave it to me." More probably, Gerard did not make known this wonderful experience until after he had become a religious; that is, when he was obliged by obedience to give a true account of the special favors he had received from God. On this occasion he also spoke of the event narrated above, and remarked that his extraordinary devotion to the Archangel St. Michael began at that time.

This reception of Holy Communion from the hands of an angel seems not to have been the only one of the kind by which God gratified, in a marvelous way, the great desire of this favored child. One day a priest found him kneeling before the altar, and as this seemed to him very strange, he asked him what he was doing there. "A little child", he answered, "came out of the tabernacle and gave me Holy Communion."

It is easy to think that such occurrences inflamed the heart of the little saint with love for the most Blessed Sacrament, and with the desire to visit his hidden Lord as often as possible. "Come! let us visit Jesus Christ, our dear prisoner," he was often heard to exclaim when the ringing of the bells invited the faithful to visit the Blessed Sacrament. He would frequently slip away from the house during leisure hours, in order to hasten to the neighboring church of St. Mark where, without being disturbed, he could give vent to the feelings of his heart and devote himself to the exercise of contemplation, — a gift which was already manifesting itself.

At last, when he was nearly ten years old, his desire for Holy Communion was heeded, and he was allowed by his spiritual director to receive the Blessed Sacrament. Naturally the day on which he made his First

THE HIGHLY FAVORED CHILD. 31

Communion, was for him a day of great joy. His innocent heart, already sanctified by mortification and glowing with an ardent love, received its Lord with such dispositions that the Eucharistic food not only nourished his soul, but also caused him to feel its sweetness sensibly.

After receiving Holy Communion, the boy became quite immovable, as if in ecstasy, and during the long thanksgiving which he made the spectators viewed with pleasure the angelic glow which was seen on his countenance. From this time forward Gerard received Holy Communion every second day. In order always to approach this holy banquet with due preparation, he went to confession. To combine sacrifice with devotion he scourged himself with knotty cords which he had tied together.

CHAPTER II.

The Apprentice.

About the time of his first Holy Communion or shortly after, Blessed Gerard met with one of those calamities which during mortal life must be expected; and yet, when it befalls us, gives as much pain as if it were unforeseen. Death took away his good father and brought great destitution on the family. The widow Benedicta found that it was necessary to enable him, as soon as possible, to support himself and others of the household. She therefore apprenticed him to a tailor, that he might learn the trade of his father and become the support of the family. Of course, this event dispelled one of his pious dreams, for he had always thought of leaving the world and entering a convent in which he might, without hindrance, devote himself to the vocation to which he felt himself called. He had not the least inclination for a secular life. However, he was obedient and yielded without contradiction to his mother's wish, confident that God would dispose all things for the best.

His conduct in the workshop of his master Martino Pannuto, was in every respect so exemplary, that his employer was carried away with love and admiration for his apprentice. Gerard devoted himself to his trade with assiduity, and showed himself tractable, attentive and docile. His interior recollectedness was not the least impaired. While his hand was busy with the needle his mind was with God and engaged in divine things; while more than once it happened that on account of his absent-mindedness the work was interrupted. However, his master was too pious a man to be displeased by such interruptions. On the contrary, he allowed him to perform exercises of piety according to his wish, and rejoiced to have an apprentice who was a saint. He also learned by experience that Gerard always made up easily by quick work the time that had been lost by those interruptions. Moreover, Gerard's spirit of sacrifice and mortification, so rarely found in youth, only inspired him with the greatest confidence. Pannuto often worked until late in the night, and on these occasions the delicate boy was always at his side. The latter, who could not return home after his master had finally left the workshop, owing to the late hour of the night, would rest his weary limbs on the bare floor. When Pannuto noticed that Gerard did not use the bed prepared for him and questioned him in regard to the matter, he received the answer that for one who was a mere apprentice, the couch that he had chosen was better than a soft bed.

But quite different from the disposition of Pannuto was that shown towards the servant of God by the foreman of the workshop, a brutal, unprincipled man. The piety of Gerard was a thorn in his sight, and excited in his bosom a feeling of hatred. Every moment which the saintly apprentice spent in the church or in saying his prayers, the foreman believed to be an unwarrantable loss of time, that should be devoted to work; and on account of what he called Gerard's sloth and aversion for work, he daily heaped on him all kinds of abuse and reproaches. This was not all. Often the man became so enraged that he struck the boy with fist clinched and trampled on him. Gerard bore everything with great patience. Sometimes he said to himself: "My God! My God! Thy holy will be done;" and frequently, when the longing for suffering took stronger hold of him, he cried out to his tormenter: "Keep on striking me, you have indeed reason to do so." To complain of such treatment never entered his mind, though he would have been justified in doing so, and his master would, without doubt, have protected him; on the contrary he sought rather to conceal these things from him. On one occasion, after the ruffian had been beating him in a most cruel manner, so that Gerard fell to the floor, Pannuto entered the room. Seeing his apprentice in so pitiable a condition, he naturally asked his foreman for an explanation about what had happened. As the latter, however, on the one hand, could not say anything to justify himself, and on the other, knew that he could count on Gerard's silence, he briefly answered that Gerard would be better able to say what had befallen him. Pannuto then turned to Gerard and questioned him; but the servant of God, whose heart was as noble as it was truthful, said with holy simplicity: "Master, I fell down near the table." Thus, while making known the truth, though only half of it, he satisfied the inquirer, and at the same time spared the guilty foreman.

Such magnanimity did not, however, subdue the ruffianism of his enemy. The acts of brutality toward the poor apprentice were continued, and all the manifestations on his part of nobility of heart, as well as of the most sublime virtues, could not protect Gerard against them. When the latter, on one occasion, seemed pleased and began to laugh after receiving a blow which the foreman had given him with his fist, he was struck most unmercifully with a piece of iron, which the man had seized in his fury. The pain which he felt and which might have deprived him of consciousness, could not disturb his charity, so that as soon as he had recovered from the blow, he threw himself at the feet of his tormenter, and said with great meekness: "I forgive you for the love of Jesus Christ," and then applied himself

to his work as if nothing had happened. That Gerard
laughed when he was ill-treated, did not proceed from
a sense of mockery, as one might have believed, but it
was the result of a reflection, which at such a moment
is as rare, as it is worthy of a saint. He himself found
an opportunity of giving an explanation of this matter.

Having one day returned home rather late from his
favorite church of Capotignagno, he was assailed as usual with every kind of insult and abuse, and finally
beaten. He was silent and began to smile, which so ex-
asperated the ruffian that he cried out: "You are laughing! tell me instantly why you are laughing." "I laugh,"
answered Gerard, "because God's hand strikes me."

How long the persecution of the innocent apprentice
lasted, is not known. God, Who thereby only wished
to try His servant and prepare and purify him for
greater favors, took care that it should cease in proper
time, and so arranged matters that Pannuto, who had
certainly noticed the hatred which his foreman bore
towards the apprentice, but could not make up his mind
to dismiss him, was finally induced to do so. Without
Gerard's knowledge, he one day followed him to church
and watched the conduct of the apprentice in prayer.
He might indeed have expected that he would be edified,
but he was to be the witness of a scene which usually
moves the religious spectator profoundly and fills him
with the highest degree of respect and veneration. After
the boy had prayed for a long time, he lay prostrate on
the floor of the church and kissed it; then, while moving forward on his knees, he at the same time touched
his tongue to the ground till he reached the foot of the
altar.[1] Here he was again rapt in prayer, which be-

---

[1] This exercise of penance was not unusual in Southern Italy. It was practised chiefly by persons who were animated by a very ardent faith, for the purpose of atoning for sins of the tongue; it was also per-formed by those who, possessing a lively imagination, strongly desired by means of these signs of humility and contempt to express in a very sensible manner the affections of their heart.

came more and more ardent, until finally he fell into an ecstasy, and remained immovable and lost in God. Being greatly affected by what he had seen, Pannuto left the church. He knew now that his little apprentice was in high favor with God, and he no longer dared to tolerate in his house a man who did not fear to treat contemptuously and to consider as an outcast a youth so highly privileged by the Almighty.

The patient endurance of the ill-treatment received at the hands of the foreman was not the only example of heroic virtue which Gerard gave during his stay at the house of Pannuto, and of which we have received information. Pannuto's son, Joseph Anthony, at a later day, often related another incident of which he himself had been an eye-witness, and which affords no less proof of how deeply and firmly the virtue of patience was rooted in the boy's heart. Pannuto had on one occasion sent him to his vineyard to do some work, and Gerard after finishing it went for a moment to the sanctuary of Capotignagno, which was not very far distant. While returning to the city he crossed the fields and unfortunately approached a thorn-hedge on which some birds had alighted. These birds were eagerly pursued by a sportsman who closely lay in wait for them. Gerard, by his approach frightened the birds away, and thus bitterly disappointed the sportsman. Unable to control his anger, the latter rushed foward unexpectedly struck the saintly youth a violent blow in the face. When ordinary mortals are surprised, their virtues, especially those of patience and meekness are usually overcome; but this was not the case with Gerard. Becoming immediately recollected, and being mindful of the teaching of the Gospel, he delayed not in fulfilling it to the very letter, and at once offered his other cheek. But the angry sportsman, who very likely at this moment did not think of the Gospel, and who thought that this act of humility was but insolent mockery, became still more excited and continued to ill-treat his supposed insulter. Fortunately, at this time, Pannuto's son came upon the scene, and having made the necessary explanation he was able to pacify the infuriated man. In this he succeeded so well that the sportsman not only began to conceive the highest esteem for this boy, who was capable of practising so much virtue, but wherever he went, became the zealous panegyrist of of the virtuous apprentice.

If anything could vie with the wonderful patience which Gerard allowed to shine forth during his apprenticeship, it was his willingness to perform any labor at the command or desire of another. When at home he regarded the will of his parents as the will of God, and now he so regarded the will of his master. Pannuto only needed to manifest his wish and the boy flew, as it were, to fulfil it; on more than one occasion people could not help taking it for granted, that God gave wings to Gerards obedience, with which even the strongest will could not have supplied him, so marvelous was the promptness he showed when he fulfilled what had been commanded.

One evening in autumn, when the grapes were ripening, Pannuto went with Gerard to the vineyard at Boccaporta, in order to watch during the night and protect his fruit from thieves. While preparing the lamp which was to burn during the night, he found that there would not be sufficient oil. Gladly would he have sent for some to his own house, but he did not wish to fatigue the boy, who would have been obliged to undertake a rather long journey in the darkness of the night. Yet scarcely had Gerard remarked the perplexity and the wish of his master than he started of his own accord for the oil and came back in so short a time, that Pannuto doubted whether the boy had obtained it at his house in Muro. But, as the apprentice asserted that it was there that he had received it, he felt obliged to ascribe this astonishing celerity solely to a special help of God Who thereby wished to reward the boy.

At another time, it was the wife of Pannuto who was wonderfully assisted by a service quickly performed by Gerard. She had sent her husband's dinner to the vineyard where he was at work, and had forgotten to put a fork into the basket. Though this oversight was trifling, the good woman feared the displeasure of her husband and became greatly agitated and confused. Gerard noticing this consoled her, saying: "Be of good cheer, I will take the fork to your husband." He then set out, and although the servant had left the house long before, he reached Boccaporta at the same time, and was able, at the right moment, to rectify the mistake.

This surprising quickness in the performance of his duties was not the only sign by which Gerard's gift of miracles was made known in Pannuto's house.

Of the several other wonderful occurrences, of which this family was witness we shall mention only the following:

One night Gerard was to watch with Joseph Pannuto in the previously mentioned vineyard. In order to while away the time that was becoming tedious the pious apprentice took some reeds and rushes out of which he made a simple cross and said his prayers before it. Then he lighted a reed and walked with it as with a torch around the bundle of straw which was to serve as his bed, and chanted the Miserere.

Suddenly the straw caught fire. He came to himself only after an outcry of young Pannuto, who seeing the danger, burst into tears and said: "Oh what have you done, what have you done!" But Gerard quickly said "It is nothing; it is nothing;" and making the sign of the Cross, struck at the flames and quenched it at the moment when a general conflagration threatened.

CHAPTER III.
At The House Of The Bishop Of Lacedogna.

The feast of Pentecost A. D. 1740 occurred during the time when Gerard was busy in the workshops of Pannuto and was of the greatest importance for the pious youth, abounding as it did in the choicest graces. On this festival June 25th — he knelt in the chapel of the poor Clares at Muro before the bishop of Lacedogna, Monsignor Claudius Albini, who had been delegated by the diocesan bishop, Melchior Delphico, to administer the sacrament of Confirmation. In the soul of the child that had already most faithfully employed the graces received in Baptism, the sacrament which completes and perfects Baptism, must naturally have borne fruit in the fullest measure. Hence the Holy Ghost, now became the master of the movements and aspirations of Gerard's heart. From this time forward he entertained an especially tender devotion toward the Holy Ghost, — a devotion which continued till the end of his life; and of the fervor of which, those who became his brethren later, used to narrate the most touching traits. "No day passed," these are the very words of a narrator — "not even an hour, during which Gerard did not invoke the aid of the Holy Ghost; and this was not omitted whether he himself needed good advice, or if others asked him to give it. On the feast of Pentecost he was seen to have so joyful and glowing a countenance, that he was like one who is unable to repress the delight that is inwardly moving him. The days preceeding this festival he spent in penance, by fasting on bread and water, by

scourging himself, and similar mortifications; and he **prepared himself for** this day with so much fervor, that **it seemed he would** be able, with the fire that inflamed **him, to** enkindle even the most tepid soul, if it had approached him."

One of the principal fruits resulting from his reception of the sacrament of Confirmation, **was** evidently the vehement and more decided yearning for the religious life, as well as the longing for the time when he might devote himself in as perfect a manner as possible to the service of God. Soon after, he made his first attempt **to be** admitted into **a** convent; he was unsuccessful because the time in which he was to complete his sacrifice in conformity with God's holy will, had not yet arrived.

In the neighborhood of Muro, the Capuchin Fathers **occupied a** small convent, called San Menna. On this convent Gerard had set his heart; for he was not only pleased **with** the simplicity, humility and seclusion reigning in this house, but he hoped that he would more easily gain admission there than elsewhere, because one of its inmates, Father Bonaventure, a learned and much esteemed theologian was his uncle. He therefore presented himself to **the** Father Guardian of the **convent, and begged to be admitted among the novices. The Superior,** however, could not make up his mind to receive him even on trial, either because he did not put **much faith in the stability of the young man's resolutions** and ascribed this request to the pressure of poverty and **a desire** to find employment, or to an exaggerated **piety rather than a true** vocation; **or** perhaps he **did not think him** strong **enough for the** religious life on **account of his** delicate frame and appearance. **In refusing Gerard's** request, the Father Guardian **mentioned this last objection.** Greatly disheartened by **this disappointment in his hope of** ever working out his salvation within **the sacred walls of** a convent, he was about to **leave the house;** but, in order to console him in some **measure and to** give him at the same time a suitable alms, his uncle, Father Bonaventure, made **him a present of a new coat. To the heart** of the young **man, who** usually thought **more of the** poverty of others **than of his own,** this gift was a consolation only **in so far as it** would enable him to console another who might be in want. Gerard had scarcely left the convent when a wretched beggar, clad in rags met him, and **in most piteous** tones besought an alms. The request **for help had** not to be repeated for it was asked of one **who had just met** with affliction, and who was therefore doubly **inclined to perform an act of** charity. Gerard quickly took **off the new coat which** Father Bonaventure had given him **and** presented it to the poor man. **This act** did **not remain hidden; it was made** known in the Capuchin convent, and Gerards uncle, as we may easily suppose, was not entirely satisfied with the great **liberality shown by his** nephew. He sent for him, and **made him feel his displeasure by a severe** reprimand. **The** young man **listened to the rebuke** with great humility, but deemed it his duty to say a word in self-defence. "**Ah! my** dear uncle," said he, "do not be angry with me; you did not see how naked the poor **man was to** whom I gave the coat, and how much more **he needed it** than I; had you seen him he would have **moved you to** the same act of charity." These **were** words that so strongly suggested the memory of the **saint of** Assisi, and were spoken so much in accordance **with his spirit, as not** to permit **Father** Bonaventure to say anything **in reply.** The Capuchin was silent, being edified by the behavior of his nephew, whose soul was animated by sentiments so holy and so noble.

Though Gerard had been unsuccessful in his efforts to begin **a life of self-denial and** of sacrifice in the silence of a convent, yet his self-sacrificing soul found sufficient compensation in the many opportunities he met to practise these virtues in a heroic degree. It was a year after his confirmation when Gerard was asked by the bishop of Lacedogna to become a servant in his house.

Monsignor Claudius Albini had become acquainted with Gerard and learnt to esteem him, not only when he administered the sacrament of Confirmation in the chapel of the Poor Clares, where the singular devotion and piety of the youth had made a favorable impression on him, but it was far more the good reputation that had spread throughout the city in regard to the young tailor that induced him to make choice of Gerard. Being a native of Muro he had heard, not without interest, of the boy's wonderful life, of his virtues, his piety, his humility, his unalterable patience and his unexampled obedience. Hearing all this from the lips of those who were able to watch the young man, as well as to form an opinion of him, he could not doubt the truth of what had been reported. He became very anxious to admit his saintly countryman into his house, and to have him as much as possible near him. In fact, the good prelate needed a saint to be his servant. Even those persons who are otherwise excellent, whom God employs in His church to do many of His great works, often have faults which, under certain circumstances gradually become unbearable. To this class belonged Monsignor Albini. He possessed so lively a disposition, was of so passionate a temper, that he often became enraged on account of the most trifling things; and then the treatment of his subjects was so harsh that they were not only grieved and humbled, but became embittered and discouraged. Hence there was a continual change of servants in his house, and no one was willing to enter the service of this ill-tempered master. When the proposal which had been made to Gerard became known, some of his friends hastened to dissuade him from engaging in such service by depicting in lively colors the daily drudgery to which he, who was so simple-hearted, would expose himself. But for Gerard, there was nothing that attracted him more than what they advanced in order to prevent him from accepting the offer. He joyfully consented, and exchanged Muro for Lacedogna, the tailor's workshop for the bishop's house.

Here he had to be the soul of the household; now he would be busy in the kitchen, again he would be at work in the rooms of the prelate, who, as he was not wealthy, had to restrict himself to what was absolutely necessary. But, wherever Gerard performed his work he showed zeal and assiduity and was extremely careful not to give his master any occasion for complaint, and not to excite his nervousness. True, he was not always successful in his efforts; in spite of all his care and readiness to serve he had to endure complaints, scolding and humiliation; and, much as Monsignor loved the pious servant in the innermost recesses of his heart, he yet overwhelmed him with most vexatious commands, and threatened to dismiss him from his service for trifling mistakes. On these occasions, the servant of God could be seen standing before his irate master with that amiable humble cheerfulness which is the fruit of meekness that holds in check and absolutely deadens every passion. He said not a word, but with eyes modestly cast down waited till the storm blew over. Then he continued to work without showing the least displeasure, as if no trouble had occurred, and a repetition of worry was not expected. Such was his humble and childlike disposition, that the thought of leaving his irascible and passionate master never entered his mind. When others, who were astonished at this power of endurance, asked him how he was able to bear with the repulsive manners of this prelate who had driven so many predecessors from the house, he usually excused his master and ascribed all the blame to his own awkwardness. "Monsignor loves me," he said; "I shall serve him with pleasure as long as he lives." Such sentiments were sufficient to suggest to the inhabitants of Lacedogna the thought that, in the new servant, a great saint had been given to them. Besides, they also saw that he was leading a very austere life, that he was practising the rarest virtues, and that he was in all things very superior to other persons.

In the episcopal house at Lacedogna, Gerard lived like a monk in his hermitage. The practices of piety to which he had accustomed himself in former days were continued with the greatest fervor, and they underwent only such changes as were required by his increased and enlightened virtue. Every morning he remained before the altar either to assist at the Holy Sacrifice of the Mass or to receive Holy Communion; and if during the day he had any spare moments he also employed them in visiting the Blessed Sacrament. This so edified the people, that they not only praised the devout young man, but cried out: "O happy Gerard! he is a great saint!" (Beato Gerardo che e' un gran santo!) and many, following his example, often visited the Blessed Sacrament during the day.

In regard to food, Gerard was as formerly, exceedingly moderate and austere. Dry bread and vegetables were considered by him sufficient; and whenever he received better food from the table of his employer, he gave it to the poor or carried it to the sick whom he greatly loved, as the suffering members of Christ. During his stay at Lacedogna he had poor health and frequently suffered great pain, which he however bore with the patience and joy peculiar to himself, and which he even tried to increase. Dr. Dominic Lamorte one day met Gerard, and as he looked remarkably pale and emaciated he asked him about his health. "My dear sir, I am very well," answered Gerard. Of course this answer did not satisfy the doctor; he thought that he could not be very well, and began to examine his breast. He then saw that the poor young man wore a hair-shirt, so that easy breathing was either impossible or very difficult.

At Lacedogna, however, the esteem of the people for the saintly young man increased day by day and was heightened still more by an event of which many persons of the place were witnesses. The bishop had one day left the house to take a walk outside of the city, and Gerard, who was about to fetch water from a well near by, locked the door and took the key with him. Accidently, the key slipped from his hand and fell into the water as he was stooping near the edge of the well. The poor servant stood for a few moments, speechless, before the well; he knew the disposition of his master,—that he would become greatly vexed if on his return he could not enter the house, and learned what had happened. After having implored heaven for help, he hastened to the cathedral, whence he returned with a small statue of the Infant Jesus, which was usually exposed for the veneration of the people during the Christmas holidays.

A considerable number of people who, from a motive of curiosity, had gathered around the well, looked with astonishment at the servant of the bishop, neither knowing nor conjecturing what he was going to do with the little statue of the Infant Jesus. He took one of the ropes of the well, and having fastened it to the statue, lowered it to the bottom, and in the meantime addressed in a loud voice the following words to the Infant which fright and his simple confidence suggested

to him: "O my little child! my little child! get me
that key; O help me to get the key, so that Monsignor
may not be angry when he reaches home!" In anxious
expectation all looked towards the statue which Gerard
had, after a short time drawn to the surface; the greater number of them, perhaps, with the feeling with
which we usually regard the issue of an affair that we
think will disappoint some one's hopes and make his
heart ache. Yet very great was their astonishment, and
transported with joy was Gerard, when the looked-for
key was seen in the hands of the Infant Jesus, and the
confidence of the pious servant was rewarded in so
wonderful a manner. Then Gerard carried back to the
cathedral the statue of the Infant Jesus in triumph;
The report of this miracle spread throughout the city
and to the well the name Pozzo Gerardiello (Gerard's
Well) an appelation that the people of Lacedogna employed for more than a hundred years.

On the 25th of June 1744, after Gerard had been
for three years in the service of the bishop of Lacedogna, the latter died and his faithful servant was among
those who greatly mourned the loss of his friend and
master, and grieved for him with the feelings of a son.
He often said: "Alas! I have lost my best friend; Monsignor really loved me." His lively faith made him entirely forget the rough exterior of his master's character, while the love for Gerard which the Monsignor
really entertained in his heart, was never effaced from
his memory and made him resolve always to count him
among those friends and benefactors whom he venerated.

Gerard now returned to his native place; he was
eighteen years old. The desire to enter a convent re-
asserted itself with increasing fervor and induced him
to apply again to the Capuchins; again his request
was unheeded. It is true, he had grown older while at

Lacedogna, but he had also become more austere, and the paleness of his face and the emaciation of his whole body, in consequence of his austerities, were no recommendation for the young man. He was supposed to be sickly, and too weak to keep the strict rule of the Convent, and was told that there could be no question of admission.

Grieved at the second failure of his design, but not discouraged, he yielded to Divine Providence and again resumed his trade in his native country. Circumstances did not permit him to begin business for himself, therefore he entered the service of Vitus Monnona until he was able to retire to his mother's house and establish a workshop for himself, about the latter part of 1745. In the house of Monnona he fared very well; he was loved as one of the family, and all esteemed him as a saint. They had heard of the marvelous life of the youthful Gerard which filled them with the highest esteem for him, while almost daily recurring signs of grace and sanctity contributed much to require their respect. One day Monnona's wife, or his mother, witnessed the extraordinary efficacy of Gerard's prayer.

About a mile from the city was the little river San Maffeo, whither Monnona's wife had gone to wash some clothes, accompanied by Gerard who was always very obliging. Later in the afternoon a heavy rain interrupted the work, and obliged them to seek shelter under a thatched roof. As it was growing dark and the rain did not cease, but the sky became still more overcast, the anxious woman wept and lamented because she could not return to town, which circumstance distressed Gerard very much.

His simple faith, or rather that innate confidence peculiar to souls upon whom God bestows the gift of miracles, soon suggested a means. Stepping into the open air he raised his hands towards heaven and cried out with childlike confidence and in humble supplication: "Dear Lord, what shall we do, to get home?" Scarcely had he uttered these words when the rain ceased, the sun broke through the clouds and the two returned home without difficulty.

Years after, old Monnona spoke with enthusiasm of his pious apprentice and never tired of extolling his obedience, mildness and compassion for the destitute, particularly for the poor souls in purgatory. Monnona was equally lavish in dilating upon many other virtues of which Gerard gave most excellent proof during his stay with his employer.

When the youth was a lay-brother of the Congregation in Caposele, Monnona visited him several times to be edified by his holy life, to receive comfort and counsel from his own lips, and to recommend himself to his pious prayers.

CHAPTER IV.

Gerard Becomes Foolish For The Love Of God.

The business in which Gerard had engaged toward the close of 1745 was prosperous; he had work to do, not only at Muro, but he also received orders from Castelgrande, a neighboring village. All loved the pious and modest young tailor; for even though many could not understand his quiet and reserved manner, and might have looked upon him as eccentric and as going to excess, yet no one could urge any well grounded complaint against him. He was kindness itself, and ever ready to render service. He was extremely patient, never quarrelled nor disputed with those who opposed him, and what pleased every one was his conscientiousness in business transactions. In this he went so far as never to keep the most trifling thing that had been entrusted to him. Some one testifies: "He never retained even a piece of thread which did not really belong to him." Withal, his prices were low, and he often worked for the poor, of whom he asked no payment. Frequently while he was performing these charitable acts, God came to his assistance in a wonderful manner. It once happened that a poor man brought him material out of which he was to make him a new garment, but of which there was evidently not sufficient for the purpose. Gerard however accepted it, and after some time carried to his customer not only the new garment which had been ordered, but a part of the material, which had been left. The material therefore seems to have grown in his hands as a reward of his charity. Not only a large part of his labor, but also a large share of his earnings were given by **the kind-hearted workman to his beloved poor, whom he usually** called "**the poor of Christ**." He divided his **earnings** into several parts, one of which was given to the poor; sometimes he gave them more, so that he himself suffered hunger that he might appease the hunger of others.

Among the "poor of Christ" whom his charity urged him to support so carefully, he counted not only those **who** were in need **of daily** bread and who were obliged **to lead** a life of privation, but also the faithful departed **who were not** able to pay "the last farthing" which **must** be paid before the gates of heaven are opened to them. Gerard considered it a sacred duty to assist these poor souls in their spiritual distress by means of his temporal gains. "Alas!" he often said, "the souls in purgatory are **so very** poor, and they call on us for help." He frequently — some have said regularly once a week — had the sacrifice of the Holy Mass offered for them, and at times he was seized with such compassion that he endeavored to practise this act of charity to a greater extent. On one occasion he received as his wages for one week's work eight gold pieces. This was his entire earning. Nevertheless he sacrificed all this **money for the same purpose** — for the redemption of those poor prisoners in purgatory. During the following week he had to fast, or to appease his hunger with dry bread.

Gerard's mother, it is true, was satisfied with his charity towards the poor, and he never gave alms without her permission. But she was more frugal and pru**dent** in the management of **a** household than her son, **and could** not approve of a prodigality that entirely **forgets one's own wants** and knows nothing about economy. Hence she often approved him on this ac**count; for she wished him to remember his condition** of life and to be mindful of the future. But what did the servant of God understand about such things? The birds of the air, that God feeds, and the lilies of the field which He clothes, seemed to him to be more worthy of imitation than those persons who are so much concerned about their future welfare. "O my dear Mother," he said to her when she brought forward her usual arguments, "God will provide for me, for to Him who trusts in God nothing will be wanting."

The great charity which Gerard entertained for his fellow-men was only the natural result of the love of God which was glowing in his heart. This love had grown since the days of his childhood and had now attained that degree of intensity which generally paves the way for the joyful endurance of humiliations, for the patient carrying of crosses, and for simple and blind obedience. In the sad hours spent during his apprenticeship and in the difficult service at Lacedogna, his love for God found abundant nourishment, with which, as a healthy plant, it was constantly and eagerly fed by means of its absorbent roots. Hence it began to blossom on all sides; it brought forth most charming fruits and emitted a fragrance which delight the strong, but which was apt to sicken the weak-nerved and cause them violent suffering. Besides his work for God and his neighbor, prayer was his greatest delight. The place where the Divine Lover of souls in all the fulness of His love has taken up His abode was therefore his favorite resort, as often as his work left him leisure hours, and that obedience or charity did not require him to render services elsewhere.

Early in the morning, at the cathedral, he heard several masses which he served when allowed to do so. He received Communion at least three times a week. The moment in which he had to separate himself from the holy tabernacle was for him as painful as the separation from a dear friend, and one could notice that he had to do himself special violence to tear himself away. If, during the day, he found any leisure moments he again hastened to the church in order to visit our **Lord,** and there he would often become ecstatic, and be deprived of sensible power whenever the eyes of his soul happened to see the depths of the power, the love and the mercy of God which are hidden from mortals at large.

His most favorite time of prayer was the night. Then **he** was free from **all** earthly cares, and the noise of the **world** was hushed around him. Don Tirico, the sacristan **of the cathedral,** a relative, sometimes gave him the **keys of the church,** so that he might without hindrance, **make his nocturnal visits to our** Lord in the Blessed **Sacrament, a favor of which he always** availed himself.

A church dedicated **to the** Mother **of God was the** place of special devotion **for** Gerard. **It was probably** the church **of St. Maria del** Soccorso, **which has now** been brought **within the city** limits. **Had the** Blessed Sacrament been **there he would certainly have preferred it to every other** church. **Still it was a favorite spot, a Paradise for him, where he would have spent entire days, had it been possible. Several times he stayed there two or three days in prayer and penance. A little bread was his food, and the bare** floor **his resting place.**

Gerard edified Muro for a year in this manner, when he left this town, necessitated, or as it is said by others, requested to do so.

The city officials had decided to tax his occupation; **on** the other hand a certain Luca Malpiedi invited him **to accompany him to San Fele,** where he had established a private school for **boys and was in need of a** tailor.

To avoid paying the heavy taxes, Gerard accepted the invitation. Towards the close of 1746, or in the beginning of 1747 he left Muro and went to San Fele. He had indeed escaped the heavy taxes but he became the victim of very disagreeable annoyances.

Luca Malpiedi was, to say the least, no educator of youth; his school was a picture of disorder and dissolution. Gerard tried his utmost to give satisfaction, but as was to be expected, soon became the butt of the ill-mannered youths and of their ignorant master.

During the six or eight weeks which he spent there, his patience was put to the test, which he, however heroically survived. It was comparatively easy to endure the scoffs and ridicule of the boys, but the ruffians abused him with blows besides; in his unspeakable meekness he offered no resistance, save an occasional pathetic, "Won't you stop?"

The most astonishing was that Malpiedi not only refused him protection against the ill-treatment of his pupils, but even followed their example and tormented and beat the simple young man most barbarously. Notwithstanding all this, Gerard lost neither his equanimity nor his cheerful temper; on the contrary, he seems to have thirsted for new sufferings and contempt. His conduct shortly after supposes such a conclusion.

In February, 1747, the servant of God was at home again. Soon after his return Lent began. Whether the reading of Fra Antonio Olivadi's meditations (Anno dolorosa,) animated him, or whether his love of the Crucified had become more intensified — it is certain he had resolved that this Lenten season should be for him a time of penance and of suffering, in order thereby to render himself like unto his despised Redeemer.

He multiplied his exercises of penance and added scourges to these tortures. The ordinary practices did not satisfy him. He frequently scourged himself till the blood flowed, and in order to make these chastisements more painful he prepared scourges out of wet and knotted ropes. To guard against self-love he besought a certain Felix Falenza his special confidant to become his torturer, who afterwards related the following: "When at his request I tied him to a pillar and most unmercifully scourged his bare shoulders, he was greatly pleased and blessed me. Moved with compassion, I desisted, but he besought me to continue the favor, until at last the blood flowed from his shoulders."

He sometimes directed his friends to suspend him from a beam with his head downwards, and to burn green wood, or rags, underneath. His sufferings then were intense; the smoke had a scorching effect on his eyes and produced all the anguish of suffocation, while his face suffered from the terrible heat. In spite of this, Gerard inhaled the ascending smoke with pleasure, remembering those martyrs who endured similar torments for the love of God. "Ah!" he said, "we must suffer something for Jesus Christ, Who suffered so much for us." The excruciating pain caused by smoke and heat seems to have had for him a special attraction. Thus on one occassion he was on a visit to a house in which some green brushwood was burning in the stove. This caused a very offensive and pungent odor. Gerard knew no better place for himself than near the stove, and allowed the smoke to pass by his face. When the mistress of the house noticed this she cried out to him: "What are you doing, Gerard? Why do you allow the smoke to annoy you?" He answered smilingly and used the proverbial: "A belli occhi va il fumo. "Smoke is good for beautiful eyes."

But these mortifications and scourgings seemed to the loving disciple of Christ to contain too little of self-annihilation, too little of the total destruction of self-love, to prove satisfactory to him. His love impelled him to go still farther and to perform an act of the most perfect self-denial, — an act which at first sight, without the consideration of its motives and its circumstances, might almost be condemned.

While considering that his loving Redeemer had gone so far in His voluntary humiliation that He allowed Himself to be not only martyred and put to death, but to be mocked by the rabble as a fool and madman, it appeared to him that he should also endeavor to impose on himself this kind of suffering and should therefore pretend to be a lunatic. It was not a difficult matter for him to make this impression on a certain class of persons. Having been reared from his childhood in places which were situated far from the ordinary paths of the people of the world, his conduct appeared to them very odd and singular. His great patience, his unparalleled endurance when mocked and beaten, his silence amid the grossest insults, his flight from every youthful amusement, and his quiet demeanor, earned for him the reputation of being a heartless, narrow-minded, silly boy. Besides, the unnatural appearance which he occasionally assumed, his ecstasies, his abstractions from the things of the world, were regarded by the rough class of people as something quite incomprehensible and even repulsive, and inspired them with the thought that Gerard was at least bordering on insanity, and that it would not be surprising if he really became insane. It was therefore not difficult for him to appear among them as really demented. Dissimulation on his part was unnecessary. All he had to do was to exhibit his singular ways more than usually, as also his insensibility, which people ascribed to him as stupidity.

All this the servant of God accomplished, and thus obtained the result at which he aimed. Very soon people said: "What has been long expected has now really occurred. The poor fanatical tailor, Majella, has **become quite** crazy!" The better class who could not see through the deception, though they believed the report, felt great compassion for him; the malicious laughed at him and numbered him among those beings upon whom they might play tricks and whom they might turn into ridicule on every occasion. Indeed, the heart of the young man, who was constantly thirsting for sufferings, was filled with joy when he saw himself proclaimed and treated as an insane person.

Hence, whenever he left the house he was subjected **to** all kinds of insults and even to cruel treatment. No sooner would he show himself in the streets than a crowd of children and grown-up boys would gather **around** him, and while yelling at the top of their voices, would attack him, throw mud at him, and pull him about or drag him along the road. **"Fool! fool!"** were the words heard on all sides. "Yes, **yes, a fool** for the love of God," he would say; and those who did not understand the words, screamed still louder, laughed and mocked **him.** With this treatment he was greatly pleased and hastened through the streets to his own house, never so satisfied and joyous as when he had a crowd of boys following **him, throwing stones** at him and shouting: "Ora si **ritira il pazzo,"** "**The fool is** running away! the **fool is running away!"** "That pleases me, I like **that,"** he was heard to say.

"We must," he also said, "suffer all these torments if we wish to please our Lord, Who suffered so much for us."

One day — it was in winter — his mother **happened to meet him surrounded** be a crowd of laughing, mischievous boys. **They had thrown him into the snow and actually buried him.** The poor woman burst into **tears at the sight, and could not restrain herself from bitterly upbraiding the tormenters of her most patient** son. Gerard, however, was radiant with joy. Sometimes he even challenged the boys to ill-treat him and to amuse themselves at his expense. Having on one occasion come to Castelgrande, he met in Le Porte street a crowd of boys who were enjoying themselves and shouting while playing their games. They appeared to him to be mischievous enough to torment him. "Here boys!" he cried out, "till now you have enjoyed yourselves, let us now do something to please God." He then begged them to tie him and drag him through the streets. The hot-headed lads did not hesitate to agree to the proposal; the crazy man had just come in time to afford them some amusement. They had gone scarcely a dozen yards when he bled profusely from his head and shoulders; yet he did not wish them to stop, but asked them to drag him to the place they had fixed upon. The poor young man reached the spot in a most pitiable condition; at the sight of him the boys came to their senses; all felt the greatest pity for him and several of them cried bitterly. But Gerard was, as one of his tormenters afterwards related, quite cheerful and happy. "Oh!" he said, "all this is nothing for the love of Jesus Christ, who became a fool on our account." He arose from the ground in evident satisfaction.

It is a remarkable thing that this event occurred just before the house of the Carusi family, where, a few years afterwards, as if in compensation for the outrage perpetrated on this spot, he was glorified by God before the eyes of men by most astounding miracles.

God also manifested great pleasure in the self-renunciation practised by our saint, and in the deep humility which he evinced by assuming, for His sake, the character of a lunatic. For it was amid the insults and outrages mentioned above that he endowed him for the first time with the gift of prophecy, and put into his mouth the words which very plainly expressed the veneration that would be bestowed on His servant. This happened on the occasion when Gerard was again the object of the mischievous tricks of the boys who kicked and beat him. He then cried out to them with more than usual energy, full of dignity, yet not knowing what he was saying: "You now despise me; the time will come when you will think it an honor to kiss my hand." The lads then laughed at these words, but when Gerard afterwards actually appeared at Muro under quite different circumstances, as one much sought after and honored as a worker of miracles, many of them recalled his words and acknowledged them as prophetic, and inspired from on high.

How long a time the servant of God sought **to impose** on himself the ignominy and outrages inflicted by others, in order to imitate Jesus Christ, is not known; it was probably not long, for it is certain that it was forbidden by his confessor. That he did not show the least repugnance in obeying with childlike submission the words of the priest, and that he gave up, in consequence, his usual practices of self-renunciation, are convincing proofs that he thereby became more thoroughly and truly similar to his Redeemer than by all **other kinds of sacrifices** and sufferings.

Nevertheless it was evident that he mortified his palate in a more heroic degree during the greater portion of Lent. He usually ate only dry bread which he **moistened** with water; he often fasted for whole days, or picked up in the streets some fruit or fragments of food, which served him as nourishment. If occasionally he **partook of the kind of food** usually eaten by others, **such as soup and vegetables,** he thought this a delicious meal and spoke of having been **at a banquet (banchettare).** **If invited to take food, he** excused himself by saying that he was not hungry; and if eatables were forced upon him he distributed them among the poor, or carried them to some sick person. — This rigid fast of Gerard cost his kind mother many tears; she often complained and gave vent to her sorrow on this account. But he said to her: "Do not be troubled, my dear mother, I am not hungry; my appetite is satisfied; I need no food."

Even though he could sometimes use these words in a general sense, his appetite was gratified only by bitter and disagreeable herbs, such was wormwood, milfoil and the like, of which he always carried a large quantity with him.

As Donna Eugenia Pasquale one day tried to persuade him to eat, and not to kill himself by fasting, he, as usual denied that he fasted too rigidly, and that he did not eat enough, and said that he always carried eatables in his pocket. Eugenia had the curiosity to see for herself, and putting her hand into his pocket, she found nothing but a quantity of bitter roots and herbs.

The approval of heaven, as well as the anger of hell, kept pace with his zeal for penance and suffering. The latter perfectly corresponded with the state of Gerard's mind at this time.

One night while speaking in the excess of his love to our Lord in the Blessed Sacrament, he heard from the altar these words: "Pazzarello! Pazzarello!" ("O you little fool! O you little fool!") The saint immediately recognized the voice of his Master, and could not restrain himself from giving the answer which his great confidence and his glowing love prompted him to make. "You are more foolish," O my Jesus! he said, "You are more foolish, since for my sake You remain here a prisoner."

On another occasion, wholly inebriated with love he came to the altar, when he again heard the divine voice saying: "Little fool, little fool, what are you doing?" "What dost Thou wish, O my God," Gerard answered,

"What dost Thou wish? why dost Thou call me by such a name? Didst not Thou put me into this state?"

The evil spirit made extraordinary attacks upon him for the purpose of destroying or preventing the holy conversation of the saint with his Savior. During these visits to the Blessed Sacrament the devil first tried all kinds of grimaces and apparitions, either to frighten or to injure him, as he has often done in regard to other great servants of God. One morning, when Gerard was about to enter the church in order to receive Holy Communion, he rushed on him under the appearance of a very large dog, howling, and showing his teeth as if he were going to tear him to pieces. Any one else would have fled, but Gerard was not alarmed, for he knew to well who was concealed under the mask; he made the sign of the cross, and the monster disappeared. The same thing happened at another time when the devil met him in the disguise of a wolf, making savage threats to attack him. At another time, while Gerard was kneeling at the foot of the altar, in the chapel of the Blessed Sacrament, the evil spirit threw down a candlestick, in order thereby to disturb him in his prayers and in his communion with God. He also threw down upon Gerard while he knelt there, one of the wooden angels that were fastened to the cornice of the chapel, and wounded him in the arm. Gerard suspected the author of all this, but did nothing except to move out of the way. As, however, the statue seemed to be under diabolical influence, and might be hurled at him he prayed, and the apparition vanished. Many years after these events, Gerard, at the command of his Superior, told the particulars of these demoniacal occurrences.

From the spirit awakened in this intercourse, and the wish to attach himself to heaven by inseparable bonds, proceeded also the holy boldness which induced him at this time to offer his heart to the Queen of heaven and become espoused to her. As we have seen, he had always borne a childlike affection towards the Blessed Mother of God, and of man. As the masterpiece of God's hand, her incomprehensible beauty and the plentitude of her goodness enraptured his soul; as the Mother of the Redeemer, she excited his admiration, his joy, his respect; and as the dispenser of every grace, she attracted with irresistible force his loving heart that thirsted for the possession of this ornament of the soul.

It often happened that he could not separate himself from the presence of the images of the Blessed Virgin, and when asked the reason, responded: "The Madonna has ravished my heart, and I have willingly yielded it up to her." It is also related that when a boy he had already dedicated to her his body and his soul with all their powers and acts; and it is probable that even in his twelfth year he presented as a friendly gift to the Blessed Virgin his vow of perpetual virginity. At least, when worldly-minded persons indiscreetly asked him whether he intended to marry, he several times said very decidedly: "I shall choose for my spouse a beautiful woman."

But as in the heart of the saintly young man, who had completely resigned himself to the inspiration of grace, all the virtues had grown, and, at the time of which we speak, had increased in intensity, so had his love for the Blessed Virgin Mary become greater, and now inspired him to perform an act of most tender and perfect consecration.

On the third Sunday of the month of May the people used to celebrate with great pomp a feast in honor of the Immaculate Conception of the Blessed Virgin. Gerard always prepared himself for it with special fervor. In the year 1747, on the day of the feast he was again devoutly praying before the statue of the Blessed Virgin, **when,** under the pressure of **the** feelings that controlled him, he felt his heart beating violently, and **as it were** bounding with the greatest joy and love. When the statue was about to be carried in solemn procession he was seized by an irresistable power, and, more in ecstasy than conscious of himself, he pushed his way through the crowd, and standing before the statue he took a ring off his finger and endeavored to put it on the finger of the Blessed Virgin, and said with **a loud voice!** "Behold! I am wedded to the Madonna." ("Ecco mi sposato colla Madonna!") By this act, he afterwards declared, he celebrated the espousals between his virginity and the virginity of the Blessed Virgin, and he believed himself from this moment **to be** consecrated in a special manner to the mother of God, just as a bridegroom is consecrated to his bride.

The blessing resulting from this consecration was not merely the expression of a transitory feeling of love, but a well developed blossom of a holy and long cultivated disposition. It accompanied him throughout life and exhibited itself in a perfect purity of soul and body. Gerard remained free not only from every grievous sin, and carried with him to the grave his baptismal robe unsullied, but he was able to avoid those stains which pave the way to voluntary venial sins. His confessors scarcely found matter for absolution, and one of them, Father Celestine de Rubertis, to whom the servant of God, towards the end of his life, usually went to confession, declared that the always felt deeply humbled when he saw him kneeling at his feet, in all the splendor of innocence, like an angel of paradise. As regards purity of body, however, Gerard was in this matter entirely free from the stings of the flesh and from the degrading **influence** of concupiscence brought into this world by original sin. This was the gift which the Vir**gin** had **presented to her virginal** client.

CHAPTER V.
On The Road To The Convent.

Not long after the event just mentioned Gerard was seized with the most vehement desire to leave the world like the old hermits, and to devote himself in perfect seclusion to penance, meditation and manual labor. Such a life seemed to him to be the only compensation for the religious life which he so ardently desired, and to which he now had not the least prospect of ever being admitted. His health and bodily strength had not improved during the last years; in consequence of his austerities and the continual exhaustion occasioned by his burning love, he had become weaker and could therefore not expect anything but a refusal if he made a third request. In a hermitage, however, he thought that his weakness would be no obstacle; there he would be a burden to no one, and could imitate to a certain extent the rule of life followed by religious, and make the sacrifices that they have to make. He therefore resolved to become a hermit. We do not know whether he obtained the permission or the approval of his director for the execution of this design, or whether he only wished to make a trial of the life of a hermit and afterwards submit its success to his confessor, with the petition to continue it.

For the establishment of his hermitage Gerard had chosen a forest situated in a mountainous district at some distance from the city. When he communicated his project to one of his most intimate friends, the latter not only approved of it but he was courageous enough to offer himself as his companion. Gerard was pleased, and readily gave consent. With very little baggage the two young men left Muro on the day they had fixed, and set out for the solitary forest.

The life of the hermits was imediately begun. The rule which they intended to observe was very strict, and was not unworthy of the anchorites of primitive times. They wished to devote the hours of the day partly to manual labor, to exercises of piety, and to devout conversation. The night, however, was set apart for meditation and for rigorous penances. Only a few hours were to be given to sleep, which they did not wish to take on a comfortable couch under shelter, but in the open air, in order that the rest they enjoyed might also bear the character of penance. Their food was to be extremely moderate. They had read that the old hermits prolonged their lives by means of roots and wild herbs, so they resolved to imitate them by selecting for their ordinary nourishment berries, roots and herbs found in the woods.

We cannot but admire the determination which prompted them to carry out this strict rule; but in the case of one, it was soon discovered that his strength was not equal to the austerities imposed upon them. After three or four days, Gerard's companion declared himself unfit to continue this difficult life; "the bow had been bent to much;" and he returned to the city. Of course the servant of God, who, from childhood had exercised himself in most rigorous fasting and severe mortifications, found in that which had driven away his associate no reason why he should follow him; he remained in the woods rejoicing on account of the increased solitude; now he could give himself entirely to God and devote more time to prayer.

The servant of God would have continued this mode of life if God had willed that he should remain in the hermitage; but this was not His design.

This secluded life, spent wholly in the service of God seemed suited to the aspirations of the highly gifted soul of Gerard. He certainly would have continued this mode of life to the end of his days had such been the will of God. A few days after the departure of his companion, his confessor commanded him to leave the forest, to return to his mother's house, and to continue his trade. The word of his confessor was for him the voice of God, he submitted with his usual exactness, returned to the home of his childhood, and again labored in his workshop.

The life which he now led in the world, during the two years intervening from the end of 1747 till his entrance into the religious state, was similar to that which he led before his retirement into solitude. He showed the same zealous fervor in the service of God and of his neighbor, the same obedience, conscientiousness, and virtue; it was remarked that his zeal for souls then manifested itself more strongly, and that apostolic bearing shone forth more prominently in Gerard's behavior. If formerly he endeavored to promote the honor of God by suffering, and by seeking every species of torture, he now labored to increase this honor by his activity, and by his salutary influence over the hearts of his fellow-men.

Upon children he bestowed the most tender care. When a boy, he used to collect them to take part in pious plays; now, he gathered them around him to disengage them from dangerous entertainments and useless pastimes. He spoke to them of God and of divine things with that affability which fascinates, and with that pleasant eloquence which arises not only from personal conviction,— and therefore produces conviction in others,— but which is also reserved, yet in harmony with the occasion, which neither annoys nor fatigues the listener. Sometimes he went in procession with the children to his dear chapel of Capotignagno, or visited an old church dedicated to St. Leo, in which he instructed the older children in the truths of religion, and taught the smaller ones to pronounce the Holy Names, to make the sign of the Cross, and to say the **Lord's prayer.**

But Gerard was not only an apostle abroad; he exerted a like influence at home, upon his mother and sisters. With the most convincing arguments, he often recommended to them the love of God and the love of the Redeemer, and encouraged them to receive the sacraments frequently. Very often they heard him say: "Let us visit Jesus, our dear prisoner;" words which he frequently spoke to his companions when a child. **He** instructed, encouraged, and advised his younger sisters, and when necessary he did not hesitate to rebuke them. He had remarked that one of his sisters was inclined to indulge in finery, and was prone to childish vanity. This displeased Gerard; and he expressed his dissatisfaction in a kind but straightforward manner, saying: "Come, now, my dear sister, throw those beautiful trifles into the fire."

That there was no decrease in Gerard's love for the Crucified Redeemer, nor in his desire of rendering him**self like to** Him, we learn from an incident that occurred about this time, probably in the beginning of Lent, 1749. When, therefore, the crucifixion was again to be represented, the privilege of personating the suffering Redeemer was granted to Gerard. He considered the matter very seriously. It was customary in Muro as well as in other countries of lively faith to represent to the people, in living pictures, scenes of our Lord's Passion. The representation took place in the cathedral; it was regarded as a kind of sermon, and as a religious drama **which pious** persons considered it an honor to take **part in. On the appointed** day Gerard had himself **bound to the cross and** begged those who were to personate the **officers of justice** to tie him in a very cruel **manner, and to inflict on him** as much torture as **pos-**

sible; he had forgotten that there was no question of torture, but merely a representation of it. As Gerard's **peculiarities were well-known,** they promised to realize **his wish. Thus the servant of God** appeared hanging on the cross in a truly suffering state. The sight of the **saintly** young man, bound and stretched on **the wood,** showing in the expression of his countenance a pious interior disposition, as well as of sufferings cheerfully borne, moved the spectators to tears; they thought that they saw before them the suffering Redeemer Himself. Gerard's good mother had also come to the play, without, however, knowing that her son was taking the chief part in it. When, therefore, quite unexpectedly, she saw him hanging on the cross, she swooned away. But the servant of God was filled with joy, and upon his return home he consoled her and said that all he had endured was nothing; that he must suffer for Jesus Christ.

Those **souls for whom "it is necessary"** to suffer for their Saviour, and who in fact suffer for Him with pleasure, the Lord glorifies in proportion to their sufferings; **not only by drawing them within the** circle of His special friends, but by allowing them to shine before the eyes of men in their intimacy with God, and in all their spiritual greatness. Thus did **our** Lord act in regard **to this** servant of God.

We have seen how the wonderful power of working **miracles** had already manifested itself in his childhood **and during the** time of his apprenticeship. But now, **it showed** itself in a still more singular and astonishing way. Of the miracles which Gerard performed at this time at Muro, **a few are still** remembered by the inhabitants, and we can therefore relate them in detail without the fear of bringing forward what is not well authenticated.

Great astonishment was created among the townspeople by the following miracle, which is attested by most trustworthy witnesses, and was performed by the servant of God. One day business induced Gerard to walk by a place where men were engaged in building a house. He noticed that something disagreeable had happened, for everybody seemed to be in bad humor. It appears that a mistake had been made in cutting the beams destined for the house, so that they were too short, and did not reach from one side to the other. Gerard remained standing near the workmen, and after he had ascertained the cause of the trouble, he had recourse to his Lord and Master, and invoked the Holy Name over the beams. He then encouraged the workmen to try to draw the beams into their places by means of ropes. That Gerard was often inspired when he spoke, and that he possessed supernatural power, every one knew; we need not be astonished therefore, that the workmen did exactly as they had been directed. The result of their compliance with his request was most marvelous. The beams were found to fit exactly; they had evidently become longer, through the prayer of the servant of God.

On another occasion he met a woman named Giuliani, who seemed to be in great distress. She was troubled about her child Amato, that she carried in her arms, and that cried and screamed most pitiously. The child had fallen into boiling water and had severely scalded its arms and breast. Oil and wax, which the mother had put on the wounds to relieve the pain, proved useless, and the poor child in excruciating suffering now cried incessantly. The pitiable condition of the child, and the tears of the mother, made a deep impression on Gerard's kind heart. He placed himself before the child, gazed at it, placed his hand on its breast, and signed it with the sign of the Cross. Twenty-four hours afterwards, Amato was perfectly well!

If our saint brought about cures by the imposition of hands and the sign of the Cross, the sign of the Cross made by his command produced the same wonderful effects. That good woman, Emanuela Vetromile, with whom we have already become acquainted as the intimate friend and confidante of his youthful secrets, had an opportunity of discovering this power. She had a servant in her house, a relative of hers named Ursula whom she loved very much on account of her excellent qualities. This girl had been afflicted with a chronic disease, which defied the skill of the physicians; Ursula was evidently near the grave and at length was given up by the doctors as hopeless. Vetromile was greatly alarmed, and had recourse to heaven. She was about to go to the church of the Conventual Fathers, in order to invoke the aid of St. Anthony for the preservation of her beloved servant, when Gerard met her. Seeing that her eyes were red with weeping, the sympathetic young man asked the cause of her dejection. After she had informed him of the cause of her sorrow and the object of her journey he consoled her and told her to go home and to make the sign of the cross upon the forehead of the dying girl three times, and she would be cured. The woman believed, went home, and did what Gerard had told her. His prediction was realized: scarcely had the sign of the cross been made on the forehead of the young girl when she rallied, to the astonishment of the physicians, as well as of the whole city of Muro.

Meanwhile, the time was approaching when Gerard should see his most ardent wish fulfilled, when he would reach the haven of the religious state. The religious Society for which God had destined him as one of its first and brightest ornaments, had, during a number of years, grown strong amid storms, visibly sustained by the hand of Providence. It was the "Congregation of the Most Holy Redeemer." Gerard was six years old when St. Alphonsus Ligouri laid the foundation of the Institute, being actuated by a merciful desire to save many abandoned souls that lived in the country, —such as he had become acquainted with among the shepherds of Amalfi. He was supported in his design by the counsel of wise and holy men, and encouraged and incited by the divinely privileged Sister Mary Cœlestis Costarosa, then living in the convent of the Holy Redeemer, at Scala. She had manifested to him God's holy will in this affair. We shall meet her again in the course of this biography. Having surmounted great obstacles, he founded the first house at Scala; soon after, he established another house at Ciorani, then followed that of Nocera, and lastly another was begun at Iliceto.

Gradually, there gathered around the saintly Founder a considerable number of priests and laymen, who, animated with his spirit, and penetrated with a like desire for their own sanctification and for the salvation of the most abandoned souls, began to realize his plans. The work of the missions increased daily and the name of Don Alphonsus was honored as that of a true apostle and friend of the poor. There were on the one hand miracles of love and zeal; on the other miracles of grace and conversion.

Eminent prelates seeing the success and zeal of this new work, hastened to avail themselves of the opportunity of securing the labors of the Fathers for the welfare of souls in their parishes, by giving missions and retreats, and began to take measures to have houses of the Congregation established in their dioceses. Among these prelates was Monsignor Nicolai, Archbishop of Conza. A mission, given in May 1746, in the little town of Caposela, belonging to his diocese, under the direction of St. Alphonsus, convinced him of the great good which the Fathers would accomplish if they had a permanent house established among the people confided to his care. He believed it to be his duty to offer to the holy Founder the sanctuary of "Mater Domini", which was situated near Caposele. Alphonsus accepted the offer.

Twenty years before, this sanctuary had been offered to St. John Joseph of the Cross, who at that time was the Provincial of the Alcantarians, in order that he might there establish a convent of his Order. But the saint refused to accept it, and while giving his reasons for the refusal, he uttered a prophecy which was now fulfilled. He said: "It is not God's will that our religious should establish a community in this place; but after twenty years, other religious will come here and will work for God's honor and the salvation of souls." At the close of 1747, St. Alphonsus sent as first Superior, his faithful companion, Father Cæsar Sportelli, a man possessed of eminent virtues, and remarkable for his unbounded confidence in divine Providence.[1]

---

[1] Father Cæsar Sportelli was born at Aqua Viva on the 29th of March, 1702, and was one of the first and most holy diciples of St. Alphonsus. Like the latter, he devoted himself to the legal profession, and was a lawyer at Naples. When in the world he led a most exemplary life. After he had become acquainted with Alphonsus he was his constant companion, and entered the new Congregation as soon as it was established. His humility, patience, obedience and brotherly love were resplendent; his faith was so lively that he often cried out: "O paradise!" His hope was so strong that he never grew disheartened, no matter how great his distress might be. He used to say: "Lasciamo fare a Dio benedetto." "Let us leave it all to the Blessed Lord." During the missions he often preached three or four times a day, and would not allow his frequent hemorrhages and asthma to interfere. He was indifatigible in the confessional, in which, on one occasion at Foggia, he sat fully ten hours without interruption. In all his public discourses, he manifested such zeal, that some one

Although the good people of Caposele did all in their power to advance the new foundation and to secure its stability, yet the funds were insufficient. The building of the house required more money than they could supply. Hence the Fathers were compelled to appeal to the liberality of the faithful living in other cities and dioceses. The Archbishop of Conza gave them a special letter of recommendation. Father Francis Garzilli was appointed to make a collecting tour, and brother Onofrio was chosen to accompany him.

In August, 1748, they arrived at Gerard's native place; they were the first Redemptorists whom he had seen. Yet he felt attracted to them, and was inclined to enter into conversation with them. This feeling was evidently sympathy of vocation. Gerard knew that this was an inspiration from on high, and did not hesitate to follow it. He then accosted Onofrio, asked him about the usual community life in the Congregation, the practices of piety, especially those of penance, and informed him that he had a desire to enter as a lay-brother. Onofrio gave him the most satisfactory information, but discouraged his desire to enter the Congregation. "Our Congregation," he said, "will not suit you,

---

said: "I had a great desire to hear St. Paul, but having heard Father Sportelli I am satisfied, for he seems to me another Paul." As a true son of St. Alphonsus, he entertained an ardent veneration for the Madonna, and was faithful in his visits to the Blessed Sacrament. During the missions and retreats he did excellent service to the Congregation as Superior and General Consultor. The time of his last illness was devoted to heavenly things, and he breathed forth his soul after having uttered the Psalm: "In exitu Isreal de Egypto." He died April 19th, 1750. After his death many miracles were wrought by the invocation of his name. Our holy Founder, St. Alphonsus, was induced to petition the Holy See to allow his beatification to be introduced. But soon, most violent storms agitated the little bark of St. Alphonsus, and he was prevented from following up this matter.

for our life is one of great suffering, and our Rule is very severe." Onofrio evidently did not know the spirit that animated the young man. Gerard radiant with joy, said "The information you have given me, is just what I would like." He hesitated to proceed any farther in this matter, either because he held in remembrance the refusal of the Capuchins, or what is more probable, he did not trust his first inclination, and wished to subject it to further proof to find out whether or not it was a divine call. In the meantime, Gerard was convinced of his vocation to the religious life. The following year, 1749, the Fathers came to Muro to give a mission.

It was Easter-time, April 13. The exercises of the mission were begun, and the inhabitants of Muro took a lively interest in them: especially young Majella. He stood near the pulpit daily, and listened with the greatest attention of the words of the missionaries, especially to those of Father Paul Cafaro, who was the superior of the mission. Father Cafaro was a man qualified to attract a saint like Gerard. He was endowed with the gift of apostolic eloquence and well versed in the science of the saints. We may judge of the spirit with which he was animated by the words which often involuntarily escaped his lips: "O death! O eternity!" He preached the truths of religion with that persuasiveness and unction that moved the erring to conversion, and filled the innocent with the magnanimous desire to devote themselves entirely to the service of God. Gerard was fascinated. These days of penance were wholly according to his taste, he rejoiced to see the fruits of the mission manifested in the salvation of so many souls, the renewal of fervor, the defeat of the evil spirit, and the triumph of grace.

There is an incident on record which very plainly reveals Gerard's penitential sentiments at this time. Among the customary exercises of penance, performed during the mission was that of scourging. In a few days the minds of the men were already disposed to contrition, and after the sermon, this penitential act was performed. Gerard was never absent. His love of penance prompted him never to neglect such an opportunity. There were others present who went to the church not in the spirit of penance but with mischief in view. Among these were two young men who were gratified to inflict pain on the servant of God. They secured a place behind him, and as soon as the lamps had been extinguished and all had begun to scourge themselves, they inflicted heavy blows on the innocent victim. Gerard might have complained of such wicked behavior, but did not even change his place in the church, and patiently bore these tortures during the four or five ensuing evenings.

In the meantime, the servant of God had become thoroughly convinced that divine Providence had ordained that he should enter the Congregation of the Most Holy Redeemer. He lost no time in responding to call by removing all obstacles. During the mission he offered his services to the Fathers, and towards the close, he distributed all that he had among the poor, to detach himself from the world and to enter the state of perfection as a truly poor man. At last he disclosed his intention to Father Cafaro, and declared that it was his most ardent desire to follow him and become a lay-brother in his Congregation. Father Cafaro was convinced of Gerard's noble disposition and genuine piety; yet the young man's weakness and his emaciated frame made him doubt that he was equal to the laborious duties of a lay-brother. Father Cafaro, therefore, refused his request, advising him to banish the thought of entering the Congregation. Gerard would willingly have followed this advice which so holy a man as Father Cafaro had given him, — yet he could not resist God's voice. He continued to importune the missionaries; beseeching them to give him a trial. He was not discouraged when he met with a refusal.

His mother had meanwhile received information of what he intended to do. One day when she asked him the cause of his extraordinary sadness he related to her his negotiations with Father Cafaro. This brought new difficulties. However pious and resigned to God's will this woman was, she could not bear the thought that her son should leave her; and listening too much to the voice of nature she began to oppose the young man's plan and to do everything to prevent him from carrying out his resolution. She undertook to cross Gerard's plans, appealing to him with maternal tenderness, and begged him several times with tears, not to abandon his mother. "He could," she said, "love and serve God as well in the world; and besides he should be mindful of her needs, and should not leave her without support." His sisters also joined his mother in her entreaties. Much as he loved his family, Gerard proved that he loved the Beloved of his soul still more, by hearkening to the voice that bade him leave house, and mother and sisters in order to devote himself entirely to God's service. He therefore conquered his natural affection, consoled his mother and sisters, and told them he could not act differently from what he had resolved to do. "I must," he said among other things, "seek an asylum where I can say: Here I am altogether for God,—for God Who asks of us and loves the sacrifice of all our feelings and of our whole heart."

Finding her tears of no avail she hastened to Father Cafaro, to prevail upon him not to receive Gerard into his congregation. The love which she bore her son made her eloquent, and in its excess she exaggerated her condition. She represented her poverty and her dependence on Gerard for support in the most glowing terms,[1] and besought the missionary **with** tears to favor her request. There was no need of appealing to Father Cafaro **to** dissuade Gerard from his purpose for he had never thought of receiving the young man; on the contrary, he was firmly resolved to oppose him though it pained him to do so. He consoled the weeping mother, and dismissed her with the information that he did not think of admitting her son. Knowing how ardently desirous the servant of God was to follow him, and to leave Muro with the missionaries, he advised the mother not to allow Gerard to leave the house when they were about to depart.

This advice was punctually carried out. When the hour for the departure of the Fathers had arrived, the servant of God was confined to a room of the house, and was not even permitted to bid them farewell. But what avail is human prudence against the bold and inventive love of the saints!

The missionaries left Muro, and had already gone quite a distance on their way to Rionero, where they intended to open a mission, when the voice of a young man who was running after them, and who was nearly out of breath, cried out: "O my Fathers! do wait for me, do wait for me!" They did not credit what they saw and heard, — **but there was** no mistake; it was Gerard's **voice!** The servant of God had found means of escaping from his prison. He had used the bed-clothes **to** lower himself from the window, and had thus secured

---

[1] The poverty of Gerard's family was undoubtedly great, still, as his sisters were already grown up and could earn their living by the work of their hands, it was not of such a **nature that** the young man, called to something higher, would have been obliged to remain with his mother. After Gerard had entered the Congregation there was no longer any question about the poverty of his family, and if this poverty had been so great, the conscientious St. Alphonsus would never have admitted him to **religious profession.**

his liberty. On the table he left a note in which he told them of his flight, and that he was going away to become a saint. He further remarked that the members of his family should never more think of him. Father Cafaro and his companions were astonished at the heroism of poor Majella, and felt the greatest compassion for him, especially since they knew for what reason he had come, and that his petition would again have to be refused. Father Cafaro tried to persuade him to return quietly to Muro. But all in vain: he cried and entreated; "Try me," he repeatedly said: "and then you may judge my case, and send me away if necessary."

In the fervor of his desire he followed the fathers as far as Rionero, where he besieged the Superior of the missionaries with entreaties and tears. Again, and again he received the fatal answer, "It cannot be done; it is impossible." Finally he threw himself at the feet of him whom he thought an unmerciful Father, with an expression of humility which would move the heart of any one to favor his petition, and began to plead in a modest but firm voice. "Well, then, my Father," said he, "if you do not receive me among your brethren, you will see me every day among the poor and beg at the door of your convent. But I beseech you, try me first, and if I shall be found unfit, then send me away."

So modest and so resolute a tone conquered Father Cafaro. Though not convinced that Gerard was fit for the position of lay-brother, he thought that he should yield to his ardent wish, in order not to wound or break so noble a heart. He, therefore, gave him a trial. He then wrote these few lines to Father Lorenz d'Antonio, Rector of our house in Iliceto, "I send you a brother, who, in regard to work will be perfectly useless. But I could not absolutely refuse him admission, on account of his many earnest entreaties, and the high reputation which he enjoys at Muro." This short letter contains, at least in the first part as we shall soon learn, an entirely erroneous judgment about the servant of God; yet it made him happy beyond measure when it was handed to him with the request that he should proceed with with it to Iliceto. It seemed to him to contain the credentials, empowering him to set out from the land of exile, and joyfully enter paradise.

CHAPTER VI.

THE LAY-BROTHER.

After having received the strange letter of recommendation, the servant of God set out without delay for Iliceto. The road leading to it was not a short one; it was a good days walk, even at a rapid pace. But for our happy traveler, who felt as if a load had been taken from him, and who was absorbed in holy thoughts, this day seemed as fleeting and as pleasant as if only an hour.

When he saw the house of the Redemptorists in the distance, he felt the greatest joy, and hastened to reach it as soon as possible. It was probably on Saturday, the 17th of May, 1749, when the servant of God set foot on the threshold of the little convent where he was to lead a wonderful and holy life, and prepare himself fully for the duties of his vocation. Let us enter with him, for it will not be without interest to us, as it later became the theatre of his virtue and miracles.

The house of the Redemptorists at Iliceto, in the diocese of Bovino, stood on a small mountain in the neighborhood of the little town from which it derived its name, in a corner of the woods which the inhabitants used to call "Vallinvincoli." In former times it gave shelter to a community of Augustinian monks, whose Founder and first Superior was Blessed Felix of Corsano. A venerable memorial of this holy man was still in existence. It was a grotto hewn out of a rock, situated below the convent, in which Felix loved to pray and devote himself to the practice of penance. Next to the house was a small church dedicated to the Mother of God, under the title of "Our Lady of Consolation," which was constantly visited by the inhabitants of Iliceto and of the surrounding country, in order to pay their respects to the miraculous picture.

Towards the end of the year 1744, St. Alphonsus had also gone **there for** the same purpose, **while giving** a retreat at Iliceto. **He was so** charmed with the devotion of the place and the solitude that reigned in Vallinvincoli that **he** yielded to the persuasion of those who wished to retain him at Iliceto, and declared **that** he was ready to accept the Augustinian **convent that** had been offered him, and convert it into a **house of** his Congregation. In the following year, 1745, he repaired to this place with a **few** companions, **and was** received with open arms and joyfully welcomed **by the** people, especially by the bishop of Bovino, **the venerable** Antonio Lucci. Iliceto then became his abode for two years. Here he devoted himself **to piety and** study.

In fact, the solitude and seclusion of the **house at** Iliceto were entirely suited to **offer to a** scientific, **and,** in a far higher degree, to an ascetical **life, the natural** foundation for its proper display **and development.** This quiet place was never disturbed **by the world and its** concerns. Besides, this solitude **was consecrated** by a holy past, so that the mind and heart **could apply** themselves calmly and unreservedly to **the most serious** affairs of **life.** "In this **new** house of **Our dear Lady** of Consolation," wrote Father Cafaro, **a short time after** its establishment, **"I believe that I am sharing the** happy lot of the **hermits of Egypt.** When we return to this place after the missions **of the winter and spring,** we live so quiet a life, **are so retired from** the tumult of the world, that **we scarcely know what is going** on there. **We are free from all intercourse with** seculars, in the heart of the **forest. Our hermitage rivals the rocky mountain which St. Peter of Alcantara chose as his favorite resort. 'Blessed be God Who has brought me to this place'!"**

So, too, spoke Gerard when **he** entered the convent

of Iliceto. How he thanked God for having at last granted him the grace for which he had prayed so long; how he thanked the Mother of Consolation, who now visited him with consolation after so many trials and afflictions!

Immediately upon his arrival, the happy young man knelt before the altar of the Blessed Mother to express his gratitude and declared that he wished to live under her protection as also to die in this house which was dedicated to her. So great was his happiness that he could hardly contain himself. He wept for joy, and walked through the corridors of the convent and kissed its walls.

The Fathers and Brothers who had an opportunity of witnessing the happiness of the new-comer thought that it would soon be changed into sorrow, and that the young man would not stay with them very long. The few lines written by Father Cafaro made them surmise this; besides, every one was convinced at first sight that the candidate was weak in body.

But his appearance and behavior soon wiped out the unfavorable impressions which Gerard's exterior and Father Rector's letter had made. In a short time every one was convinced that the servant of God was far from being a "useless brother," and that they had received into the house not only a saintly young man but a very excellent workman.

We need not add that Gerard, during the first days, charmed every one by his humility, his spirit of mortification, exact obedience, and his other virtues. Ere long he convinced them that in considering him unfit for work, they had misjudged him. While working, he was active as if he were in the best of health and possessed a robust constitution.

When Father Cafaro, who had sent him to Iliceto, came there in October 1749 in the capacity of Rector of that parish, **he heard quite the** contrary of what he had anticipated, for Gerard was lavishly praised by all.

We know not the exact time when Gerard received **the** religious habit. It was always a rule in the Congregation, that those who wished to enter as lay-brothers had to wear the secular dress for at least six months, and under some circumstances even longer, before they could receive the religious habit. During this time they were under the direction of the Master of Novices whose business it was **to test** them and to teach them **how to** practise virtue. If they were equal to the trial, they received the habit and made their first novitiate **of six** months. After some time, they **were** admitted to the second **novitiate,** which was concluded by the **making** of the vows. We have no reason to think that **an exception** was made in Gerard's case, but we may, **however,** suppose that the preliminary trial did not continue beyond the usual six months. Consequently **he must** have received **the** habit towards the end of the **year 1749.**

From this time he was looked upon as a novice of **the** Congregation, and his next duty was to enter into the spirit of **the** religious life in general and into the **spirit of the Congregation of** the Most Holy Redeemer **in particular.** Gerard found no difficulty in doing this, having already passed through an excellent school of **the** spiritual life. During **the first days of** his religious career he comprehended what it means to be a serving-brother of the Congregation, **and** the ideal which he **should** strive to attain was quite vividly before his **mind.**

According to his notion — and it **is a perfectly correct one** — the good lay-brother is a man who understands **how to** unite to the work of his hands, prayer and the exercises of piety, so that if work claims most of his time, his heart inclines constantly towards prayer and exercises of piety. **The** good lay-brother is able **to sanctify every kind of** work, and as it were, seasons it and changes it into prayer by intercourse with **God,** by a good intention, and by ejaculatory prayers. From morning till evening **he is at work;** he knows nothing of idle moments. Always **ready to** serve others, he finds no work too insignificant, no occupation too lowly: **he is ever ready to** come to the assistance of others. **Impatience which** his work is apt to create, he suppresses with the cheerfulness of a self-sacrificing heart, and smiling, he accomplishes whatever has been enjoined upon him. He is **in the kitchen,** the refectory, **the** workshop, **at the door, in** the sanctuary, — always at the right time, according to the orders he has received; **and he never** interferes in the affairs of others. He is not attached to the office which he holds; he is **not absolutely** tenacious of the work in which he delights. He is distinguished by modesty, humility, simplicity, a certain quiet behavior, love of silence **and recollection.** In obedience and **respect** for Superiors he does not wish any one to surpass him. The good lay-brother believes himself to be the hand or the foot **of the** Superior, which moves without asking questions or without resistance, at his will; he submits his judg**ment to** the judgment of those who are in authority. A model of brotherly love, he is anxiously concerned about the wants of all. His own wants are the last he thinks of, and for these he provides, with great austerity, in strict observance of holy poverty. If sick persons are confided **to his charge,** he nurses them with maternal care; **if he has to** wait upon strangers, he does **his** work in such **a manner that he not only** serves, but edifies them; **and they go** away strongly persuaded that there is a **vast difference between a servant** in the world and a serving-brother in the convent. Of the outside world, **the** good lay-brother knows very little; he has no intercourse with the world except that which the business of the house may require. If occasionally he can say an edifying word or do something else for the salvation of souls, he does it without arrogating to himself the office of priest; he is at his best when like St. John the Baptist, he prepares the way of the Lord in humility and simplicity. Such is the pious lay-brother of the convent. This was the ideal which Gerard endeavored to reach in the beginning of his religious life.

There were lay-brothers in the Congregation who had already realized this ideal, whom he could imitate in the practices of virtue. Although the Congregation was still in its earliest youth, being not yet twenty years old, a few of its saintly lay-brothers had already departed this life in the odor of sanctity.

The first fruit plucked by Almighty God in the garden of St. Alphonsus was such a saintly brother. This was amiable brother Joachim Gaudiello, whose pious life was followed by a holy death, on the 18th of April, 1741, eight years previous to Gerard's entrance in religion. This lay-brother served him as a model in every respect. He was an Aloysius in his zeal for penance and the purity of his morals, a Francis in his ardent love of God and divine things, a Giles in his simplicity and obedience, a Bernard in his love for the Madonna. Though he was extremely fond of prayer and of intercourse with God, his favorite maxim was: "Work is the test of the lay-brother," — an expression which convinces us that he fully understood what it is to be a lay-brother. When dying in the house of Ciorani, in view of the circumstance that he was the first Redemptorist passing into eternity, he was so full of joy that he repeatedly cried out: "It is I who carry the standard." (Io porto lo stendardo.)

Another holy lay-brother who was highly esteemed for its virtues, having died four years before at Iliceto, but still living in the memory of all, was no less an ideal for imitation. We mean Brother Vitus Curzius, in whom there is manifested, perhaps less than in Brother Gaudiello, the practice of virtue in all its loveliness and gentleness, but who is more conspicuous as an example of heroic self-control, and perfect obedience. He was born of a respectable family in 1706. Imbued with false notions of honor, he lived the life of a proud and haughty worldling. A dream, directing his attention to the holy Founder, St. Alphonsus, effected a complete change in his soul. He joined the saint and was as zealous to acquire true honor as he had formerly proved himself in his effort for the acquisition of worldly renown. He wished to serve God as a poor lay-brother, and entered the Congregation in this capacity immediately after its establishment. During the first part of his religious life he had many temptations and conflicts; later, God elevated him to the highest degree of prayer. His humility and mortifications were sublime; but he distinguished himself chiefly by his obedience. This virtue was not natural to him — it was the fruit of grace, — a victory over nature. Vitus used to say: "A lay-brother should resemble the bell which is fastened to the neck of an animal that is grazing: this bell never rings unless it is moved. So a lay-brother ought never to do anything unless he is prompted to do so by holy obedience." This principle he observed most perfectly during his whole life; and St. Alphonsus himself remarks, — one may say that he died a victim of obedience. Obedience demanded of him to make a journey on foot, and while he was returning he came to a house where he expected to spend the night. Though he was exhausted from the heat of the day he was refused admittance. Patiently bearing the affront he went into the open air and lay down to rest. The cold air was a serious injury to him: he was seized with fever and could scarcely drag himself along. Almost within sight of our house at Iliceto, he found that he could proceed no farther. A good priest received him into his house, in which he lay sick during forty-nine days, and at last, on Saturday the 18th of September 1745, he entered the joys of the Lord. When the people heard of the death of this lay-brother they said: "The saint is dead." The corpse was solemnly carried to the church of the Redemptorists. St. Alphonsus, who was then at Iliceto, offered up the Holy Sacrifice of the Mass for him, and was so grieved at the loss of the holy brother, that he burst into tears several times during the obsequies. People vied with one another for the possession of the things that had been used by Vitus, as if the were holy relics. Monsignor Amato, at that time Vicar General of Conza and afterwards bishop of Lacedogna, had entertained so high an esteem for the deceased, that after the lapse of a few years he obtained permission to keep the skull of the saintly brother which he placed on his desk; it was the subject of his daily meditations. After the death of the bishop, this venerable relic was restored to the house of the Redemptorists.[1]

Thus had the servant of God very distinguished models on whom he might adapt himself to realize his ideal of perfection. Besides these favorable circumstances, the young novice enjoyed the privilege of being guided by the eminently spiritual director, Father Cafaro.

Father Paul Cafaro, who was born on the 5th of July, 1707, at Cafari, spent his childhood and youth in innocence, and entered the ministry of which he became a bright ornament at an early age. It was his custom daily to devote two hours to prayer before the taber-

---

[1] Among the works of St. Alphonsus there is also to be found a sketch of the life of the saintly Brother Curzio.

nacle. He was quite familiar with all kinds of penances; he often fasted on bread and water, wore a hair shirt, and chastised his body not only with ordinary scourges, but sometimes with a bundle of sharp thorns. In his twenty-eighth year, by order of his bishop, he was obliged to take charge of a parish for five years. He labored among his people so zealously and conscientiously that he was called by his colleagues: "Sollicitudo omnium ecclesiarum" "The watchful guardian of all the churches." In consequence of scrupulosity, he resigned his benefice, and soon afterwards entered the Congregation of St. Alphonsus. Here he made rapid progress in all the virtues. While he was indefatigable in laboring for the salvation of souls, he found time to hold intercourse with God in secret prayer; and if in former years he spent two hours of the evening in its exercise, he now devoted himself to it every day during seven or eight hours. The will of God was everything to him, so that St. Alphonsus could testify of him: "The only passion of Father Paul was, to fulfil the will of God." Towards the end of his life God tried him, as He only tries great saints. He encountered those spiritual nights, those sufferings, those interior trials of which even the experienced can scarcely give a discription, so great is the woe that accompanies them. St. Alphonsus, who was well informed of the suffering condition of Father Cafaro, but was prevented by the secrecy with which he was bound, from disclosing its nature, says, that if he were permitted to reveal it, a description of it would move the very stones. This terrible martyrdom continued during the last six years of his life; and when Gerard intrusted the direction of his soul to him, he had already entered upon his trial. St. Alphonsus regarded **Father Cafaro as** a prop of the Congregation, always asked his advice, and was governed **by** his direction in the affairs of his own conscience.

When **Father Cafaro** became seriously ill, and danger of death **became apparent, the** holy Founder did **all in** his power **to** prolong **his** life. He not only prayed **himself, but** had prayers offered up **in** all the houses of **the** Congregation. Especially did he **apply** for this purpose to other convents, including **several convents of** nuns. But God had ordained otherwise. **On the 13th.** of August, 1753, Father Cafaro, **who** had lived the life of a saint, died the death **of a** saint at Caposele. **In** the course **of** this biography **we** will again refer **to** his death which was a heavy blow for St. Alphonsus. The **saint** humbly submitted to God's decree and sought comfort by writing a beautiful hymn **on the** conformity of our will **to** the **will** of God. He afterwards wrote the life of this holy priest.

This was the man **to** whom Gerard **instrusted** the **care of his soul,** when he began **to put into** practice **the** resolution of becoming a holy **lay-brother.** As regards the direction of his soul it **was** very severe. A biographer assures us, Father Cafaro kept the servant of God, "sub virga ferrea" (under the iron rod), and all his care was aimed **at** the total suppression of natural inclination and **of** self-will. He never wished that Gerard should flatter **his** nature in any way, and also took **measures that he should never** want for humiliations. **He** gave his **full consent to** the mortifications to which Gerard **had** accustomed himself and **even** urged him to practise **them;** yet everything that Gerard did **was to be subjected to** his judgment **and** approbation. **Father Cafaro** exercised **such** severity, not to discour**age or inflict** pain upon so noble a soul **as** Gerard's, **but only to** keep him in humility and obedience, to **establish these virtues** firmly, **and to secure** them against **the attacks of** the devil. His austere manner of directing **corresponded** with the wishes of the servant of God, **who treated** himself with equal severity.

When he made his first spiritual retreat at Iliceto he wrote the following impressive admonition which he believed necessary for himself. "Posuit me Deus in paradiso voluptatis," (God has placed me in the garden of delights.) "Consider it well Gerard, that the Lord has taken you out of the world and placed you in the paradise of the Congregation, there to labor, to keep the commandments and to practise the evangelical counsels contained in your rule. If you were to neglect this you would be most unhappy; the punishment thereof would be (which God may avert) the abandonment of the Congregation."

The servant of God carried out this resolution without delay. His diligence and love of work were not a whim, or of short duration, his fervor was never diminished. Gerard was always an able and industrious workman; it was said that he did more than any other brother; even that he could do the work of four men. During the first period of his stay in the convent he was occupied in the garden. This kind of work was quite new to him, and therefore very difficult. He was lively and cheerful however, and handled the spade and the rake as if he had been accustomed to such work all his life. He was so successful that he finished the task allotted him in a shorter time than any of the other brothers at work with him. When the soil had to be dug up and the ground laid out, Gerard always completed his share of work before his companions; he then hastened to assist them saying: "Let me do that, for I am the youngest." When he could not help others during the leisure moments at his disposal, he found occupation elsewhere; he repaired parts of the wall that were damaged, collected building materials, or made himself useful in some other way.

The work in the garden proved too difficult for the young man. One day Father Cafaro accidentally looked into the garden, and noticed that the good novice was working with a fervor that was actually wearing him out, and that he did not take his failing strength into consideration. He called him immediately and told him that he should discontinue working in the garden, and that another kind of work would be assigned to him.

As soon as he had finished his first novitiate, which covered a period of six months, the office of sacristan was entrusted to Gerard, early in the summer of 1750. This change pleased him very much. To work in the church, — to him the dearest spot on earth, — he considered an honor and a pleasure. We may therefore imagine with what care he exercised the duties of this office. He did his work in so perfect a manner that the little church of "Our Lady of Consolation" never had a better sacristan; and even after the lapse of fifty years the people at Iliceto spoke with admiration of the holy and conscientious brother. Never had the church been so clean, never had the altar been so beautifully and tastefully decorated as when he had charge of it. The poverty of the house did not prevent him from doing all this; his piety was fertile in expedients, and he well understood how to arrange the few articles at his disposal in such a manner that all who visited the church were charmed and edified. "All our old Fathers," says Father Camillus Ripoli, in the process of the beatification, "related to me that the saintly brother was an accomplished sacristan. He knew how to decorate the church with so much taste; he kept it so exquisitely neat and clean, that since his time they have never found his equal."

Besides the office of sacristan, Gerard had also to make and mend clothes for the community. In this new duty he also showed himself exemplary in every respect. He sought to provide for the wants of all in every particular; for his lively faith saw our Lord in the brethren whom he had to clothe; and, with the eyes of faith, he perceived that in his occupation a service rendered to them was at the same time a service rendered to Jesus Christ Himself.

The zealous lay-brother was accordingly constantly occupied with the duties of his office. There was occasionally a little free time which he did not dare to devote to recreation, but which he employed, when necessary, in assisting the other brothers. It was a principle with him to render aid wherever aid was required, and not to permit any one to ask him to offer it. One of his resolutions, afterwards recorded, and which even then had become his rule of conduct, was the following: "Whenever I see a Father or brother in need of assistance I will lay aside everything to help him, if obedience does not prevent me from doing so." Hence, when he was not engaged in the church or in his workshop, he was seen helping the cook, the brother who had charge of the refectory, and sometimes the brother who held the office of porter, each according to the best of his ability. As the brother who baked the bread for the house had to exert himself very much at his work, Gerard would come to his assistance as often as he was free, and show himself most assiduous. "Let me do something," he would say to the brother, "I am younger; go now and rest yourself."

While anxious to assist others he was extremely careful not to violate charity, and the desire to render service was removed from the arrogance and false zeal of those who pretend to know everything better than others, who are always intruding and meddling with the business of others. In regard to this matter he made the following rule: "I will never meddle with other peoples' concerns; I will never attempt to say, 'I do not like that,' 'That is not done properly,' or the like." In his anxiety not to molest any one, or to tempt others to impatience, he went so far as to lay down for himself the following resolutions: "When, in company with others, I am sent to discharge any duty, however mean or lowly it may be, such as sweeping, etc., I will never take precedence, or make use of the best tools; but I will give up my own comfort in all things."

This modest and unpretentious behavior of so able a lay-brother as Gerard was not affected; it was not that smooth, false, and abject cringing which we often find among persons who serve to gain, or to please others. What appeared in his exterior, lay deeply rooted in his interior.

True humility was a characteristic of Gerard: but in his new state of life he practised it in such a high degree that we can say "he no longer possesses it, but he was possessed by it." His brethren gave him the name: "Il simbolo dell' umilta" (the image of humility), a title truly deserved. As all those who at that time enjoyed his society unanimously testify, his conduct, bearing, language and all his actions bore the impress of unfeigned humility. Though he usually said nothing concerning himself, a brother who was very intimate with him found means of extorting from him what opinion he had of himself and thus became, as he says, a witness of the skill with which "Gerard would exhaust the dictionary of terms, of contempt and depreciation." He called himself the worst and last brother, a miserable wretch, a dreadful sinner, a mere nothing.[1] All the good that he possessed he ascribed solely to the

---

[1] If the saints call themselves "great, or very great sinners," we should not regard this mode of speaking either as untrue or as exaggerated. From their point of view — that of the liveliest faith and deepest humility — they could indeed speak thus. It is true that if in doing this they had a really existing state of sin in view, that way of speaking would be inadmissible and untrue. But who could believe that the saints

exceeding great goodness and mercy of God. He believed himself unworthy to appear before God, and at prayer he was often seized with consternation, fear and confusion. Even hell, he thought was to good a place for him. "I find myself," he once wrote, "full of sin; pray to God that He may pardon me. All are converted, I alone remain hardened. I beseech you to perform some act of penance for me, that God may have mercy on me and receive me again into His favor." On another occasion he thus expressed himself to an intimate friend: "Alas! I am no longer a human being, for I permit myself to be overcome by my passions and evil inclinations."

In view of these sentiments of humility, which reigned in the heart of the servant of God, we can easily imagine the discomfort he felt when any one praised

<small>intend by the expression "great sinner" to point to a really sinful state of the soul? If they call themselves sinners, they have not before their eyes the sinful act, but the tendency to sin, that continually existing frailty of the human soul in the present state of probation; that possibility of falling into sin, which is prevented only by the grace of God. This tendency they have before their eyes, and because their eyes are purified by deep humility, sharpened by heroic faith, they behold it as a yawning, infinitely deep abyss. They see that they are capable of falling into an infinite number of sins, of becoming addicted to endless malice, and in all this they see only perfect truth. From this point of view they then rightly call themselves "sinners," namely, beings who in themselves and in consequence of their weakness can produce only what is bad, and who would without God's grace plunge themselves from one sin into another. They call themselves "sinners" in the same manner as one calls every creature a nothing. For as it is nothing, not in reality, but only so far as it does not carry in itself the cause of being, and consequently can sink into nothingness whence it was taken, and from which only God's omnipotence separates it, so also are saints "sinners" not in realty, but so far as they have not in themselves the cause of sanctity, and consequently can sink into sins whence God's grace has drawn them, and from which it alone separates them.</small>

his virtue, or spoke of his extraordinary gifts. Such language appeared to him sinful and as it were blasphemous; accordingly, he quickly put an **end to it whenever it** was in his power **to** do so. He rejoiced when he was insulted; and whenever he was called a fool or a block-head he was pleased to listen to this abuse as if it were delicious music. He used to say that he was undeserving the bread which was given him, and that he was imposing on the Community. He was delighted when permission was granted him to eat the fragments left after meals, and said, "it was proper that he should take his meals on his knees among the lowliest." When slighted and treated as a beggar, or employed **to do** menial and most despicable work, he was much pleased, and never exhibited the least sign **of** annoyance. On the contrary, he eagerly sought to engage in those employments for which others had an aversion, **and** which afforded no occasion for the display of vanity.

The humiliations to which he was frequently subjected by his superiors, either to chide a mistake **or** a fault, or to try him, he submitted with that happy tranquility which proceeds only from the conviction that they are deserved. He did not exonerate himself, even when he could easily have done **so.** It was his opinion that, strictly speaking, no person **should speak** of humiliations, as **nothing can prove a humiliation for a** creature. **"Man," he said, "is a worm,** a mere nothing, **if God does not govern and protect him by his power and providence.** Therefore he should not say: 'I **humble myself,'** for whoever speaks in this manner believes that he is something. Jesus Christ alone could **say that** He was humbled; for though He was the infinite **God, He became man;** and though **He was** the Lord, **He made Himself** a servant."

The servant of God did not show himself less perfect in obedience than in humility. Later on, the good brother was called a "saint of **obedience.**" **During his novitiate and while at** Iliceto, he distinguished himself **in a most heroic degree, by his obedience.** Gerard paid **the most childlike** obedience to all points of the Rules of **the Institute.** He valued them so highly that he was **not satisfied to** read and reflect on them often, but he applied himself to the task of committing them to memory. Owing to his diligence he succeeded so well, that he knew them by heart, not only as to their meaning, but word for word. "If the Rules should be lost," said **one** of his brethren, "Brother Gerard could easily restore them, and not an iota would be wanting; he knows them so well." By this exact observance of the **holy Rules,** he proved how highly he esteemed them. **In this he was a model** for all, **and was** regarded by **everyone as** a mirror of regular observance. He was **so exact and** scrupulous in keeping the Rules, that when sometimes he was not able to perform certain exercises prescribed during the day, he employed the night to supply the loss, though he was not obliged to do so. **Even in** trifling points he adhered strictly to what the Rules commanded, and did not dare transgress **them.** He believed that a little fault is followed by a **great fault, the first** by a second and a third, etc., "Give me, O Lord, the courage faithfully to observe **Thy holy** law! Oh, if it were my misfortune to deviate from it the slightest I should very soon remove far from it; for Thou permittest those who despise that which is little to fall into that which is greater." In speaking of **faults** against the Rule he once gave expression to the following: "Dear **brethren! let** us fulfil everything, even what is most insignificant with solicitous **exactness, if we do not wish** to fall into great sins; **God permits this in order** to punish us." On another occasion he said: "**If** we **are** careless in committing **little faults,** God may punish us, by allowing us to fall into great sins. David, who was a man according to God's heart, is a proof of this."

Faithfully obedient as Gerard was to the holy Rules, he was not less faithful in obeying the commands of his Superiors, because he recognized in both the manifest will of God.

"My God! for the love of Thee I will obey my Superiors, and I will obey them as if Thou wert speaking to me. I will so abandon all self-will, that I will act as if my judgment and will were to be found only in the judgment and will of him who commands me." He also said: "Obedience toward my Superior must be my guide to Paradise. The will of my divine Master, and the will of my Superior, are to me one and the same thing."

Sustained by these exalted sentiments in reference to holy obedience, he surrendered himself perfectly to the direction of his Superiors, and wished to do the most trifling things from a motive of obedience. "Ah!" he said, "why should we loose the merit of obedience for such a trifle!" It was therefore an easy matter for him to acquiesce with docility to the wishes of the Superior: a nod, a gesture, a look sufficed. "In a certain way," says the biographer, Father Tannoja, "he worshipped the thoughts of his Superiors." Gerard's Superiors had to be very cautious in giving orders; they were obliged to use very definite and plain terms, if they did not wish him to perform things which indeed corresponded to the literal meaning of the commands, but were in accordance with their wishes. The force of the inclination to obey, completely repressed the inclination to reflect on the signification of the command; nay more, it did not even permit him to examine into the meaning of the words.[1] It seemed to him that Jesus

---

[1] This manner of practising obedience, which we meet in many holy privileged souls, is to be admired, but should by

Christ stood before him and gave him the commands in person; so that there was nothing on his part left to be done except the accomplishment of what the words of the order conveyed. He never doubted that the command was right, proper and feasible. Gerard, therefore, obeyed all the commands of the Superiors with the most astonishing simplicity.

When, one day, Father Cafaro told him that he should make his manifestation of conscience to another lay-brother, Gerard did so immediately, without repugnance, and performed the duty with as much exactness as if the brother were his director, and knew his interior.

More than once, God acknowledged this great simplicity in a very wonderful way, to show that he was pleased with the exactness of Gerard's obedience. On one occasion he received from the Superior, Father Cafaro, the positive order that as soon as the bell would ring no means be imitated. It is the fruit of an exceedingly ardent, living faith, of perfect self-denial, and we might say, of an ecstatic joy in doing the divine will as manifested in the will of the Superior. What these souls omit unconsciously under the pressure of the Holy Spirit, namely, the reflection about the value and the meaning of the words spoken by the Superior, we are not allowed to give up knowingly and voluntarily. To him whom a higher power, an impulse of the Holy Ghost, does not prevent from rightly fulfiling the duty of obedience, this reflection is just as necessary as readiness, exactness, promptness in executing the order that has been given. For obedience does not require that we should perform what the words of the Superior express in their literal meaning, but that we should act according to his will, of which those words are the signs, and that we consequently should examine in which sense he employed those words. This examination is not in the least opposed to the blindness which is demanded of religious obedience: for this blindness does not at all consist in this, that we omit to inquire into the meaning of the order received, but solely in this, that in regard to the motives or intentions of the Superior we pass no judgment, but simply obey orders, for the reason that they are given by the Superiors, who take the place of God.

he should leave every thing and immediately hasten to the door. Soon after he had received the command, he had occasion to go down into the cellar to draw some wine. While standing before the cask and receiving wine into a vessel the door-bell rang. Instantly without taking time to close the faucet, he hurried away with the half-filled vessel. When he reached the door he was met by **Father** Rector, who reprimanded him for going about with the vessel in his hand, and asked him why he did so. "Your Reverence," Gerard answered, "told me to discontinue my work and answer the call of the door-bell without delay, I heard the bell ring when I was getting wine from the cask; this is the reason why I have come here in this condition." "Oh! you are an awkward man," said Father Cafaro, with a gesture of disapproval — "go, and creep into the oven!" (Va t'informa!) This jocose expression, which Father Cafaro liked to use to give vent to his displeasure in regard to the conduct of others and which was used by way of mere exclamation was literally accepted by Gerard, and he actually crept into the oven. A short time afterwards the baker came to light a fire in it, and was astonished to find the servant of God in it as immovable as a log of wood. He could not, of course, understand why Brother Gerard had selected this strange place for a hermitage, and he wished to persuade him to come out of it. But Gerard would not do so, and said that he was there by the command of the Superior, and only at his command could he leave the place. The baker then hastened to the Superior and informed him of his discovery; he stated that Gerard was in the oven and would not come out, because he was there in obedience. "O my God!" cried Father Cafaro, when he heard this, remembering his words; "with this brother one must weigh every word, for he obeys blindly. "But," said he, turning to the baker, recalling the circumstance of Gerard's coming from the cellar, with the half-filled vessel, "go quickly into the cellar; I told him that he must leave every thing at the first sound of the bell; it is possible that he did not even turn the crank of the cask." The brother hurried to the cellar before he called Gerard from his place of concealment. It was really so; the faucet had not been closed; but, wonderful to relate, not a drop of wine had run out of the cask. Greatly astonished, he related what he had seen to Father Cafaro. The latter struck his forehead as if in self-reproach, and raising his eyes to heaven he said with emotion: "God is dealing with this brother in a singular manner! We must let him act according to the spirit that is leading him."

Many similar incidents of blind obedience occurred during Gerard's stay at Iliceto. We shall relate one more. One day he received the order to go to Ascoli, a little town near Iliceto, to attend to some business. He was told to set out "immediately." He started on his journey without exchanging the large house-shoes which the brothers were accustomed to wear in the house at that time. No doubt, brothers of the convent of "Mary of Consolation" had often been seen in the public square of Ascoli, but none of them wore such shoes. A crowd of merry lads gathered around him laughing and jeering at Gerard's shoes. Though the merriment was at his own expense, the pious religious was much amused.

The servant of God at one time found an excellent opportunity to prove the purity and sublimity of the motives which influenced him in the exercise of obedience. This happened towards the end of his first novitiate, in April, 1750. Father Cafaro was absent on a mission in Melfi, which St. Alphonsus was invited to give by the bishop, Monsignor Basta; and as all the elder Fathers of the house took part in the mission, the care of the house was confided to a younger Father, named Matthew Criscuoli. Father Criscuoli was of a melancholy temperament, given to extravagant ideas, and capricious in the highest degree. A few years afterwards (1754) he was obliged to leave the Congregation, because he did not wish to exert himself to correct his faults. No one was less competent than Criscuoli to direct even so small a community, as was afterwards clearly proved. Previously, however, one would not have believed this, and Father Cafaro, who appointed him to substitute him for a few weeks, did not suspect that he was unfit for such an office. Perhaps God permitted this error on the part of Father Cafaro, in order to bring to light the virtues of Brother Gerard. The perverseness of Father Criscuoli, his fickleness, his bitterness and his measureless humiliations proved keen suffering for the whole Community. Precedence in all this was given to the saintly servant of God, who became the butt of his daily reproofs and accusations; he never had a kind word for him. The poor brother could not stir without exciting the anger of the ill-tempered Father. The corrections that he received never came to an end; penances were heaped upon penances, and nearly every day Gerard was forced to take his meals on his knees. Besides fasting on bread and water, the good brother was obliged to make fifty or sixty crosses with his tongue on the floor. This penance lasted for a whole month, and ended only when his tongue became so lacerated that he stained the floor with blood. All this would not have been painful to the servant of God, who was accustomed to the practice of the most rigid penance; but Father Criscuoli in his unreasonable zeal presumed to forbid him Holy Communion; and this was incomparably more bitter than if he had suffered hunger and thirst for days, and had been subjected to the most outrageous treatment. Gerard, however, was so calm and resigned that his brethren were not only astonished, but filled with the greatest reverence towards him. Father Tannoja, who was at this time a student at Iliceto and a witness of all this declared: **"Either this** brother is **a fool, who does not** understand the humiliations to which he is uselessly subjected, or he is a saint, who has arrived at an eminent degree of the love of God." **The latter was** indeed the case. **It was** the advanced **sanctity of the holy** brother and his great love for God **which made** these humiliations easy and supportable. **It was his lively faith that** strenghtened him not to **view things wrongfully** and not to fail to see in the unworthy **instrument the hand of God his Master Who used it.**

CHAPTER VII.
THE CELESTIAL LIFE OF THE NOVICE.

What mainly distinguishes the lay-brother of the convent from the ordinary workman in the world is, as has already been remarked, the facility to bring into an easy, sweet, and harmonious union, manual labor and prayer, so that prayer, as it were, penetrates and purifies the work, and mingles with it good intentions, frequent ejaculatory prayers, as also the spirit of devotion, of reverence for God, and of longing for sacrifice.

Brother Gerard had pretty well acquired this facility while yet in the world. This was perfected in the novitiate. As to his external occupation, he attained the highest eminence in the art of leading an interior life.

"With Gerard," says Father Tannoja, "labor was not separated from the spirit of prayer. Though he worked hard during the day, he retired to the church at night, and shed an abundance of tears before the Blessed Sacrament. The practices of piety prescribed by the Rule did not satisfy his heart; he therefore applied himself to interior prayer with such zeal and perseverance, that in the morning he was often on the very spot where he had been seen the evening before. Prayer was everything to him, and however distracting the labors which he had to perform, he walked in the presence of God. He was always profoundly recollected, his ejaculatory prayers were frequent, and the words 'Jesus and Mary' were ever in his heart and on his lips. At times he was so absorbed in God that he would suddenly cease to work, as if he had forgotten it."

The servant of God was imbued with the spirit of

recollectedness to such an extent that Father de Rubertis thought himself justified in asserting that Gerard had attained, in a high degree, the practice of constant and uninterrupted communion with God. Moreover, from Father Giovenale, who lived with him at that time at Iliceto, we have preserved a statement which confirms this assertion.

"I remember," says Father Giovenale, "that one day in Chapter, Father Cafaro commanded him not to think continually of God. But what could he do? God drew him with an irresistible power. And yet he did not wish to disobey. He would then walk through the corridors of the house, sighing 'O my God! I do not want You now; I do not want You!'"

Sometimes the contemplation of God threw him into an ecstasy and deprived him of the use of his senses. Gradually, the soul of the servant of God became so susceptible of divine love, that often a picture, a sound, a pious word, were sufficient to snatch him from the external world, and to throw him into an ecstasy. Thus he was once going down stairs to take some gentlemen who were making their retreat in our house to the dining-room, when he accidentally glanced at a picture of the Immaculate Conception, hanging on the wall opposite the stair-case, when he fell into an ecstasy which lasted a considerable time, to the great astonishment of those who were present.

On another occasion he was appointed to serve at table while several young men were making a retreat, previous to their ordination. In this room there was a picture of the Ecce Homo hanging on the wall. While Gerard was performing his work, a glance on the picture was sufficient to rouse his love of God, and he fell into an ecstasy. His eyes were rigidly and immovably fixed on the picture, his arms were outstretched, his whole body motionless. In one hand he held a napkin, in the other a fork. In this condition he was found by a lay-brother. When the latter saw that Gerard had not yet finished his work, and there was very little time left, he wished to awake him from his ecstasy, and called him by name. But Gerard heard nothing. The brother then raised his voice, yet Gerard did not move. Father **Cafaro** had to be called. The latter then seized him by the arm, and commanded him to revive. Gerard regained consciousness immediately. Father Cafaro, however, in order to humble him gave him a sharp reprimand, which the servant of God received with his usual calmness and resignation.

While engaged in very ordinary occupations, which afforded no occasion for any special emotion of the heart — for instance, when he was taking his meals — such a plentitude of sublime thoughts and sentiments often surprised him that he could not resist them. The Fathers Giovenale and Cayone, as also Brother Rendina, testify that at table Gerard frequently burst into tears, and whether he was thinking of the goodness of God Who furnished him with food, or that some other holy thought suddenly and powerfully took possession of his mind, he was not far from falling into an ecstasy. He raised his eyes to heaven, and his whole demeanor betrayed an expression of the deepest devotion and astonishment. The secret of his extraordinary interior recollectedness was his intimate union with the will of God. He did not aspire to ecstasies and spiritual consolations, but rather to accomplish the will of God in all things as perfectly as possible.

"I wish," he said, "to love God, I wish always to be with God, and to do every thing for the love of God."

"The centre of all love for God," he however said, "consists in giving ourselves entirely to God by being in all things conformable to the divine will, and remaining in this conformity for all eternity."

"O will of God!" he once cried out, "O will of God! how happy is he who understands how to wish nothing else than what God wishes!"

To obtain a higher degree of love for the adorable will of God, he united all his meditations, devotions, penances, and pious exercises with the great mysteries in which God manifests His love. It afforded him a delightful opportunity of living as it were the life of the Church, in her annual celebrations of these mysteries.

It was above all the Mystery of the Redemption by which he sought to enkindle the fire of his devotion, and from which he eagerly drew interior vigor. The Crucified was the favorite subject of his meditations; to hear any one speak of the sufferings of Christ, or to see a picture of Him, was sufficient to throw him into an ecstasy; and during the time in which the Church reminds the faithful of this great mystery, he entered into the meditation of it in such a manner that he himself seemed to suffer with our Saviour. He seemed on these occasions, especially in Holy Week, like a man in his agony, and about to breathe his last. Again, when the church was celebrating the closing of our Lord's tomb, it appeared as if he were no longer among the living, but that he was buried with our Lord. "Alas!" he was heard to say; "Jesus Christ died for me, and I do not die for Him."

But the Passion of our Lord had moved Gerard while yet in the world, not only to sympathy, but to endeavor as far as possible to show it in himself, by becoming also exteriorly like our divine Saviour. It was a yet stronger factor in his religious career.

"Christ crucified," says Father Tannoja, "was a book, from which he constantly read; the more he read in it, the more it appeared to him necessary that he should torture his own body."

In fact he believed that a love for our Lord could not be acquired without mortification of the body. "The love of God" he used to say, "cannot enter a soul if the body is too well treated." (se il cannarone è ripieno.) He therefore treated it, we might say, not unlike the manner in which the executioners treated our Lord. We will simply make mention of the fasting on bread and water, of the practice of rendering his food and drink distasteful by means of wormwood and aloes; of the hair cloth which he wore; of the little iron chains which he used to fasten around his limbs. We do not wish to speak at length of the scourgings which he now undertook not less unmercifully than in former days, and for which he often used the most frightful instruments, such as hard knotted cords or scourges furnished with twelve sharp-edged iron stars, which he used in such a way that the place where he performed this penance was bespattered with blood. We shall speak of one torture only which the saintly brother inflicted upon himself by way of imitatating the sufferings of our Lord, which is unexampled. Had we not authentic testimony concerning the matter we should regard it as incredible, and should pass it over in silence.

The reader will remember the grotto situated at the foot of the hill on which the convent stood, and in which Blessed Felix of Corsano had devoted himself to contemplation and penance. This grotto had become a favorite resort for Gerard; here he meditated and prayed in solitude and quiet. Inflamed with the desire to become like our suffering Redeemer, he wished to inflict sufferings in which he might approach as near as possible the tortures of the scourging, the crowning with thorns, and the crucifixion. In order to accomplish this, he induced a young man of Lacedogna, Andrew Longarelli, a Postulant of the house, to take the place **of the cruel** executioners who ill-treated **our Lord,** and to do **from a motive of** love what they did through hatred. Longarelli **knew the** extraordinary piety and **the spirit of penance of Brother Gerard to** bear the **most intense** sufferings with patience; **and he also** knew that the servant of God never practised penances without the permission of his spiritual **director. He** therefore yielded to his earnest entreaties, and **assisted** him in the performance of bodily affliction.

When Gerard wished to begin his meditation on the **sufferings of Christ, he went** with Longarelli into the **grotto of Blessed Felix.** Here the Postulant had first of all to **tie Gerard's fettered hands to a** beam, which **was to represent the pillar** of scourging, and then he **had to strike him with** wet cords until the blood trick**led to the ground** from his shoulders. After the scourging followed the crowning with thorns. A bundle of thorns reminded him of the crowning of **our Lord with** thorns. Gerard relentlessly **pressed it on his head,** and his companion had to **strike it with a cane.**

Gerard, however, was not yet satisfied. One day he **wished to represent in his person,** as far as was possible, **the crucifixion.** For this purpose he succeeded **in procuring one** of those large wooden crosses which **the** missionaries were accustomed to use in the erection of Calvaries, and took it to the grotto. Longarelli had to fasten him to it with ropes; and as he had read **that** when our Lord was nailed to the **cross His limbs had to be forcibly drawn to their places,** he also requested **that** his companion should violently pull and **stretch his** hands and feet. The pain which he suffer**ed must have been great,** but for this diciple of the Crucified, ever thirsting for suffering, it was not intol**erable.** He then ordered that a crown of thorns should be placed on his head; and thus the picture of the Redeemer was completed.

When, occasionally, Longarelli moved to greater compassion, hesitated to scourge and bind him as cruelly as he desired, or if he began to perform his task with greater pity and indulgence, Gerard burst into tears and begged and implored Longarelli to continue the work of charity which was so meritorious for him.

The tortures in the grotto of Blessed Felix, lasted during a considerable time, but were afterwards forbidden by Father Cafaro. From this time they ceased until a new Superior came and Gerard found new reason for repeating them, as we shall see later.[1]

"Gerard's desire to participate in the sufferings of Jesus Christ was not without reward," as Father Tannoja remarks. "It pleased the Crucified to favor him with a grace which He bestowed upon but few of His servants, such as St. Francis of Assisi and St. Catharine of Sienna: namely, of experiencing mystically the sufferings endured by Jesus Christ in His Passion. For this grace he had earnestly asked, and he received it. Although he looked strong and well on other days, he presented a changed appearance on Friday nights in consequence of this grace; he seemed to be a man oppressed with pain, very sick, and a great sufferer; nay,

---

[1] The awful tortures to which the servant of God submitted, and the peculiarity of using the help of others in inflicting them, may seem to many a reader excessive and eccentric. That such a thing may be regarded as a general rule, we can easily admit. However, in order to form a correct judgement of the permissability of those tortures in the case of the servant of God, we must consider that in passing judgment on forms which the saints have given to the practices of piety, and especially of penance, we must act just as we do when we pass judgment on the manners and customs of peoples. As in regard to the latter we are never permitted to use our own tastes, habits and inclinations as the rule for finding out what is right or wrong, so we are not allowed to do so when we are judging about those forms. Not every thing in the manners and ways of living that is suitable to one is suitable to another, and even where there is often the same urgent

he even seemed to be in the agonies of death, and he often spat blood while in this state. But the interior sufferings which he had to endure, and the desolation of his spirit, were so great, that as he told his directors, they were beyond description. But on Saturday night he was quite himself again; the weakness vanished, and Gerard was able to perform the usual duties of the house."

Besides the sublime mystery of the Redemption and of the Passion of Our Lord, which the servant of God made the subject of his meditations with special fondness, there were also three other mysteries of religion in which the thoughts and sentiments of his soul were occupied, and on which he was anxious that his spiritual life should depend. These were the mysteries of the Incarnation, of the Blessed Sacrament, and God's masterpiece of power and grace, — the Immaculate Conception of the Blessed Virgin Mary.

Apart from the fact that the Child Jesus — the embodiment of benevolence and loving condescension on the part of the Most High — has always manifested reason, there are developed, in consequence of different tendencies of mind and heart, different manners and customs. The same thing happens in the case of the unessential forms of piety and penance which are, in their development, left to the individual. With the greatest unity in fundamental things there may be developed in this respect, owing to different tendencies of mind and heart, a great diversity and even a certain opposition, which causes one form to create a dislike in the follower of another form. It would, however, be wrong to be misled by the feeling of dislike into passing a condemnatory judgment about these different forms of piety and penance. In pronouncing judgment in reference to the peculiarities of certain saints, we should moreover remember the saying of St. Agustine: "Give me one that loves and he will understand me." Again, in regard to these penances of Gerard, we must remark that other saints were herein his models. To speak of one more example: In the life of the missionary and spiritual man, Father Paul Segneri, S. J., are related practices of penance which are almost similar to those above described.

the most fascinating attraction for holy souls, it was this same Child that at an early day had visibly approached Gerard, and had led him into the extraordinary path on which he was now walking. The remembrance of this benefit and grace was indelibly impressed upon him. Besides, the servant of God seemed subsequently to have been found worthy of being frequently visited by the Holy Child. The latter was, however, the object of his meditations and veneration, which he needed not to select, because, having from the beginning loved and cherished Him, he kept Him always in sight. In his religious life he availed himself to this dear object with greater zeal, in order to inflame his love, to strengthen his desire for sufferings, and to acquire humility and simplicity of heart.

His biographer, Father Tannoja, and others who were acquainted with him, narrate that his devotion to the Divine Child afforded him inexpressible consolation. The festival of Christmas filled him with holy joy, and he took special delight in decorating the crib and the church. The preparation of his soul for the graces of the feast was however, the greatest object of his desires. For this purpose he made a special novena, during which he observed a strict fast, and allowed himself very little sleep. Christmas-day he passed in the church, rapt in prayer, or in his cell, engaged in practices of penance. It was for him quite a heavenly night, and caused him to be as joyful as if he had heard the Hymn of Peace sung by the angels.

The Most Blessed Sacrament had the same attraction for the servant of God as the Crib; it had influenced him not only since his entrance into the convent, but he had long before felt its power. It now increased, and considerably strenghtened its efficiency in our laybrother. His devotion became incomparably ardent and tender. Perhaps in the convent he was not able to spend as much time before the altar as he was able to do previous to his entrance into religion, yet he supplied in fervor what he lacked in time. Before the altar he seemed to be aflame. Sometimes when the Most Blessed Sacrament was exposed for the adoration of the faithful, he could not conceal his interior ardor; he lost consciousness and was absorbed in an ecstasy of love and joy. The time during which the Church represents to the faithful in a special manner this most adorable mystery produced in him the most lively feelings. On the feast of Corpus Christi and during its octave, Gerard walked about in a frame of mind the counterpart of that indescribable sadness which seemed to change him into a dying person on Good Friday. A visit to the Blessed Sacrament was one of his favorite practices. He generally employed every spare moment for this purpose. The office of sacristan was therefore that which particularly gratified him, since it gave him the opportunity to be near the altar, where he could pay homage to Jesus in the tabernacle, while at work. He also found free moments which he devoted to this holy occupation of love. For this he generally used the time which, according to the custom of the country, was allowed to the Fathers and brothers for their mid-day rest. Thus, while the others slept, he went to the church and prayed. He often did the same during the night. "It was a touching spectacle," says Father Tannoja, "to see how Gerard struggled sometimes, in consequence of his love for Jesus Christ and his spirit of obedience; the latter, however, always gained the victory. Once when I was in the church unobserved by him, I saw that while he was bending the knee at the foot of the altar in order to leave the place, he was struggling to rise. As he did not feel himself free to do so, he cried out: 'Let me go, I have something to do.' He then hastily retired, as if he were tearing himself away by main force from the Divine Presence."

The love which the saintly brother entertained in his own heart toward the mystery of the Blessed Eucharist, he also endeavored to infuse into the hearts of those whom he met. It grieved him to see the churches empty and the public places thronged with people, and he could not withstand his longing to induce and lead to our Lord as many as possible, to visit and adore Jesus in the Blessed Sacrament. In order to effect this, he not only gave the good example himself, but he also had recourse to gentle encouragement and kind solicitation. Wherever he went, either at home or abroad, he sought to gain guards of honor for our Lord in the Blessed Sacrament. "It was to his efforts," as Father Tannoja testifies, "that the inhabitants of several districts are indebted for their present assiduity in visiting the Blessed Sacrament."

Finally, as regards his devotion to the Blessed Virgin, he gave convincing proofs of its reality, ardor and activity, at an early age. While at Iliceto this devotion became more fervent and universal.

The vigils of the feast of the Blessed Mother he always spent in church in prayer and meditation; also, he was accustomed, like a true son of St. Alphonsus, to celebrate with special prayers and all kinds of penitential exercises, those days of the novenas held in her honor.

There were, however, three glories of the august Virgin Mary toward which he was more affectionately disposed, and which he always contemplated: the divine Maternity, her dignity of Queen of Martyrs, and the Immaculate Conception. This last mystery had not then been solemnly declared a dogma of faith, but like all those souls who had penetrated more deeply into the life of the church, Gerard was always among the defenders of this most noble prerogative of Mary, regarding which he was of the same opinion **as his brethren** of the priesthood who bound themselves by a vow **to defend it.**

The office of sacristan afforded him the desired opportunity to show in various ways his love **for Mary and his zeal** for her honor, — an opportunity which he never failed to turn to account. In the same manner in which he encouraged others to visit the Blessed Sacrament, **he led** them to honor our Blessed Lady. **He** sought occasions to say a word about the devotion to her, and to recommend the making of sacrifices in her honor. He always had rosaries and scapulars on hand, and distributed them wherever he hoped to enkindle or to increase the devotion to Mary. When he was not able to influence the minds of the people in favor of his Queen, he at least **decorated** her altars with the same **care and** happy skill with which, in later days, and in his travels to different places, he understood how to arrange and direct so many brilliant and edifying processions, **grand** fireworks, the firing of guns and the like.

We cannot doubt that this zeal bore fruit, and gained **not a few** persons, who became very devout to the **Blessed** Virgin. Certain it is that his efforts did not remain without a special reward. More than once, our Blessed Lady expressed her benevolence toward her faithful servant in an extraordinary manner, during his **stay at** Iliceto. We have already mentioned that Gerard fell **into a** long and sweet ecstasy while he was one day looking at a picture of the Immaculate Conception; we may reasonably suppose that this was not the **only** occasion **on which** he received so signal a **favor.**

The Reverend Fathers Giovenale, Petrella and Cayone **tell** us that the servant of God once enjoyed the great **happiness** of seeing the Mother of God, face to face. While he was keeping his usual nightly vigil in the **church before** her picture, she appeared to him in all her dazzling beauty, and assured him in a most tender manner of her love and favor. More than once she glorified his love and devotion to her in a striking manner. A surprising incident of the kind is related by Father Tannoja, who states the sources from which he has drawn his information.

One day Gerard was returning home accompanied by two young peasants, when he came to a church dedicated to the Blessed Virgin which was situated near the road. Gerard made use of the opportunity to speak of the glories of his august Queen. He began therefore to speak of the Blessed Virgin, and was ere long overcome by an exuberant emotion. This joyousness increased to such an extent that he appeared transformed. Suddenly he seized a piece of paper, and having written a few words upon it, he threw it into the air as if he wished to send a letter from this world to his heavenly Queen. The love, the joy of his soul overcame the law of gravitation in a wonderful manner; he leaped high into the air, and hurried forward, to the great astonishment of his companions, who were able to follow him only with their eyes. Not till the servant of God had passed over the distance of about half a mile in his ecstatic flight did the marvelous power which had raised him abate, and Gerard again approached. This event contributed much to make him known in the whole district, and to earn for him the reputation of being a great saint; for both the young men who were witnesses of the miracle spoke of it wherever they went.

This ecstatic flight seems, however, to have awakened in the servant of God all other marvelous powers. Having reached the door of the convent he found a young man of wretched appearance sitting there. The poor sick man was afflicted with a dreadful cancer in the leg, which seemed to be incurable. Having heard of Gerard's great sanctity, he resolved to have recourse to the servant of God. Owing to his earnest entreaties **his parents had, with great** difficulty, carried him to **the** door of the convent; as Gerard was not at home, **the** afflicted man remained there awaiting his return. The patient's pitiable **condition induced Gerard to ask** him what was the matter. **The suffering** petitioner told him of his suffering **and trials: he had always** been very poor, but now since God **had afflicted him** with this ailment he was condemned to beg his bread. Gerard embraced the deeply distressed man, and ask**ed to see the** diseased leg. He loosened the bandage **himself and** found that the limb was eaten away by a horrible, **cancerous ulcer.** He then stooped, and **applying his lips to the ulcer,** heroically suppressing **all natural disgust, he sucked** the nauseous matter **from the wound. "Trust in** God, my dear brother," he said; "your wound will heal." Then he carefully bandaged the leg. At the same moment the young **man felt** freed from all **pain. His** joyful surprise **at the happy change was so** great that with tears of **gratitude he cast himself** at the feet of his benefactor. He called him a saint, — an angel of God. Gerard exhorted him to practice virtue, gave him an alms, and dismissed him. The next morning, when the young **man** removed the bandage from the leg, he really found **what Gerard** had foretold, — the wound quite closed **and healed.** It was a source of unbounded joy and heartfelt gratitude. The young man who had been **cured also began to** proclaim Gerard's praises, and to demonstrate **his** sanctity and power, as seen in **the** miracles of his benefactor.

The previously mentioned case of ecstatic flight was not the only one of the kind during Gerard's stay at **Iliceto.** A certain person named Magdalena de Flumeri narrates an occurrence not less wonderful, of which her aunt Rosaria Bertucci, was an eye-witness. It is recorded in the acts of the process of beatification. Magdalena narrates as follows: "Rosaria," she said, had led a pious life from her youth, and often visited the church of 'Mary of Consolation' for the purpose of going to confession. Now it happened that on one of those occasions, she met the great friend of God, — who was returning from Iliceto. He was well acquainted with her, and asked her to carry a garment (capotto) with which he entrusted her, to the house of the Fathers. Then, through modesty, he walked a little in advance of her, until he came to a chapel which he entered. When he again left her he was raised into the air with outstretched arms, and thus was carried for about a mile, from the chapel to the church of 'Mary of Consolation.' My aunt who was a witness of this miracle, stood there transfixed and amazed, observing this wonderful flight. As long as she lived she regarded this memorable coincidence as most extraordinary and astonishing."

CHAPTER VIII.
Austere Life And Charity Towards Others.

It is characteristic of genuine piety that it awakens and nourishes in the heart of its possessor two desires which are apparently incompatible, but which are in reality in perfect harmony. We refer to austerity towards one's self and a tender and considerate love of our neighbor. We know of Gerard's severity towards himself while he was still in the world; it increased considerably after his entrance into religion.

Whether we consider Gerard's cell, his garments, or his other personal wants, we shall everywhere find that he was contented with the least as well as the worst things.

With the permission of Father Cafaro, he had chosen a dark corner of the house which was formerly used by the Augustinians as a store room. His bed strictly speaking, might be called an instrument of torture. It consisted of a mattress padded with straw only along the edges, the middle being filled in with sharp stones; two tiles serving him for a pillow. On this hard couch he took a short rest, which he endeavored to lessen and interrupt by an inconvenient posture.

This austerity he practiced till the end of his life. It was in Caposele that one of his brethren, actuated by curiosity, found upon examining Gerard's bed that it was filled with stones and thistles.

The only piece of furniture which Gerard had in his cell was a miserable chair. He had placed a number of skulls around his bed.

He thought he was deserving of such austerity and poverty, and considered a better dwelling too good for him. When asked by one of his brethren why he wished to live so poor a life he answered: "I do it for the love of God and my Creator. I deserve it."

When Monsignor Basta, Bishop of Melfi, and Monsignor Amato, Bishop of Lacedogna, came to Iliceto to make their retreat and saw Brother Gerard's cell, they did not find words to express their astonishment at the sight of such extreme poverty and austerity.

Later, however, to the great regret of the servant of God, an ordinary cell was assigned him, but he rarely occupied it. When strangers came to the house to make a retreat, or otherwise availed themselves of its hospitality, Gerard was always ready to give up his cell. If he found no hiding place that afforded him the desired mortification he would sleep in any other corner of the house, or on the floor of the church. The high altar was hollow and the space which was shut off by a little door was large enough to lie in. He was happiest in the church near the Blessed Sacrament, just under the altar on which the sacrifice of the Mass was offered daily. Once, however, this pious practice caused him great annoyance. Probably after too long a vigil, Gerard had lain down there towards morning, to rest. Very much fatigued, he had fallen into so deep a sleep that he did not wake till after the first Mass had been begun. The little bell that rang at the Consecration roused him. But now he could not come out of his hiding place without betraying his practice of mortification and causing astonishment and distraction to those who were present in the church. He was therefore obliged to remain under the altar still longer.

On other occasions when Gerard had to give up his cell to strangers, he retired for the night to the stable, and lay down to rest on the straw that was intended for the beasts of burden.

When the Superior directed him to sleep as others did, to use a simple straw mattress and not to sleep on the hard floor or on stones, Gerard begged so earnestly and perseveringly that he might be permitted to continue his ordinary way of taking his rest that he finally prevailed on his spiritual director to allow him to sleep on a board three times a week, and to use two tiles for his pillow. He also received permission to fasten stones to his feet, and to encircle his temples with little iron chains while he was taking his nightly repose.

The same austerity which Gerard practised as to his lodging and bed, he also showed with regard to the clothes he wore. Being the tailor of the house, it was his duty to distribute different articles of clothing, and he was thus enabled to clothe himself according to his own taste. While he gave to others new and good clothes, as a rule he selected for himself the oldest and worst. How poorly the good brother was often clad may be inferred from the fact that he was sometimes not recognized by outsiders familiar with the religious garb. The poverty of his dress gave rise to many mistakes which were occasionally very comical, as we shall see further on. With all his poverty, he always had the highest regard for cleanliness, and was very far from seeking virtue in negligence and slovenliness.

We have already had occasion to mention how austere he was in regard to food, and merely wish to add that in all things he depended on divine Providence. It is true, he never neglected anything that was entrusted to him in this matter; but he was never anxious as the generality of people are even to provide for his necessities.

When he was sent from home to attend to some business, the Superior had always to give him directions as to how he should provide for his wants, for he himself thought as little about them as sparrows think of their food, relying with childlike simplicity upon the Providence of God.

One day he was sent to Terra d' Accadia. He set

out early in the morning, and as Father Minister had forgotten to give him his breakfast before he left, he made the long journey without breaking his fast. When the good brother had arrived at the end of his journey he was so tired and weak that he fainted. To procure food for himself on the way had never entered his mind.

The measure of austerity which the servant of God exercised towards himself was also the measure of the charity which he exercised on behalf of others. Towards himself he was hard and rigid, even while he manifested to his neighbor a kind of charity resembling maternal solicitude, which being sustained by the most sublime motives, extended to all persons.

It is quite obvious that his own brethren were, in a pre-eminent degree, the first objects of Gerard's charity. We have already described how readily he assisted the lay-brothers working with him, and how anxious he was to do their work. We have also quoted the principles which he had laid down for his guidance, with respect to his intercourse with the lay-brethren. We only wish to remark here that he conformed most perfectly to these principles, and that he therefore became a model of brotherly love.

In the position of tailor he had the best opportunity to practise this charity, and we are told that he never missed it; that each day he gave proofs of attention and readiness to do favors for others.

As glad as he was when he suffered personal want, so did it seem insupportable to him when others suffered. One extremely cold winter he deprived himself of his warm waistcoat to give it to another who was in need of it, satisfied with his wretched threadbare outer garment. He never desired to have any thing more convenient than others had, and joyfully gave up what was better, being satisfied, as he expressed himself, "with whatever God allowed him to have. For then all will be contented, and I myself will also be satisfied."

Gerard was particularly charitable towards the sick. If one of his brethren was sick, the saintly brother, though not appointed to nurse him, went to see him at least once a day to console him and to perform some little act of kindness. In general he showed attention and sympathy which were prudent as well as tender.

Though Gerard's charity was directed to his own brethren in preference to others, the latter were not yet excluded from it. He gave the clearest proofs of this during his quiet life in the novitiate, and during the time that immediately followed it, even before he was obliged to associate with the outside world.

Canon Francis Anthony Sebatelli of Melfi was taken seriously ill on a visit to the house at Iliceto. He had not been particularly acquainted with the servant of God. The latter was nevertheless ready to render the sick man the necessary service, and watched day and night at his bedside. Sebatelli did not know that the obliging brother was depriving himself of his night's rest. His astonishment was therefore great when, one night, suddenly waking, he saw at the foot of the bed the good brother, who was anxiously watching him. Such great charity springing from the purest virtue edified the Canon in the highest degree, and in order to compensate the good brother he ever afterwards, extolled the holy brother's charity and goodness.

Still more wonderful was Gerard's charity manifested on another occasion; a hermit lay dangerously ill in our house at Iliceto. The unfortunate hermit had hitherto only deceived the world and had by no means led the life which his dress betokened. The disease of which he was slowly dying was as horrible as it was fatal. His body diffused so offensive an odor that no one could approach him without feeling the greatest disgust, and he was shunned by all unless they were obliged to visit him. Gerard bestowed the most magnanimous attention upon this poor man. How the servant of God yearned to save the wretched soul of the hypocrite! However, his love and efforts were fruitless. In vain did he represent to the dying man the reasons for contrition and confidence in God; in vain did he try to fan into flame the last spark of faith. The dying reprobate's heart remained insensible; and as the imposter had despised so many graces, so he also dispised this last and greatest of all graces. He died impenitent, a most wretched death. Gerard nevertheless thought he could continue the exercise of his charity, and recommended the soul of the deceased with great fervor to God. While he was once more praying for him, the miserable man appeared to him and said in a terrible voice: "Cease to pray for me; I am damned and I am damned by the just decree of the Almighty!" Gerard was so horrified and frightened by this revelation, that during his whole life he remembered this occurrence with terror.

Just about this time, perhaps to console him in his sadness and to increase his confidence, God permitted him to know that the divine power and help were still in an astonishing manner within his reach.

In the little town of Iliceto there lived a young man who was lying hopelessly ill of consumption. His physician had declared his inability to do any thing for him. "In order to help him," he said, "I should have the power to make a new lung." The sick man and his family, in their terror at so sad a prospect had recourse to heaven; they had heard of Gerard's great sanctity, and of the power he possessed of working miracles. They asked Father Rector to give the brother permission to visit the sick man. The Rector acceded to their wishes and the servant of God came to the house just as the physician was making his visit. In his presence

Gerard now consoled the young man, encouraged him to become pious, and told him to place his confidence in God, "in Whose hands," he said, "are the destinies of men, and from Whom he might also expect the recovery of his health." These words which were opposed to the verdict of the physician naturally displeased the latter, he could not refrain from renewing his previous statement in which he declared the invalid to be in a dangerous condition in the presence of the sick man and of the whole family. "He cannot recover; the lung is too far gone."

"Well," said Gerard, who looked at things from a different point of view, "the lung may be decayed; but do you believe that God Who is the Creator of all things could not supply a sound lung or restore the diseased one to its former healthy condition? May it be pleasing to God to work this miracle in order that confidence may be instilled in the hearts of His faithful, and they may be encouraged to call on Him for help, from Whom alone they can obtain it!" Having said this, he arose to depart. The parents of the sick man then asked Gerard to pray for him; to which the latter acquiesced. He kept his word, and his prayers were wonderfully efficacious. From this moment the condition of the sick man improved, and after a few days he was well. Everybody was astonished, especially the physician who now admitted in the presence of all, that this cure was an undeniable miracle and that without a miracle it could never have been accomplished.

The poor, as well as the sick, were the objects of Gerard's charity. Every poor man moved his feelings, and if help could be afforded it was always given. Even those who were placed in a momentary perplexity could rely on the servant of God as a most ready helper.

One day he met a poor man who was carrying a bundle of dry wood on his head, on his way to the convent, he was walking along with great difficulty, under such a load. Gerard immediately came to his assistance, put the bundle on his shoulders, and carried it to the old man's hut. The same thing happened at St. Agatha di Puglie. Ascending a steep hill, he noticed a poor woman who had just been washing clothes in the river; the effort to walk up the hill with the wet and heavy clothes on her head almost took away her breath. He took the bundle from her at once and put it on his own head. On entering the town he felt some repugnance to appear publicly in this fashion. He overcame human respect most heriocally and carried the bundle through the public square of the town, and did not give the clothes to the owner until he had reached the door of her house.

"In this act of charity," say Father Tannoja, "he most faithfully imitated Brother Curzio, who used to exercise the like charity towards the street porters at Scala."

We have another example of his charming readiness to serve others, when on a certain occasion he had to accompany several candidates for ordination he met a number of workmen between Melfi and Atela who were in great perplexity in consequence of the overflowing river. They had been engaged to do some work on the other side of the stream, but were afraid to pass through the water. Gerard was ready to help them immediately. He was on the other side of the stream and crossed it without delay on a horse; one after the other, he carried them in succession safely across the river. Don Michele Pinto who was present, assures us of Gerard's confidence; that he rode not as through raging torrents, but as if over solid ground. The holy brother anticipated no danger. To those who cautioned him not to be too daring he made answer: "Carita del prossimo!" (Charity towards my neighbor); and encouraging his horse; he said: "Now my little horse, let us do something to please God." ("Cavallo mio, diamo gusto al nostro Dio!")

In the course of the journey he and the candidates came to another river which they had to cross, and which, like the first was very much swollen. No ford could be seen. Gerard, however, was not perplexed. He acted towards the candidates as he had acted towards the workmen, and carried them separately in safety to the other shore.

But, if charitable in temporal concerns, he was more zealous in his charity when eternal goods — the interests and salvation of souls — were at stake.

Hence he constantly prayed for the Church, for her **duffusion throughout the earth, for** her chief Pastor the Pope, for bishops and priests, for the missionaries, especially for his own priestly brethren who were laboring in the pulpit and in the confessional for the honor of God and the salvation of souls.

The thought that the world is so cold, that it is a stranger to God's love, was peculiarly painful and insupportable to him. He longed to inflame the earth with the fire that he felt burning in his own bosom. Those souls who followed the inspiration of grace, who loved and served God with a generous heart, were to him a charming spectacle. It was difficult for him at times to conceal the joy it afforded him.

On the contrary, the mere mention of sin **caused him** great sadness. He would willingly have given his life **to prevent** such an **evil** as sin. He often lost his **habitual** cheerfulness instantaneously, when he reflected that God is so often offended by man, and that the sufferings of Christ are rendered fruitless by sin. Then he would heave a deep sigh, and tears would trickle down his cheeks.

We can therefore easily understand that poor sinners

were the principal objects of his charity. In fact, he would make the greatest sacrifices for their conversion. His good works, his prayers, his communions, his sufferings, — everything — he offered up to God for them.

We may justly say that at this time his sentiments were not different from those to which he afterwards gave expression in the following words: "O my God! would that I could convert as many sinners as there are grains of sand on the sea-shore, leaves of trees and blades of grass on land, atoms in the air, stars in the firmament, — as many as there are rays of the sun and of the moon, and creatures which the world contains!"

If the servant of God met a sinner and discovered the possibility of saving his soul, the simplicity of the brother was changed into energy, under the influence of hope and charity; his taciturnity into eloquence, his modesty into assurance; he then spoke in such a manner that no one could contradict his convincing arguments nor resist his holy importunity. Rarely did Gerard work in vain for the conversion of a sinner; seldom did those who had been converted by him fall back into their old vices. When there was question of the saving of a soul, the servant of God knew neither human respect nor threatening danger, though he never transgressed the limits of his humble station, and he always retained that calmness which is peculiar to virtuous zeal, and which exerts such great influence over others.

Between Iliceto and Foggia there was a tract of land which belonged to the Duke of Bovino, which was intersected by a road leading to Foggia. Owing to this fact the duke's land suffered considerable damage and he wished to prevent persons from trespassing upon his property. He therefore hired a few guards, whose duty it was to warn travelers not to trespass. As it usually happens, these men, in obeying orders, exceeded the power which they had received, and treated people with great harshness, and even with blows.

One day Gerard, who had been sent by his superior to **Foggia to attend to some business**, returned home by the forbidden road. He was riding on his horse, **wholly unconscious** that he was injuring any one, **when** suddenly the guard rushed upon him in great excitement and with a furious look. The guard was a ruffian; a monster of cruelty rather than a human being. **The fact that he treated the poor lay-brother so inhumanly,** proved that what had been reported was true. Amid horrible curses he attacked the unsuspecting young man, began to strike **him with the butt-end** of his **musket,** and finally **inflicted** a blow that **broke one of Gerard's ribs,** and caused him to fall senseless **from his horse. With all this the fiend** was not yet satisfied. **He still continued to strike** him without mercy, and **finally he thrust the end** of his weapon into his breast **and sides.** "I have long been wishing to revenge myself on a monk," said the infuriated monster, "you have **just** come, and have most opportunely thrown yourself into my power."

As he relaxed in his ill-treatment, Gerard cast himself at the feet of his enemy, to ask pardon. "I do not want either excuses or pretexts," the guard answered, more furious than ever, and began to beat him again most unmercifully. When Gerard saw that he had **a man before him whom fury had rendered quite insensible,** he resigned himself to his fate, and clasping **his hands** he said "Strike, **brother,** you have reason to do so; continue to strike!"

This act of humility and of patience produced the **same effect as cold** water poured upon seething and foaming water. Such resignation, such calmness, so inconceivable a desire for sacrifice, vanquished the angry man; he came to his senses, and as often happens with such persons, the frenzy of passion was followed by most vehement self-condemnation and heartfelt sorrow for having allowed it to control him to such an extent. The guard threw away his musket, struck his breast, and cried out with a voice choked with sobs: "What have I done! Alas! What have I done! I have killed a saint!" He then threw himself at the feet of Gerard, begged his forgiveness, and asked him to forget all that had just been done.

The request was heartily granted. The servant of God embraced the penitent sinner, now doubly rejoiced on account of his wounds and pains, as he entertained the hope of winning the soul of the unfortunate man. He reiterated his excuses in all humility, and only requested the guard to help him mount his horse and to accompany him to the convent.

While riding home no complaint about the treatment escaped Gerard's lips. He sadly lamented the pitiable condition of the soul of his guide; he therefore spoke to him of those things which might induce him to reflect seriously on his conversion. He impressed upon him, as well as he could, the heinousness of mortal sin, spoke of God Whom he had offended, and spoke of the fire of hell which he had deserved. He was only concerned about the salvation of this soul; the thought of rescuing it from destruction constantly occupied his mind.

He arrived at the convent half dead. He was at once questioned concerning the cause of his pitiable condition. Gerard, however, not wishing to expose his companion, and desiring to complete the work of love with the greatest tenderness, said nothing about the outrages he had suffered, but only spoke of a fall from his horse. Moreover, he praised the kindness shown him by the guard in accompanying him home, and knew how to exalt this slight kindly act in such a way that the guard received a recompense. Gerard left him with the following words: "Brother, **what you have done to me, do to no other, lest** you have cause to regret it."

These new proofs of an unspeakable charity produced a salutary effect on the intractable mind of the guard, so that he fully opened his heart to grace, and after he had publicly made known the whole occurrence **to the honor** of the servant of God, he came **to our house** at Iliceto, where he made a general **confession amid many tears** and other extraordinary signs **of contrition.** Happy would he have been if he had never again left the road of penance. But he was a **man of** such character and disposition that perseverance in a good life could have been gained only by the **exertion of an iron will**; he was one of those unhappy beings who can disengage themselves from evil which has penetrated all their inclinations and desires, only by constant and fervent prayer. This exertion was too **much for the man, he had no desire** to engage in a battle with himself, **and thus** again fell into the vice which he had lamented and detested with so many tears.

One **day while he was again** discharging the duties **of** his office, he met a traveler, who was treated in the same manner as Gerard. He made a furious attack on **him, and also** began to ill-treat him, as he had done to **Gerard, with blows and** thrusts, because **he** had trespassed on the grounds. The latter, however, was not **so lamblike as the poor lay-brother of Iliceto,** and **jumped from his horse, snatched the musket from the guard, and struck** him a blow that threw him to the ground half dead. The unfortunate man should have regarded this as a warning from God, but he did not, and though he soon recovered from his bodily wounds, his soul still remained wounded and miserable. A short time afterwards the tyranny of this incorrigible man bore its last sad fruit. In a new quarrel, a ball fired by an enemy struck him and deprived him of life as well as of the time for grace which he had so much abused.

The lay-brother bitterly lamented the death of the guard. As long as Gerard lived, he remembered the unfortunate deceased, for, in consequence of the cruel blows which the man had inflicted upon him his breast was so affected that he frequently spat blood, and was often overcome by extreme weakness. He never spoke of the cause of this trouble. When one of the brothers surprised him while he had another hemorrhage and was going to tell the Superior of it, Gerard prevented him from doing so. "O my brother," said he to him, with that humility which deems itself unworthy of any care and attention, "you will confer a great charity on me if you say nothing about this. Do not speak of it, I beg of you, for I have often had such attacks, and I never felt myself obliged to mention this trouble to any one."

Though the charity which Gerard revealed in the conversion of the unfortunate guard was not accompanied by a permanent result, his zeal was crowned in a hundred other cases with success in the realization of his wishes. His efforts brought conversions which were as complete and lasting as they were wonderful, and the house at Iliceto was in this respect a witness of the most astonishing occurrences in regard to changes that were wrought in men's souls.

Among those who had come to Iliceto to make their retreat there was a gentleman of high standing. He wished to put the affairs of his conscience in order, and began the spiritual exercises with a good intention. But scarcely had he begun them than he lost his peace of mind by a continual and vehement temptation to despair. The devil excited this in him, by pointing out the many sins he had committed, his ingratitude, and the difficulty of effecting a true and perfect amendment of life. **The poor sinner** lost all courage. He lost hope **and the inclination to work successfully for** the salvation of his soul, which appeared to him quite useless. **He** finally resolved to return home and not to trouble himself about this matter. Gerard met him in this frame of mind. Being inspired by God, the servant of God knew the storm that was raging in the heart of the unhappy man, and observed his increasing despondency. He therefore hastened to offer him relief. Without making a long introduction, he thus addressed him: "What is the matter with you? Banish this mistrust; it comes from hell; for God and the Blessed Virgin are **obliged** to help you." This kind of language made the nobleman blush; he felt that his interior had **been** read, and he was consoled and strengthened in such a manner that he was at once free from the temptation. He then banished all gloomy thoughts, and grace triumphed.

Another person, while making his retreat, had yielded to the temptation to make an insincere confession, and yet he wished to participate in the general Communion which was held in the church, and had already gone there, when Gerard, who was praying in the gallery, became enlightened from on high in regard to the interior of this man. Going down to him he called him aside and represented to him with impressive words the **dreadful** crime which he was about to commit. Great was the astonishment, and overpowering the confusion of the sinner. The scales fell from his eyes, and what he formerly knew but did not regard, — the enormity of his malice, — he now realized, and hastened to seek a confessor, to whom he sincerely and humbly acknowledged all his sins. In the excess of his repentence he immediately went to the church in which all had assembled, fell on his knees, and said in an audible voice: "I have been ashamed to confess my sins to the servant of the Lord, but Brother Gerard made them all known to me, and now I acknowledge them before all men, to my own confusion." The repentant man would really have made a public confession of his sins, had not a Father who was present emphatically forbidden him to do so.

The servant of God performed a similar, yet greater and more wonderful act of charity, in behalf of a priest whom Monsignor Amato Bishop of Lacedogna, had sent to our house at Iliceto, for the purpose of making a retreat. This man had brought great shame upon his sacred calling by a public scandel that had lasted many years. Severity and kindness failed to produce any effect. Exteriorly, he made the spiritual exercises that had been forced upon him, in such a way that all were edified; but interiorly he was unchanged, and ready to continue his disgraceful mode of living.

In order to wear the mask of the hypocrite till the end, he also wished, like the others who were making retreat, to approach Holy Communion on the appointed day. On his way to church for this purpose he was met by the servant of God. Gerard detained him and said: "Where are you going?" "I am going to Communion," said the wretched man. "To Communion!" answered Gerard, in a tone of voice which expressed horror, indignation, and reproof at the same time. "To Communion! you are going to Communion! And this sin and that and that you did not confess! Go back and make your confession, but make a good confession, if you do not wish the earth to open and swallow you!" Greatly moved by language so powerful, which presupposed a supernatural insight into his interior, the priest repented, confessed his sins, and made a firm and sincere resolution to change his life.

With the best resolves he then left the house of the Redemptorists, and returned to his home. However, **the fervor of** his zeal lasted only a few months. Later on, it again grew cold and the unfortunate man turned back to the evil which he had left, becoming worse than formerly.

Nevertheless, the following year, he again came to Iliceto in **order** to make his retreat with the Fathers. Human respect had forced him again to assume the mask of the hypocrite, and as if he had forgotten the power of Gerard's eye, he dared to say to him in answer to a question about the state of his conscience, that all was well with him, thank God, and that he had not relapsed into his former faults. Yet the servant of God could **not be** deceived. Inspired by God, he knew as well as he did before, the real condition of the man's **soul, and was deeply** grieved at the bold lie, which convinced him that the wretched man had again fallen into the snares of the "Father of lies."

His zeal for souls encouraged him **to hope** for **the salvation** of this soul, however discouraging the prospect seemed to be. He now employed the most efficacious means to accomplish this difficult undertaking. He most fervently begged God to furnish him with power, charity, and patience. Then he took a crucifix, and proceeded to the room which had been assigned to the **priest.**

Having entered, he immediately shut the door and **windows.** He was very much agitated; in his heart **there was** an ebb and flow of the most ardent zeal, the **most tender love** and just indignation, which were reflected in his eyes, his manner, and his bearing. Without any introduction, the servant of God began the subject and thus addressed the priest: "What does all this mean, my dear sir? You have dared to offend God in this manner! Alas, you ungrateful and wretched liar! How is this? You have done nothing? You have not relapsed? Look at these wounds of Jesus Christ! **Meditate** on them! Who caused them, if not your wicked deeds? You have made this blood flow from His veins?" Saying this Gerard held the crucifix before the eyes of the sinner; and behold! from its hands and feet there flowed real blood, — a miracle which did not fail to make an impression on the mind of the poor priest.

But the lay-brother continued his soul-stirring appeal. "What evil has your God inflicted upon you?" he said with increased energy. "For you He wished to be born an infant in the stable; for you He lay on the straw, deprived of all things!" While Gerard was speaking, the priest saw the Infant Jesus in the hands of the brother.

Yet Gerard ceased not to speak. "What!" he again said to the sinner, "you dare to insult your God, to insult Him in such a manner! Alas, you remember that no one can do this with impunity! God is good, but in the end He chastises and punishes. You also, if you do not put an end to your wickedness, will surely experience this. What then will await you — see here!" Gerard made a sign with his hand, and before the eyes of the sinner there stood a horrible demon, who with threatening aspect turned towards him as if wishing to attack him and carry him off. The sinner trembled, and was struck dumb with terror. "Begone, you unclean beast!" said Gerard, when he noticed what effect had been produced on the unfortunate man; and the vision disappeared.

But now the heart of the sinner was shaken as it were in its innermost recesses; he was filled with fear and contrition. The image of celestial love as well as that of diabolical hatred, which had been palpably represented to him, had completely softened him.

He could no longer resist. After Gerard had left him, he hastened without delay to Father Petrella, made his confession, narrated the miracles which had converted him from his hypocrisy, and gave him permission to make them public for the edification and instruction of all. This time the amendment of his life was perfect and permanent; the converted man never more deviated from the right path, but till his death led a truly edifying and exemplary life. In this way he blotted out all traces of former scandals.

As the servant of God converted this sinner by a mysterious representation of the blood of Christ, of the Infant Jesus, and of the devil, so on another occasion, by a similar mysterious bringing forward of a soul from hell, he moved another man to contrition.

This was a man who while making retreat intended to approach holy Communion in the state of mortal sin. Luckily Gerard met him at the right moment, and taking him aside he called him to account. He spoke to him in a kindly manner and said: "My dear brother, you are going to communion, and there is still a grievous sin on your conscience which you have not confessed. Do you not know what a great crime it is to commit a sacrilege? Ah, if you do not know, I will show you; see the hideousness of a sacrilegious soul!" At this moment a lost soul appeared! The sight of it was so terrible that the poor sinner trembled in every limb, and burst into tears. He hastened back to the confessional, made another confession, and amended his life. This admonition given by Brother Gerard, and the vision of the lost soul was a salutary remembrance during the rest of his life, and helped him to persevere in subsequent temptations to sin.

A great number of similar conversions were brought about by Gerard's wonderfully sustained zeal. They all bear witness of the love the servant of God had for poor sinners.

There does not exist a more effective proof of the zeal of the servant of God in this respect than the fury of the evil spirit, who now annoyed the good brother unceasingly, and even more than when he was still in the world. The evil one augmented his attacks in proportion as Gerard increased in zeal for the conversion of sinners, and succeeded in this kind of work.

During the night, he was often attacked by a whole army of evil spirits; they presented themselves to him under the most frightful appearances; howled, yelled, and threatened, as if they wished to tear him to pieces. Once, while the servant of God was working in the kitchen, they assumed the appearance of furious dogs, and endeavored to push him into the fire. They often dragged him through the corridors of the house, struck him violently, or seized him by the throat and nearly choked him. The Friday nights, during which Gerard was accustomed to devote himself to practices of penance for the atonement of sin and for the conversion of souls, were especially noisy and stormy.

It is remarkable that they often told him in plain terms why they annoyed him. One of the evil spirits once said to him: "You do not wish to desist from robing us of souls -- I shall not desist from tormenting you till I have put you out of this world."

In spite of all this, they were not able to inspire him with fear for any length of time. What he at that time wrote to a distressed soul in regard to the terror which is usually inspired by the devil, was for him a leading principle. "If the devil," "seeks to fill our soul with fear, let us not be disturbed. It is his part to frighten us; our part is, not to allow ourselves to be deceived by his tricks. It is true, there are times when we feel confused and weak. Yet if God is for us, if we have recourse to His power, we need not be confused and faint-hearted, for there is no doubt that in these struggles we are sustained by the Almighty's arm. We can afford to remain calm, and rely more securely on the divine will."

However furiously the evil spirits might attack him, he still despised their want of power. "You can bark," he cried out to them, when they surrounded him like hungry wolves, "but while Jesus Christ and my dear Mother Mary are with me, you cannot bite me." And when they attacked him somewhat boldly, he dipped his finger into holy water, springled them with it or made the sign of the Cross, and the infernal band was dispersed as is the morning mist before the rising sun.

"How many possessed persons," says Father Tannoja, "did he not deliver by one word! On one occasion, when he had been sent for by one of these unfortunate beings whom the devil refused to leave he put his cincture around the waist of the person, and thereby put the enemy to flight."

The servant of God also possessed the faculty of being sensible of the presence of the spirit in any place; no matter how the evil one was disguised, Gerard could not be deceived. Thus, one Sunday, two young men were seen in front of the church; no one knew who they were and whence they had come. Gerard saw them and knew them immediately. "What are you doing here?" he said to them, "this is not your place; in the name of God go back to hell." At the same moment the two unknown men disappeared. They were evil spirits. What reason they had in boldly placing themselves near the church is unknown, yet the fact is established, as more than one of the residents of the convent were eye-witnesses.

CHAPTER IX.
FIRST PUBLIC APPEARANCE. RELIGIOUS PROFESSION.

In June 1751, Father Mazzini[1] visited the house of Iliceto as Inspector. This visit was of great consequence to the servant of God. Having but recently entered the community as lay-brother, he had not the slightest prospect of being permitted to take his vows. According to a custom hitherto observed in the Congregation, the time of probation for lay-brothers had been extended to a longer period of time, and there were grave reasons for making only occasional exceptions to this rule. Gerard was not physically strong, yet his health had been exceptionally good during the past year. Although his Superiors recommended him and his co-brothers spoke highly of him, this was not sufficient to prevail upon the holy Founder to admit the servant of God to profession sooner than any other member. One of the Consultors of St. Alphonsus, Father Mazzini, a very influential adviser, personally observed

---

[1] John Mazzini was born at Naples in the year 1705. Having been ordained priest, he distinguished himself by a great devotion to the Most Blessed Sacrament, which he frequently visited, especially in those churches in which the devotion of the Forty Hours was celebrated. As St. Alphonsus, who at that time was at Naples preparing himself for the priesthood, had the same pious habit, they could not fail to become acquainted with each other at the foot of the altar. This acquaintance soon led to an intimate friendship, which proved afterwards to be of great importance to Mazzini as well as to St. Alphonsus. When the latter was called to establish the Congregation, and communicated his plan to his friend, Mazzini not only encouraged him, but declared that he was ready to follow him as his first companion. He faithfully kept his promise, although for the purpose of doing this he was obliged to remove many obstacles which were thrown in his way

the servant of God and was thus convinced of the genuine virtue and extraordinary spirit of the young lay-brother. Father Mazzini maintained that the Congregation received in him a heavenly treasure whose intrinsic value could not be doubted; nothing would be more reasonable than to receive him without further hesitation. He therefore appealed to the holy Founder to make an exception in Gerard's case; and encouraged those who made propositions to the Superior to that effect.

St. Alphonsus consented, and in January or February of 1752 a letter was received from the Saint at Iliceto, permitting brother Gerard to enter upon his second novitiate preparatory to taking the holy vows.

With what delight the servant of God obeyed this direction can easily be imagined. In the meantime a change had taken place in the house of Iliceto which considerably affected the young novice.

On the 30., or 31., of October 1751, Father Cafaro resigned his office as Superior, to assume new duties as rector at Caposele. Father Giovenale substituted him for a short time, being succeeded by Father Salvatore

by his parents, relatives, and even his own director. "No one," he himself relates, "can form an idea of the distress to which I was subjected. Only after many entreaties and tears was I allowed to join Alphonsus. This was in the year 1733." Father Mazzini was thenceforward the constant companion of the holy founder. Besides the office of Rector, which was several times intrusted to him, he was chosen to be a General Consultor. His life was entirely worthy of a friend and first companion of St. Alphonsus. He died in the odor of sanctity, December 2. 1792, after he had the happiness of giving his brilliant testimony in the process of the beatification of St. Alphonsus. In the account of the latter's virtues he also speaks of Brother Gerard in the following terms: "This Brother died many years ago. He left behind him a high reputation for sanctity, and worked a great number of miracles, not only during his life but after his death." (Process of beatification of St. Alphonsus, summ. Sup. virtut., p. 747.)

Gallo for a few weeks. In February 1752, Father Carmine Fiocchi took charge of the house in Iliceto, which office he held until October 1755.

The separation from Father Cafaro, who had been a wise director in every respect, was very distressing to the servant of God; in fact, he could not resign Father Cafaro's direction entirely, but continued his former relation to him till his death. Father Cafaro on his part did not fail to assist this privileged soul by his counsel and instructions. "The Lord," said Father Cafaro, when speaking of the servant of God, "has exalted this brother above all other men; his life has been a continuous miracle."

In the meantime Gerard chose Father Giovenale to be his confessor, instead of the much loved Father Cafaro. Father Giovenale, born at Lacedogna in 1719, entered the Congregation as a young priest in 1746, and had resigned himself unreservedly to the direction of Father Cafaro in Iliceto since 1749. The spirit of this pious young religious was communicated to him. In order that he might better be able to direct Gerard, God sent him a series of the severest trials; this experience rendered him an excellent director of souls. Henceforth he labored indefatigably on the missions. "Were it only granted me," he was heard to say, "to die with the weapon in my hand in the battle for the salvation of souls, redeemed by the blood of Jesus!" He died renowned for his great virtues, in S. Angelo a Cupolo, on the 1st of May 1782.

When brother Gerard commenced his second novi\-tiate, is is very probable that Father Giovenale was his novice-master. Later, when Father Giovenale (in April 1752) was removed to the house in Caposele, the Rector, Father Fiocchi, seems to have assumed this office.

The servant of God did not suffer any loss by the

change. Father Carmine Fiocchi, although younger than Fathers Giovenale and Cafaro, was nevertheless equal to them in virtue and the faculty of guiding souls; he was just the man to gain the sympathy and confidence of the servant of God. The chronicle of the Congregation speaks of him in such manner, that we do not hesitate to number him among the most important disciples of St. Alphonsus.

Father Fiocchi was born of virtuous parents at Cajano, June, 1721. He gave proof of genuine piety in early childhood, loved intercourse with God, and was so devoted to practices of penance that his mother was obliged to take certain instruments of penance from him so that he could not exceed the proper bounds. After he had attained the age for study he went to Naples for a more advanced course in the sciences. The vanity and frivolity of the capital exercised no evil influence over him; he preserved his innocence, his pious disposition, and made as much progress in virtue as in the sciences. Having entered the clerical seminary at Salerno, he was soon ordained sub-deacon. But, he had a higher aim in view, he felt that he was called to the religious life and did his utmost to correspond therewith. After inquiring into the merits of the different religious societies which he might enter, he felt especially attracted to the Congregation of the Most Holy Redeemer which had been recently established by St. Alphonsus.

He therefore wrote to the holy Founder, made known to him his thoughts and desires, asked him to test his vocation, and petitioned to be admitted among the members of his Congregation.

The saint complied with his request, and after some time wrote him that "his vocation was from God; that the Lord wished to have him entirely for Himself and for the good of souls; and that he should therefore correspond to the divine call, since these calls are transient graces which may easily be lost." Thereupon Fiocchi set out immediately, and hastened to the novitiate at Ciorani.

Fiocchi's parents, who though otherwise pious, were very much displeased on account of his departure. In consequence they became so exited that they not only appealed to the resolute young man with entreaties and threats to induce him to give up his resolve, and to return to the seminary, but they also called upon the secular authorities for aid.

They succeeded in having Fiocchi removed from the house of the Redemptorists, and sent by the authorities to a convent at Salerno to test his vocation; but, it was not in their power to make him change his resolution. The blows of the hammer had only hardened the steel, and Fiocchi, after having endured many annoyances and vexations, came back to the novitiate the more courageous, the more cheerful and, the more desirous of self-sacrifice. This happened in 1743.

After zealously and fervently passing through the year of probation, he made his profession and completed the course of studies. He was then ordained priest, and despite his youth was immediately employed in the work of the missions, for his maturity of character supplied the want of years. He was one of the greatest missionaries trained in the school of St. Alphonsus, and in this field of labor spent a period of thirty years, unceasingly active, burning with zeal, fortunate in results; captivating and savings souls not as much by his great eloquence as by the power of his virtues. In his twenty-eight year he was appointed Rector of the house at Nocera, and after the death of Father Sportelli (1750) St. Alphonsus admitted him among the number of his General Consultors.

All virtues, especially poverty, humility and obedience, shone forth in Father Fiocchi. We have already made mention of his ardent love for the Blessed Sacrament and the Blessed Virgin. He was a master in the art of walking constantly in the presence of God. His favorite ejaculatory prayer — just the prayer of a missionary — was: "O Lord! spirit and courage!" ("Signore! spirito et animo!")

Father Fiocchi died a holy death, in 1776, while uttering the sweet name "Mary." Several wonderful incidents are recorded of prayers that were heard through his intercession. Four years after his death, his body was found incorrupt.

Under the guidance of such spiritual directors as Father Giovenale and Father Fiocchi, is was not difficult for the servant of God to continue in his second noviciate what he had begun in the first. Again it was to the practice of obedience and penance that the pious brother devoted himself most zealously.

Father Giovenale gives us several examples of the simple and humble obedience of the novice. We cite them in the words of the priest. "One day," Father Giovenale relates, "I called Gerard to serve my Mass. I knew well, for it was a notorious fact, that after receiving Holy Communion he usually fell into an ecstasy. Nevertheless I told him to receive Communion before Mass and to make his thanksgiving during Mass; then he might return to his work. Remembering what generally happened to him, he could not refrain from saying to me; 'But my Father!' I immediately interrupted him and said; What do you mean by saying, "But my Father?" Do you not wish to be obedient? This was sufficient. He obeyed tremblingly. However, as soon as the Holy Sacrifice was over Gerard hurried away to hide himself on his knees and remained there a considerable time without giving any signs of life."

Of his docility and disposition to obey, Father Giovenale, in an account written by himself, relates the following incident: "Gerard had received special grace from God, and in consequence of this divine privilege he was perfectly free from temptations against holy purity; so free, that he was wholly unconscious of their nature. Not apprehending danger any where, he did not find it a necessity to guard his eyes. When I observed this I called him and asked: "Why have you so little regard for modesty as not to cast down your eyes?" "Ah, my Father!" he answered in all simplicity, "why should I cast down my eyes?" In order not to deprive him his simplicity, I merely said: "Because it is my wish that you should cast down your eyes."

"I remember being called to him one day, when he was ill. Repairing to his room, I found him prostrated with a violent fever. In the capacity of spiritual director, I commanded him to rise and go to work. He arose, and the fever left him. I was about to depart for the missions, when he came to me and asked: "Father, shall I not be ill, hereafter?" 'You are to remain well, until my return from the missions,' was my reply. And so it happened."

Father Fiocchi learned, as Father Cafaro had learned before, that the obedience of the servant of God was sustained by a supernatural knowledge of the thoughts of the Superior. On one occasion a letter had to be forwarded to Lacedogna. The Superior gave it to Gerard and told him to set out immediately. The obedient lay-brother had already gone a distance from home, when the Rector remembered that he had forgotten to mention an important matter in his letter. "Oh, if I only had that letter back again!" he thought within himself; and behold, in a short time Gerard entered the room, and handed the much desired letter to the Superior. Father Fiocchi feigned to be ignorant of the reason why the brother had returned, and therefore asked an explanation. Gerard made no reply but smiled so significantly as if to say that he had known his desire, and it was this knowledge only that induced him to return.

The following gives evidence of the remarkable obedience of the servant of God. In March 1752, Father Fiocchi went to Melfi to visit the Bishop of the place, Monsignor Basta, who was a great friend of the Congregation. The holy life of the lay-brother Majella naturally became the topic of their conversation. For a long time, the Bishop had desired to become acquainted with him. This desire was now increased still more, and induced him to ask the Rector to permit the brother to stay with him for some time. The reasons which he gave for making this request and the consideration which his dignity and friendship deserved, moved Father Fiocchi to yield to the desire of the Bishop.

Greatly pleased with his success, the Bishop wished to send a messenger to Iliceto immediately, to tell Gerard of the arrangement that had been made to bring him to Melfi. "Monsignor," said Father Fiocchi, "it is not necessary to send for him: it is sufficient for me to think that I desire him to come, and he will be here in a short time. I will show you how far his obedience goes, and in what manner he is favored by God." After he had spoken thus, he reflected for a few moments, and gave Gerard the command to repair to Melfi.

At the same moment Gerard who was at Iliceto went to Father Minister who replaced the Rector during his absence, and asked him for permission to go to Melfi; "for" said he, "it is there the Superior wishes to see me." Permission was granted, and Gerard set out accordingly arriving at the episcopal palace at Melfi while the bishop was speaking to Father Fiocchi. "What brings you here?" said he to the brother, with some bitterness when he entered to kiss his hand. "Obedience to your Reverence's call," modestly answered Gerard. "What? Obedience?" continued Father Fiocchi, "I called you here neither by letter nor by messenger." "Surely you did, Reverend Father," he answered. "In Monsignor's presence you gave me the express command that I should come, as he desired to see me. Alas, Monsignor!" he said, turning towards the bishop, "who am I that you should wish to speak to me? I am only a worm of the earth, a miserable being who needs the fulness of God's mercy."

Gerard's coming and his humble words made quite an impression upon the bishop who found the guest such as public opinion had described him, — a miracle of obedience, of simplicity and of humility. The Prelate was now still more anxious to have Gerard for some time in his own house, and to keep him under observation. The soul of this young man seemed to him worthy of study, and he hoped also to derive many useful lessons from his supernatural wisdom, for the benefit of his own soul as well as for the souls of those intrusted to his care.

He therefore asked that Gerard might be allowed to remain with him for a few days, and his request was granted.

The prelate, whose hospitality Gerard enjoyed, was of a cautious and quiet disposition. For although he presumed that by his first impression of Gerard he had received excellent testimony of the brother's virtue, he wished to examine into it more critically, that he might the better appreciate it.

He began to test the spirit of the holy lay-brother in various ways, and most eagerly traced the deeper motives which animated him in order to see whether or not Gerard's interior dispositions corresponded with their external splendor. This test was decided in favor of the **servant of God.**

The prelate was now most lavish in his attention to his guest, and sought to turn to account the supernatural science and prudence of this highly favored religious. He had daily conferences with him, and directed them in such a manner that Gerard was obliged to express his judgment in regard to matters concerning the welfare of the diocese, and to communicate his views in reference thereto.

Persons who lived with the bishop were equally anxious to avail themselves of the gifts of the servant of God. Gerard who had **come to** Melfi, through obedience remained there in obedience, and God's blessing **ever attended him.** No one ever tired of listening to him or consulting him. A priest with whom he often **came** in contact in the bishop's residence says: "He treated religious subjects and especially the Mystery of the Redemption with **such facility, that** he seemed to be another Augustine or Jerome.

The life led by Gerard, as well as his supernatural wisdom, astonished and edified all. He lived in the **palace of the bishop as he lived in** his cell at Iliceto. He engaged in labor, prayer, and different practices of piety; was continually collected in God, and appeared to live among men only for the **purpose** of enkindling in them the fire of divine love.

An incident is on record **to verify this.** One day a certain Nicholas Martini, who was cook at the bishop's **house, met him.** The servant of God was just then engaged in his accustomed spiritual delights, inflamed like a seraph. In this condition he walked up to Martini, put his hand on his breast, and said in an impressive tone of voice: "**Let** us love God! oh, let us love God."

Gerard also became known outside the prelate's residence; he was especially esteemed in the convent at Ripacandida and Atella which belonged to the diocese of Melfi, and with which, as we shall learn later on, the servant of God was at that time brought into closer relation.

The three weeks which Gerard was permitted to spend at Melfi passed too quickly for his friends. They endeavored to detain him a little longer. But, the servant of God would not be detained a moment longer than his Superior had permitted.

On the evening of the last day which he was permitted to spend in their midst, he put the bridle on his horse and prepared to return to Iliceto. It was late, and a heavy fog had risen; besides, a heavy rainfall threatened.

The heavy fog had made the road almost invisible. Soon he lost his way, and found himself in the thicket which lined the banks of the Ofanto, and through which it was dangerous to travel, on account of the innumerable ravines caused by many heavy rains. Gerard's situation was critical, on account of the darkness, and of the rain that was now pouring down in torrents, he could no longer see anything; hence he had to trust entirely to the instinct of his mount.

Suddenly, he noticed a human being directly before him, apparently determined to hinder his advance. It was a demon who wished to make use of this occasion to destroy his enemy whose life was now in the greatest danger. The evil spirit was, however, obliged to help the man of faith out of his difficult position, and lead him to his destination.

At a late hour at night Gerard arrived safe at Lacedogna; he knocked at the door of Constantine Capucci, a friend of the Congregation, in order to avail himself of his hospitality for the rest of the night.

Let us hear from his lips, or rather from the lips of Gerard, how it was possible that he arrived without accident, and escaped the hostile designs of the evil spirit.

"It was about four o'clock in the afternoon," (ten o'clock according to our reckoning) says Capucci, in a report which has been handed down to us, "I was sitting with my family around the hearth, and we had already thought of retiring, when I heard a knock at the door. To have some one calling at the house at so late an hour and in such weather startled me. I asked who was knocking. 'Brother Gerard,' was the answer. The voice was familiar to me. I quickly opened the door and saw the brother before me, thoroughly wet, and bespattered with mud from head to foot.

"'O my dear Brother Gerard,' I cried out, and having embraced him I added 'What brings you here at such an hour, and in such weather?'"

"'The will of God be done at all times, my dear Constantine,' he answered; 'I have returned from Melfi; but in the darkness, fog and rain, I lost my way. I found myself on the banks of the Ofanto so close to the ravines that I would have lost my life, if God had not come to my assistance. While I was in the greatest danger on the brink of a precipice, somebody stepped up to me and said: "Here it is that I wish to secure you; now I am your master; you did not obey your Superior, and God will not forgive you this!" I was at first a little startled, but I had scarcely recommended myself to the Lord when I perceived that the speaker was a demon. "Miserable fiend," I said to him, "I command you in the name of the Blessed Trinity to take the bridle of my horse and to lead me straight to Lacedogna without doing me any harm." Thus led by an evil spirit, I was saved from the danger that threatened me. Without this guide I should not be alive, and my body would be buried in the ravines of the Ofanto.

After we had reached the church of the Holy Trinity, the strange guide said to me in evident ill-humor: 'You are in Lacedogna', and instantly vanished."

With the same simplicity and frankness with which Gerard related this adventure to his friend Capucci, he also related it, upon his return home, to Fathers Fiocchi and Giovenale, from whom he thought he ought not conceal anything of this nature.

During the time of his final probation, he considered obedience and the practice of severe penance a sacred duty.

For a long time the grotto of Blessed Felix had served him as a secluded place of prayer. This was the order of his Superiors, and he obeyed. But now, he thought the time had arrived when he might repeat his former inflictions and petition that the prohibition be rescinded. He therefore presented this request to his Superior, and to his great joy it was granted. Thus the grotto again became the theatre of unheard-of mortifications, which perhaps differed from the former only by the fact that they were more severe.

The place of Lougarelli was now taken by a certain Francis Teta, a tailor by trade, and a native of the city of Nusco; at this time he was leading a retired life, and was working in the convent. Gerard could promise himself much from the service of this man who was greatly indebted to him.

The reader will allow us to explain in a few words how he became acquainted with Teta. One day Gerard, entrusted with a commission from his Superior, found himself on the road which leads to San Agata di Puglie, a small town not far from Iliceto, when he came to a place where two roads cross each other. He thought he heard an interior voice saying: "Stop here; a great sinner will come to you soon." He stopped, and waited. Presently, he saw a man approach whose countenance expressed the deep melancholy that had taken possession of his soul; his features bore the stamp of guilt as well as of remorse. "This is my man," said Gerard within himself, when he perceived the condition of the stranger.

The man, however, hastened his steps as soon as he noticed the lay-brother, and endeavored to pass by him rapidly. Still more convinced that the right person was before him, Gerard accosted him with this friendly question: "Where are you going, my friend?" The mild tone of the question made no impression on the dark-visaged man. "That is none of your business; let me alone," he answered abruptly. Gerard, however, did not allow himself to be disconcerted. "I beg you," he continued, "to have the goodness to tell me who you are, and where you are going. Perhaps I may be of some use to you." "I am going my own way; you go your own; do not trouble me," the man replied, angrily, and was about to rush past him. But Gerard held him fast. "I know," said he, "that you are in despair, and on the point of giving up your soul to the devil. You are doing a great wrong, and God has sent me to this place just on your account! Have confidence in Him!"

These powerful but kind words effected a salutary change in the disposition of the unhappy sinner. His heart was softened, and opened to God's grace. With tears in his eyes, he revealed to Gerard the sad and troubled condition of his soul, and desired that the servant of God should form his judgment about these matters, and counsel him. The saintly brother encouraged the penitent sinner, and pointed out the means which he should employ. "Go," he said, "to Iliceto; try to find Father Fiocchi, make a good confession, and all your troubles will cease." The sinner obeyed, went to Iliceto, made his confession, and showed such fervor that his petition to obtain work in the convent was granted, and he was allowed to remain in the house for some time. He became the model of a pious penitent, a man of prayer and mortification. After four years he went to Naples, where he devoted himself to the care of the sick.

This converted sinner was no other than Francis Teta, whom Gerard had chosen for his task-master. After what had been narrated, we shall understand that Teta was obliged to acquiesce in Gerard's wishes and commands, however difficult these might appear.

Teta also exerted himself to render to his holy friend the service which he asked of him as well as possible: he scourged him to blood, crowned him with the favorite crown of thorns, and fastened him to the cross just as Lougarelli had formerly done. It sometimes happened, that Teta's courage failed him, and in spite of the joy manifested by Gerard amid his tortures, he stopped and did not wish to continue, being overcome by compassion. Then Gerard who found delight where others could see no cause for it, began to entreat and implore him. If entreaties were of no avail, he had recourse to what he thought was his right as far as Teta was concerned, and said: "Oh, if you do not wish to do what I have asked of you, — then I command you to do it! Strike me, yes, strike me, by obedience!"

In order not to lose the merit acquired during his second novitiate, he added penance to this life of obedience and modest retirement. He felt the necessity of this seclusion the more, since he had become known to the world. His time would have been greatly trespassed upon by externs, had he not absolutely withdrawn himself. His greatest desire was to be forgotten; and he rejoiced that the Superior assisted him to attain this end by depriving him of intercourse with seculars.

The Prioress of the Carmelite nuns in Ripacandida had asked Gerard to present her regards to a certain hermit. "In order to comply with your request" he wrote to her, April 16., 1752, "there was no other means for me to adopt, than to give your letter to brother Cajetan. At the present time, only the language of signs is open to me; I have been dumb for a considerable time, because this is God's holy will. My Superiors have forbidden me to speak to any one outside the Community, and in this prohibition have excepted only the case when I am out of the house. Do pray to our dear Lord that He may destroy the erroneous opinion which people have of me, that they may give up the desire to see me and to converse with me."

The long-desired month of July, 1752, had come at length, when he was to consecrate himself as a holocaust to his Lord, by making the vows. On the feast of the Visitation of the Blessed Virgin he began the customary retreat of fifteen days, and on the 16th. of July, the feast of the Most Holy Redeemer, and of our Lady of Mount Carmel, he made his religious profession.

Unfortunately, the details of this celebration have not been preserved. The only special item recorded is, that the saintly brother offered his sacrifice with great joy, and that the entire Community at Iliceto participated in his happiness. We can, however, easily infer from the already well known dispositions of Gerard, what emotions of gladness, love and gratitude must have filled his heart during this most sublime act. Moreover there are in existence two letters, written by the servant of God shortly after his profession, when yet full of the impressions that had been made upon him, in which he clearly expresses his sentiments in regard to the great priviledge that had been conferred upon him. The first of these letters is addressed to St. Alphonsus, Superior General of the Congregation.

It is a true mirror of the soul of the good brother, and reads as follows:

"Jesus, Mary!

"The grace of divine love be always in the soul of your Paternity, and may the Immaculate Virgin Mary preserve it for you. Amen!

"Most Rev. Father: Prostrate at the feet of your Paternity, I thank you most heartily for the goodness and love you have bestowed on me, without any merit on my own part, in receiving me into the Congregation, and in allowing me to be numbered among your sons. Blessed be for all eternity the goodness of God, Who has permitted me to participate in so many mercies and favors, among them being the inestimable privilege of making my profession, and of consecrating myself entirely to Him, on the feast of the Most Holy Redeemer. O God! who was I? and who am I? that I should dare to consecrate myself to Thee!

"I should like to speak of the greatness and goodness of God! but it is useless under the present circumstances, and you would call me a foolish man. Most Rev. Father, I beg you, for the love of Jesus Christ and of the Most Blessed Virgin Mary, to give me your blessing, and to place me at the feet of His Divine Majesty. I kiss your hand. I remain your Paternity's unworthy son, Gerard Majella, of the Congregation of the Most Holy Redeemer."

The second letter, dated July 26., 1752, is addressed to Father John Mazzini, one of the General Consultors. We quote it:

"Jesus, Mary!

"May the grace of the Holy Ghost fill the soul of your Reverence; may it always remain in it, and may Mary Immaculate preserve it. Amen!

"My dear Father: How much I love you in Jesus Christ and the Blessed Virgin Mary, with a love which is pure and founded in God, I cannot tell you; God alone knows it. Most cordially do I thank you for the goodness and love with which you exerted yourself in my behalf, in requesting our much beloved Father to allow me to take the holy vows. I made my religious profession on the feast of the Most Holy Redeemer, and I hope that the Divine Majesty will not forsake me, but will always sustain me in doing His holy will.

"My dear Father: For the love of Jesus and the Blessed Virgin Mary, I recommend my soul to you! Do not forget to commend me frequently to God, just as I shall never, never, never forget your Reverence.

"I kiss your consecrated hand. Et perpetuo permanemus in corde Jesu et beatae Mariae. (Let us always remain in the holy hearts of Jesus and Mary,) I remain, your most unworthy servant and brother, Gerard Majella, of the Congregation of the Most Holy Redeemer."

As was to be expected, the perfect sacrifice of himself by the holy vows intensified his love of God. In his note book we find the resolution frequently to renew his vows, in the following words: "At every memento for the dead (at holy mass) I will declare to the Lord my desire for martyrdom, and fervently renew my four vows."

Another passage reads thus: — "On September 21., 1752, I understood the following truths better: To suffer, and not to suffer for God, is an infinite torment. — To suffer everything, and to suffer for God, is nothing!"

Moreover, in imitation of St. Teresa, he made the vow, at this time, "always to do that which he knew to be most perfect," — a vow at which the weakness of human nature recoils, and which is the expression of a heart that lives entirely for God and for His interests.

As this sublime and most difficult vow was in perfect harmony with the life and endeavors of the servant of

God, it was, as his biographer remarks, "well adapted to raise him to a very high degree of perfection. Henceforth, nothing could be seen in him except what was heavenly, — a heart entirely open to every influence of the Holy Spirit, a religious of incomparable purity, and an armament of God, which possessed all the qualities requisite for the great things to be accomplished in the souls of men through his humble labors."

CHAPTER X.

The Gatherer Of Alms.

According to the plan of divine Providence, the beauty of Gerard's virtue was to be displayed not only in the seclusion of the convent, but he was to become in no slight degree, as far as the rank of a simple lay-brother permitted, an apostle, and a saver of souls among the people of his native country.

From his childhood, he had cherished an inclination for apostolic labors. How he displayed his zeal in the beginning of his conventual life, has just been told. After his profession, there were many opportunities of laboring for the salvation of souls, which had been denied him previous to his taking the vows.

A very favorable opportunity to evince his zeal was afforded him by the custom, followed by the Neapolitan Fathers, of taking a lay-brother with them on their missionary tour.

He had to discharge the duties of steward, to render the Fathers every kind of domestic service, and also to attend to the business outside of the house. As our saintly Brother Gerard united in himself these qualities in an eminent degree, it was quite natural that the Fathers chose him to accompany them on the missions. Gerard on his part did not neglect so grand an opportunity to display his zeal for souls.

Without trespassing the limits of his office, he labored more than many a preacher, by the example of his virtues as well as by his pious conversation with all classes of persons. "He was," says a witness of his activity, "a most assiduous co-laborer of the priests, especially in his love for instructing the poor people. He was very attentive to those who had strayed from the path of duty, he communicated with them privately, and reclaimed them to virtue. His peculiarly pleasant and engaging manners ensured him perfect success; the Fathers used to say; "The example and labors of Brother Gerard do more good than a thousand missions and sermons!"

A word from his mouth, a glance from his eye, could scarcely be resisted by the most hardened sinner; so that when the confessors did not succeed in infusing into any unhappy man the proper dispositions; if his hardness of heart set at defiance all their exhortations and entreaties, they endeavored to persuade him to have a short interview with the servant of God, Gerard, or at least to call and see him. If the sinner agreed to do this, it usually happened that he returned after a short time, but in a quite different frame of mind: softened, converted, determined, reformed.

What learned and zealous priests could not accomplish, he brought about by a few words, the simplicity of which was truly marvellous. He generally spoke to poor sinners calmly and gently; but when he deemed it necessary, he knew how to be severe, and addressed them with an earnestness which made them tremble.

In this way, he effected the most remarkable conversions. "This holy brother was a visible instrument in God's hands," says a missionary; "we could do nothing but gaze at him in amazement, and endeavor to imitate him."

Not only on the missions, but at other times, the Fathers frequently desired the servant of God to accompany them, namely, when they had to leave home for the purpose of giving novenas, triduos and similar exercises. Every one regarded the success of his labors insured if he could have this highly favored brother at his side. Such anticipations were never disappointed.

Although blessed with good results in his apostolic labors during the missions and on similar occasions, Gerard's influence was still more productive in other undertakings. A more extensive field of labor was open to him when the poverty of his community compelled him to beg for alms. "Let us fortify ourselves with courage," St. Alphonsus wrote to Father Xavier Rossi, when the house of Iliceto was established, "for our life here will be a life of poverty." The prophecy was fulfilled. The disadvantages under which the work in Iliceto was begun multiplied from day to day. It was useless to depend upon the other houses of the Order for assistance, as they themselves often suffered want.

Thus the Superiors had to submit to the unpleasant necessity of availing themselves of the help of the benefactors of the Institute; for this purpose they sent out some of the brothers to different parts of the country, to gather alms according to the recommandations and instructions given by the bishops and pastors.

Among all the brothers, none seemed to be better fitted for this difficult and delicate business than the servant of God. He displayed charming modesty, tender blending of affability, simplicity and earnestness, which distinguishes the mendicant lay-brother from the common beggar; that piety, purity of morals and freedom of rudiness which are as effective as a sermon whereever the mendicant goes; finally, prudence which is of absolute necessity in his intercourse with the world. In the meantime the reputation of his sanctity had already become generally known; every one esteemed him highly; he was regarded more as a messenger from heaven than as an ordinary mortal. Hence the hope that he would not only attain, in a most satisfactory manner, the main object, — that of gathering alms, but that he would draw upon his work that blessing and unction which such labor once received through St. Francis of Assisi and St. Felix a Cantalicio.

Truly, a representative of the holy Capuchins seemed to have been resuscitated when Gerard, in obedience to his Superior, assumed the office of an alms-gatherer.

On such occasions, Gerard manifested a true apostolic spirit, and great love for his fellowmen. In the course of three years, he passed through hundreds of places, hamlets, villages and cities leaving everywhere a rich treasure of heavenly graces in return for the alms which he gathered. A detailed account of the long journeys made by our saintly alms-gatherer would be highly interesting, instructive and edifying. We regret, however, that but little of this wonderful and efficacious work is on record; nevertheless, from the little we do know, we marvel at his untiring zeal.

Before we describe the life which Gerard led, and the labors which he performed in different places to which his office and the circumstances connected therewith led him, we shall endeavor to give a picture of the manner of life observed by the holy brother during his journeyings.

The art of arts of the religious, whom necessity compels frequently to hold intercourse with the world, is no other than this: in spite of bodily absence from one's quiet cell, to preserve its spirit, not to allow it to evaporate in the bustle and turmoil of the world.

The saintly brother possessed this art in an exalted degree. His life outside the convent conformed exactly with that within its sacred precincts, — ever the same strict, simple, poor and amiable brother. Evidently, he was a man of prayer, possessed of divine gifts and graces. None but a saint could thus go from village to village in poor, wretched garments, walking by the side of his horse, and begging alms with incomparable modesty and simplicity. He was always recollected, yet friendly, saluting those whom he met, and exchanging a few kind words with everyone; every child that hurried to kiss his hand received his blessing.

On his journeys he practised the same severe mortifications as when at home. From the time he made the vow always to aim at perfection, he had become still more exact in this matter, and the fatigues of travel, the hardships of begging, and the many different privations connected therewith, he thought no reason for less austerity. It is true, he endeavored as carefully as possible to hide his fasting, his vigils and other mortifications from the eyes of men, but the benefactors in whose houses he had to take shelter during his travels, and who were already informed of his great sanctity, observed his very step, so as to learn the minutest details of Gerard's mode of life.

We are therefore enabled to speak of his practices of piety and mortification on these journeys, and also of those things which doubtless he strove most carefully to conceal from others.

He constantly thwarted his sense of taste, rendering his food unpalatable by mixing it with bitter herbs. Though he did not always pass the night in vigil, he refused to use the bed which had been prepared for him, and slept on the bare floor. Not to let any one know of this, he usually disarranged the bed in the morning as if he had slept in it. Sometimes, when he was not able to stay at the houses of the benefactors and friends of the Congregation, he took up his quarters for the night in the open air, for he did not wish to dwell in the houses of strangers.

In a preceding paragraph we have made use of the phrase, "When one saw him going from village to village by the side of his horse." The fact is, he usually did this; he walked by the side of the animal, as he did not wish to ride. Riding, he considered too great a convenience, and as not becoming him. Sometimes the Superiors enjoined upon him the duty of riding. Then, of course, he did so. If perchance he met any one heavily laden, who was travelling the same road, his compassionate heart induced him to offer the use of the horse. The man had to place his burden on the horse, and could not refuse Gerard the pleasure of accepting this kind service, at least for a short distance. If any one of the brothers accompanied him, he was obliged to ride, while Gerard walked by his side.

A distinctive characteristic of this traveller was his unobtrusive appearance. He came in contact with women very often, but never deviated in the least from that delicate modesty which was peculiar to him. He had framed a rule for himself that as often as duty would bring him in contact with persons of the opposite sex, or that he would meet any of them, he should say a Hail Mary in honor of the purity of the Blessed Virgin; he was always faithful in observing this rule. He avoided speaking to any woman alone, if possible; when speaking to several, though he was able to converse with them without embarrassment, he was so reserved, that no one could be scandalized. Less on his own account than to sustain the virtue of others, and to give an encouraging example, he usually cast his eyes down, and when most actively engaged with the world, was a model of innocence and purity.

Wherever he went, his appearance produced a moral effect. After he became better known, he was often received with great enthusiasm by entire communities. All were zealous in giving him alms; and Gerard said, "the women of his native place to which he had come, would have deprived themselves of their ear-rings, and the men of their silver buttons, had he not checked their fervor." In return, all zealously received spiritual alms from him.

His spirit of prayer was particularly edifying. Every leisure moment was spent in presence of the Blessed Sacrament; not unfrequently, in ecstasy. It was evident to all who met him that his mind was bent on things supernatural, while he was making his way through the crowd.

Frequently it happened that Gerard entirely forgot where he was going, moving onward as if in ecstasy. Thus, one day (no doubt an exceptional day in this respect), he rode during several hours, quite absorbed in thought, without remarking that he was going to Foggia, though he had to go to Melfi. "When I noticed this," he afterwards related, "I recommended everything to the suffering Redeemer."

As soon as the business of begging was finished, besides making generous returns by way of offering spiritual alms, he became an apostle.

The renown which he enjoyed, his undeniable sanctity, as well as his attractive manners, were the cause that wherever he went the people had recourse to him, and overwhelmed him with petitions. Some wished him to pray for them; others desired his advice; others sought consolation and instruction. It often happened that after his day's work they came to him in great numbers. No one had to regret importuning Gerard; the servant of God was never happier than when he could communicate to others the gifts which God had bestowed upon him. Every one went his way rejoycing, satisfied, astonished, and imbued with a true love for God. The subjects upon which Gerard spoke were what a true service of God demanded, fidelity in the discharge of the duties of their state of life, the frequent reception of the sacraments, the love due to Jesus Christ, devotion to the divine Mother, the heinousness of sin and like subjects appertaining to a Christian life. All were astonished at the attractive and captivating manner in which he was able to discuss these subjects.

The lay-brother so mastered the art of consoling that one who experienced his power speaks of it in the following terms: "Gerard, with a heavenly countenance, consoled all sufferers." Those who are very much depressed in spirit, those who were in the deepest melancholy, he drew forth from their dangerous conditions, encouraged them by pointing out the example of patience shown by Jesus Christ, and succeeded in persuading them to resolve to bear their trials with humility, and resignation to the mostholy will of God. Differences, enmities, and various other scandals, Gerard could never tolerate. When informed that such an evil existed, he did all he could to restore peace, and many families owed to him the return of happiness, which had been apparently lost forever.

One day, while he was going through San Menna, he noticed that his horse had lost its shoes. He called on a blacksmith of the place to have the animal shod. The man, who was covetous and without conscience, thought that he might exact something for his own benefit from the simple brother, and accordingly having shod the horse, asked an exorbitant remuneration for his work. Gerard could not agree to this unjust demand without violating poverty and also encouraging the man's avarice. In holy anger he ordered his horse to throw off the shoes that had been put on under these sinful circumstances, and the horse actually shook them off, taking a leap and giving a most vigorous kick. The avaricious man stood speechless for some moments; only after Gerard had mounted his horse and had gone some distance did the blacksmith's speech seem to return; seeing the wrong which he had done, he cried out to the servant of God: "Gerard,

Gerard! Oh wait! I beg of you to wait!" But Gerard proceeded on his journey without looking back.

Once, having returned from his journeys and arriving at the Bovino Bridge, the servant of God heard loud cries. Turning towards the place whence the sounds proceeded, he saw near the bridge a wagon which had sunk so deeply in the sand, that the horses could not drag it out; there was great danger of the wagon and the horses being lost. The driver began to curse like a demon, and endeavored to urge his horses forward.

The blasphemies which Gerard had to hear pained him in the extreme. "Do stop cursing, you miserable wretch!" Gerard cried out to him with a loud voice. "I will stop, if you save my wagon and horses, for they will be lost," answered the driver. "Very well," said the servant of God, turning towards the horses: "I command you, in the name of the Blessed Trinity to move on." These words he accompanied with the sign of the Cross. At the same moment the wagon seemed to become lighter, and the animals drew it through the sand without an effort.

The driver was astonished. It was a favorable opportunity for Gerard, and he made use of it. He reprimanded the man, exhorted him to give up the bad habit of cursing, and concluded with the words: "Henceforth refrain from blaspheming, and if ever an accident should befall you like this one of to-day, throw this handkerchief that I give you on your wagon, and God will come to your assistance."

Having presented the handkerchief, Gerard proceeded on his way. The driver subsequently found an occasion to heed the counsel of the servant of God, and to learn by experience the truth of his prediction. For later, happening to find himself in a similar predicament, he thought within himself: "Let us see whether the lay-brother is really a man of God;" and threw the handkerchief which Gerard had presented to him and he always carried with him, on the wagon. Immediately, his team gained new strength and the wagon that before was immovable was dragged without any difficulty.

Not only casually, and as it were by accident, did the saintly and zealous mendicant carry on war with sin. It is safe to say that he actually gave chase to poor sinners, and that he left nothing untried to convert them. But it was always the charm of his charity that attracted the hearts of men more than anything else; possibly, his wonderful penetration of men's consciences may have contributed largely to his success.

In order to make a breach in the hard hearts of sinners, he often resorted to the oddest methods of attack. One day, when a few miles from Iliceto, he met a young adventurer, who steadily fixed his eyes upon him, and surveyed him from head to foot. Gerard's attire had very little to recommend it; an old patched cloak was hanging from his shoulders; under it could be seen a short cassock just as old; and on his head, a most wretched hat. No wonder that the young man was somewhat startled, and did not know how to classify the servant of God. Truly, Gerard looked like a gypsy.

To meet a man, who he thought must be in league with the devil, was not welcome to the adventurer, who had already fallen into the most grievous irregularities. "Can I go with you?" he said, while moving towards Gerard. "I think," he continued, "that you are a necromancer." This strange language must have puzzled the brother; and yet informed from on high, he knew the interior state of his questioner. In short, the words spoken by the young man were grist to Gerard's mill; and he thought of a method af attaching him to himself for a short time, in order to bring him back to the right path. He therefore gave an evasive answer, which, without being affirmative, could however not be regarded as a negative answer.

The young man, who was only greedy for money, did not allow himself to be deterred by this answer of the saintly brother, and thinking it to be in the affirmative, uttered in a timid manner, now began to offer his services. "If, perhaps," he said, "you are in search of a treasure, let me assist you. Will you do so?" "Of course," said Gerard, "but are you a man of courage and common sense?" "Certainly," declared the adventurer; you do not know who I am; listen to the story of what I have already accomplished." The stranger then began to relate all his shameful acts, with that boasting and detail usually indulged in by those who tell of their great deeds. Among other things he said that he had not received the sacraments for six years.

After finishing the anything but edifying history, Gerard said, very encouragingly: "Very well, then, the treasure I am seeking shall be yours; we shall soon have it." This gave the poor sinner still more courage; he continued to relate new crimes, while the servant of God was quietly planning a method to entangle him in the nets of grace.

In the meantime both arrived at a dense forest. Gerard was the first to enter. His companion followed, believing that now the digging for the treasure would begin. Having reached the heart of the woods, Gerard said: "We have arrived at the spot." He then spread his cloak on the ground, and bade the young man approach. The latter began to tremble in every limb, for in his superstition he thought that he would presently see a demon. He followed the directions that had been given. Gerard then told him to kneel, and clasp his hands as if in prayer. He himself then turned his eyes towards heaven, with a look which expressed most earnest solicitation, and said to the adventurer in a solemn tone of voice: "I promised that I would permit you to find a treasure; I am keeping my word. But the treasure is not of this world; it is the treasure of treasures, the treasure of paradise. If you wish to see it, here it is!" At these words he drew forth a crucifix. The young man looked at it dumbfounded; he had not expected this. "Yes, just look at it," continued Gerard, "this is the treasure which you lost many years ago, which you have exchanged for the most worthless things." In most glowing colors he described to the poor sinner the wretched condition of his soul, represented to him the enormity of his infamous deeds, and earnestly besought him to return to God.

The holy brother had spoken in this manner for half an hour, when the man stood before him, weeping and lamenting; he was no longer the same person he had been an hour before; the young man who had asked so many sinful things of Gerard, and had so insolently boasted of his crimes. The adventurer sincerely and heartily repented of his sins. When the servant of God remarked this change in him, and that his words had penetrated his heart, he lovingly embraced him, and persuaded him to come with him to the convent. The penitent did not hesitate, and humbly and repentingly followed the brother. Here he found the treasure which he had lost. A good confession reconciled him with God, and the peace which he afterwards enjoyed caused him ever after to be a grateful admirer of the servant of God, and enabled him to keep the promises which he had made.

The journeys of the saintly gatherer of alms were replete with such conversions. We shall find occasion to mention some of them elsewhere. A large number are lost; perhaps the greater number are known only to God.

As the zealous servant of God profited by his travels to deliver souls from the morass of sin and vice, he was no less anxious to win such as might become followers of a perfect life. With special fondness and tact he knew how to prevail upon young girls to bid farewell to the world and to enter the religious state. His power of persuasion was one of his principal gifts; and just as he became known in a short time as a man who understood how to lead sinners to the confessional, so he very soon gained the reputation of one who had made it his special business to win spouses for Jesus Christ.

The Carmelite nuns of Ripacandida, the Benedictine nuns of Atella, and the nuns of Saragnano increased in number by the zeal of the servant of God. The convent at Foggia especially was indebted to him for a number of distinguished subjects. Besides his own niece, he sent there two daughters of Constantine Capucchi, as also twelve other girls who were relatives of this family.

Indeed, God regarded this work of gaining souls for a more perfect life with so much complacency that He manifested it several times by evident miracles. Thus it is related that several girls who were going to the convent were wholly protected against the rain during a fearful storm, having spread Gerard's cloak over them.

Still more wonderful is what happened to the daughters of Constantine Capucchi, when they left their father's house to enter the convent at Foggia. With their father and Gerard they came to a swift-running river that had overflowed its banks. This circumstance would have prevented their further progress if Gerard's confidence and faith had not come to their aid. But this holy brother, whom no difficulty could deter, did not hesitate to command the agitated waters to stand, as Josue had done to the waves of the River Jordan.

And behold! the waters were separated, and permitted the pious travellers to cross without hindrance. However strange this event may appear, we have the testimony of the father of the two girls, a sober-minded as well as learned man who often in his old age spoke of this occurrence as a great miracle.

The journeys of the servant of God were an almost uninterrupted chain of miracles. We will mention a few. One day Gerard was in the house of a worthy Canon, Calvini, in Venosa. A poor mother who heard of this and who had a little son whose limbs were quite crooked, took the sick child in her arms and carried him to the house of the Canon. There she asked to see the servant of God, to whom she showed her child, with the earnest petition to have pity on him and on herself, and to pray to God for her. "It is nothing," said Gerard with his usual simplicity, "the limbs are sound." At these words he touched the feet of the child, and immediately they were restored and made straight.

It once happened that blessed Gerard having knocked at a very poor woman's door to ask for some bread, received the pathetic reply that she had not a morsel for herself. In fact the poor woman had but little flour, which had just been brought from the mill. The servant of God acted as if he were astonished at the excuse which the woman had made. "What!" he said, "you have nothing! Is not your cupboard full of bread?" "It is empty; there is not even the smallest piece of bread in it," the woman answered. That he might see the truth of her assertion, she led him to the cupboard and asked him to open it. Gerard did so, and behold! a large quantity of the most excellent bread lay before them. A cry of terror at witnessing such a miracle was all that she could utter. It is certain that the happy woman joyfully and reverently furnished the mendicant brother with some of the bread which had been given to her in so wonderful a manner.

A similar miracle wrought by the servant of God during his journeyings is related by the lay-brother Antonio de Cosimo, who, long after Gerard's time, visited the places where the latter had been collecting alms. His account runs as follows:

"While I was attending to some business in the province of Basilicata, I came to a house in Ferrentina inhabited by an old blind woman, named Lucretia, whom I addressed as follows: 'I am a lay-brother of the missionaries.' Then the blind woman cried out: 'Ah it is Brother Gerard! Oh, my dear Brother Gerard! let me kiss your hand!' But when I informed her that Brother Gerard had died many years before, she burst into tears and said: 'He is dead, yes, he is dead! Good God, he was a great saint!'

"She then narrated to me that Brother Gerard had once come to her when there had been a bad harvest, and asked her for an alms. She had to excuse herself, and to admit that she had but three measures of flour which would scarcely suffice for the space of a week to support her family and her fieldlaborers. The new harvest could not be expected for a long time, and she begged him to excuse her if she did not offer him anything. 'Oh, no matter,' said Gerard: but allow me to tell you, give more generous alms to the Blessed Virgin this year than usual, and you will see that what is left the Madonna will increase in such a manner that it will go far enough to support your family till the next harvest.' 'If this be the case,' answered Lucretia, 'take as much flour as you please.' The remainder of the flour, the good woman related with tears and great emotion really lasted as Gerard had foretold, till the next harvest. Though this seemed incredible, it was an undeniable fact, and she regarded Gerard as a saint. 'Oh, certainly!' she concluded, 'he was a great saint, else he could not have worked that miracle.' As a remembrance, Lucretia gave me a considerable amount of corn, and from that day forward I began to invoke and venerate Gerard daily as my patron."

In this way the servant of God labored with great success, under the humble exterior of alms-gatherer, for the glory of God and the salvation of souls. His travels were those of an apostle, who by the example of his brilliant virtues, as well as by the power of his words and of his miracles, revives everywhere the true faith, and makes most unexpected conquests of souls.

"In every place, where he gathered alms," says an eye-witness, "he earned the reputation of being a man of God, an angel of purity, and a saint rich in miracles, in charity towards his neighbor. This reputation and high esteem continued after his death."

In consequence of his travels, the servant of God found an occasion for another kind of labor of which we may speak here; we mean his epistolary instructions.

Whoever made the acquaintance of the saintly brother experienced the power of his words, his instructions, his consolation. He had also tasted for his own benefit the spirit of wisdom which animated Gerard, and also conceived a great desire to enjoy this happiness oftener, and was not unfrequently obliged to continue in communication with so extraordinary a judge of his heart. So it happened that Gerard was asked by many for advice by letter, was requested to administer consolation and instruction, and as he could not satisfy them by a personal interview, he was obliged to pen his thoughts, in order not to abandon a work that had been begun so auspiciously, and not to forsake his "dear penitents" — to use Father Tannoja's expression — on the road which he had assigned them.

These productions of his pen are the expression of

the soul of this simple, seraphic brother. The orthography, style and connection of thoughts betray the artless, uneducated lay-brother; while the spirit that pervades them is not unworthy of a master of the spiritual life. They are hidden pearls.

The greater number of the letters which were written by the servant of God have unfortunately been lost. Most of them were addressed to pious virgins who had consecrated themselves to God. We shall afterwards make special mention of his directions of these religious. Many of these letters have been preserved, and in the course of this biography we shall quote what is most edifying in them. Some few letters were written to persons living in the world, but only fragments of these are in existence. At the end of this chapter we intend to reproduce these few remnants of Gerard's labors for the benefit of the reader. His apostolate was as rare as it was rich in blessings. May his letters serve as a memorial of his divinely-given wisdom and of his unbounded charity towards his neighbor! We pass over only one letter, which, though it breathes apostolic freedom and true charity in a high degree, yet, is rather obscure on account of its many references to unknown events.

We begin with the short but beautiful letter of the saintly brother, written to a nobleman who was almost in despair. It is a tender exhortation to prayer, and to confidence in the providence of God.

"I have received your esteemed letter. If, my dear sir, you are only faithful to God, He will sustain you. God knows how painful your trials have been. May the holy Ghost furnish you with the knowledge of our great obligation to suffer for Him Who suffered so much for us! O my brother in Jesus Christ, have patience: God has permitted all this for your own good; He wishes you to save your soul, and to enter into yourself. Only one thing is necessary; bear every trial with resignation to the divine will, to attain your eternal salvation. Be courageous; you will overcome your temptations. Hope with a lively faith and you will recover every thing from Almighty God."

He gave similarly consoling advice to a person who did not secure a desired situation, and who for this reason gave way to great dejection.

"Try to have patience if you do not receive what you desire immediately. Perhaps our dear Lord prefers to humble you. God often forces people to enter into themselves by means of suffering and bitterness, that they may understand what a dreadful thing it is to offend Him. In such a case the best thing we can do is to weep over our sins without intermission and to pray incessantly to the Lord to prolong our days that we may have time sufficient to weep and suffer for Him. Why do you wish to despair? Your sufferings are nothing in comparison with those which you deserve for your sins. Would it not be much worse if you were now in hell? My son, be careful; the evil spirit is cunning, and if you do not show yourself more faithful to God, He will soon find means to plunge you into misery. Moreover, be of good cheer; have confidence in the Lord; He will give you the strength to bear every thing. I recently recommended you to the duke, yet he is unfortunately not in a position to gratify your wish. Leave all to God; He will come to your assistance in proportion as you are faithful to Him."

Finally, we must speak of a letter which Gerard addressed after the manner of a wise director of souls to a priest of Caposele, Don Cajetan Santorelli. The latter — a member of Dr. Santorelli's family, who afterwards became so devoted to the servant of God — had recourse to the saintly lay-brother in consequence of very great troubles of soul, having been convinced that he was gifted from on high. Hereupon Gerard answered him by letter. This was the last which he wrote at Iliceto, namely, on the eve of his departure for Nocera, whither the holy Founder had called him in order that he might defend himself against a dreadful calumny of which mention will be made later on.

The letter reads as follows:

"Jesus, Mary!

"May the grace of the Holy Ghost always dwell in the soul of your Reverence, and may the Blessed Virgin preserve it! Amen.

"I write you in a great haste, my dear, most esteemed Don Cajetan. With the greatest consolation I received your kind letter, and I thank you for the special charity which you showed to that servant of God. God will reward you for this; I know He will.

"But now you must listen to me with great attention. What I shall say to you, I say in the name of the Most Blessed Trinity, and in the name of my dear Mother Mary; see to it that this may be the last letter that I shall ever write to you on this subject, for I shall never more speak as I intend to do now.

"As to the scruples in respect to your past life, I know that your Reverence have examined your conscience with all diligence more than once; therefore, I say to you, think no more about them. Your fears and doubts are nothing else than a stratagem of the evil spirit, who is anxious to destroy the sweet peace that reigns in your heart. Do not any longer notice his suggestions, and seek to preserve your interior peace, so that you may advance on the road that leads to perfection.

"In regard to the anxiety which is occasioned by the administration of the Sacrament of Penance, I must say in all truth that even this is only a temptation. The evil spirit wishes only to make you give up the office to which you have been destined from all eternity, for your own benefit and the greater benefit of souls. Take care not to yield to this temptation: I say this to you in the name of God. If your Reverence would give up the administration of the Sacrament of Penance, your spiritual life would suffer great injury and God would have to diminish the reward which He is ready to give you in eternity. To resign this office would be nothing else than not to do God's will, for I repeat, it is the will of God that you work with great zeal in the vineyard of our Lord. The faults that you may commit in this work should not discourage you; it is sufficient that you have the earnest will never to offend God; the rest should not trouble you. As for the knowledge which you are expected to have, God has given to you what is quite sufficient for the discharge of this office.

"The visit which you intend to pay me in company with Don Nicholas (it is evident that Dr. Santorelli is meant) appears to me not to be feasible at the present time, for, as my Superior says, I must set out for Pagani. I thank you for the kindness you have shown to me, though I do not deserve it. "Pray for me I beg of you, for I need prayer very much. Praised be forever the goodness of God, which sustains me in all my trials! Give to the members of your whole house my kindest regards.

"While I embrace you 'in corde Jesu' (in the heart of Jesus), and humbly kiss your hand, as also that of Don Nicholas, I remain, your Reverence's unworthy and wretched servant and brother in Christ, Gerard Majella, of the Congregation of the Most Holy Redeemer."

CHAPTER XI.
Labors At Muro And Corato.

The first excursion of the servant of God was to his native place, Muro. In all probability this journey took place a few weeks after his profession, during the autumn of 1752.

Only three years had elapsed since Gerard's departure from his native place; nevertheless within this short space of time the respect which the people of Muro had entertained towards their townsman while he lived so piously among them, had already developed into the veneration that is usually paid a great saint. The fame of his virtues and of his hitherto-wrought miracles had penetrated as far as their town and had filled all with astonishment.

When it became known that Gerard was to visit them, his coming was looked for with anxious expectation, and when he actually made his appearance he was received as a messenger from God. The Franciscan Fathers whom he visited after his arrival received him with unmistakable veneration and awe.

Among those who rejoiced most were the members of his family. We refer to his sisters, his mother Benedicta having died a few months previous, (April 10., 1752). Though they did not have the happiness of extending him their hospitality during his stay in his native place, it is by no means to be inferred that it was a matter of indifference to Gerard; it was his desire to practice the virtue of obedience and self-denial that prompted him to forego this pleasure.

We wish to remark that in this self-denial which is becoming to a religious Gerard did not intend that the souls of his relatives should suffer any disadvantage as a result; for the affectionate manner in which he at that time interested himself in behalf of a young girl, his niece, who thought of becoming a religious, serves as a convincing proof that the servant of God was as much concerned about the welfare of his own family, as he was about the welfare of others. He not only encouraged her faithfully to carry out the plan which he had proposed, but he was also solicitous in regard to her reception into the convent of the Most Holy Redeemer at Foggia. After she had received permission to enter he accompanied her to the convent.

The joy which he experienced at the happiness of his niece was so great that on the road from Muro to Foggia he scarcely spoke of anything else than of the duty of aiming at perfection, and that thus she should become a great saint. In his emotion he made use of strong expressions: thus he said to her when they had arrived at the banks of the Ofanto, while pointing to the river: "Do you intend to be a saint? See! if I knew you were not resolved to do so, I would immediately throw you into the water."

Scarcely had Gerard begun to gather alms at Muro than he was enabled to exercise his apostolic activity and to reveal the gifts which he possessed. The people followed him in crowds. Children and adults alike hastened to meet him, and to kiss his hand. Men considered it an honor to accompany him.

"When he was at Muro," said one of his townsmen, "very many citizens went to him: some to find relief in their troubles; others to obtain spiritual consolation.

Even during the first days of his sojourn his prophecy to one of his townsmen on an occasion when they teased and ridiculed him as a crazy man: "You despise me now: a time will come when you will kiss my hand," was fulfilled.

Not only laymen pressed the saintly brother with petitions and questions; priests and clerics also appealed to him. "Many ecclesiastics," says Father Tannoja, "paid the greatest respect to Gerard, and gave him the strongest proof of their confidence. Some of the ablest confessors of the secular as well as of the regular clergy called upon him for the purpose of obtaining from his supernatural wisdom an explanation of difficult matters connected with the direction of souls. Gerard solved their doubts as if he were a master in theology, and like a teacher well-versed in the spiritual life he discussed the most intricate questions of asceticism and morality."

One of those who heard him speak in this manner could not refrain from crying out in astonishment: "Father, Lord of heaven and earth, glory be to Thee, that Thou hast concealed these things from the wise and hast revealed them to the lowly. So it is Father, so, it has pleased Thee." Among those who most admired the servant of God in this respect was the director of the seminary, Canon Joseph Pianese. The wisdom of the uneducated lay-brother who spoke like a Doctor of the Church, made the deepest impression upon him. Desiring to afford his colleagues and the seminarians the same useful and salutary impression, he one day asked the servant of God who had come to the seminary, to address the young people. He proposed that he should explain the words that open the Gospel of St. John: "In principio erat verbum" (In the beginning was the Word, etc.), which is one of the most difficult passages to explain. Gerard obeyed the command of the priest. The words propounded referred to his favorite mystery which had so often stirred his heart and put him into ecstasy. He loved to speak of it. He therefore began to speak of the generation of the Word, and he did this with such loftiness and such exactness of expression that the audience was carried away with admiration. The bishop of the city, Monsignor Vitus Mujo, a very learned and discreet prelate, also cherished the greatest affection for the servant of God. His general bearing, his profound humility, his great love for God, and his piety charmed the bishop when he first met him. Not satisfied with this interview, he often sent for the brother, and as formerly the bishop of Melfi had done, conferred with him on different important matters. As he himself testified later, the manner of speaking, so worthy of a teacher, which Gerard employed when he had to speak on theological subjects, filled him with astonishment, while his humility and simplicity of heart inspired him with love. "As often as he came to me," said the Monsignor to one of our Fathers, "he consoled me by his heavenly countenance."

At Muro, his winning manners and extraordinary wisdom increased day by day the respect with which he was regarded; yet that which contributed mostly to this reputation was the manifest miracles by which God wished to glorify His servant before the world. One miracle especially, attracted general attention.

The son of his host, Piccolo the watchmaker, had generously offered to collect in different houses, provisions that were destined for alms to be given to Brother Gerard. For this purpose he hurried through the town with such excessive zeal, that a serious accident befell him. The poor youth stumbled in the street and fell to the ground, his head striking a stone with so much violence that he became unconscious. He was lifted up and carried to the nearest house, while people gathered around in large numbers. The father of the unfortunate man came at the same time accompanied by the servant of God. In the exitement Piccolo could only hear: "He is dead; he is dead!" In his anxiety to know to whom these words refered, Piccolo asked the name of the one who had met with the accident. He was told that it was his son. What dreadful news for the poor man! The father had not the courage to look at his dead child; in his distress he turned to Gerard and asked him to enter the house. The servant of God entered, and found the young man lying on the floor, apparently dead. He calmly went up to him, made the sign of the Cross on the forehead of the boy, and said; "It is nothing, my son, it is nothing." Immediately the youth opened his eyes and awoke as if out of a swoon, and was as well as he had been before.

Of the gifts of penetrating the hearts of man and of prophecy, Gerard also gave many convincing proofs in his native place. This increased his reputation among all those upon whom Gerard bestowed his favors.

Worthy of mention in this respect was that which happened to a certain notary, Pietro Angelo de Rubertis. This man had committed a crime many years previously, known to none but God and himself. Rubertis had in his vineyard a cherry-tree, the excellent fruits of which often proved a temptation to others. He was therefore accustomed to watch this tree, especially during the season when the fruit was ripe. While watching one night, he captured a thief, whom he however dismissed after giving him a reprimand, and threatening to punish him severely if he were again found stealing the fruit. Unfortunately, however, the man did not heed the warning, but came again. Though Pietro was very angry he did not carry out his threat; but when the bold man attempted to steal a third time, the notary became so enraged that he carried his threat into execution. He murdered the culprit. Rubertis buried the dead body in his vineyard with his own hands, and having resolved to conceal his deed, he spoke to nobody about what had happened, not even to his own wife. Unfortunately he also wished to lie to God, and persevered in concealing the terrible act, even at confession. It is true, the disappearance of the murdered man created some excitement at first, and accordingly a search was begun. Yet, as no light could be thrown on the subject, and no traces of the missing man could be found, no mention was any longer made about the matter; and at the time in which we find Gerard at Muro, it had been entirely forgotten.

The servant of God, however, had scarcely seen Rubertis, when he perceived the wound that was rankling in the heart of the unfortunate man; and though but little acquainted with him, he said, as soon as he could speak to him alone: "My friend, your conscience is in a bad condition. Your confessions are worthless, for you have not yet confessed the murder which you committed near the cherry-tree in your vineyard, where you buried the murdered man." It can be easily conceived that this revelation must have filled the notary with great terror. After his first excitement had abated, he communicated the mystery which had been hitherto so carefully concealed, to his wife. Probably she told it to those persons through whom it came down to us. "Yes," Rubertis asserted on this occasion, "Gerard must be a great saint, for he revealed something to me, which was known only to God and myself."

It need hardly be mentioned that Rubertis now confessed his sin, and thus regained that peace of mind of which he had been so long deprived.

One day Gerard visited the house of a citizen named Carmine Petrone. His son aged three years soon drew Gerard's attention entirely upon himself. For some minutes the servant of God rested his eyes upon the child at play, and then said to his father: "Little Anthony will soon be taken from you; he will die with a musical instrument in his hand." Not long after the boy was taken sick; his illness became worse, and one day apparently already in his agony, he asked for the guitar which was near him. While he was touching the strings with his little fingers, after the manner of children, he yielded up his soul to the holy angels.

On another occasion the servant of God was going to pay a visit to the Poor Clares in company with Pianese, the director of the seminary, when he met a man who was uttering the most terrible blasphemies against the Blessed Trinity. Gerard and his companion were terrified at such language: "These blasphemous words will not remain unpunished; you will see." Three days after the wretched blasphemer was shot in the street, and died without having time to call upon God to have mercy on his soul.

We have just mentioned the convent of the Poor Clares, and we must not leave Muro with the servant of God without saying a few words concerning his labors in that convent. The fact is, this convent was like other parts of the city, the scene of miracles performed by the saintly brother.

The renown of the first marvelous deeds which were accomplished in the city had thrown the good nuns of St. Clare into pious excitement. All wished to see the holy brother, to converse with him, and to draw profit from his peculiar gifts; and if we still remember that it was in their chapel that Gerard had received the Sacrament of Confirmation many years before, we shall not think it amiss to hear that they were of opinion that they possessed a certain right to be visited by the servant of God. Gerard, however, always refused to accept their invitations.

The nuns, who ascribed this refusal to the modesty

and humility of the servant of God then applied to the bishop, in order that he might comply with their wish. Monsignor Mujo was not at all opposed to such a request; on the contrary, he encouraged it, since he hoped for the best results to be derived from an interview of the saintly religious with the nuns. "A chat (chiacchierata) with this brother," he wrote to them, "will do more for you than a long series of Lenten sermons."

Gerard could not refuse obedience to the prelate, and therefore paid the long wished-for visit, and often repeated it, at which he generally addressed the nuns in a short discourse, "which," to use Father Tannoja's words, "put the nuns into an eden-like mood." (Restarono imparadisate le monache.)

The saints are at all times practical, and a glance from them quickly discovers certain sore spots which it is necessary to heal. So it was with Gerard, especially when he spoke of the obstacles to sanctification in virgins who live in solitude; of the dangers which are too often overlooked; of the means of removing these obstacles and of resisting these temptations. On the one hand, he vividly portrayed the injury that is caused by attachment to creatures, and by the evil habit of frequenting the parlor; and on the other hand, the advantages of a total detachment from all earthly things, and of a perfect love for solitude. "In the silence of the cell," said he, among other things, "God speaks to the faithful religious. Here, where she can pour out her heart to Jesus Christ her Lord, and to her sweet Mother, the Blessed Virgin Mary, she finds true consolation."

The words of the servant of God spoken in the parlor, soon produced a wonderful effect in the cells of the convent, as well as in the hearts of the religious themselves. Many abuses, which the confessors had tried in vain to remove, and which had done a great deal of harm, entirely ceased after the humble brother warned the nuns against them.

Among the religious in the convent there lived a nun who cared very little about the spirit of poverty. With that incomprehensible pettiness which always takes possession of those who, though called to what is great, neglect to strive to attain it, she had conceived a great attachment for an ex veto, — a small gold heart. She would by no means give it up, always carried it with her, and was as fond of it as a miser is of his money. Several confessors had tried in vain to persuade her to surrender it, but she obstinately turned a deaf ear to every entreaty. When Gerard came, one single conversation with her was sufficient to break asunder the chains which bound her soul. The nun entered into herself, gave up what she had loved so inordinately, and became an exemplary and exact observer of the Rules.

In the convent of the poor Clares, God also confirmed the exhortations of the brother by several extraordinary proofs of his higher mission. One of these was Gerard's cure of the Superior of the convent, Maria Josepha Salines. This nun had suffered from intermittent fever for a long time; she therefore asked the brother to recommend her to God. Gerard promised to do so, and after he had prayed for the sick person, he sent a little of the dust taken from the grave of St. Teresa. Immediately after she had swallowed it the fever abated. This precious dust the servant of God had received from the Carmelites at Ripacandida, and generally gave it to the sick to conceal his own power of performing miracles. We shall see how he used some of this dust when he was on his death-bed.

Another cure effected in this convent by Gerard was not so well known, but was far more extraordinary. It concerned a nun who was suffering from an evil that affected her soul. She had, either through negligence or for some other culpable reason, concealed a sin in confession for a long time, though she had made a general confession three times. The wound was deep and old; therefore very dangerous. The servant of God, however, perceived it, and was filled with compassion for her. He had an interview with the nun, and made known without circumlocution what he knew of her interior. Moved to repentance, she acknowledged her fault, and hastened to cleanse her soul in the crucible of confession.

In this manner Gerard worked miracles, and saved souls during his stay at Muro. The inhabitants of the city were filled with respect and veneration for him. They found in him far more than they had expected, and regarded his words as coming directly from God.

The profound humility and unaffected modesty of the servant of God exercised the greatest influence over all, but while receiving the clearest proofs of the high regard in which he was held, he did not wish to appear to be any other than a poor beggar, and a laybrother of the Congregation of the Most Holy Redeemer. He was constantly annoyed with invitations, and therefore had the best opportunities to dine at the tables of the first families; but he declined all, and prefered to mingle with beggars: he often stood at the door of the seminary, where the poor usually received a piece of bread and some broth as an alms.

Soon after his sojourn in Muro the servant of God encountered great dangers in his travels, of which a contemporary, Canon Serio, gives us a detailed account. He relates as follows: "It was in the year 1751 or 1752,[1] — it is impossible to specify the exact time, I was in Carbonara with my father, who was exercising

---

[1] Certainly, in 1752, as Father Fiocchi mentions in the following report.

the high office of governor. He was an intimate friend of the physician, Don Antonio Dominico. This physician, a man of excellent qualities, was accustomed to offer hospitality to all the monks and missionaries who happened to pass through Carbonara, and he entertained the highest regard for them.

"One day, about the hour of dinner, he invited me to dine with him, in order that I might bear Gerard, who was staying at his house, company.

"He thought I would be pleased to make the aquaintance of the servant of God, and that the latter would also be greatly pleased to meet with an ecclesiastic.

"I joyfully accepted the invitation, and we immediately started, and went to the house together.

"On entering the room, Don Antonio cried out in a joyous tone; 'Be of good cheer, Brother Gerard! it is rainy and stormy, and it is dangerous for you to proceed on your journey. I have brought you a companion, so that you may not be alone. Dinner will be served shortly.'

"I thank you for your kind attention, my dear Don Antonio,' said Gerard, 'but I must hasten, for I must be at Melfi this evening. Obedience requires it.' 'But my dear Gerard,' replied Don Antonio, 'one should understand how to interpret the command of a Superior. If the Superior who gave you the command were now here, he certainly would not allow you to go away in this kind of weather. After dinner we shall see how the sky looks, and the matter will be arranged.' Gerard concluded by saying: 'I hope that the weather will be finer; and I shall then set out on my journey.'

"At this point I also engaged in the conversation, and asked the brother a few particulars in regard to Father Giovenale and Father Cafaro; I had gone to confession to the latter when at the seminary in 1750. Gerard's answers proved very satisfactory to me. Soon afterwards we sat down to table, and dined with holy cheerfulness. Don Antonio's efforts as well as mine were meanwhile directed to prolong the dinner as far as possible, so as to prevent the brother from departing. And he on his part gave us some hope that we might detain him for the night. But in due time he interrupted the conversation, and firmly declared that he was going away. 'That cannot be,' said Don Antonio, 'it would be highly imprudent on my part to allow you to travel when it is raining in torrents. You will have to cross the Lausento, the Ofanto, and the bridge of the Oglio. You will lose your way, and then — the hour is already too far advanced!' I also tried to persuade Gerard to remain.

"But the latter arose and said: 'For the love of our Lord, take pity on me, and do not urge me any more. Father Fiocchi expects me this evening at the episcopal palace at Melfi. As for the Lausento, I do not fear: my horse is good, strong, and fearless in crossing streams. As regards the Ofanto, if the rain should continue and I find the river too swollen, I shall follow the road and cross the bridge; should the weather prove favorable, I shall choose the shortest way. Be kind enough not to detain me. I tell you the weather will not change until I shall have left the house!'

"He then went out and saddled his horse. His last words seemed spoken in so positive a manner that we said to each other: "Let us see whether the weather will really change before he departs. Let him go; but let us provide him with an escort as far as the ford of the river.' Meanwhile Gerard was ready to set out. 'My dear brother,' said Don Antonio, 'if you wish to go, set out without delay, for it is getting late, and you will arrive two or three hours after sunset. I will order my servant to accompany you till you have crossed the Lausento. But I am quite sure that you will return. The rain is falling in torrents, and the whole country is flooded. Gerard mounted his horse and while we bade him farewell rode away.

"Two men had received orders to accompany him as far as the Ofanto. As soon as Gerard left the house, the rain ceased and the sun began to shine, so that Don Antonio looked at me and said: 'Don Matteo, what think you? is not this brother a saint? You see that his assertion was very correct; he has departed, and the weather is fair. Is not the obedience of this brother worthy of admiration!' I was of the same opinion, and then left the house, inwardly praising God.

"The following day I learned that the two attendants who had been sent with Gerard had crossed the Lausento without hindrance upon his invitation. But when they had come to the Ofanto they saw the waves rise and the storm was rapidly washing great uprooted trees down the stream. They therefore advised the servant of God not to cross the river; it would be to expose himself to certain death. He however answered that his horse could swim very well. Then making the sign of the cross, and calling to his horse he said: 'In the name of the Blessed Trinity, let us go ahead!' Whereupon he rode into the water. The noble animal pushed forward, but soon sank in the waves, and a moment later nothing was above water, except its head. The river moved so impetuously, that the brother seemed to be lost. The attendants were horrified, and cried out: 'O holy Virgin, help him!' In the meantime the horse swam on. It had nearly reached the middle of the river when an immense tree, tossed by the waves, was swiftly bearing down upon both horse and rider. The two men seeing the danger, thought all was lost. They shouted: 'A tree, a tree, Brother Gerard!' The latter, however, very calmly made the sign of the Cross, and the tree which was approaching at a fearful rate stopped short, than moved aside, leaving the rider and his horse untouched. Gerard reached the other side of the river soon after, whence he called out to our frightened people: "Now you may go home. May God protect you; fear no longer." Gerard knew how wonderfully he had been saved on this occasion, but he ascribed his deliverance to obedience which prompted him to undertake the dangerous journey. One day when speaking to the Bishop of Lacedogna, Monsignor Amato, of the power of obedience, he narrated this occurrence in order to prove its wonderful effects. Some months later during the last week of Lent, 1753, we find Gerard in Carato, a city in the province of Bari. Although he may have been known there as a collector of alms it was not alms-gathering that induced him to come here at present.

Some priests and laymen of this city had made a retreat at Iliceto, and had become acquainted with the servant of God on this occasion. They were so captivated with his sanctity and his wonderful life that they spoke of him at home with the greatest enthusiasm, and awakened in all their friends and acquaintances the desire of seeing Gerard and of speaking to him. Thus it happened that they applied to Father Fiocchi to permit the servant of God to come to Corato for a short time. The reasons which they advanced in support of their request were by no means to be despised; yet Father Fiocchi was not inclined to grant the request which he had been obliged to deny so many others. Was not the task imposed on the brother wholly contrary to his proper sphere of life?

After duly considering the arguments for and against the petition, Father Fiocchi finally resolved to give Gerard permission to spend a few days at Corato. He did not regret it. Gerard also met all expectations in

Corato. Even his journey there was rich in blessings, and distinguished by an evident miracle.

On the road which leads from Andria to Corato he noticed a poor farmer who was looking at his field most dejectedly and uttering loud complaints. Gerard stopped, and asked him the reason of his sorrow. "Oh, my Father!" said the farmer," even though you knew it you could not help me." "What my good friend," said Gerard, "cannot Almighty God?" "No doubt, but just look at my barren field: the mice have ruined it entirely! Oh my Father, my family will die of hunger." Moved with compassion, Gerard turned towards the field, and made the sign of the Cross over it. The farmer who had been surveying his field from morning till night, perceived a sudden change. The mice were fast disappearing; they were lying in heaps either dead or dying at the farthermost end of the field. Filled with excessive joy, he cast himself at the feet of Gerard and thanked him most cordially. "My good friend," said the brother, "you must not give thank to me, but to God."

He then mounted his horse and rode away in order to escape further demonstrations of gratitude. The astonished farmer now began to walk through his field. What he had seen on the outskirts of the field, he saw everywhere. The mice lying around in great numbers, dead or just dying. Overwhelmed with joy he could no longer contain himself. He pursued the servant of God, crying aloud: "Wait, man of God, wait!" But Gerard urged his horse on, and was soon out of sight. The farmer, however, when he reached the city, related what had happened, and everywhere proclaimed that a great servant of God had come to Corato.

Gerard had received instructions to stay at the house of a certain nobleman by the name of Papaleo. But as it was his first visit to Corato he did not know where he lived. So he gave the reins to his horse and quietly rode on. He did not wish to inquire in the public street, lest he should attract attention. For some time the horse continued his way through the streets, when all at once he turned towards a house, taking his rider directly into the court-yard. "Can you tell me," said Gerard to those who hastened to meet him, "where Don Felix Papaleo lives?" "Why, Father," they answered "this is the place." Grateful to heaven, Gerard alighted. He had again experienced the delightful guidance of his good angel.

In the meantime, the report of the wonderful destruction of the injurious field-mice had spread throughout the city, and people hastened in crowds to Don Papaleo's house to see the performer of miracles. Everybody rejoiced at his arrival, and thanked those who had called him. What they saw in him, and what they heard of him, pleased them so much that they expressed their grateful appreciation of the privilege granted the good brother to remain among them for a few days; and they most cordially thanked those who had been instrumental in procuring the favor. The conviction that they should avail themselves of the counsel, exhortations and consolations of this extraordinary man forced itself upon the minds of all and caused Don Papaleo's house to be the most frequented place in the city. Priests and laymen, noblemen and the poor paid him daily visits; some to tell them of their trials and to seek consolation; others to speak to him about the affairs of their soul and to ask his advice. Everyone went away highly edified by his virtue and his divine eloquence.

The life, however, which Gerard led in Don Papaleo's house, was not essentially different from that which he was accustomed to lead at Iliceto, He ate little, slept on the hard floor, scourged himself most severely at a late hour of the night, always appeared humble, pious, patient, amiable, and conspicuous by the charm of his winning simplicity and meekness. He united to his teaching and exhortations the best example, and thus enkindled in the hearts of the people of Corato the fire of divine love; they regarded and esteemed him "as a learned and holy director of souls."

The special object of his holy zeal were the two convents of nuns in Corato; the one belonged to the nuns of St. Dominic, the other to the nuns of St. Benedict.

In this place he also gave to the nuns the same impressive exhortations that he had given to the poor Clares in his native town. He spoke to them of flight from the world and its spirit; of the necessity of avoiding useless conversation in the parlor, of total detachment from creatures, and of union with the Lord in prayer, and by means of Holy Communion. Here, too, his simple and holy words produced the most wonderful results.

In the convent of the Dominican nuns, the original austerity and regularity flourished no longer. The spirit of the world had sadly encroached upon it, and with this came tepidity in the performance of all religious duties, as well as that astonishing thoughtlessness which makes it possible for religious to wear a habit and to life in a place in glaring contrast with their life and their sentiments.

Gerard knew this and made up his mind to grapple with the abuses which existed among these nuns, and with God's help, to awaken in the convent a new religious life. He brought about what a hundred others had failed to accomplish, if not perfectly, at least in part.

At his first interview he already skillfully drove a wedge, as it were, into their hearts; he opened their hearts daily more and more to grace; the will that was good in the beginning, gradually developed more and more into a true, firm resolution, which was finally carried into effect. Thus Gerard affected a general reform, a thorough change of the life led in the convent, and the total abolition of the most deeply-rooted abuses. The nuns resolved to give up their frequent intercourse with the outside world, to restore community life, to remove all that was contrary to poverty, and to conform in every thing to the religious spirit.

Several times when the old leaven showed itself and threatened to impede and lessen the good work that had been begun, Heaven came to the assistance of the reformer, and gave to the irresolute nuns such hints as could not be misunderstood.

Thus, — to mention only one incident of the kind, — there was a window of the convent which faced the public street; Gerard desired that it should be removed. He took his crucifix, and while fastening it to the window said: "The nuns who wish to be saved should look at nothing but at Jesus crucified." But they feigned not to understand him, for they did not wish to make this sacrifice.

Yet how great was their astonishment and shame when they found the window entirely walled up one morning? Who could have done this? It would not be reasonably supposed that some one had entered the convent during the night and walled it up without making a noise. They finally acknowledged that the angels had done the service of masons for Gerard; however this may have been, this wonderful occurrence created a profound impression in the convent, and greatly aided the general reform. The evident marks of the pleasure of God toward him contributed to this.

One day Gerard was giving his usual discourse and was speaking of the love of our Lord towards man and of his death on the Cross, when quite an extraordinary joy seized him and his soul became thoroughly penetrated with an excess of heavenly desires. His heart was so agitated that he could no longer restrain his feelings. His bosom heaved, his face was all aglow, his eyes were raised to heaven, and with his hands he seized the iron bars of the grate, sighed, and appeared about to succumb to the attacks of sweet and powerful emotions.

After a little while he recovered consciousness, became quiet, and asked for some water. He drank a few drops of it, and washed himself with it in order to cool the ardor of his love. A lasting and effective remembrance of Gerard was associated with Vincentia Palmieri, a young lady, who was receiving her education at the convent. She was the daughter of a rich family at Naples, and an heiress of great wealth. She was anxiously looking forward to the hour when she would return to the world; she did not manifest the least sign of a religious vocation.

Gerard, who, as we have already mentioned, entertained a great desire to win virginal souls to be the spouses of our Lord, having heard of young Palmieri, wished to see her and to speak to her. The girl came, acknowledged to the brother, among other things, the extreme disgust which she felt for monastic silence and for a life between four impenetrable walls. Gerard listened quietly to all that she had to communicate; then he said: "You desire, my child, to leave this house? No! here is your place; just here you will be a nun." Vincentia answered that her ambitions and inspirations did not tend to a religious life, she loved the world too well. "Well," said Gerard, "you will abandon this idea and purpose; you will become a nun in this convent, and live long for the edification of others."

And really, when the mother came to take her daughter back to Naples with her, Vincentia did not wish to go home; she was now quite changed; instead of Naples she now desired the novitiate. She was received, made her profession, and led, as Gerard had foretold, a holy life in the Order. She was nearly a hundred years old when she died, and was consoled in her last moments by a vision of the glorious Patriarch St. Joseph.

The convent of the Dominican, as well as that of the Benedictine nuns derived the greatest profit from Gerard's sojourn at Corato. He visited them frequently, and his words, spoken with so much unction and ardor, produced innumerable fruits of salvation.

The pious abbess of the convent felt the greatest confidence in the servant of God, so that she made known to him her interior. The office of directress weighed heavily on her and she would have been happy to be relieved; she therefore asked Gerard at every visit to pray to the Lord that the heavy and responsible burden might be taken from her shoulders, and that her prayers in this regard might be heard. "Your prayers will be heard, and very soon," said Gerard, "but the Lord will take from you this cross only to give you another, which you must carry to the end of your life." The resignation of the abbess was accepted a short time after; but very soon after her most ardent wish was granted, her foot became affected with a cancer, and this disease caused her the most dreadful sufferings, borne till death with most edifying patience and resignation.

It was also in the church of the Benedictine nuns that our Lord wished to glorify His servant in such a manner that the veneration which the people of Corato already entertained for the saintly brother should reach its crowning point.

In the year 1753, Good Friday fell on the 20th. of April. On the afternoon of this day, according to an old custom, there was a tenderly expressive image of the crucified Redeemer carried in solemn procession through the streets of the city. When the procession arrived at the church of the Benedictine nuns the servant of God was engaged in prayer and meditation on the sufferings of the Son of God. As soon as he saw the image of the crucified Lord, being seized by some supernatural power, he was visibly raised in the air, and remained in this position for some time; his eyes fixed on our Lord. Those who were present gazed at him astonished, and regarded the saintly young man with reverent awe, deemed worthy as he was, of these extraordinary favors from heaven.

Meanwhile, Gerard's stay at Corato was drawing to a close. As soon as the Easter holidays ended the good brother announced that he must set out immediately for Iliceto. His friends wished to dissuade him from his purpose; there was no need of hurry said they; neither a messenger nor a letter had come from his Superior demanding so speedy a departure. Gerard, however, said in reply to all their arguments: "I am called; I must go."

In fact, Father Fiocchi — as he himself admitted subsequently to Canon Giove — had given the command, in spirit, that Gerard should come home, just at the time when the servant of God became restless at Corato, and declared that he wished to depart.

In regard to Gerard's labors so rich in blessings, at Corato, we are in possession of a short account by an eye-witness, Don Francis Xavier Scoppa, a priest of Melfi, who was at that time in the city, and who wrote to the Father Rector at Iliceto. The biographer of Gerard, Father Landi, and also Father Tannoja, have transmitted the account to us. It is dated April 24., and is as follows:

"Divine Providence had led Brother Gerard to Corato, for the salvation of a large number of souls. His appearance and his good example have edified the whole city, and have effected most wonderful conversions. Ladies and gentlemen of high rank have approached him, and a word from his lips was often sufficient to penetrate them with grief, and to move their hearts.

"It is impossible for me to speak of this matter in detail. Your Reverence can scarcely imagine the number of priests and noblemen who visited him, and the zeal they displayed to accompany him everywhere. He was actually carried about in triumph, like a saint just come from heaven. Many could not resign themselves to a separation from him before a very late hour in the night. His words penetrated the heart like a dart, and often, among the vast multitude, one heard nothing but sighs.

"Not only were the people moved to hate vice; even a convent in which the nuns did not lead an edifying life reformed in consequence of his admonitions. A single interview with Gerard turned them from every species of vanity, and made them submissive and obedient to their Superior.

"All the inhabitants of Corato are enraptured with Brother Gerard, and the whole city has been thrown into salutary exitement by him, so that about twenty or more priests and noblemen are preparing to hasten to your house to make a retreat. They desire that a mission be given in November.

"I hope that I shall find an opportunity to kiss the hand of your Reverence, and be able to report every thing by word of mouth."

From this time forward, says Father Landi, the city of Corato was especially attached to the Congregation of the Most Holy Redeemer, and the intercourse of its inhabitants with the convent at Iliceto became more frequent. In spite of the distance, at least forty men from Corato made an annual retreat. The mission was most astonishingly successful; and to the present day—Father Landi wrote in the year 1780 — two Fathers preach every year at Corato; their sermons during the past eight years always bearing abundant fruit.

Gerard's name was on the lips of all, and his edifying behavior during the few days which he spent in the city, was marked by very extraordinary results even in later years.

"On the occasion of Gerard's stay at the house of Papaleo's family," — such are the words of Father John Camillus Ripoli in the process of beatification — "he became known to the whole city. He was a model of virtue and penance, a man distinguished by the gift of miracles and by his knowledge of hearts; he was venerated everywhere as a saint. His memory was blessed among us for a long time, and inspired me, in 1798, to enter the Congregation of the Most Holy Redeemer."

CHAPTER XII.
THE ANGEL OF PEACE AT CASTELGRANDE.

On Tuesday, the 24th. of April, 1753, Brother Gerard came from Corato to Iliceto where he was enabled to spend nearly the whole month of May in solitude, excepting a few days during which he was in Atella on business. In June however, we find him away from home for quite a while in Castelgrande, a short distance from Muro.

The servant of God was well known in Castelgrande. In his capacity of tailor he had a number of customers in that place. When he allowed himself to be ridiculed and beaten as a fool, for the love of his Redeemer, one of the most touching scenes of his patience and self-denial was here enacted. The street Le Pietre then saw Gerard dragged over the stones by a crowd of mischievous boys; and it was at the house of Carusi, in the same street, where he arose covered with blood and horribly wounded. It was in this house at Castelgrande, that Gerard was wanted.

For a considerable time Marco Carusi's house was the abode of the most bitter, deadly hatred. A young man of twenty-one years, the son of this prominent family, had become involved in a quarrel with a notary named Martino Carusi, a few years before. They probably belonged to the same family, and in the duel which followed, Martino killed his opponent. In consequence of this, the parents of the young man conceived so great a hatred towards the murderer that they would not listen to any proposal for reconciliation. The relatives of the guilty one did all in their power to establish peace and to remove the scandal which this enmity had caused. All was in vain. Marco Carusi and his wife rejected all entreaties with unyielding perseverance. Their grief for the loss of their dear son had made their hearts insensible and unyielding to everything except revenge. It was justly feared that the evil, however great it already was, would not rest here, but would produce additional trouble.

Gerard was asked to intercede for them and to help them in restoring peace. A few prominent persons called upon Father Fiocchi to allow Brother Gerard to go to Castelgrande to reconcile those that were at variance.

The request would hardly have been granted had Father Cafaro not very strongly supported the petition. The latter was just then giving a mission in Guardia, in the diocese of San Angelo dei Lombardi, and found an opportunity to examine the state of affairs more closely. In a letter which he wrote to Father Fiocchi he represented the matter in all its details, and also gave his own views on the subject, so that the Rector finally consented.

Gerard, accompanied by Brother Francis Fiore, set out at once for Castelgrande.

As the heat at that time was very oppressive and the distance great, many great difficulties had to be encountered in making the journey, but the zealous servant of God regarded this as unworthy of notice.

The devil was preparing more serious difficulties than those of the journey for the servant of God. No doubt, the evil spirit had a presentiment of the defeat which he was to suffer at Castelgrande. He attacked him more severely than usual, and permitted him no rest during the whole journey. It was the devil's intention to confuse Gerard's mind by illusions and to frighten him by terrors, so as to divert him from his undertaking.[1] But it was of the greatest benefit to Gerard to

---

[1] What those terrors and illusions of the evil spirit were, has not been recorded in the sources of information handed down to us.

have undertaken the journey merely out of obedience.

"Out of obedience," said he to the tempting and annoying oppressor, "I am fulfilling the command of God; but you, O hellhound! may devour yourself in impotent rage, and return to the infernal abyss."

On the way to his destination the servant of God was obliged to pass by Ruvo, a town in which he was highly esteemed. Knowing this, and disliking nothing so much as the honor and respect paid him, he did not wish to travel through this place, but endeavored to escape notice, by following another road. The inhabitants, however, had received information that the saintly lay-brother was on his way to Castelgrande. They were aware of the humility of the servant of God, and placed guards in the fields around Ruvo; this circumstance made it impossible for Gerard to pass by without being noticed.

Though he had taken a solitary path, of a sudden he saw himself surrounded by a number of country people, who led him in triumph, as it were, to their little town. Here he was obliged to spend a few hours in answering questions and in hearing the complaints of the good people. This he did in so affable and gentle a manner, that they were greatly consoled and satisfied by the instructions he gave them.

The day was declining when Gerard proceeded on his journey with his companion. It was his custom to travel a foot, as he always offered the use of his horse to his companion. When they arrived at the base of the mountain called de Rapone, which they were obliged to climb, Gerard began to feel very tired. All at once a white horse approached him as if it had come to be at his service. Whence it came, and to whom it belonged, no one ever knew. The servant of God mounted the mysterious horse [1] without exhibiting the

---

[1] We say "mysterious;" for whether it was an animal sent to the servant of God by Divine Providence, or whether

least fear, and could now keep pace with his companion. But the animal soon left the road leading to Castelgrande, and carried the rider to a place surrounded by precipices, which the people called Difanci. Gerard noticed the danger, and sternly commanded the animal to proceed in the direction of Castelgrande; and behold! the horse obeyed the order. Without further trouble, the servant of God reached the town late in the evening.

We have a detailed account of the arrival of the saintly brother, written by Doctor Cajetan Federicci, at the time mayor of Castelgrande. He was a special friend of the Congregation, and therefore offered Gerard hospitality.

"It was," he says, "in June, 1753. Brother Gerard arrived at my house after the Angelus. One of my neighbors, Isabella Sebastiano, had a daughter who suffered from very strange attacks of madness, which appeared to have been superinduced by diabolical influence. When she heard that the saintly brother was coming to the city, she implored me to intercede for her with Gerard, to deliver her daughter from the great torture which she was suffering. After supper I retired for a short time in order to muster up courage to accomplish the task which had been imposed upon me.

"On my return, the love of God was under discussion. Gerard had raised his eyes towards heaven and his cheeks were red as roses. I addressed him, saying: 'Well, my dear Brother Gerard, it is necessary that for the love of God you should free a poor girl who is possessed by a devil.'

"At first he was somewhat reluctant, saying it would cause too great excitement. The more he objected,

---

it was an illusion of the devil, annoying him on his journey to Castelgrande, is not known; it seems probable that the latter was the case.

however, the more I importuned him. Finally, I sent word to Isabella that she should bring her daughter.

"When the poor girl reached the door she cried out with a loud voice: 'He has already conquered the beast!' Then the girl without being led, ran into the room where Gerard was, and fell to the ground on her face. We recited the Litany of the Blessed Virgin; thereupon Gerard took his cincture, and a few other blessed articles, and applied them to the possessed girl. He moved away from her and sat down. He seemed to be speaking to her, for he moved his lips, though no one could understand what he was saying. The girl arose, took a chair, and approached the brother.

"At a sign given me by Gerard, I left the room, but kept the door ajar so that I could easily see what was going on. I now noticed that the brother continued to move his lips as if he were speaking, and then listened to the answers of the possessed girl. This interview lasted about twenty minutes and then Gerard dismissed her with these words: 'My child! go now, and be afraid no longer! Love Jesus Christ most ardently, and have confidence in Him.'"

"The girl who before could neither go to confession nor visit the church, nor work in the field, was now released for a long time and received the Sacraments again, and worked as she had done before her illness. In the meantime, Gerard informed me confidentially that it was not the will of God that she should be delivered entirely from the torture."

The evil spirit who had taken possession of this girl yielded much more readily than the evil spirit that had inspired the hearts of Marco Carusi and his wife with hatred and revenge.

In order to deal prudently in so delicate and difficult a matter, Gerard sought above all to obtain an interview with the offended family. This interview was cheerfully granted him, and at the appointed time the servant of God called upon Marco Carusi.

In the meantime, Brother Francis was told to pray before the Blessed Sacrament; for Gerard was convinced that a heart once possessed by hatred can be changed by no other than by Him Who alone can mould the hearts of men like wax.

The prayer offered by Fiore seemed to have attained its end. Everything went on very well. At the first interview with the father of the murdered young man, Gerard gained so much confidence that he was enabled at its close to make an offer of effecting a reconciliation. But, however great the impression which the words of Gerard had made, this offer was not heeded by Carusi. Still, the former bitterness had vanished, and at the end of the conversation Gerard was hopeful of the unhappy father resolving to make the sacrifice which was demanded by Christian charity and true honor.

In fact, this was accomplished by another meeting. Don Marco declared that he was ready to forgive the murderer of his son, to shake hands with him, and to forget the past. The affair seemed to be settled; only the solemn act of reconciliation had not yet been performed.

In the meantime, Gerard was urged to visit his native place; as it was so very near he availed himself of the opportunity. He charged his host, Don Cajetan, to make the necessary arrangements for the solemn act of reconciliation, and then started on his journey to his native place.

His sojourn there was short, yet not without special blessings and miracles.

Bishop Vitus Mujo was sick at this time, and Gerard, when he visited him, found him in bed suffering very much from gout in his hands and feet. The prelate was very glad to see the brother again, and recommended himself to his prayers, after having had a long conversation with him. "My dear Gerard," said he to him, "do pray to the Lord to relieve me of these pains." "Monsignor," answered Gerard, "bear them patiently; it is not for the honor of God that you should be freed from them." "Without these sufferings," he added, "your grace, would not be saved." At another visit the saintly brother found the sick bishop suffering still more. "Oh!" cried Gerard in a joyful tone, "how happy is your lordship that you are able to suffer for the love of God! Alas! I, — I am suffering nothing for my God!" These words consoled the sick man, and pleased him so much that they remained indelibly fixed on his memory.

Gerard's visit to Muro proved a specially kind dispensation of God for the wife of Alexander Piccolo at whose house the servant of God lodged, as on a former occasion. This poor woman, whose name was Catharine Zaccardi, had been living at enmity with God for many years; she could not be persuaded to manifest her interior by a sincere confession. On his former visit to Muro, Gerard had not said anything to her about this matter. The hour of grace had not then arrived. It had now come. Enlightened by God, Gerard remarked the sad state of Catharine's soul.

He sent for the woman, and, while he revealed the great sin to her which she had long before committed, and which she had always concealed, he exhorted her emphatically, yet kindly, to approach the tribunal of penance with a sincere heart, in order that she might not lose her soul. "Make your confession, and prepare yourself for death," then, he concluded by adding; "for in a short time you will have to appear before God." The fact is, Catharine, who then was in the enjoyment of excellent health, became sick and died a few days after the disclosure which Gerard had made to her.

We have reason to hope that her conversion was sincere, and that she died a happy death.

Meanwhile, the evil spirit had been active at Castelgrande in every possible way to destroy the work of peace which Gerard had nearly completed. He availed himself of the absence of the servant of God to wipe out the good impression which he had made on the heart of Don Marco, and to dissuade him from carrying out his good resolution.

As an instrument for this diabolical undertaking, he used Don Marco's wife. The destroyer of souls well knew the mother's heart, its weakness, and its sensibility. These were the points which he attacked. He inflamed the deeply offended woman with new hatred, and aroused in her a thirst for revenge, so much the more since her husband was inclining to peace and reconciliation. She yielded to the temptation and as Marco had expressed the resolution to effect a reconciliation with the murderer of his son, she violently opposed it and would not on any condition hear of it.

In her fury, she determined upon a plan which she believed would be most efficacious for her purpose. She collected the bloody garments of her murdered son which she had sacredly preserved and, accompanied by her daughters who shared the hatred of their mother, she carried them to her husband. More like one of the furies than a mother who carries in her hand the effects of her deceased child, she held the blood-stained garments before him. "See here!" she cried out in her fury, "see the garments which the blood of your son has reddened! Look at them, and then go and be reconciled with the man who killed him! The blood of your own child demands eternal enmity with the murderer, and cries for vengeance, and you!— you are going to embrace him! Alas, the prayers of a despairing mother shall yet find an avenger of her son!"

To this violent outburst of passion, Marco's heart could not remain insensible, especially as it had but lately been healed of the same passion; kindred emotions were still fluctuating in it. In fact, Don Marco now forgot entirely the exhortations of Gerard. His wife had well known the proper way to fan into a blaze the fire that was still smouldering. The old hatred, the former revengeful thoughts were again enkindled; of reconciliation there was no longer any question; he was, it appeared, more obstinate than ever.

Of this sad change of Carusi the servant of God was informed as soon as he returned to Castelgrande. Should he now desist from performing the work of reconciliation? Should he retreat before the evil spirit? Should the latter come forth victorious from the battle? "No!" cried out Gerard, after the state of affairs had been explained to him, "no! the devil shall not be the conquerer."

Animated with a zeal, the servant of God hastened without delay to Carusi's house. That the first appeal to Don Marco and his wife should be fruitless, was to be expected. Though Gerard spoke most earnestly and convincingly, his words produced no effect on the hearts of these insensible people. The servant of God then fell on his knees. Taking his crucifix, he placed it upon the floor and invited them to trample upon it if they could, saying: "Come, come, and tread upon this crucifix." Such language caused terror and confusion. Both became deadly pale, and dared not accept the invitation. "Well now," continued Gerard, "just try to trample upon it! — Why do you not obey? You seemed to be filled with horror. You must know there is no other way: either you must forgive, or you must tread under foot our Lord Who has commanded us to forgive, as He forgave His executioners on the cross. Now take your choice!"

Don Marco and his wife were much affected and agitated. But hatred had sunk so deeply into their hearts that even the emotion which they now felt could not dispel it. Partial victory had paved the way for grace and Gerard continued: "Whether you will or not, you must forgive! Listen to me: When I first came to you, I came to you in compliance with the request of men, to-day I come by the command of God, and not at the request of any one. Hear what I say:—your son is in purgatory, and must remain there so long as your obstinacy lasts. Do you wish to release him from prison? then become reconciled. It is absolutely necessary. You must also have five Masses said for the repose of his soul. These are the last words I shall say to you, in the name of God. If you pay no regard to them, you may be prepared for dreadful punishments."

After saying these words, Gerard turned away to leave them. They were greatly moved and would not let him go. "Yes," they cried out, "yes, we wish the reconciliation to take place, and it shall be done at once!"

Immediately after this interview the reconciliation was celebrated, to the greatest satisfaction of all the inhabitants of Castelgrande. The two families ever remained in the most harmonious relation to each other; the sad event, which had created the feud was entirely forgotten.

Gerard repeatedly defeated the evil spirit in Castelgrande. On one occasion, the servant of God was praying in church, when two mothers entered, each leading by the hand a daughter possessed with an evil spirit. The presence of the servant of God tormented the evil spirits that dwelt in these girls, and they cried out in a loud, piercing voice, "Who is that person that is persecuting us?" The cry of the possessed girls roused Gerard from his meditation in which he had become absorbed. He hastened towards them, and when he perceived the poor mothers and the cause of their grief, he felt compassion for them. He encouraged them to have confidence in God, and then taking his cincture he gave it to the women saying: "Go home with your daughters, put this cincture around them, and they will soon be released. Do not be afraid when you see them faint; for that will be the moment in which the devil will leave them. But as soon as they are freed, they must go to confession and Holy Communion. Then the devil will never more molest them. Have confidence! The Almighty is good and nothing can withstand Him." The women obeyed, and their obedience was rewarded in the manner announced by Gerard.

The presence of the saintly lay-brother was also a source of consolation to the sick people of Castelgrande, in many ways a cause of salvation. Every one wished to see him, at his bedside or in his sick room, and to receive his blessing. Many cases are recorded in which his blessing effected a sudden cure. We will here describe only one of them.

Among Doctor Cajetan Cianci's patients there was a boy, three years old, named Felix Pace, whose hands and feet had become crooked in consequence of dreadful convulsions. He led the holy lay-brother to this child. The latter placed his hand on the boy's head and made the sign of the Cross on it as was his custom. Then the servant of God said to the broken-hearted mother: "My good woman, cheer up! your son will no longer suffer from this evil." In fact the boy became well, strong and robust, and grew up without experiencing the old trouble.

At times, however, Gerard did not wish to cure every sickness, and refused the petitions that were offered for this purpose.

This was the case with Giuditta (Judith), the little daughter of his own host, Don Federici. The poor child had been suffering from a malady, which culminated in blindness. Her mother, who greatly grieved on account of this misfortune, begged Gerard to intercede with the Lord in behalf of the poor girl, in order that she might regain her health. The servant of God promised to do his part, and requested her to pray. But he soon afterwards told the anxious mother: "If Giuditta recovers her sight she will be ruined. Be resigned to God's will! The child will be compensated for her loss, and will be able to perform the kind of work usually done by women, much better than others." The event proved that Gerard's words, the consoling ones as well as those that were less so, turned out to be true. The girl remained blind, but showed great skill in domestic duties; she also taught her younger sisters. Besides these and other wonderful deeds, Gerard's presence and his conduct while at Castelgrande assisted greatly in consoling, edifying and saving souls.

"His stay at Castelgrande," says Father Tannoja, "was in truth a mission for the inhabitants. To many of them, Gerard manifested the condition of their conscience. Moreover, his discourses were so efficacious as to produce a general change. Among others there were fifteen young persons who by their scandals had ruined many, and whom no one dared to check on account of their standing in society. These Gerard brought to the knowledge of their sins and to sincere contrition, and gained them over to Christ."

It may easily be understood why the entire population of Castelgrande became exited when it was made known that Brother Gerard was about to depart. More than three hundred people accompanied him for quite a long distance, showering prayers and blessings on his head. So high a reputation had he gained among the people that the laborers in the field, noticing Gerard passing by, left their work, and ran after him to receive his blessing once more. Brother Francis Fiore walked a hundred paces ahead of the crowd that surrounded Gerard, and was therefore often taken for Gerard, and honored in every possible way by the country people who were hurrying from all sides to meet the saintly brother. In order to escape the unmerited demonstrations, he cried out whenever he saw a number of people hastening towards him: "I am not the saint, there he comes! there!"

From Castelgrande Gerard repaired to Caposele, which was near by, partly to conduct the fifteen young men whom he had converted thither, that they might make a retreat; partly, and perhaps chiefly in order to see and speak to his reverend director Father Cafaro, who was the Rector in our house at Caposele. Then only, he hastened back to Iliceto.

"The fruits of his labors at Castelgrande," thus concludes Father Tannoja in his narration of Gerards stay in this place, "were so permanent that, for a long time after, every Saturday, a great many of its inhabitants used to come to confession to our Fathers. They came, not heeding the distance, which was seven or eight miles, nor the necessity under which they would be to spend the night in the open air. This great concourse of people made such an impression on Father Cafaro, that he cried out: "It is really wonderful; wherever Brother Gerard goes, he occasions the greatest commotion."

CHAPTER XIII.
Sojourn At Melfi. Death Of Father Cafaro.

The servant of God enjoyed but a short rest after his return from Castelgrande to Iliceto. Shortly after, he was appointed to accompany Father Stephen Liguori who was in delicate health, and two other priests who were to take the baths at Melfi. They left Iliceto on the 16th. of July. Brother Gerard was well known in Melfi. He had been there more than once, although only to travel through the place, or to stay for a short time. Having wrought so much that bordered on the extraordinary, he was well remembered, and was often the subject of conversation.

But for an unfortunate circumstance, it would be possible to give a definite and most interesting account of Gerard's doings in Melfi. The Scoppa family, at whose hands the servant of God had received hospitality, were in possession of a journal, containing an account of the works, teachings and miracles of Gerard, as recorded by Mrs. Scoppa. We regret that this precious document was lost in a fire in 1838. Owing to this, we only know of an ecstasy and a prophecy during his stay with this family in Melfi.

A picture of our blessed Lady was the cause of the ecstasy. The picture was in the house of Donna Anna. It hung quite high on the wall, and seems to have been shown to him by the owner; at least his attention was rivetted on the picture, and he immediately felt himself deeply moved. His heart became inflamed with love toward the Queen of Virgins, his spirit was transported to the celestial world, and exclaiming: "Ah! Donna Anna, what pretty things you have!" he flew like a piece of straw from the ground into the air, as high as the picture, which, with glowing countenance and enraptured, he seized with both hands. This spectacle so agitated the woman who was present that she fainted.

The prophecy pertained to the father of a family who was very ill. In her distress his wife hastened to Scoppa's house where the servant of God was, and confidently asked him the simple question, whether her husband would die.

"Do not fear", said Gerard, consoling her, "your husband will not die of this illness; but it will be prolonged." The prediction was literally fulfilled.

In the summer of 1753 when Gerard arrived at Melfi with the sick Fathers, he did not stay with Mr. Scoppa, but at the house of a very pious widow, Victoria Bruno, whose son, Mauro Murante, a young man of twenty, had entered the Congregation of the Most Holy Redeemer. Only a few incidents relating to this sojourn have been preserved.

The good brother took delight in cheering the suffering fathers, and therefore frequently sang some well known song. Thus he once sang the following favorite stanza from Metastasio:

> "Se Dio veder tu vuoi
> Guardalo in ogni oggetto,
> Cercalo nel tuo petto,
> Lo troverai con te."

(If thou wishest to see God, seek Him in everything; seek Him in thy heart; thou will find Him with the!)

He was accompanied on the piano. The words of the song, and the soft tones of the instrument, inspired him with holy excitement. He seized Father Stephen Liguori, who was standing near him, and putting his arms around him began to dance, and in an ecstasy he moved in a circle with the poor Father, who was trying in vain to release himself.

On another occasion, he was on a visit to the house of Canon Leonard Rossi, when the latter turned the conversation upon the divine perfections. In an instant, the brother was aglow; his exterior betrayed great inward agitation, and he seemed to have lost consciousness. The Canon perceived Gerard's condition, and having procured some water, he refreshed and restored him. When Gerard noticed that he had again been detected on his way to paradise, he became quite confused, and left the house.

He was subjected to similar confusion on another occasion, when invited with Father Liguori to dine at the house of a priest, a great friend of the Congregation, Don Marco Murante. Whether he forgot where he was, or supposed that no one would see him, he acted as he usually did at home; he threw into the food some of the bitter herbs which he generally carried with him. Of course this action was noticed. Curious to know how the lay-brother seasoned his dinner, the mother of the host asked to taste some of the food on his plate, and Father Liguori also tasted it. But the food was so distasteful that Father Liguori testified if he had swallowed the little he took, he could not have retained it.

The servant of God gave proof of the power he had to heal the sick, and of his knowledge of the future, by what he did for Don Michele di Micheli, a young man, who, while Gerard was staying in the city, was confined to his room by sickness. In his love for the sick, the brother visited him, and while taking him by the hand and feeling his pulse, he said: "What! you say that you have the fever? No, you have not, you are well." It was a fact. The visit of the servant of God had restored him to health. Henceforth Gerard kept him in sight: and on meeting him one day he fixed his eyes upon him, and said emphatically: "A day will come when you will be one of our number." "Oh yes," said Michele, "that will happen when I shall be able to touch the heavens with my hand." It had never entered his mind to become a religious. The name itself was offensive to him; and above all, he felt a special aversion for the Congregation to which Gerard belonged. The words of Gerard were, however, verified. "When I was about to choose a state of life," Michele himself said to Father Tannoja, "for six months my mind was agitated by a thousand contradictory feelings; but finaly, I do not know how it happened, I found myself ready to enter the Congregation, though several religious disuaded me from doing so, especially Monsignor Basta, who had a great regard for me."

In the latter part of 1753 di Micheli was in the Noviciate at Ciorani, to enter upon religious life. He was faithful in the discharge of his duties during his career as a religious, and died the death of the just on the 3rd. of June 1795.

In the beginning of August, Father Liguori and his companions had taken the water-cure, and Gerard returned to Iliceto with them. A few days after his arrival it was reported that his spiritual director, Father Cafaro, was seriously ill; he was then in Caposele. Father Cafaro knew it would prove fatal. He seems not only to have had a presentiment, but a conviction that his earthly career was drawing to a close.

"More than once," says St. Alphonsus, "he predicted his death. Eternity and paradise were his one unchanging theme for some months before he died. He often said to his companions: 'Tell me, what do they do in paradise?' On one occasion he positively said: 'I shall die this year.' On the 5th. of August, he spoke more definitely about his death and said, 'I shall die this month. The fever will come on to-day.' That very day, after dinner, he was taken with the fever, and on the third day the doctors despaired of his life.

"During his whole sickness he was an object of astonishment to all who knew him; .... ever gentle, patient and obedient, and remaining in a state of constant and silent recollection. He constantly kept his eyes fixed on an image of Jesus crucified, and on that of the Blessed Mother. ....

"When one of the Fathers begged him to command the Community in the capacity of Superior, to pray God that he might be restored to health for the good of the Congregation, he said: 'No, no! it is expedient for me to die.'

"When I heard of his dangerous illness, I sent him an obedience by virtue of my authority as his Rector Major and Superior, to get well, should such a thing be the good pleasure of God. When he heard of this command he raised his hand in silence, thus signifying that his recovery was not the will of God.

"In the beginning of his illness he was somewhat tormented by his habitual fears; but after his director had admonished him to have confidence, he became quite calm, resigned himself to the hands of divine mercy, and with eyes fixed on the crucifix surrounded by his weeping brethren, he peacefully surrendered his pure soul to God, about three o'clock in the afternoon, August 13th. 1753, being only forty-six years of age.

"We confidently trust that he is now united with his God, Whom he strove so earnestly to please, and Who was the sole object of his life.

"When the tolling of the bell announced his death, general sorrow was expressed not only among his brethren but among the strangers who were then in the house. Before he was buried, one of his veins was cut and immediately the blood gushed forth. After his death, a large number of the faithful obtained great favors by having his relics applied."

The pious hope to which the holy Founder gives utterance, that the venerable Father Cafaro was immediately after his death, united to God, seems to be confirmed by what happened to his disciple at Iliceto at the time of Father Cafaro's death. Gerard was just then in prayer and rapt in profound ecstasy. Having recovered, and being asked the cause of his joy, he said: "I saw the the soul of our Father Cafaro going to heaven. He occupies a place next to St. Paul, because he always preached with zeal and ardent love, and gained many souls for Jesus Christ."

CHAPTER XIV.
PILGRIMAGE TO MOUNT GARGANO.

A few weeks after the death of Father Cafaro, blessed Gerard had the privilege of visiting the famous shrine of Mount Gargano.

The scholastics of the Congregation who were studying dogmatic theology at Iliceto under the guidance of the young, and afterwards very celebrated Father Alexander de Meo, wished to take advantage of their summer vacation to make an excursion to the well-known pilgrimage of Mount Gargano; they proposed the matter to the Rector of the house, Father Fiocchi. The latter gave his consent, but expressly wished that Gerard should be their guide and that he should take entire charge of the pious band. Gerard was well acquainted everywhere; besides, Father Fiocchi knew this privileged brother could produce something out of nothing, and could multiply bread in their hands; for, as we shall presently see, much could not be provided for the travelers.

Nothing could have been more welcome to the servant of God than this. We know that from his childhood Gerard entertained great veneration for the archangel St. Michael, especially as the latter had brought him Holy Communion one night in so wonderful a manner.

As is related by pious tradition, the Consecration of St. Michael occurred in a very remarkable manner, during the pontificate of Gelasius, who lived in the last decade of the fifth century.

At that time, Mount Gargano, at the foot of which was situated the little city of Siponto, belonged to a rich man named Garganus, from whom is derived its name, and who used it as a pasture-ground for his large herds of cattle. It happened one day that a steer separated itself from the herd and ran away. After a long search the herdsman found the animal lying at the entrance of a cave. In order to rouse the steer, one of the men drew an arrow, which, however, was turned into the air as if by an invisible hand, and thrown back toward the one who hurled it. This occurrence created terror among all those who saw it, but no one dared to approach the mysterious cave. Finally, the matter was reported to the bishop of Siponto, who, having been fully convinced of what had happened, proclaimed a three days' fast and prayer that God might enlighten him what to do under these extraordinary circumstances. At the end of three days, the archangel St. Michael appeared to the bishop and declared that the cave was under his special protection, that he and other holy angels should be venerated there in a special manner, for the greater honor and glory of God. After this revelation the bishop and the people repaired to the place designated, in order to dedicate it for the purpose mentioned by the holy angel. Having arrived at the cave, they found it wonderfully arranged for a chapel; accordingly, the holy mysteries were immediately celebrated in the sacred spot. From this time forward, Mount Gargano became a favorite resort for pious souls, and the frequent miracles that were wrought there attracted innumerable pilgrims every year.[1]

The lapse of centuries could not weaken its power of attraction, and even during Gerard's time Mount Gar-

---

[1] The Church commemorates the feast of the apparition of St. Michael, on the 8th. of May.

gano was highly esteemed as the throne of the great archangel.

What therefore must Mount Gargano have been in the eyes of the servant of God? It is easily understood that he hailed the announcement of the excursion with great joy.

The whole company left Iliceto towards to close of September 1753. It consisted of ten persons, two priests Father de Meo and Father Spera, six students, blessed Gerard and a hermit, named Brother Angelo di San Girolamo.

They journey, from beginning to end, was accompanied by the most extraordinary incidents; as a witness in the process of beatification well expresses himself, it was nothing else than an uninterrupted series (complesso) of miracles of faith, hope and charity.

When the pilgrims were about to set out, Father Fiocchi appointed Gerard treasurer, and gave him some money to pay the traveling expenses; but it was not the requisite amount, for it consisted only of thirty carlines, -- a little over two dollars. This was a very small sum to defray the expenses of a party of ten, who were going on so long a journey.

Gerard did not offer the least objection, and when his brethren told him that thirty carlines would not be sufficient, he used his familiar expression: "Iddio provvedera," (God will provide) He knew how to communicate his own confidence in God to all, so that they looked forward to their journey without fear or anxiety.

Two donkeys were hired to carry the small amount of baggage, or possibly one of the pilgrims who might become too much fatigued. Brother Angelo took charge of them.

Foggia was the first stopping place.

As is perhaps known to the reader of the life of St. Alphonsus, this city, the capital of Apulia, is in possession of an old, remarkable, miraculous picture of the Blessed Virgin. It was in the presence of this image that the saint, when preaching, was favored before the assembled people with the expression of the esteem of his Queen. For while he was praising the prerogatives of our Lady, and exhorting his hearers to love her, a brilliant ray of light was reflected from the picture on the face of the saintly preacher, and he fell into a profound ecstasy. The same favor he received a second time.

The sons of St. Alphonsus could not neglect to visit this picture. Gerard was particularly anxious.

In the city of Foggia the servant of God was no stranger. During several of the former excursions he had remained here and permitted his virtues and gifts to shine forth. Scarcely had the lay-brother arrived, when the clergy and laity came to enjoy his conversation, at least for a few minutes. They proposed different ascetical and theological questions; both mind and heart received genuine pleasure, for Gerard spoke about these matters in his usual masterly way, and answered these questions with great clearness and most astonishing wisdom.

In the convent of "the Annunciation of the Blessed Virgin" (dell' annunciata), a nun wished to speak to him. She had many things on her mind about which she thought it would be beneficial for her to consult him. The servant of God complied with her wish, and conversed with her about the affairs of her conscience. In taking leave he advised her to prepare to appear before her judge, — an advice which no doubt startled her greatly. The nun was young, in good health, and of a lively temperament; it seemed impossible that death was near. Gerard had, however, given counsel at the right time, for after four months God called her to Himself.

From Foggia, where the pilgrims had spent the night, the journey was continued to Manfredonia. But very soon Gerard noticed that the young men were not accustomed to take long walks, and were considerably fatigued. So he resolved to hire a conveyance that should take the whole party as far as Manfredonia. When he mentioned what he intended to do, all cried out: "Where will you get the money to defray the expense?" He answered as usual: "Iddio provvedera," (God will provide,) and actually hired a wagon that carried them to the place of destination.

In the meantime the two donkeys fared very badly. They and their leader Brother Angelo could only with difficulty follow the wagon. The poorly-fed animals were not able to run; they dragged themselves along at a very slow pace; and finally grew so weak that Angelo had to remain behind with them. When the party had arrived at Condela, where refreshments were to be taken, neither he nor the animals could be seen. They waited and looked but all in vain. At last they descried the poor leader, covered with dust and bathed in perspiration. Gerard on his arrival made him take a rest, so that both he and the donkeys might be revived; soon after, he gave the signal for departure.

The hermit, however, objected; the animals were too tired, he said; they must rest longer; he would stay with them a little while and follow later on. But Gerard did not agree to this. "No, they must not stay here longer;" he said; "come, you will see that I shall get them to move on." The anxious hermit had to yield, and mounted one of the donkeys. On the other was mounted, by the order of Gerard, the son of the owner of the hired conveyance. The animals were then harnessed to the wagon. When Gerard was seated he gave the donkeys a vigorous blow with the whip, and said in a loud voice: "In the name of the Blessed Trinity, I command you to move on!" The animals seemed to have new life; they galloped with the horses, as if — to use Father Tannoja's expression — "they were race-horses."

In this way all arrived safe at Manfredonia. After the expense of hiring the wagon had been defrayed there remained in the never well-filled purse the small sum of seventy "grains" — about nineteen cents.

This however, did not discourage the man of providence. He thought of his good heavenly King, and was anxious to have an audience with Him. On his way to the chapel of castle Manfredonia, he bought a beautiful bunch of carnations on sale in the market, and took it with him to church. Having arrived there, he paid his respects to the Most Blessed Sacrament, and mounted the steps of the altar, on which he placed the bouquet of flowers. While doing this he looked towards the tabernacle as if in supplication, and said with touching simplicity: "Good Lord and Saviour! Thou seest that I have thought of Thee: now it is Thy turn to think of my little family." The chaplain of the castle, who was present in the church unnoticed, remarked this act of childlike confidence, stepped up close to see the pious adorer and his companions. When he recognized them as members of the Congregation of the Most Holy Redeemer, of whom he was a special friend, he called Gerard aside and gave him a most cordial invitation to be his guest. "May God reward you," said Gerard most gratefully, "but there are many of us." "That is of no account," answered the kind-hearted priest, "I beg you to come. Everything will be provided for all of you, if you will only be satisfied. My good mother, who is with me, has, however, been ill these past two months, and cannot wait upon you. She is confined to bed and very weak." "But this can be remedied," interposed Gerard.

"Believe what I tell you; go home, make the sign of the Cross on your mother's forehead, and she will recover." The priest trusted in the words of the servant of God, and was not disappointed. Scarcely had he made the sign of the Cross on the forehead of the sick woman when she felt well and strong, arose from her bed and was able to wait upon the guests.

Of course the services rendered them were so unexpected, the pilgrims could not even have dreamt that such treatment was in store for them at Manfredonia. Besides, the chaplain could not dismiss his guests without giving them a handsome present to enable them to continue their journey.

But this extraordinary assistance was not the only advantage which the bouquet of carnations produced for the pious servant in Manfredonia. Another priest who had also heard of the touching appeal which the servant of God made at the foot of the altar, came to see the lay-brother, and to speak to him. The interview was very satisfactory, and full of emotion. When taking leave he promised to make a present of a silver censer to the church at Iliceto. The good priest kept his promise, and a short time after sent the censer, which was worth about sixty dollars, to the convent at Iliceto.

The prophecy made by Gerard, that God would provide, could not have been filled in a more satisfactory manner. Therefore the minds of all, especially of those who had looked upon Gerard's arrangements with considerable distrust, were relieved of their anxiety, and they began to breathe that atmosphere of confidence in which the servant of God was constantly moving.

The following day they set out in good spirits, in order to ascend Mount Gargano. This ascent was very difficult; in a short time the young men complained of fatigue, and now one, then another, had to ride part of the way. Gerard alone walked as he was accustomed to do, and seemed to feel no fatigue, no weakness. His thoughts were devoted to his beloved patron, whose sanctuary he was approaching.

What joy when at last it was reached! Then every one attended to his devotions according to the promptings of his own heart. Gerard was soon so rapt in quiet communion with the holy angel that he did not know what was going on around him.

In the meantime the young men had finished their prayers and were waiting for their leader, but he did not move, and when they approached him they noticed that he was in an ecstasy. As usual, his face was turned towards heaven, his eyes were open, and resting on one spot; his breathing was scarcely perceptible. For a while they left him in this condition; they then resolved to rouse him, for fear that he might become too much exhausted. To call him by name proved a useless task; and shaking and raising him up had no effect. When he finally awakened and saw his companions around him, he was greatly confused, and said: "It is nothing; it is nothing! Let us now think of getting something to eat." After saying these words, he arose and left the church with the entire party.

The following day was also spent in devotions. At an early hour in the morning the pilgrims paid their respects to the Prince of angels. Although Gerard said his prayers with the same joy and the same fervor as he had done the day before, he did not forget the wants of his brethren. At the appointed time he gave them an excellent breakfast, and when the dinner hour had arrived, he acted as if a grand dinner was to be given.

The young men were just then assembled around Father de Meo. Brother Gerard entered to announce that dinner was ready, and that they should sit down to take it. As they knew that there was very little money left in the purse after supper and breakfast which they had eaten, they did not show any inclination to accept the invitation, and looked at one another embarassed. "O you of little faith," the servant of God cried out to them, "is this obedience? Come now! sit at the table." While all were complying with this categorical command, and Father de Meo and the students entered the dining room, Gerard took from his pocket twenty-four "grains" — a few cents of our money — and gave them to Brother Angelo and told him to buy some bread. The latter obeyed, came back with what he had bought and joined the company at table. What a surprise for all! They found Gerard busily engaged. The table was laden with different kinds of fish. It was a day of abstinence, and the good brother, like a well-to-do head of a family, placed before each one a goodly portion.

But now Father de Meo asked the hermit who had ordered all things. Angelo could not give an answer. But one of the students named Ricciardi asserted that Gerard had had no more than four "grains" in his purse the day before, and could certainly have nothing where with to pay for the dinner. The hermit then gave them information which threw light upon the mystery.

He then related that on the day before, Gerard had really no more money than four "grains," but that seeing this deficiency he went immediately to the altar of the archangel St. Michael in order to pray, and soon after a man approached who handed him a roll of silver coin, with the request to remember him in his prayers. According to another version, the unknown man said: "Take this and always love God." However that may have been this much is certain: the servant of God could not have been able, without the extraordinary help of divine Providence, to regale his brethren in so magnificent a manner.

When the time had arrived for them to leave Mount Gargano, Gerard wished to settle his account with the innkeeper. The latter, a man without conscience, thought only of his own profit, and demanded an exorbitant sum. All representations and entreaties to moderate his demands were fruitless. "Very well," said Gerard, incensed at the mercenary spirit of the innkeeper, "if you do not reduce your rate, or if you ask more than is due, all your mules will die."

This threat had scarcely been uttered when the man's son rushed into the room, and with tears in his eyes cried out: "Father! for God's sake come quickly; I do not know what is the matter with the mules; they are rolling on the ground in a most frightful manner! Come, come quickly!" When the man heard this he was very much alarmed, and acknowledging his guilt he cast himself at the feet of Gerard and asked his pardon. "I gladly forgive you," the servant of God answered, "but never forget this: God is with the poor! Things will fare badly with you if you ever dare to ask more than is due to you."

The innkeeper did not wish to accept anything now, but the servant of God placed on the table the money to pay the board, and hastened to the stable, where he found the sick mules. He made the sign of the Cross over them, quieted and restored them to perfect health.

The pilgrims paid another short visit to the archangel, and then began their march homewards.

After they descended to the foot of the mountain they all felt very thirsty. "We shall soon come to a well," said Gerard, "there you can refresh yourselves. Have a little patience!" After a little while they reached the well; but when they tried to draw water, they noticed that the ropes that let down the buckets had been removed. On account of the drought then prevailing throughout the country the owner of the well had taken them away, because he feared that the water might give out, if every one were allowed to use it.

The servant of God who was not concerned about himself, but about his thirsty brethren, called upon the man and asked him humbly to give him the ropes for a few minutes, and to be kind enough to allow the young people to refresh themselves. But he received only a gruff answer, and was turned away insolently.

This man too had to be convinced of the wickedness of his behavior by a manifest miracle. For while Gerard was going away, he said, under the influence of a higher power: "You refuse to give water to your neighbor whom you should love as you love yourself. Well, then! the well will now refuse to give water to you." Having said these words, he left the place with his brethren. Only a short time had elapsed, however, when the man came running after them at full speed, and cried out: "Oh, have pity on the poor people who need the water of the well; it is the only well in the whole district." Now what had happened?

From the time Gerard had uttered the threat, a remarkable change was taking place in the well; its water began to diminish, and appeared to be drying up. This opened the eyes of the owner, and he acknowledged that there were evident signs of a marvelous punishment of his uncharitableness and of his avarice. He was willing to give water not only to the religious, but to the two beasts of burden that accompanied them, if the man of God would prevent the drying up of the well.

The students could scarcely believe what the man said: they had just before looked down the well and had seen plenty of water in it; how could it be in danger of becoming dry after so short a time? Still, they convinced themselves of the truth. For, when overcome by earnest entreaties of the man, they had returned, they actually noticed nothing, but mud and sand in the well.

Gerard, who had conquered the stubborness of the owner, and thus saw that the cause of punishment was removed, now fastened the bucket to the ropes and let them down into the well. At the same moment water again appeared. After all had quenched their thirst the servant of God turned to the owner of the well and said to him with great earnestness: "In the name of charity, my friend, never refuse water to any thirsty man from your well, as it belongs to all; otherwise God will refuse it to you. Or does not our Lord command us to love everyone? Be full of charity, if you wish that God should have mercy on you."

The man never forgot this lesson. From that time forward the ropes were always left near the well, and everyone that passed by could refresh himself with a drink of water.

Having arrived at Manfredonia, the party again called upon the chaplain of the castle, who a few days before had received them with such warm hospitality.

The journey thence as far as Foggia, which had before been made in a wagon without much fatigue, had now to be made on foot; and, on account of its length, — it was over twenty miles, — was very severe on the travelers. Even Gerard was at this time among those who were exhausted and seemed to be in a worse condition than any one of the party. He was unexpectedly seized with a hemorrhage from which he often suffered, as has been mentioned; and the consequent exhaustion was so great that every step which he took was extremely painful to him.

In spite of all this he did not wish to think of being relieved, and while his brethren used the donkeys in turn, he made the way on foot, and endeavored to conceal his suffering condition from those around him. He never uttered a word of complaint; and if it had not been accidentally discovered that he was spitting blood, he would have said nothing about what had happened, and would have borne his sufferings in silence.

This trouble could not prevent him from showing his brethren the most delicate attention and effective charity, and from doing everything that he hoped would give them pleasure. Scarcely had they arrived at Foggia, where he might have found some rest, when he expressed himself desirous of making an excursion to the sanctuary of the "crowned" Virgin (incoronata), which was situated at some distance from the city.

Because his companions knew what he would like most, and were aware that it would not improve his health if they did not agree to his proposal, all were unanimous in approving of Gerard's plan. Therefore, under his guidance, they set out for the sanctuary.

What happened to the saintly brother on Mount Gargano was here repeated. No sooner had he knelt in the church and said a few prayers, than his spirit was rapt in the sweet bonds of ecstasy. The young men, however, had witnessed in the servant of God during the previous days so many wonderful things that they did not specially remark this new favor granted him by Almighty God. Only one of the students spoke of it after Gerard had come to himself, and asked him what had been the matter with him. "Nothing," said the brother, "it is a weakness from which I must suffer."

After the visit to the "crowned" Virgin, the pilgrims turned aside from their homeward march into a road leading to Troy, in order to venerate a wonderful and very beautiful image of the crucifixion which was there exposed to the veneration of the people.

In fact the students took the liveliest interest in this sanctuary, and derived great comfort from their visits to the holy image, which they prized as a sacred treasure, it being a remembrance of the saintly relative of their holy Founder. Father Tannoja says: "Gerard experienced greater consolation than others upon visiting the image of the crucified. He was transported with rapture."

This pilgrimage was, in truth, an uninterrupted series of miracles and extraordinary events which aided them very much to confirm their faith, to strenghten their vocation, as it also helped them to acquire that spirit of piety and union with God, which must be the chief characteristic of the apostolic life for which they were preparing.

Among the young men there was one who must have vividly remembered this journey with Brother Gerard, because a prophecy which was made to him at that time, and to which he paid but little attention, was actually accomplished. We mean Father Peter Blasucci, who was still a very young man, and had taken his vows a month before. He was the brother of Dominic Blasucci, who seven months before, in the flower of his youth, had ended by a holy death, and innocent and virtuous life. He was the Aloysius of our Congregation.

To Peter Blasucci the servant of God had said durring the pilgrimage to Mount Gargano that he would be appointed Superior-General of the Congregation. Forty years afterwards the prophecy was actually fulfilled, for on the 24th. of April, 1793, the chapter elected Father Blasucci Rector Major of the Congregation, which he governed for twenty-three years, till his death in 1816.

The journey of the saintly brother had covered fully nine days. When on his arrival at the convent he handed the purse to the Superior, it was found to be heavier than on the day he received it from him. Father Fiocchi was therefore not disappointed in his expectations that the confidence in God possessed by the brother was the most valuable purse he could have given to the pilgrims.

CHAPTER XV.
LABORS AT MELFI AND LACEDOGNA.

During his stay at Melfi in August, Gerard had made a favorable impression upon Monsignor Basta, the bishop of that place, who, in consequence, was most desirous of again seeing him, as soon as possible in his diocese. The solemn novena celebrated annually in the church of St. Theodore at Melfi afforded him an opportunity of effecting this. He invited Father Fiocchi to preach, and begged him to allow Gerard to accompany him. The Rector of Iliceto acquiesced, and arrived in Melfi towards the close of October, 1753. The feast of St. Theodore was celebrated on the 9th. of November.

This visit of Gerard was hailed by the inhabitants of Melfi with acclamations of joy. Never before had so many persons attended the novena. Everybody wished to see the holy brother, and to learn something from him.

Monsignor Basta proved himself most enthusiastic in this matter. He confered with the enlightened religious for many an hour as he had done on a former occasion, and confiding in his extraordinary gifts, his clear insight, and the wonderful accuteness of his judgement, he did not hesitate to submit the most intricate cases to his decision.

The clergy faithfully imitated the example of their bishop. Able priests, and especially confessors hastened to Gerard to propose to him their doubts and difficulties in regard to the care and direction of souls. He answered all with the wisdom of a saint, solved their doubts in all sincerity, and explained things to the utmost satisfaction of those who appealed to him.

His influence over the laity was not less great. Whoever was troubled by any fear, or had a request to make, called upon him. Prominent men and women, as well as simple workmen and the poorest among the people, had recourse to his charity and were not disappointed.

It is hardly necessary to mention that the children could not resist his holy attraction. Ninety years after Gerard had labored at Melfi, one of the children had still a vivid and pleasant remembrance of him. We mean the hundred-year-old Xavier Pascucci, who gave testimony in regard to the servant of God, during the process of beatifiation, in 1843.

"When Gerard was at Melfi," he relates, "I was ten or twelve years old, and had the happiness to speak frequently to the servant of God. He always conversed with the young people who were accustomed to be around him, about the love of God and of the fidelity with which they should discharge the duties of their holy religion. He once asked us: 'What do you give to Almighty God? What do you give Him?' And then he would sign our foreheads with the sign of the Cross, and he often distributed small pictures representing the sorrowful Mother, among us children. He led a very austere life. Several of us noticed that he always wore a rough hair-shirt. He also did very much for the poor. He frequently shared his food with them. I myself once saw him, while going to school, taking off his shoes, and giving them to a poor person. His great interest in the salvation of souls, and his zeal for the conversion of sinners were very great."

What Gerard then accomplished in this respect was so admirable and of such great importance, that for a long time afterwards people spoke of the conversions which he had effected, or for which he had paved the way, and the happy fruits which they now enjoyed.

Whoever knew of a sinner endeavored to lead him to the brother, and the conversion was only a matter of time.

Father Tannoja says: "A simple word spoken by Gerard was enough to make sinners contrite. If they were ripe for the reception of grace in the holy sacrament of penance, he joyfully led them to Father Fiocchi. Among others, this happened to several distinguished noblemen who had for years neglected the concerns of their soul, and had sunk deep in sin. A single interview with Gerard brought about a complete change in them. Afterwards they served as public models."

Gerard's intimate knowledge of hearts contributed greatly to his success.

Thus, at Melfi there lived a man who, concealing his sins for several years, had used the means of salvation to his own spiritual destruction. When Gerard met him, he knew at once the sad condition of his soul: "My son," said he, full of compassion, to the man, "you are living in sin; why do you wish to die a reprobate? Confess the sins which you have for so long a time concealed, and concern yourself about God's grace." The poor man could not deny the truth of these words, was very much ashamed, and called upon a priest to restore his peace of conscience.

The same thing happened to an unfortunate woman who had not been able to remove a burden of conscience, in spite of frequent confession, because she foolishly persisted in concealing her true condition in confession. "My friend," the servant of God said to her, "how can you live in peace while you are an enemy of God? Why do you not confess the sin which you have concealed for so many years?" This disclosure made the poor woman blush for shame. She resolved to hesitate no longer, and to fulfil the duty she had so long neglected. Gerard encouraged her, and she went to a confessor who took an interest in her soul.

Essentially similar, but more wonderful in its circumstances, is the following conversion. One day when the servant of God was about to leave the episcopal palace, he was accosted by a woman belonging to that class of persons who pride themselves on their external piety, and do not hesitate to display it. The virtue of this person was only assumed, and in order to increase her renown the hypocrite sought to associate with all those who enjoyed a reputation of great sanctity. Among these she would dispose of what she called her mysteries, and play the part of a conscientious, pious soul. It was a matter of course, that her choice of a director was the most celebrated confessor who was then at Melfi, Father Martino of the Order of St. Augustine.

This unfortunate woman, Teresa Morante, also called upon Brother Gerard. Gerard listened to her patiently and silently. After she had finished her hypocritical discourse, he said in a very earnest tone of voice: "What! you have a scruple: do you also wish to impose on me? For many years you have confessed and communicated sacrilegiously, and now you act as if you were a saint. Go and make a good confession, if you do not wish to die the death of the damned!"

Such an unexpected disclosure confused the woman and filled her with shame. The words "you will be damned!" terrified her. They were like a flash of lightning from a clear sky. She immediately went to her confessor, Father Martino. Without telling him about the pitiable condition of her soul, she merely said: "Oh, my Father, I am damned! Do help me. I wish to make a general confession."

It was pardonable that the confessor, believing that Teresa had merely trivial fears, reproved her for being so easily confused and disturbed, and then sent her away with these words: "Go, you are a fool." It was less pardonable, that in spite of the penitent's repeated and calm declaration that she felt her soul to be in a most wretched condition and that it was only the supernatural knowledge of Gerard which enlightened her and aided her to become contrite, that he refused to hear anything more about the matter, lost his temper, and afterwards so far forgot himself as to censure the holy brother in the presence of several persons, and to call him an ignorant and imprudent man and a disturber of consciences. Luckily, Gerard's words exercised a greater influence over Teresa than those of her irascible confessor, and the hypocrisy to which she had been previously addicted was no longer powerful enough to resist the truth which had been so plainly made known to her. There was no rest for her, and she went to Canon Leonardo Rossi, to whom she sincerely confessed that for ten years she had concealed a sin through shame, and had thus committed sacrilege upon sacrilege. Her contrition was now so great, and the detestation of her former hypocrisy so sincere, that she permitted the Canon to manifest to her ordinary confessor, Father Martino, the real condition of her conscience. She also expressed the wish — nay, she intimated that it was her positive desire — that in case the virtues and miracles of the servant of God would be published, what he had done for her should not be concealed, but should be told just as it happened. Thence-forward, Teresa led a life which was both edifying and exemplary. It is easily understood that such remarkable conversions rendered the actions of Gerard productive of much good. To these were added other, not less evident proofs of his sublime mission. Among the miracles which he wrought there is one recorded which took place in the house of Donna Bruno, of whom we have previously spoken.

This widow had sold a considerable quantity of her wine; but when the customer came to take it, the wine in one of the larger casks was discovered to be sour. The man now refused to accept it, and the woman was not a little confused. Fortunately Brother Gerard visited the distressed woman that same day. Having been informed as to what had happened he made the usual reply: "It is nothing;" then he ordered one of those papers on which the name of the Immaculate Conception was written, then in very frequent use, to be thrown into the cask. He promised that the wine would again be palatable.

Donna Bruno hesitated. "Oh," said the servant of God, "why do you hesitate; are you to change the wine? No, God will do that; therefore, do as I said." She obeyed and Gerard's promise was fulfilled.

At the close of the Novena, Gerard accompanied Father Fiocchi and the other Fathers to Atella, where they were giving a mission, not far from Melfi. In Atella the missionaries lived with Don Benedict Grazioli, a friend and benefactor of the Congregation, who took entire charge of the priests, so that the servant of God found leisure time for his pious occupations. While the missionaries were in the pulpit and in the confessional, laboring for the salvation of souls, he prayed before the Blessed Sacrament to aid them. He was particularly fond of doing this in the little church of the Benedictines, where he prayed so fervently that it was still remembered by these nuns in 1843, at the time of the process of his Beatification.

From Atella the servant of God returned to Iliceto; however, only to leave it again after a few weeks.

The inhabitants of another city, who were prostrated

with sorrow, soon after asked for Gerard, that he might come to console them. This was at Lacedogna, where Monsignor Amato, a great friend of the servant of God, a man whom Father Tannoja calls "the crown of bishops," discharged the office of chief pastor.

A devastating epidemic had broken out in the city; it was regarded by good citizens as a scourge of God, Who was punishing them on account of the many scandals that existed among them. Penance and a thorough amendment of life they thought would be the best means to remove the dreadful plague.

One of the ablest of them, truly a man of God, the arch-priest Dominic Capucci, in whose family we have already met Gerard as an honored guest, was energetic in assisting the zealous bishop in his endeavors to remove the scandals, and to bring the guilty ones to a sense of their duty. But all the efforts of the pious and zealous shepherds of souls were frustrated by the stubborness of these people. They did not heed them; and in spite of the fact that the fatal disease was raging, the most scandalous disorders prevailed.

Under these circumstances, the bishop as well as the arch-priest believed that the best and only means to stem to tide of evil was to send for a man, who, endowed with unusual powers, could change the hearts of evil-doers. The bishop, therefore, applied to Father Fiocchi to allow Brother Gerard to come to Lacedogna for a short time.

The request of so eminent and noble a patron and friend as Bishop Amato, who as grand-vicar at Conza had given effective aid to the establishment of the house at Caposele in 1746, could not be refused. The arch-priest Capucci, who was a spiritual son of Father Cafaro, also deserved that others should comply with his wishes by zealously co-operating with him in the good which he had undertaken.

Accordingly, the servant of God set out for Lacedogna, where he arrived, probably in January, 1754.

What joy all the well-disposed inhabitants of Lacedogna experienced when they again saw the good man, who three years before had edified them when he was in the humiliating and difficult service of Bishop Albini, — what consolation they felt when this holy man again dwelt among them, and called down upon them God's mercy, — what great veneration they paid when they received within their walls a religious who was everywhere prized, cannot be expressed. Gerard's biographer, Father Tannoja, relates that the servant of God was received at Lacedogna rather as an angel than as a man.

The epidemic then prevailing gave Gerard opportunity to render service to the sick, and by these proofs of charity to pave the way to the hearts of those whom he wished to convert.

Thus he was seen hastening through the city, and from house to house visiting the sick. He made no exceptions. He visited every one, the poor man in his hut as well as the nobleman in his mangnificent dwelling. One, Gerard would encourage to be patient; into another he would infuse sentiments of contrition for his past life; a third he would prepare for the journey to eternity; many he cured in a wonderful way. Among the latter was the arch-deacon of the diocese, Canon Anthony Saponiero, who has given us a written account of his cure which we shall describe in his own words.

"A very violent fever," he says, "had reduced me to extreme weakness. Lying abed had become a torture to me; my stomach refused to perform its functions and my head ached violently. Every day I believed to be my last. I received information that the servant of God had arrived at Lacedogna. I sent him word immediately that he should offer up a prayer for my recovery. Thereupon he sent a messenger to tell me that I would recover very soon, and that all I needed was to have great confidence in God. On the following day he called to see me. While approaching my bedside he said: "Praise God! You are already well." And in saying these words he made the sign of the Cross on my forehead with his thumb. I immediately felt quite well and would have left my bed if he had not told me to do so only on the following day; and this actually happened. Thus was my cure effected in a moment, by a miracle performed by Brother Gerard."

By making the sign of the Cross, he cured a poor woman, in whose case the skill of the doctor had failed, and who greatly lamented her unhappy condition. "Courage!" said he to the sufferer, while making the sign of the Cross on her head; "arise in the name of God, and come with me to the church where I wish you to go to confession." Wonderful to relate! The woman who had hitherto suffered so much torture was able to comply with this command. She went to confession, and returned home perfectly well.

Another sick person whom the miraculous power of the servant of God restored to health, was a certain Lella Cocchia. This poor creature was suffering from the most grievous of all diseases: she had been wasting away from the terrible effects of insanity. It was not possible to look at her without the most heartfelt compassion and without shuddering, for the demented girl was violent and often uttered the foulest language. She was, however, well known to Gerard, having met him before.

For, when on one occasion he had come to Lacedogna on a collecting tour, Lella hastened to call upon him to seek some consolation. Her mother had just died, and the fate of her departed soul weighed heavily upon the mind of the bereaved daughter. Thanks to his higher gifts and his supernatural knowledge, he could afford her real consolation. He said: "your mother is in purgatory; I advise you to offer for her forty Communions, then she will be released from her sufferings." Lella did as Gerard had told her; and after the fortieth Communion the soul of her mother appeared, and giving thanks said that entrance into heaven was no longer refused her, that she was then going there.

The sad state of this poor child was a source of great grief to the servant of God. As soon as he had been informed of the particulars of the case he visited her. He saluted her in a very friendly manner; then as was his habit, he made the sign of the Cross on her forehead. Scarcely had he done this when Lella began to sing, and praised God and the glorious Virgin, the Mother of God. Henceforth, no foul expression crossed her lips, she was entirely cured, and fully recovered her mental powers.

He was equally successful in treating those who were spiritually sick. Thus, he was enabled to fulfill the task which had been imposed upon him by the bishop and the arch-priest Capucci, to their fullest satisfaction, however impracticable it might at first have have seemed.

He chastised those who gave scandal, not with reserve and in an indirect manner, but with all freedom and sincerity. This he could do, armed as he was with the power of God. If persons avoided him, he knew well how to find a pretext for visiting them at home. Though this did not decide their conversion at once, it contributed largely towards it. He stopped many in the street, and while speaking to them either in joke or in earnest soon succeeded in studying their disposition. If he found them ready for further conversation he accompanied them home to further his plan. His lively faith made him a most convincing speaker: With ardent zeal he represented to sinners their folly and malice; impressed upon their minds the strongest motives for changing their wicked lives, and sometimes he cast himself at their feet entreating them with tears in his eyes; nor did he cease until they yielded, and were won for Jesus Christ. If this mild treatment was not sufficient, he also knew how to raise his voice in most earnest reproach; but sometimes it was a threatening look that attained success.

Among those who gave scandal was a very prominent man who seemed incorrigible. His excellent wife who was deeply grieved on account of the condition of her husband, begged Gerard with many tears to bestow his charity upon her husband, and to do what he could to bring him back to the path of duty and to the fear of God. The servant of God consoled her, and bade her pray. He then made it a point to meet the man, and spoke most kindly to him. His words seemed inspired by God, so great was the impression which they made. Even while Gerard recalled the enormities of his life, the sinner was changed from a wolf into a lamb, and expressed sentiments which plainly indicated sure marks of conversion. The servant of God was very much rejoiced when he saw this, but was not satisfied with these manifestations of contrition. Before leaving the converted man, he made him promise that he would go with him to Iliceto in order to make a retreat. The man went with him, and the fervent retreat which he made was the beginning of a new life.

Another equally notorious sinner, on his death-bed had already refused to see the priest at Lacedogna, and no one could induce him in this supreme moment to be sorry for his irregularities, and to make amends for the scandals which he had given. The whole city was thrown into excitement on account of such hardness of heart. Gerard came, and having cast a glance at the obstinate man he knelt and said a Hail Mary to the "Refuge of sinners." The consequence was that the hard heart became as soft as wax. The servant of God accomplished his work without difficulty and was so successful that he soon prevailed upon the man to send for a priest and to make his confession. The priest came, and he that had been the prey of the devil so long was snatched from his hands before it was too late.

The servant of God was just as successful in effecting the conversion of a priest who, unmindful of his holy calling, had been leading a sinful life for many years. Gerard met him in the sacristy of a church just as he was about to go to the altar to say holy Mass. He beckoned him to follow, and having led him aside, he threw himself at his feet and represented to him the enormity of his sin in going to the altar to offer the holy sacrifice to God while guilty of grievous sins which he would not confess. Gerard's humble and earnest entreaty made a favorable impression. The priest repented, and ever after led an exemplary life, and was most enthusiastic in sounding the praises of the servant of God.

The servant of God had again taken up his abode at the house of Constantine Capucci, the brother of the arch-priest. As before, this worthy family was a witness of the grand virtues and the extraordinary gifts of this highly-privileged religious. They were highly edified by his spirit of collectedness, his continual prayer, his pious affections, his severe penances! The days during which Gerard was at Capucci's house, were, for the members of his family, rich in fruits of grace. Nothing rendered them more fervent and helped more to advance them on the road of perfection than the different interviews which they had with the brother, and at which all without exception delighted in being present. The short discourses of Gerard about the love of God and on the necessity of saving one's soul had always a peculiar effect: they convinced by the simplicity of the disinterestedness and humility of the speaker, and by the fervor of his love for God and for his neighbor, and therefore penetrated deeply into their hearts. At times he betrayed a supernatural knowledge which greatly enhanced the impression effected by his discourse.

One day, the conversation turned as it usually did, on the grandeur of eternal life, and on the felicity that is enjoyed by the saints in heaven. The servant of God spoke as he generally did, with an eloquence which enraptured all those present. Among them was a man whose baptismal name was Angelo, and who, while listening to Gerard thought of his wife, wishing that she also might be present and hear the charmingly beautiful discourse. But just as he conceived this thought the servant of God turned to him and said: "But, Angelo, my friend, why do you not think of your own affairs, and derive some profit for yourself? Why are you thus concerned about your wife? As long as you think of the absent, you remove yourself from that which is here said for the benefit of all." The good man blushed, and was too much astonished to make reply. He subsequently told Constantine Capucci that Gerard had justly addressed those words to him, as in reality his thoughts had been busy elswhere.

Many similar incidents occurred. This alone would naturally explain the great concourse of people that flocked to see him; and so many visited him, that Capucci's house resembled a public meeting house where people were constantly coming and going. He gave counsel, encouragement, and reproofs — everything with his usual admirable clearness and power. He had scarcely a moment that he could call his own, and was often kept busy till late at night.

A certain lady of Lacedogna had also come to ask his advice; being constantly troubled with great temptations, she felt quite unhappy. After she had manifested her interior to the servant of God he saw at once that she brought about these sufferings herself and said to her plainly and sincerely: "The fault, my good woman, lies with you, and only with you. You are not faithful to the Lord Jesus, in such and such a matter. Shut the door of your heart, then you will have peace." The lady was surprised, not so much at what had been said, but that Gerard read her soul so quickly and so well; for she had to acknowledge to herself that her earnestness in breaking off a certain attachment, and in avoiding every dangerous occasion had been rather lukewarm.

One of those who most frequently asked counsel of Gerard, was Bishop Amato. He consulted him about important affairs, and one might say that he actually put himself under the direction of this simple brother. Hence he never allowed any of Gerard's subsequent visits to Lacedogna to pass by without having a long interview with him. "To enter into a spiritual and theological conversation with Gerard" he used to say, "means to become his disciple, but he who becomes a disciple will leave him as a true theologian so great will be the light which he will receive from him."

The most distinguished priest who followed the example of their Bishop was Canon Capucci. He never tired of conversing with the servant of God about his spiritual concerns. This intercourse affected lasting results. Although the Canon had been under the spiritual direction of Father Cafaro since the mission of 1746 conducted by our Fathers at Lacedogna, he had not yet secured that interior peace in the spiritual life, which his dignity demanded. This deficiency was remedied by his intercourse with the privileged brother. Gerard taught Capucci the ways of the spiritual life; pointed out those points which he should always bear in mind; instructed him how to purify his aims and sentiments from what is worldly and earthly; and succeeded so far with him by his exhortations and counsels, which the pious priest accepted in humility, and with the docility shown by chosen souls, that the latter subsequently led a truly apostolic and virtuous life, and died a most holy death.

While Gerard was laboring at Lacedogna, a sick man from Bisaccia, a neighboring city whose inhabitants had heard of the miracles, came to him and was cured. Hereupon Canon Cella, the Primicer of the Cathedral of Bisaccia went to Lacedogna and besought the brother to go with him to this city where an unfortunate man, Bartholomew Melchionne, was in great need of his assistance. He had been married but a year. Soon after his marriage he was taken with a very strange malady, wasted away, appeared to be half-witted, and showed signs of being possessed. A visit to the shrine of St. Anthony in Campagna proved useless; the evil was not remedied. St. Anthony remained deaf to the prayers which were offered by the friends of the unfortunate man, because the honor of the cure was reserved to another saint. When Gerard visited Melchionne, he approached him and uttered the words which were peculiar to him: "It is nothing, it is nothing; you are well." He then said a few prayers over Bartholomew, and the man was relieved. Gerard desired him to come with him to the Canon's house to dine there.

At table Bartholomew ate like a man in robust health, and being in the best of spirits sang a hymn with the servant of God. Besides the works of mercy, and the miracles connected with them, Gerard exhibited his higher gifts at Bisaccia by several prophecies and manifold proofs of his knowledge of hearts. When returning to Iliceto the servant of God was obliged to pass through Rocchetta.

In this place there was a Calabrian workman who had been living with a dissolute woman for a considerable time, to the great scandal of the inhabitants of the town. Upon Gerard's arrival there he was naturally informed of this great evil. He immediately sent for the man. The latter obeyed the summons. The servant of God began to speak to him in a manner so impassioned that he stood before him quite humbled and abashed. Gerard also exposed to him the secrets of his conscience, mentioned things which no one could know, and proved that he knew his interior so perfectly that the guilty man was astonished, put to shame, and very much frightened. He solemnly promised to change his scandalous life, and to remove the object of his unbridled passion at once. While Gerard saw the man humbled, repentant, and fully resolved to better, he directed him to an excellent confessor, and instructed him how to complete the work of his salvation as soon as possible. The conversion of this man was permanent, and from that time he frequently came to Iliceto to settle the affairs of his soul. He subsequently married, by the advice of Gerard, and returned to his own country.

Probably towards the end of February 1754, the servant of God came back to Iliceto. Meanwhile Satan had devised artifices which were to cause the servant of God many bitter hours during the following months.

Before we mention the particulars of the dark days which came upon Gerard in consequence of this satanic resolve, let us cast a glance at the labors of the servant of God, which we have already noticed, but the nature of which we have had no opportunity to describe to its full extent. They belong in a special manner to the vocation of this extraordinary brother, and should not be treated superficially. These labors consist in his apostolate, exercised in the convents of nuns, — his glorious work among virgins consecrated to God.

CHAPTER XVI.
APOSTOLATE AMONG VIRGINS CONSECRATED TO GOD.

The same intense love of God which made Gerard the friend, preserver and guide of poor sinners, also excited in him a special interest in those who were resolved to walk in the road of perfection, particularly those souls that served God in the religious state.

Those women who had consecrated themselves to God and were leading an austere, retired life in well-regulated communities, were, in his opinion, worthy of esteem and veneration. He never regarded them in any other light, except as the spouses of Christ.

"Do not be astonished," he writes in a letter to the Superior of a convent, "that I am writing with so much pleasure; I recognize in you the true spouses of Jesus, and this fills me with so much reverence that I wish I could always continue with you in the same holy relationship. Being spouses of my Lord, you remind me most vividly of my good Mother, the Blessed Virgin Mary."

How anxious, therefore, the servant of God was to people the convents with noble-minded subjects has already been mentioned. But he was not satisfied simply to do this, as we have already had occasion to say; he also took an active part in the sanctification of those who had consecrated themselves to God, and likewise became the guide of a large number of them on the road to perfection.

However opposed this occupation may appear to his state, the humility of his rank, and his immediate vocation, we cannot entertain the least doubt that God willed it.

Gerard was convinced that in assuming the spiritual direction of the nuns he was simply corresponding to a divine call. Had he himself occasioned the unusual occupation, had he recommended himself to his Superiors as one called to such an office, and ready to assume it; the genuineness of his vocation might have been doubted. But this was not the case.

The first opportunity for Gerard's labors in this respect was afforded him by some bishops who believed him extraordinarily qualified for such work; they therefore sent him to different communities, and his efforts were crowned with the best success.

Gerard submitted to the authority of the Church when he engaged in such work; accordingly he was convinced that it was the holy will of God.

The approval was determined upon, after a conscientious, severe and calm consideration of the subject, by his immediate Superiors, Father Cafaro, Father Fiocchi and St. Alphonsus, — men who abhorred what was unseemly and unbecoming, as readily as they recognized merit.

To Gerard's Superiors nothing could give more convincing proof of his vocation than his spirit, wisdom humility, and later on the glorious results of his labors. This vocation was also proved by the testimony of all those who were able to observe him, and who unanimously praised, not so much his zeal, as the prudence which he showed while engaged in so extraordinary an occupation.

Strange as it may seem that the poor lay-brother was a director of souls, and also the spiritual guide of nuns, there cannot be the least doubt that he had a true vocation for such an office.

In regard to the fulfilment of the duties of this vocation, the servant of God labored in these different convents as an awakener of souls.

What he accomplished in the convent of the Poor Clares at Muro, how he stimulated the Dominican nuns at Corato to renewed fervor, and edified the Benedictine nuns of the same place, has already been mentioned. We shall afterwards relate in detail what he effected among the nuns of the same order at Calitri. Of his labors among the religious of Atella we have received but little information.

Father Margotta, a holy zealous priest, whose acquaintance we shall soon make, had restored community life in this place and had endeavored to confirm this awakened zeal by the spiritual exercises which he conducted for these religious. It was he who brought the servant of God in closer relation with the nuns at Atella. The bishop of Melfi was particularly pleased, and therefore encouraged Gerard to promote the holy work. Gerard spared neither interviews nor letters, and kept up an active communication with the convent. The nuns soon numbered him among their truest benefactors, for besides offering them exhortations which were of the greatest benefit to them, he also induced several noble ladies to enter their convent. After his death, Gerard was honored among these nuns as a patron saint, and many of them had reason to rejoice in seeing their confidence often rewarded with success. The process of beatification brought to light several miracles which were operated by the prayers of these pious nuns.

Of two convents in particular, Gerard became the spiritual director, a fountain of wisdom, zeal and consolation. They were the convent of the Most holy Redeemer at Foggia and that of the Carmelite nuns at Ripacandida.

At the time there flourished in each of them a soul distinguished for sanctity, endowed with the most extraordinary gifts of heaven, well versed in the higher branches of the spiritual life, congenial in mind with the servant of God, and hence desirous of his counsel, instruction and influence. In the convent of Foggia it was sister Mary Cœlestis Costarosa; in that at Ripacandida, Sister Mary of Jesus; both were Superiors, and strict upholders of the monastic rule.

Sister Mary Cœlestis Costarosa, in whom the gifts which heaven and the sufferings which the world bestowed upon her were equally balanced. More than twenty years before she lived in the convent at Scala, where on the 3rd. of October, 1731, she had the famous ecstasy which had so decided an influence over the destiny of St. Alphonsus. In this state she saw a band of apostolic men moving with great zeal through cities and towns, offering and rendering their services to the most abandoned souls. At the head of these men, she saw Don Alphonsus, and heard a voice which said: "Behold! this one I have chosen to be the founder of a work which is to promote my honor." Cœlestis communicated this vision to the saint and thereby essentially contributed towards establishing the Congregation.

However, she was not to follow her vocation in the convent at Scala. After having spent some time at the conservatory at Nocera in which young girls were educated, and having infused it with new life, she founded the conservatory of the Most Holy Redeemer at Foggia in 1738, over which she presided with the greatest success, in Gerard's time. The excellent education which under her direction the daughters of the most respectable persons of the country received, was deemed a blessing not only for the city of Foggia but for the whole of Apulia.

The esteem with which Sister Costàrosa regarded the servant of God, originated in the reading of one of his letters, in which we find: "I desire to love God; I desire to be united with God at all times; I desire to do everything for God." The spirit of which these words gave evidence, corresponded entirely to her own. As soon as she found occasion for an interview with the servant of God, she revealed the similarity of her soul with that of Gerard, and the advantage which could be derived for herself and her community by a closer union with him.

Gerard, on his part corresponded most perfectly with the confidence of the Superior at Foggia, and did not refuse to render the services which she requested. During his journeyings, or on other occasions when he stopped at Foggia and had a few moments to spare, he visited Sister Costarosa. One saw renewed in these interviews, those wonderful conferences of St. John of the Cross and St. Peter of Alcantara with St. Teresa. They encouraged each other to love God, and knew well how to communicate their thoughts and the emotions of their souls.

This comforting intercourse with Sister Costarosa caused him to be more and more attached to the little convent at Foggia, and the invitation of Monsignor Peter Faccoli, Bishop of Troy, under whose jurisdiction the convent was, induced him to interest himself more zealously in behalf of all the members of this community. He accepted the invitation with pleasure. He sought to enkindle in the hearts of all the fire of zeal, and to urge and lead these good spouses of Christ to the acquisition of solid virtue, to a love of sacrifice, to regular observance, and to an intimate love for their holy bridegroom. He accomplished this partly by letters, by short discourses which he gave to all the nuns in common, and partly by conversation which he held with them individually. His efforts in this respect made a deep and lasting impression, as the testimonies which the nuns subsequently gave, clearly prove.

"The discourses of Gerard," as told by one of the nuns, "generally treated on the wonderful attributes of God, of the Blessed Virgin Mary, and of the saints. When he thought of God and spoke of Him, he immediately became unconscious, ardently inflamed." "His heart," says another of his disciples, "was a volcano of the love of God, his countenance glowed like an angel's who comes from heaven to speak to us."

These good nuns were witnesses of one of the most remarkable ecstasies that ever sized the servant of God, and this contributed in no slight degree towards promoting the right spirit in them. It occurred in 1753, on the eve of Trinity Sunday. Gerard came to the convent in order to console one of the sick sisters, just as they were chanting the first Vespers of the great feast. The solemn chant could be heard at a distance in the silence of the holy place. Gerard was suddenly powerfully affected, his spirit followed the chant, and he became rapt in a meditation on the sublime mystery which the nuns were about to praise. And as he penetrated into it more and sank into those abysses which are inconceivable but refreshing, unfathomable but attractive, immense but sweet, his soul soared to heaven and was infused with joy that can only be drawn from the fountain of all happiness. Quick as a dart, the brother hurried through the corridors of the convent, while saying aloud the words of the liturgy: "O altitudo divitiarum sapientiæ et scientiæ Dei; quam incomprehensibilia sunt judicia ejus et investigabiles viæ ejus." (Oh the depth of the riches, of the wisdom and of the knowledge of God! how incomprehensible are His judgments and how unsearchable His ways!) In the meantime the office in the choir was progressing. But the servant of God remained in ecstasy, and after the sisters had finished and left the choir, they found him in the same state. While they were looking at him, he seemed to come to himself. He addressed them saying: "O, Sisters, let us love God!" Then he became ecstatically immovable; as usual his look was fixed on heaven and his eyes were sparkling. Suddenly he was raised from the ground to a considerable height. He then recovered, very pale and quite exhausted.

This ecstasy was followed by still greater proofs of the extraordinary gifts of Gerard.

He cured a sick lay-sister with the sign of the Cross, when all seemed lost. With the sign of the Cross he likewise cured a malignant fever from which a girl was suffering, and for which medical skill found no efficacious remedy. The one little word "well", from his lips, was sufficient to restore health.

He also manifested his gift of prophecy. On one occasion while he, Sister Cœlestis Costarosa and other religious were engaged in pious conversation, he suddenly interrupted the conversation and turning to one of the nuns he asked her whether she often went to confession. After she had answered in the affirmative, the servant of God begged her to become more intimately united with God; "for," said he in confirmation of this request, — "the day of your death is not far off." The nun who was still young and in good health, was very much astonished at such language, as were also the others present. Many of them regarded the words of the servant of God as nothing but a joke. Gerard, noticing the incredulity of those around him, repeated his exhortation, and asserted that he had spoken seriously. "Even the most robust health," said he "often vanishes in a moment; therefore my dear Sister, endeavor always to be united with God; in eight days God will call you to Himself." The Sister then looked at the matter in a very serious light, and carefully prepared herself for death. And this preparation was not useless. Eight days after the interview with Gerard she died a holy death.

During the interviews which the nuns had with the servant of God in the parlor they were often accompanied by a pupil of their house, young Gertrude de Cecilia.

On one of these occasions Gerard turned to Gertrude and asked her to sing for her. Being very shy, the girl did not immediately comply, but was finally persuaded by the brother and sang the favorite verse taken from Metastasio: "Se Dio veder tu vuoi." We know that this song had already caused this impressionable man of God to fall into an ecstasy. And now the same thing happened. The beautiful words which he heard penetrated his heart like darts of love. The four verses had not yet been finished, when Gerard grew very thoughtful, then immovable, the while his eyes beamed like a seraph's. The girl finished the song, but the brother continued ecstatic for some time after.

From this time the servant of God took a special interest in the child whose singing had made him think so much of God. Ere long he had occasion to evince his interest by rendering her the services of a paternal friend in the most wonderful manner.

One day Gertrude went to confession. Whether her confession had not been sufficiently exact, or whether youthful levity had taken possession of her, she had not made her confession in such a manner as is required by the dignity of the sacrament. When she was about to receive Holy Communion, Gerard, no doubt enlightened from on high, met her and said in a very serious tone of voice: "My child, you think that you are in a fit condition to receive Holy Communion? Alas! you did not make a good confession. See the sin which you have neglected to tell! Go back immediately to the confessor, and make a general confession." The poor girl nearly died when she heard this; she could not utter a word; ashamed and confused, she hurried away to recollect herself. After a careful preparation, she made a general confession.

Very soon, her former levity was changed into the opposite; Gertrude became a prey to scruples, mental troubles, and lost all joy of heart. A deep melancholy took possession of her heretofore happy disposition, and no one could account for the change. Then again it was the servant of God who came to her assistance; for when he had to pass through Foggia, he hastened to visit the convent in order to console the distressed girl. "My child," he said, "your confession was very good. God is quite satisfied with it." Nothing more was wanting. These words drove away all melancholy thoughts, and Gertrude was again happy and contented.

The servant of God had more knowledge of the girl than she may have suspected, and when he allowed her to perceive it, Gertrude was incredulous.

Although pious and educated in a convent she did not feel the least inclination to continue to live in it and to serve God in the solitude of the cloister. She thought of her return to her family, and could scarcely wait for the end of her stay in the institution. The servant of God who knew this impatience and this desire, told her repeatedly that she should not think of the world; that she had been chosen to be a spouse of Christ, and must stay where she was. But Gertrude did not wish to hear this, and in spite of her high esteem for the servant of God, his advice in this matter did not please her. Then Gerard allowed her to notice that in this point also he was not without supernatural knowledge, and that the counsel which he had given her was a call of God. He concluded with these earnest words: "If you leave the convent, you will surely repent of the step; in the world you will be exposed to the greatest danger; in the end, whether you will or not, you will have to come back here." The girl who was frightened by this threat, remained in the convent. She received the habit and everything went well with her.

After her profession she was seized with an illness which, according to the advice of her physician, could only be cured by the air of her native place. Though her stay at San Severo, which was her home, may have been beneficial to her bodily health, it exerted a baneful influence upon her spiritual vigor. Surrounded by the vanities of the world, too little confirmed in the spiritual life, the poor nun was exposed to the greatest temptations. Her fidelity began to waver, and without any support, deceived by the persuasions of false friends, she grew tired of her holy vocation and resolved not to return to the convent. But after a short time, remembering Gerard's prophecy, and the dreadful threat which it contained, she was overcome by the greatest sorrow for what she had done, shed bitter tears, and did immediately what was most expedient for her. She returned without delay to the convent and again entered upon the service of God with renewed fervor. During the rest of her life, — she died only towards the end of the year 1830 — she never ceased to extol the sanctity of the servant of God, whose miracles she did not only witness, but to whose influence she was indebted for her vocation, and for saving it from shipwreck.

The servant of God rendered good services to the convent at Foggia; those which the pious community of Carmelite nuns at Ripacandida received were more numerous.[1] He was more closely related to this con-

---

[1] The convent of the Carmelite nuns at Ripacandida was organized in 1735, by the saintly Arch-priest John Baptist Rossi.

vent because of the circumstance that the Carmelite nuns of Ripacandida were in more frequent communication with the Fathers of his Congregation, who had many times labored among them.

In the year 1750, the holy Founder St. Alphonsus had personally given the retreat which the nuns made with such fervor that the saint was greatly astonished and said: "I would not have believed that I could find such beautiful flowers on this rock." (Non avrei mai creduto trovare un garofano, come questo, sopra una rupe.) Instead of urging them onward, he had rather to check them, especially in regard to the immoderate fasts to which they were accustomed.

Besides the holy Founder, there were other Redemptorists who were occupied with the spiritual care of the convent at Ripacandida, especially Father Margotta, who manifested such great interest in this community, that he received from the bishop of Melfi the name of the "guardian angel of Ripacandida." Father Fiocchi was also a frequent spiritual adviser at this convent and, as has been said, directed two of the nuns for twenty years.

The servant of God soon became well known to the religious of this convent. Even in the second year of his religious life he came in contact with them, as may be seen from his letter addressed to Sister Mary of Jesus, dated December 17th., 1751.

Sister Mary of Jesus was at that time Prioress. She brought into Ripacandida a revival of the spirit of St. Teresa and of the virtues of the daughters of this saint, and was greatly pleased to find in Gerard a man who showed that he was quite capable of giving her great assistance in her labors.

Like Mary Cœlestis Costarosa she had soon recognized the highly privileged servant of God who came to the convent with the Fathers.

A short interview was sufficient to convince her of his powerful mind, and to fill her with esteem and confidence in him. The saintly brother, on the other hand, understood the relationship of sentiment, of aims, and of light which the Prioress of Ripacandida bore to him, and thus in a very short time there was formed between those two souls one of those noble, spiritual unions, of which we so often read in the lives of the saints, and which have mutual assistance as their object.

As often as circumstances rendered allowed, the servant of God came to Ripacandida, to visit the Superior of the Carmelites and to converse with her about those subjects in conformity with their holy desires and aspirations. "Then one could see," as Father Tannoja expresses himself, "two concave mirrors which reflected on each other in full splendor, the rays of divine light which fell upon them."

The esteem and confidence which the Superior entertained towards the servant of God were soon communicated to all her daughters, who also desired to have recourse to him in spiritual matters. Monsignor Basta had urged the saintly brother during his first long stay at Melfi to employ his gifts in favor of the nuns at Ripacandida. Gerard therefore took great interest in those daughters of St. Teresa, helped them when he could, urged them to advance in perfection, strengthened and consoled them by words as well as by letters. Father Cafaro said that no one could read these letters without being astonished, especially when considering that Gerard was an uneducated lay-brother, who had scarcely found an opportunity to acquire a perfect knowledge of reading and writing.

Nothing escaped the vigilant eye of this extraordinary director of souls, and to his charity nothing appeared trifling that refered either to the spiritual or the temporal welfare of the convent.

His chief and most ardent desire was, to make them all true spouses of Jesus Christ. "O my divine love," he says in a letter addressed to Mary of Jesus, "be always in the hearts of these Thy beloved spouses! .... Oh, how much do I desire that you and your very good Sisters should dwell in the pierced and open side of Jesus Christ and in the sorrowful heart of the Blessed Virgin! It is there we can find all sweetness and rest."

"My Sister," he writes to Sister Mary Baptista of the Holy Trinity, "let us conform to the divine will. The true love of God consists in entire submission to God and His holy will. Let us take care never voluntarily to commit a fault; such faults afford God the greatest displeasure." Gerard not only exhorted the Sisters to aim at perfection, but he assisted them with his prayers.

"Believe me dear Sister, in Jesus Christ," he writes to the Superior, Sister Mary of Jesus, "I do not cease to pray to the Lord for you and your whole community, that it be His holy will to make you His true spouses. I say it in all truth, I think of you at every visit to the Sacred Heart. I find you all enrolled in His most holy side."

He looked upon the difficulties and sorrows of these pious souls as his own. "God knows the pain I feel," he writes in the aforesaid letter, "because you are in great distress; but it is not exactly pain; no, it is envy. Praised be the Lord Who keeps you on the high-road of sanctity!"

To show that temporal matters did not escape him, especially if regarded as the certain preliminary condition of the spiritual, he found opportunity to enable competent young women to enter the convent.

Not only did he himself frequently collect money for poor candidates so that the dowry might not be wanting, but if it was impossible for him to do this, he petitioned others to do it. It was above all to his influential brethren that he applied in this respect.

We often find him very attentive to the slight wishes of the nuns. Thus we read in a letter which he addressed from Naples to a Sister at Ripacandida the following passage: "My dear Sister, I remember that you asked me for a little book with hymns. You expressed this wish last year, but as it was not repeated, I did not comply with your request. I was waiting for a good opportunity. But as I am at Naples now, I am again mindful of it. I send you what you want. Sing the hymns in your cell, so that you may be a great saint, and always pray to the Lord for me. Your brothers send you greetings. They are all well."

As a compensation for the charity and attention which Gerard devoted to the most important as well as the most trifling affairs of the convent at Ripacandida, he asked nothing except an occasional fervent prayer, that by sacrifice and prayer he might be supported in his great undertakings for the honor of God.

While most humbly asking for such a favor he writes to Sister Mary of Jesus as follows: "The great kindness and many favors which you have shown me are a great consolation to me, but at the same time a source of humiliation and sorrow; for if I compare myself with these spouses of Jesus Christ, I find that I am full of unworthiness. I am compelled to accuse myself as guilty; I must ask everywhere for mercy and humbly implore forgiveness for Christ's sake. I very much desire your prayers, as also those of your spiritual daughters that I may correct my faults. I firmly trust that these united prayers will enable me to fulfil most exactly the will of our common Father in heaven."

His joy was unbounded when he was assured by the nuns that they would joyfully support him by sacrifice and prayer, and that they would offer up Holy Communion for his pious intention.

"The promise," so he writes in tendering his thanks, "which you have made to receive Holy Communion for my intention, has filled me with unspeakable consolation; but it also made me feel ashamed and confused. I was strongly reminded of the truly incomprehensible goodness of God Who makes even his dear spouses care for the salvation of one who has so often offended Him. O excess of love! O astonishing miracle! O love of the true Shepherd, Who with such tender care looks for the lost cheep! Here I can say nothing else than that His love which is bestowed upon me, comes from our Redeemer; it is the fruit of the blood of Christ, and of the sorrows of the Blessed Mother."

To another nun of Ripacandida, Sister Baptista of the Blessed Trinity, he writes as follows: "My dear Sister, recommend me to God now more than ever, as I am in the greatest distress. I can not forget you, because your surname "of the Blessed Trinity" constantly reminds me of the Lord our God. How much I esteem you, my dear Sister, because you are so faithful a spouse of Jesus Christ, God only knows. Love God with your whole heart; become a saint and suffer for Him only. All the sufferings which you have to endure for God, will convert even this earth into a real paradise. (Via su patite per Dio, che le vostre pene vi seranno qui in terra un secondo paradiso)."

Another petition, which Gerard addressed to Sister Teresa of Divine Love, is a follows: "My dear Sister in Christ, I am mindful of you because I believe that you will also be mindful of me by praying to God and loving Him for me. I tell you in all sincerity, you can help me; for you are called 'of divine love,' and I am of opinion that you have become entirely changed into the love of the infinite being of God and into His most holy will. Oh, endeavor to become a saint, and that very soon!"

In the postscript of a letter which he wrote to Sister Mary of Jesus, the servant of God speaks of his death and applies to the nuns for a pious remembrance of his departed soul. Just then a very zealous nun, named Sister Oliviera, had died. In connection with this death he presents his petition. He writes: "Although I am good for nothing, yet I offered up Holy Communion eight consecutive days for the repose of her soul; and I intend to do the same for every one that dies, so that she may enter paradise. Tell this to all the nuns, in order that they may be inclined to do the same for me, when I have passed into eternity."

The charity which the servant of God believed he could claim for himself, he also solicited in behalf of friends and others who were dear to him, and begged spiritual alms of the nuns for others as well as for himself. Thus in a letter written to Sister Mary of Jesus, he recommends to her the soul of a person whom he had won for God and who had always made rapid progress.

In his joy at the success of their mutual efforts in behalf of this soul, he writes: "Our dear friend, Don Luigi, no longer finds any rest; he has become foolish for Christ's sake. He has become entirely absorbed in God, and cannot separate himself from Christ. The world appears as nothing to him, and he regards creatures only as existing in God. He loves Him, and it is his sole endeavor. More than this I cannot say."

To the same Sister he recommends on another occasion a sick nun in the convent at Foggia, whose loss he would sorely feel. "I wish," he writes, "that you would use your influence with the Lord, in favor of a Sister who is at the point of death. Alas! her death is altogether undesirable; tell this to Almighty God. Therefore besiege the omnipotence of God with prayer that our request may be granted. I command you in the name of God, do not let her die, and I desire that you begin a novena in honor of the Divine Power to obtain for this nun the restoration of her health." The novena was held in compliance with his urgent request, and the sick nun recovered.

The reputation and influence which the servant of God enjoyed in the convent at Ripacandida constantly gained ground. His appearance there was hailed by all like the advent of an angel, and completed the impression which his letters, so full of charity and tender solicitude, had produced. His mortified exterior, his devotion in prayer, his modesty, his humility, all this was well adapted to edify, to stimulate in the highest degree, and to inspire confidence and veneration.

Besides, the servant of God was also known in the little convent at Ripacandida as a worker of miracles, and as a man who had received most extraordinary graces.

Twice — to our knowledge, — the Lord glorified his servant by permitting him to fall into an ecstasy while he was speaking to the nuns in the parlor.

One day he was engaged at the grate in a conversation with the Superior, when he was seized with so holy a joy and such happy emotions, that he feared he would not be able to resist them. He grasped the grate with his hands that he might not be carried aloft. Yet so strong was the power of his emotions, that the iron bars by which Gerard held himself, gave away, and were bent in his hands as if they were wax. When the Superior saw this, she called aloud to make him aware of the damage, which he was causing. The loud voice brought him to himself, as if it were from a deep slumber, and when he perceived what had happened, he was greatly confused and in his simplicity begged that the injured grate might be quickly repaired. Sister Mary of Jesus had, it is true, the grate fastened and repaired in accordance with Gerard's wishes, but a few bars were allowed to remain bent as they had been by the ecstasy of the servant of God, to commemorate the event. Even in the year 1853, when on account of the process of beatification, an investigation was made at Ripacandida, the bent iron bars in the parlor were yet to be seen.

On another occasion, Gerard had assembled all the nuns before the grate, in order to give them a short conference. "To-day," he said, "I will lead you into the wine-cellar of divine love." Then he spoke of the infinite prerogatives of Jesus Christ. While speaking, he felt the power of divine love and in presence of all the nuns fell into an ecstasy during which the parlor was illuminated as if it were in flames.

Gerard's knowledge of the future was displayed in such a manner as to increase the confidence reposed in him by the Carmelite nuns. Having one day gone to the convent, he heard that a sister was ill, and that all were anxious about her recovery. After a short pause which the servant of God passed in recollection, he confidently asserted that the illness of this sister would not prove fatal. But the nuns replied that the Sister was already in her agony, so that they did not feel inclined to believe him. "But you will see," said Gerard, "that what I have said is true; the sick Sister must continue to live, for she must still take many a step towards perfection." His prediction was fulfilled; the nun became well, and her subsequent life was even more virtuous than the past had been.

Monsignor Basta, the admirer and friend of the holy brother, was the bishop to whose jurisdiction the convent at Ripacandida was subject, and whom the nuns had to obey as their highest Superior. Whether he wished to test their obedience or to prevent abuses, he one day forbade all correspondence in regard to matters of conscience. As he intimated no exception to this rule, the correspondence with the servant of God had also to cease.

For weak souls, even a just prohibition becomes a stumblingblock; how much more that which is unreasonable, or for which there is no cause! Thus it happened that many good nuns were displeased with this prohibition, and began to murmur.

Intelligence of these complaints, their murmurings and their sadness, soon reached the ears of the servant of God. An ecclesiastic whose sympathy the Prioress had gained, became the informer and narrator of the distress that reigned in the convent at Ripacandida on account of the bishop's prohibition. Not the prohibition, but the distress of the nuns was a source of sorrow to Gerard.

To the Superior of the Carmelites he wrote the following letter:

"My dear Mother: If Monsignor has forbidden you to write, it is well; it is the will of God; and I rejoice very much that hereby many dangers have been removed. This is a sign that he loves you very much and that he wishes you to be closely united with God. Be of good cheer; take courage! These things should not cause you any trouble. They should rather awaken in you a joyful frame of mind. When there is question about doing the will of God, everything else must yield. You, my dear Mother, know this better than I, or any one else. What do you wish me to say? I have already told you, and will tell you in all confidence, though you could instruct me yourself in regard to this matter. I cannot understand how a soul perfectly dedicated to God can find any bitterness in this world, and how she can feel anything but joy in the fact that

God's will is accomplished in all things. The will of God is indeed the only support of our souls. Cursed be self-love which deprives us of so great a treasure, of paradise on earth, yes, of God Himself! O how wretched is human folly that permits us to neglect such great advantages! How can we better please God than to fulfil in all things and at all times His holy will; to do all that He wishes and when He wishes it; so that we may accomplish it perfectly?

"Let us therefore be totally indifferent in regard to all things, in order that we may be able to carry out the divine will with that highest purity of intention which God asks of us.

"What a great good is the will of God! O what a hidden and inconceivable treasure! O will of God! thou art worth as much as my God Himself; who can understand thee except God?

"I assure you, my dear Mother, it affords me great consolation to know that you are one of those souls who seek their only comfort in the most adorable will of my God. Your heroism in this point is well known to me. Oh! continue in your efforts to become united with God by a perfect transformation. What are the angels in heaven doing but the will of God? Now what the angels are doing in heaven, that we should do on earth. Yes, let God's will reign on earth! Let paradise be in heaven, and let paradise also be on earth.

"Permit all your daughters to read these few lines. I am of opinion that Monsignor's prohibition to write to me extends not only to yourself but to all the Sisters. He was right; and I sincerely hope that no one may be sad on this account, for this would be complaining of God. Let God's holy will be always done! And I declare to you that I am quite satisfied that you no longer write to me; this I say to all the Sisters. And if there should be the least shadow of disobedience in their sending me their regards, for the love of God avoid doing so. I am satisfied; it is enough for me if you recommend me to the Lord in your prayers.

"This therefore is my wish. Besides, I know very well the excellent intentions of this holy prelate who wishes that all should be closely united with Jesus Christ. If my Superior should send me to Ripacandida for any reason, I shall refrain from asking permission to speak to you. It is not necessary that we see each other here below, since we shall see each other in paradise. While we are in this world, let us sanctify ourselves according to the will of others, not according to our own will, for the former is the will of God."

That this letter, which was inspired by faith and true religious spirit, acted as balm upon a wound, quieted all mental disturbances and cheered and consoled the nuns at Ripacandida, is easily understood. All were ready to make the sacrifice.

But on this occasion the Lord was satisfied, as He often is, with the good will and required no more than unconditional and calm submission. After Monsignor Basta had tested the obedience of the nuns, he repealed the prohibition in regard to the servant of God, and even expressed to the nuns the pleasure he would feel, if they would seek counsel and help from the religious, who understood their spirit so well. That the bishop did not aim at the brother by this strict prohibition is proved by the circumstance that not long afterwards, on the occasion of an investigation which he undertook in regard to the extraordinary life and spirit of Sister Mary of Jesus, he desired not only Father Fiocchi's but also Brother Gerard's company and advice.

Though this salutary connection of the servant of God with the religious community at Ripacandida had begun in consequence of his closer union with its eminently spiritual head, Sister Mary of Jesus, it did not cease, when two years after Gerard had become acquainted there, May 1752, a new Superior, Sister Mary Michela of St. Francis succeeded his friend.

This Sister realized what support was given by Gerard to zeal, charity and the monastic life; instead therefore of withdrawing herself from his influence, she was rather inclined to strengthen the old, happy understanding, with him.

Gerard, who in rendering services, did not consider the persons, joyfully responded to this manifestation of confidence and was also very soon one heart and one mind with the new Prioress.

Scarcely had he been informed by the former Superior that Sister Michela had been chosen Superior, when he expressed to the latter his satisfaction at her appointment; he desired her, as he was in the habit of doing, to become a saint, and promised that he would write to her in a short time, "for," said he, "such is the will of God."

A few weeks afterwards she actually received the first letter from him. In it he again expresses the joy which he felt on account of her appointment. He then says: "I shall ask our Lord to sustain you, in order that you may discharge the duties of your office in a proper manner, and watch more carefully over the many spouses of Jesus Christ. I hope that His divine Majesty my give you the spirit which that seraph of love, St. Mary Magdalene de Pazzi possessed, who was so great a servant and lover of the Lord, and of the Blessed Virgin ...... so that you and your daughters may also become seraphs of the love of God." This noble desire is followed by the earnest request that he may frequently be remembered in her prayers. Moved with tender care for the former Superior — the venerable Sister Mary of Jesus — Gerard concludes with the following words: "I beg you to have regard for Sister Mary of Jesus. You know that she has been your Mother from the beginning, and has nourished you with the milk of the love of God."

Though this recommendation may have been superfluous, the servant of God wished to give it, chiefly to throw out to the new Superior a gentle hint which she should not disregard, and perhaps in order to give expression to the promise which he had made a few days before to the former Prioress. The latter, with the humility peculiar to the saints, who usually see nothing commendable in themselves, had expressed to the saintly brother her apprehension that when she would cease to be at the head of the community, all, even the servant of God, would forget her, and thus deprive her of a great help; she hoped, however, that he would not refuse to visit her. Gerard answered: "You say that I should visit you, yes, my dear Mother, I shall come to console you with my whole heart, whenever it is the will of God. Be not disheartened, and be without sadness if you do not wish to make me sad. You tell me that now when you are no longer Superior, all will forget you. As for myself, I assure you I have not forgotten you. I desire that you should also remember me. Well then, magnanimously love God, and you will become a saint. Since you are not now so much occupied, you will have more time for this purpose. Pray earnestly for me, who need so much spiritual help and who — God knows — am so sad and without consolation. If you wish, you can do very much for me by your prayers to God; render me this act of charity."

Thus did the relation which Gerard bore to the convent at Ripacandida remain unchanged under the new Superior; and he continued the spiritual adviser and extraordinary director of the nuns till the end of his life. The reader may learn the excellence of his guidance from the following chapter in which we have recorded a few extracts of his instructions and sentiments, gleaned from some of his letters.

The holy relation of Gerard to the nuns at Ripacandida continued till the end of his life, and bore abundant fruit.

Even after the death of the saintly brother, these religious looked upon him as a protector and friend, invoked him and paid him the most childlike respect and veneration. "Oh, how many novenas" — thus one of them expresses herself in the process of beatification — "did we make in his honor! We all have chosen him to be our special patron, and we still recommend ourselves to his intercession, in order to obtain every necessary grace. He, on his part, condescends to grant us assistance from heaven. A young man whose life was despaired of, is indebted for its preservation to the prayers with which we invoked the saintly brother."

CHAPTER XVII.
SPIRITUAL COUNSELS.

Soon after the election of a new Prioress in Ripacandida, Gerard found occasion to explain through a series of letters, the duties of a Superior. Only a few of these letters have been preserved.

Sister Mary Michela applied to Gerard, requesting him to give her some instruction in regard to her position as Prioress, and to furnish her with a spiritual guide or compass. The servant of God did not refuse to comply with this humble request, and wrote a treatise on the duties of the Superior of a religious community, which we will quote.

"My dear Mother:

"Pardon me for the sake of Jesus Christ and the Blessed Virgin Mary for not having immediately rendered the service asked of me. My habitual sloth was the cause of my tardiness in sending you the rule. God's will be done! You will also forgive me for writing you in great haste.

"As the Prioress takes the place of God Himself, she must fulfil the duties of her office with the greatest exactness, if she wishes to please the Almighty, Who has selected her to fill His place. She needs perfect prudence, always acting according to the dictates of the spirit of God. She should be endowed with the noblest virtues, give the best example, so that her daughters may have no cause to find fault with her. Her heart should be a pure vessel filled with the balm of virtues; these virtues should be communicated to her daughters, so that like their Mother they may advance in perfection.

"The Superior should never lose sight of her own unworthiness, and should always remember that of herself she is able to accomplish only what is evil. She owes the honor and dignity of her office entirely to God: for there are many others who would fill it just as well, and better for the greater glory of God. In view of her imperfections, she should always humble herself and have compassion on those who commit faults. She should fulfil the duties of her office in the spirit of love, and not shrink from it as from a burden. In consideration that God has destined this office for her from all eternity, she must feel the necessity of performing its duties with angelic perfection, and must adhere closely to the divine will, but remain at her post with entire indifference, and without any attachment.

"In doubtful matters, and when she cannot decide herself she should have recourse to one who is enlightened by God. But after having once determined what course to pursue, she should have God's glory alone in view, and without human respect carry out what she has resolved to do, even if she should have to shed her blood and loose her life; for there is question of doing the Lord's work.

"She should always remember that she is the Superior, and frequently say to herself: 'God wills that I should fill this post, and therefore I must do His will in all things, and watch over all the souls confided to my charge. It is my duty to serve all, to counsel all, to be the Mother of all, to console all, and to give satisfaction to all. I must give the best of everything to others, and keep the worst for myself, in order that I may please God. Finally, I must suffer something everywhere, that I may rejoice in following the example of my beloved and divine Spouse, Jesus Christ.'

"The thoughts of the Superior should be like a wheel continually in motion, without intermission revolving around the wants of her daughters. Her daughters she must love in God, with a pure love without distinction of person. Considering rightly that they can procure only by obedience what they need, she should forget herself and bestow all her thoughts and care on them. If eatables, clothes or other things be presented to the convent, she should take nothing therefrom till she has supplied others.

"She should endeavor to inspire confidence, especially if she notices that there is a want of it in some of her daughters. In this case she should summon all her strength and prudence to gain their affection. Even though she should not feel inclined to do so, she should show them kindness, and for the love of God do violence to herself. If she does not do this, if she does not exhibit the tenderness of a mother, the distress and discouragement of her subjects will increase. Even though this may not happen, the subjects will not advance in the love of God, because there is a thorn in the heart that gives them constant pain. Women are very prone to discouragement.

"A Superior requires firmness and gentleness. As the representative of God, she must know how to exact obedience and to punish, but with prudence. The reproof must be given with meekness and sweetness. If this is done, peace and happiness will be restored to the soul. A correction might for instance, by given in the following manner: 'My daughter, you do not seem to understand that your bad example is a source of scandal to many holy souls. It might have been better had you remained in the world, and had not come to this place, which another might now occupy to the edification of all. I tell you this, and I must tell you, because, I am your Mother! God knows how devoted I am to you, and how much I desire your sanctity. I beg you my daughter, resolve to become a saint, and promise the Lord that you will lay aside your imperfections. Do all that I have said, and if you think that I can do anything more for you, call upon me with childlike confidence.'

"If the reproof is given in this way, then, I believe, the daughter will not avoid the Mother, and while the latter shows confidence in the daughter, she will be able to induce her to resolve to walk in the path of perfection. One gains more by mildness, than by severity. Severity creates confusion, temptation, darkness and indolence. Mildness, on the contrary, awakens peace and rest, and encourages the Sisters to love God. If all Superiors would act in this manner, all their subjects would become saints; the disorder and disturbance noticeable in convents arise from a want of prudence. Where there is confusion, there is the devil, and where the devil is, God is not."

Here, most unfortunately, this excellent instruction is broken off. What prudence, what moderation, what knowledge of the human heart in this simple rule! One almost believes that he is listening to a venerable, experienced, priestly ascetic, and not to a simple young lay-brother. One is reminded of St. Jane Frances de Chantal, who in the attractive manner which she has learnt from her spiritual Father, instructs a Superior as follows: "Your office my dear daughter, is the office of a Mother of a family......Your solicitude should be assiduous, yet gentle. Make your daughters pious so far as lies in your power; their welfare depends on this; for if they find pleasure in being familar with God, they will become reserved and mortified. Do not be like those tender mothers who are afraid to punish their children, nor either like those passionate mothers who are always screaming."

In another letter, the servant of God describes the dignity of the vocation of a Superior as follows: I wish

I could see you like a seraph, filled with the love of God, that when your daughters look at you, they may be enkindled with the same love."

According to the views of Brother Gerard, the happiness of a true spouse of Christ is inexpressible; happy is she who has received such a vocation and who faithfully lives according to it; on the contrary, unspeakably unfortunate is she who has received this vocation, but abandons it and prefers the world.

The servant of God found a special occasion to express thoughts on this subject, when he was one day informed that at Ripacandida there was a novice who had the greatest temptation to give up the work of sanctification, and to return to the ordinary life of the world. With a holy zeal he wrote to the novice the following long letter:

"My dear Sister in Jesus Christ: I say to you in the name of God, 'remain in a deep holy peace.' This whole storm is nothing else than the work of the evil spirit, who wishes to drive you away from this holy place. My child, be careful, for the cunning deceiver who is inflamed with envy is laying snares; he is displeased to find you here, for he would like to prevent you from becoming a saint. We all have to endure temptations in regard to our vocation, and God permits these to test our fidelity. Only be cheerful and give yourself up entirely to God; He will then aid you. And how is it possible that you can forget the beautiful resolutions which you have so often made, to belong entirely to God, and to become a true spouse of Jesus Christ? If formerly you desired so much to deserve this honorable title, why do you wish to be rid of it now?

"O my dear Sister, who, except God, can grant you peace? Has the world ever been able to satisfy the heart? Has it ever been able to satisfy the heart of a princess, a queen, an empress? Neither tradition nor history record such a thing. What we know of the world is, that it knows how to sow thorns and thistles in the heart of its followers, and that the more its children give themselves up to the pursuit of wealth, honors and pleasures, so much in proportion are they inwardly tormented and annoyed. Indeed I wish I could permit you to speak to a child of the world, so that you might find out how those things are in reality, which now appear so brilliant and attractive. But, believe me who have had experience in this matter. Life in the world is a sad affair. May God preserve you from it!

"God has the best intentions on you; therefore He has permitted the temptation to try you. Have courage. Drive away all temptations by generously renewing the intention to be a spouse of Christ! In it we find happiness, peace, tranquillity, every good. Alas! what are the transitory goods of the world in comparison with that heavenly and eternal felicity which is enjoyed in heaven by a soul that has been dedicated to the service of Christ! I do not say that she who lives in the world cannot save her soul, but I assert that in the world one is constantly exposed to the danger of being lost, and that in the world one cannot become holy as easily as in the convent.

"Consider, I beg you, the flight of time, the length of eternity, and reflect how transitory is everything here below. At the close of one's life, everything in the world is for us at an end, as if it had never been. Of what use is it to lean upon that which cannot give support? Indeed, all things that do not lead to God are vanities, which are not available for eternity. Unhappy the soul that confides in the world, and not in God!

"I entreat you, my dear Sister, go for a short while

to the vault in which rest the remains of so many nuns who died in your convent, and there consider what all these would have gained if they had been most estimable ladies in the world. Oh! how much it has profited them to have lived poor, mortified, despised and secluded lives in this little convent! Perhaps they had to suffer much, but what peace did they not experience at the hour of death, when they knew that they were dying in the house of God! At the hour of death every one wishes to be a saint; but at that supreme moment, only what we have done for God is of any consequence.

"Should the storm in your heart not yet be over, than have the greatest confidence and unshaken hope in the Most Blessed Trinity and in my Mother Mary, that you will yet become a saint in your convent. But, do what you can, so that I may not be disappointed. Crush the head of the monster who is trying to drive you out of this holy place. Despise him; tell him that you are the sponse of Jesus Christ, in order that he may tremble. Be of good cheer; love God with your whole heart; devote yourelf entirely to Him without the least reserve, and see that the demon may be crushed and die with disappointment! Pray for me, as I always pray for you."

These impressive, paternal words, had the desired effect. The girl to whom they were addressed happily survived all disturbing thoughts and temptations and after having courageously conquered the evil spirit she began to make great strides in the path of perfection. Great was Gerard's joy when, after some time, he received the information that the novice had taken the vows; that she was happy and contented in her vocation. He was at that time at Naples, whence he wrote the following lines to her:

"Dear Sister in Christ Jesus: Your esteemed letter gave me the greatest consolation and pleasure, for it informed me that with God's grace you have made your profession. May God and you yourself be praised! Now that you have had the grace to dedicate yourself to God by means of the vows, you have been raised higher than ever before, since now you are a perfect spouse of the Lord. You will be happy, if in continued reflections on the greatness of your vocation, you humble yourself before the Lord and endeavor to acquire the perfection which your sublime state demands of you. Open your eyes and see the graces which have been bestowed upon you, and be thankful every day to the divine goodness. Well then, become a great saint! You have the best opportunity to become a saint. Pray for me always, and tell Almighty God that He should also make me a saint."

The true spouse of Christ must walk the path of perfection by faith which eventually leads to God.

"In order to love God," writes Gerard to the Prioress at Ripacandida, "one must believe, for he who is weak in faith, is weak in clinging to God (chi manca di fede, manca a Dio.) As for myself I am resolved to live and die, penetrated with faith. Faith is life to me, and life is faith to me. O God! who would live without holy faith? I would wish always to cry out, and to cry out so that the whole world should hear me: May our holy faith live! God alone deserves to be loved."

This life of faith, according to the view of the servant of God, must not be satisfied with any degree of advancement however considerable. The highest point of perfection should be aimed at by an uninterrupted increase of virtue. In a letter in which he mentions the death of Sister Oliviera, he speaks of this duty. He desires that her successor in office should be equal to the fervor and virtues of the deceased nun, because those who do not wish to use their great gifts generously will have to give a severe account on judgment-day.

"I had already heard," he says, "of the death of Sister Oliviera; I hear that Sister Maria Antonia has taken her place. Tell her from me that I have heard this with great pleasure. In order to complete my joy, she should now carry out the holy resolutions which she made when in the world, and let her be a saint as Sister Oliviera was; for if she does not become a saint, then truly God will call her to a severe account."

Storms, temptations, anxieties are, however, the companions of souls that are resolved to walk in the path of perfection. Nevertheless, they should not be discouraged. After all, these things are not the worst. On the contrary, even peace, quiet, freedom from the devil's assaults, should be regarded suspiciously, since snares are often concealed in them.

"Be courageous," he writes to a Sister who is troubled in mind, "do not be cast down; trust in God and hope that He will grant you every grace. Do not rely on yourself, but rather on the Lord, and if you imagine that all is calm, then be assured that the enemy is quite near. Do not put too much confidence in peace, for in the midst of rest war may break out. Live carefully, always recommending yourself to the Blessed Virgin, and putting all your trust in her, that she may keep away the enemy with her powerful hand. What you suffer should not make you dejected; it should only humble you before God, and stimulate you to greater confidence in His mercy. To brood over your troubles will do no good; this comes from the devil, who wishes to rob you of your time. Do not let your courage falter; confide in God, He will help you to become a saint."

These emphatic and gentle exhortations, these solid principles and effective arguments of divine love were the ordinary food with which the servant of God was always anxious to nourish the soul of these spouses of

Christ. For them it was certainly a delicious food. He was moderate in his requirements, and possessed the power of convincing in so eminent a degree that Gerard's influence over the good nuns was extremely salutary and contributed powerfully to make the spirit of St. Teresa grow and flourish.

The efficacy of Gerard's labors in the convent of Ripacandida became better known during a trial which they could not have survived, had it not resulted from the purest motives of faith.

The Prioress, and her daughters were convinced of the advantage they derived from their intercourse with Gerard.

CHAPTER XVIII.
Stormy Days.

The year 1753 had procured for the servant of God an abundance of glory and honor; the following year proved him worthy of such esteem and veneration among men, and that he was not metal of an inferior quality having only exterior glitter.

Divine Providence wished that during this year a trial should befall him which is seldom wanting to great saints.

During the Easter holidays the storm was to overtake him. Gerard was at Atella during Lent, attending to the business of the Congregation in his usual manner. Here he made the acquaintance of Canon Camillus Bozzio, a prominent man of Caposele and a zealous priest, who was preaching the Lenten sermons in this place.

The first meeting of Gerard with Bozzio was one of the most pleasant episodes of this year. We must not omit to relate it in the Canon's own words:

"I have had occasion," he writes, "to converse very familiarly with Father Cafaro of saintly memory, about Brother Gerard. He spoke to me of the ability and sanctity of this brother, who was a penitent of his. I had the happiness of meeting the man of God at Atella, in the year 1754, whither he had come to attend to some business concerning the Congregation, and while I was engaged to preach the Lenten sermons.... From this time forward there existed between us a close friendship, which, springing from supernatural motives, was founded on the love of Christ."

This friendship, however, was not formed in consequence of a transient, favorable impression, which the good brother had made, but was the result of a severer test to which the Canon one day subjected his virtue. "I saw Gerard," thus relates Bozzio, "standing one day in the sacristy of the church, surrounded by several priests, engaged in conversing on holy subjects. I approached and began to excite him with words which betokened very little respect for him. 'What are you talking about? You are, after all, only an ignorant lay-brother, and are playing theologian. Indeed! I do not understand why these gentlemen lose their time, listening to you; they deceive themselves in having an elated opinion of you; I — I look upon you as a vain man; I regard you as a hypocrite and nothing else!'

"This language unexpected, unmerited and abusive, did not, however, disconcert the habitual cheerfulness and equanimity of the good brother. He smiled modestly, embraced me, and in this way proved his entire satisfaction with my strange behavior. 'You are right,' he said, 'I am a poor, ignorant man, and it is necessary that you should pray to God to have mercy on me. I beg you to forgive me!'"

Though this incident was sufficient to make Bozzio feel inclined to regard the servant of God as a saint, he found other opportunities to discover in him marks of most extraordinary sanctity.

Thus, one day he entered the room of Gerard unexpectedly. Like himself, the brother was living in the house of a man named Grazioli, who was a friend of the Congregation and the father of the two girls whom Gerard sent to the little convent at Ripacandida. On opening the door, he found the pious religious rapt in deep ecstasy, and saw him, to his greatest astonishment, raised in the air.

"On another day," continued Bozzio, "I remarked

that his soul was agitated by most extraordinary emotions. I asked whether he had not received Holy Communion that morning, and he acknowledged that he had not done so; he felt something troubling his conscience. This trouble was of course only an effect of his humility. In the afternoon he called to see me in my room at the appointed time, and I could immediately perceive that the desire for Holy Communion was continually creating in his soul the most intense longing for the Most Blessed Sacrament. He himself endeavored to distract his mind and turn his heart away from the great desire with which it was filled. For this purpose we left the house to take a walk through the meadows, and sang some verses of the Lamentations of the prophet Jeremias; but all to no purpose. I then conducted him to the principal parish church. Having locked the door, we sang, accompanied by the organ, which he played pretty well, the hymn, that begins with these words: 'Fiori felici, voi che notte e giorno.' ('Ye Flowers! which day and night watch with dear Jesus, how I envy you!') [1]

"My voice was cold; but his expressed a heart that was wounded with love for Jesus. He would have no one notice the fear and longing which filled it."

While Bozzio was learning to know Gerard better at Atella, and was convinced of his solid virtue and sanctity, a storm was gathering over the man of God. Holy Week was one of peace for him. It was his custom to retire into solitude during these days to meditate upon the sufferings of the Redeemer, and to do penance; frequently he fell into ecstasies. During this year he visited the chapel of the nuns at Foggia, as indeed he

---

[1] One of the simplest and most beautiful hymns which St. Alphonsus composed. It is a tender apostrophe to the flowers which are destined to adorn the altar on which is kept the Most Blessed Sacrament.

had done in former years, where the Lord had several times filled him with His light, he remained within the precincts of this sanctuary a part of Holy Week. While he was thereby edifying all by his piety, he gathered for himself that supernatural strength of which he was subsequently to stand in need. His intercourse with his divine Saviour seems at this time to have been more intimate than usual, and his soul tasted new joys. For Gerard, who was usually silent about his interior favors, allowed a few words regarding this matter to escape him in a letter: "This day," he says, "has been of infinite consolation to my soul."

Did this excess of spiritual consolation intimate the bitter moments which were approaching? Did he conclude that a heavy cross was impending? For it is well known to all that are in any way familiar with the spiritual life, that similar sweetnesses are the forerunners of trials and sufferings, and that such a dawn usually announces a stormy day. It is certain that Gerard was not unprepared when the hour of severe trial came, and that the evil spirit could not assail him unsuspecting and unarmed.

The instrument which the evil one resorted to in order to cause the servant of God pain, temptation and shame, and to cripple his efficiency in behalf of souls was a certain Neria Caggiano. [1] The servant of God had, at the expense of much care and trouble, brought this girl to the conservatory at Foggia, from which, however, Neria after a short time again returned to the world. To justify her inconstancy, Neria reported various calumnies concering the nuns at Foggia. Finally

---

[1] According to Father Cajone's account. Father Tannoja, whose report we took in the first edition, tells the event differently. But as Father Cajone wrote his account by order of St. Alphonsus and according to close investigation, his report seems to deserve the preference.

urged by the father of lies, she ventured to direct her poisonous tongue against the servant of God. She soon found matter for accusation. We have already stated that whenever Gerard came to Lacedogna he stayed with his intimate friend Constantine Capucci; thus, we find him there in the beginning of 1754. This gentleman had four daughters, two of whom had been influenced by Gerard to enter the Conservatory at Foggia. One of these **two** was Nicoletta. Nobody seemed less likely to be the subject of so vile a calumny than Nicoletta who **was** reputed a most honorable and pious girl. Nevertheless, the slanderous tongue of Neria reported the innocent girl as being the unfortunate victim of the servant of God's seduction. Under the circumstances it was easy to clothe the basest lie under the disguise of truth, and thus Neria succeeded in spreading the report. She even convinced her confessor, the honorable Don Benigno Bonaventura, of the truth of her accusation against the servant of God. As Don Benigno highly revered St. Alphonsus and his Congregation, he was much concerned about informing Gerard's Superior of **the event, as soon as** possible, that the hypocrisy of the brother might **not undermine** the entire Congregation. He therefore not **only** commanded Neria to communicate the occurrence **to** the holy Founder, but it seems he himself wrote **to** St. Alphonsus about it. What a painful impression the calumnious letter of Neria and that of her confessor made upon the holy Founder, can easily be imagined. It is true, the charge in itself would strike **one as** incredible, but the evidence that was forwarded seemed so strong and convincing at the **time, that** it completely **concealed** the shameless falsehood. Besides, Don Benigno was a man whose **unfeigned** virtue claimed credibility, so that St. Alphonsus entertained the greatest respect for him.

That the saint, however, did not accept the **cunning**

accusation of the calumniator as truth, can in no manner be contested, and that he did not regard it as clear evidence, is not to be doubted. Had he felt really convinced of the guilt of the brother, he would have dismissed him without mercy from the Congregation. It is certain that he did not pass an unqualified judgment as to the guilt of the saintly brother. But to which side did his doubt incline? Was he inclined to believe him guilty, or innocent? Did he not, perhaps, fear that the servant of God was really guilty of the crime of which he was accused, that he was to be ranked among those souls who succumb to a terrible delusion of Satan after they have arrived at a high degree of sanctity, and that he had at least committed an unpardonable indiscretion and had occasioned scandal, which gave rise to the accusation, and was in part evidence to be studied? It was difficult to decide, since at the one hand the saint subjected the servant of God to the most severe punishments, and on the other, he did not think it prudent to give his reasons for such treatment. Though it is very probable that the saintly Founder even entertained some doubts as to the innocence of Gerard, and imposed those punishments in order to obtain from his lips an open confession, yet there are grounds for believing that he looked upon the accusation as false, and that he inflicted those trials simply to test the virtue of the servant of God.

However, this may be, the Rector Major, as soon as he had received the letter of accusation, sent a messenger to Iliceto, and ordered the basely calumniated brother to come to Pagani. Gerard received the order with great calmness, and the following day left Iliceto, which he was never more to see, and repaired to the place of destination where St. Alphonsus impatiently awaited him.

What a melancholy surprise, when he was told of

the accusation that had been made against him. To be accused of a crime for which he entertained a most decided, indescribable disgust! To be charged with having so disgracefully violated that virtue of which he himself had testified that he regarded it as a virtue which he prized and loved most dearly! "O my God!" so he writes in his notes, "among all the virtues which please Thee especially, are holy purity and innocence! O infinite purity! I trust in Thee that Thou wilt preserve me from every, even the least impure thought into which I, a miserable being of this world, may fall." And it was now boldly asserted that he had been entirely faithless to these sentiments, that he had converted his love and esteem for its very opposite! The accusation was made in such a way that one who knew what manner of life he had hitherto lived could be misled to believe him guilty.

The servant of God had a difficult task before him. Should he try to save his honor that had been attacked, to defend his innocence, to redeem his good name from a horrible calumny, or should he silently take up the cross, quietly bear with the hatred, scorn and contempt of men, and leave his reputation entirely in the hands of Providence? There were many excellent reasons why he should favor the former course; yet his humility and intense desire to render himself more conformable to the Divine Redeemer bade him be heroic, and bear it in silence.

Mindful of his vow, always to do what is most perfect, Gerard decided upon this course, and in spite of the consciousness of his untarnished innocence, he listened to the charges made against him without uttering a word, just as if they rested on evident truth and as if he were worthy of punishment. However meritorious this silence of the servant of God may have been in the eyes of **Him Who is able to fathom** the depths of hearts, under the circumstance it wore in the eyes of men an appearance of equivocation. It was not by any means an acknowledgment of guilt; yet it could not be deemed a defence against the accusation, and therefore justified the trial to which he was subjected.

Saint Alphonsus reproved the brother most bitterly, expressed his grief and his indignation, and humbled him with the severity which is usually employed against any one who has actually fallen. He finally forbade him to approach Holy Communion, and under the severest penalties to have the least intercourse with the outside world, even by letter.

The humble brother bowed his head, accepted all this in silence, and preserved in this dreadful moment, a cheerful countenance and his peace of soul.

In this delicate situation the spirit of murmur could not take possession of his heart; nor did he feel any aversion to the saint, who had so humbled him. On the contrary, Gerard exhibited the greatest respect for him in everything, and it was just at that time, and soon after his arrival at Pagani when a brother heard him express this love and affection for his Superior. Happening to meet the latter in the corridor, Gerard gazed at him with the humility and love of a child, and cried out, when St. Alphonsus had passed him: "O my Father! you have the face of an angel. When I see you I am overwhelmed with consolation."

If it was possible for Gerard to preserve interior peace in spite of his interior suffering, if he calmly bore the interior pains, perplexities, doubts, anxieties and similar emotions which were harassing him, it was due in no slight degree to the fact that he was no longer a beginner in these matters.

In fact, through all the favors of heaven, the ecstasies which were bestowed upon him, the visions which refreshed his spirit, and those wonderful moments of intercourse with the super-terrestrial, blissful world, of which we have often been enabled to make mention, there was extended a long chain of interior sufferings. It would be quite a false view of the life of the servant of God, if we supposed it a life of mere spiritual and heavenly consolations. His life was the life of a saint, a life of extraordinary gifts; it could therefore not be void of thorns and crosses.

Even previous to his entrance into the Order, interior sufferings were well known to the servant of God.

Besides those sufferings which transformed him every Friday into a picture of death, and by which he took part in the agony of the Redeemer, and that terrible woe into which he was sunk by the thought of sin, which like a fearful pestilence renders millions of immortal souls eternally unhappy, the good brother had to suffer, if not continually, at least very often, those cruel torments which are created in faithful and tender souls by the anxiety that they might yet be separated from God and not enjoy Him in eternity. In consequence of his great humility, which is ever alive to one's own unworthiness, deficiencies, malice, indolence and sinfulness, — the torments increased in proportion as his humility became more perfect; they often plunged him into a sea of discouragement and temptation, in which he became disconsolate and as it were annihilated, without the least prospect of relief. The waves of despair were pressing upon his heart from all sides; nowhere was there any support or consolation for him, except in simple faith.

In the midst of these bitter trials, Gerard usually applied to those whom he regarded as the special friends of God, and entreated them to offer prayers for his poor soul. Sometimes, in consequence of these prayers, the Lord deigned to alleviate some of his sufferings.

During the first years of Gerard's stay at Iliceto, there lived at the convent, Dominic Blasucci, one of the students of the Congregation who was engaged in his studies for the priesthood. The servant of God took delight in making him his confidant, since he knew that this pious youth stood in high favor with Almighty God. One day he came to Blasucci when he was interiorly troubled. The good student at once remarked by the paleness of the brother's countenance that he was suffering. Gerard candidly acknowledged that he was suffering unspeakable trials, and then begged him most earnestly to help him in this distressing condition. Filled with compassion, Dominic made the sign of the Cross on the heart of the poor brother, and, behold! such interior consolation filled his bosom, that all troubles vanished, and he felt relieved.

Similarly extraordinary alleviations were not, as a rule, of long duration; they were like cool drops of water upon the parched tongue of a thirsty man. The sufferings soon returned, often with greater violence, and his soul was again burning in the consuming fire of doubt and perplexity.

Gerard's letters show, in many passages, marks of this painful condition of his interior; and sometimes he knows how to describe them in words which, despite their brevity, produce the most heartfelt compassion.

Thus, while gently mentioning his sufferings, he writes for prayers to the venerable Sister Mary of Jesus: "Do not, I beseech you, forget to recommend me often to the Lord. I stand in the greatest need of prayers. Oh! God knows my continual trials."

He speaks more clearly of the bitterness of his soul in another letter to the same religious: "O God!" he says, "how gratified I was to receive such a letter as I have been desiring so long to receive. I tell you in truth and before God: this longing and great desire do not come from myself; they come from the Lord Who has referred me to others for help. Since I cannot help myself; it is His will that I should travel the path assigned me, amid storms and waves. Alas! I wish that His holy designs may be perfectly accomplished in me."

"I am full of sin," he sadly writes to Sister Mary of Jesus, "all are being converted; only I remain hardened. Do penance for me, that the Lord may pardon me and receive me again. I beg the same of all your daughters."

In May 1753, he again implores the nuns at Ripacandida: "Pray very much for me to the Lord, for I suffer great spiritual trials. God knows in what distress and in what a disconsolate state I am. If you wish, you can do much for me with God. Do this act of charity for me."

He expresses the exact nature of his sufferings in the following words addressed to Sister Mary of Jesus: "I know what sufferings you have endured; but I tell you, my own heart suffers more bitterly. You cannot imagine the depth of my sorrow and how keenly I feel them. When I tell you that I suffer more than you, it is no exaggeration, for divine justice has nailed me to the cross in such a manner that it appears to me no one else could evermore be nailed to it. Ever praised be the most holy will of God! But what makes me constantly tremble and inspires me with the greatest terror is the thought that I shall not persevere till the end."

The torture of this thought pursued the good brother till the close of his life. As a proof of this, and at the same time in order to describe in his own words mental sufferings which are unparalled and incomprehensible to him who has never endured them, we quote two other letters which he wrote, in the year 1754, to the congenial Sister Mary of Jesus. Even the superscription of the first is the expression of an anxious, distressed heart: "My God! have mercy on me!"

Then Gerard begins: "Alas! my dear Mother, how can you make game of me by writing me such a letter? You know very well that by doing so you intensify the sufferings which I am always enduring on account of my sins. You are in good spirits: that is why you are jesting with me. But as for me, what shall I say? God wishes your happiness, and I am glad of it. Yes, may the Lord help you in that happy condition, you whom He loves so much! Thus it usually happens: when one rises, the other sinks. I have sunk in such a way that I believe there is no more rising, and the years of my suffering are to last forever. Let them continue. Even this should not trouble me; if only I love God and please Him in all things, this is enough. But here is the cause of my suffering without God. My dear Mother, if you do not help me, woe is me. I find myself in an utter prostration of spirits, in a sea of perplexity, and as it were on the brink of despair. It appears to me that there is no longer a God for me, divine mercy is at an end for me and now nothing awaits me but justice. See and consider my unhappy condition! If the sacred compact of faith still exists between us, then you must know that now is the moment in which you should come to my assistance and pray to God for me, a miserable sinner. I beg you, have pity on my soul, I have not the courage to appear before creatures."

The other letter, dated at Naples, was written ten months before the death of the servant of God. The same state of mind, the same interior trials, are expressed in it. Its reads as follows:

"Jesus, Mary!

"My dearest Sister: While I am nailed to the cross

I write you in haste, for I have very little time. Alas! have pity on me in my agony! I have little to say, and if I did not do violence to myself I could not write; tears would prevent me from doing so. My trials are so bitter that they cause me the fears of a death-agony! and when I feel as if I could breathe forth my soul, I find myself again in life to endure more sufferings. I suffer. I know not how to express myself otherwise. It is impossible for me to communicate in words the gall and poison that trouble me, so that you may understand how bitter they are. I know that you are happy; your contentment somewhat encourages me, and makes me revive in God. Praised be the Lord for the many graces which He has bestowed upon me! Instead of permitting me to die under His sanctifying blows, He still gives me strength to live. If He sends me sufferings, it is only because He wishes that I should become a follower of my divine Redeemer. Oh! He is our master; I am his disciple. It is proper that we should learn of Him and walk in His footsteps. But, oh! now I am not walking at all; I am motionless on the cross with Him, buried in deep sadness and in unspeakable torments. It appears to me as if a lance were piercing me, so as to deprive me of life; and yet again it seems as if the cross on which I am hanging were only prolonging my life and my sufferings. All — so I believe — have forsaken me. But I do not wish to oppose the designs of my divine Saviour; I wish to suffer with Him, nailed to the cross; I bow my head and say: **Yes, this is the will of God**; everything that He enjoins upon me, I will perform with joyful obedience.

The servant of God had not been living in a sphere quite unusual and unknown to him, **when** calumny **filled his soul with pain** and sorrow; and consequently he could stand firm, for a not inconsiderable **time, in** admirable silence, and without the loss of the interior peace.

Humanly speaking, an expression of pain, a gentle complaint, a word of indignation about the malicious lie might have been justifiable from the lips of Gerard; but the perfect follower of our Lord wished to continue in silence, and desired to drink the last drop of the chalice of bitterness.

The misfortune which had befallen him, as well as the cause of his humiliations, very soon became known to his brethren. The impression which the affair made upon the most of them was, however, quite different from that which the wretched calumniator had thought to attain by her bold, cunning letter. Every one at large felt great compassion for the servant of God, for no one would believe that he had committed such an offence. Some of the Fathers who knew Gerard thoroughly, wished to persuade him to justify himself by speaking in defence of his innocence. But the humble brother did not wish to hear anything about justifying himself. "Let Almighty God provide," he used to say, when others were endeavoring to persuade him. "If He wished to see me humbled, why should I take the trouble of withdrawing myself from His will? If, however, it is His will that my innocence should be brought to light, ah! who will better understand how to accomplish this than He? Let God do with me what He pleases; I wish nothing else than what He wishes." "My affair," he was heard to say in prayer, "is Thine. If Thou wishest me to be humbled, I shall be glad of the humiliation; Thou also didst walk this path!"

Accordingly, he did nothing to put an end to his trials, but he redoubled his penances and his prayers. Visits to our Lord in the Blessed Sacrament served to ease his mind, and the union of his own sufferings with those of the Redeemer was his sweetest consolation. He prayed much during the night. When everything had become quiet and the brethren had gone to bed, he ascended to the flat roof of the house to breath the invigorating cool night air. He looked up at the stars that seemed to shine upon him from a land of peace, and to speak to him of the tender providence of God; he stretched out his hands towards heaven, and prayed and sighed and wept. Communing with that which is above, in this manner, he derived strength to bear on; as a flower, exhausted by the heat of the day, imbibes in the silence of the night, the fresh dew of heaven.

Having finished this nightly prayer, he descended to take a little rest, not in a bed, but in the coffin in which the remains of the saintly Father Sportelli had been preserved four years before.

"His humiliations," says Father Tannoja, "did not make him shed tears; on the contrary, he was filled with joy. Nature rebelled against it; and amid the noise of passion, mistrusting his own strength, he often recommended himself to the prayers of others. If he lamented anything, it was the sad condition of the soul who had calumniated him. He did not cease to offer up to God his own penances, and to ask for light and grace for her."

Gerard's most painful trial was in not being permitted to receive Holy Communion. The sentence pronounced against him, depriving him of the love and esteem, and partly of intercourse with his brethren might have been supportable; but that which deprived him of his dear Lord in the Blessed Sacrament seemed to him beyond endurance. "Do not ask me, I beg you," he said to a priest who wished him to serve at his Mass; "do not tempt me, for I might snatch the Lord out of your hands (che ve lo strappo dalle mani)." Nevertheless, he did not desire to ask for a mitigation of the punishment, but wished to bring his will and the will of God into the most perfect harmony. "It is sufficient for me to have Jesus Christ in my heart," he said to some one who compassionated him on account of this deprivation. On one occasion he remarked: "The Lord has punished my little love, and now withdraws from me; but I still visit Him interiorly, and I shall never miss Him in my heart."

One day his friends wished to persuade him to ask St. Alphonsus to communicate again. Gerard was somewhat astonished, and at first hesitated; but he soon after came to a decision: "No," he said, while striking his hand on the rail of the stairs near which he stood, "no! I must die under the pressure of God's holy will!"

Among his friends outside of the house, Gerard's non-appearance created painful surprise. No one knew what had become of him. Strange rumors about the brother's punishment had reached some of them. Among the latter was the venerable Sister Maria Cœlestis Costarosa, who was greatly grieved thereat, since she could not suspect the exact cause of Gerard's isolation. She imagined that some liberty which he had taken in the exercise of one of his pious works performed for the common good, had given occasion to the trouble, and under this impression she wrote to him as follows: "We have heard of your trials with great sorrow. It is always your love that brings woe upon you, and this time 'Fra Zulfo' (the devil) has succeeded in preventing you from visiting us at Foggia. We have not, however, ceased to pray for you, and I hope that the evil spirit may eventually be baffled. Wherever we are, wherever we live, let us visit each other in God, and, united, love our only beneficent Jesus Christ, Who loves us so much."

Father Margotta, whom Gerard had informed of what had happened him, wrote the following paternal letter: "My dear Gerard: Your letter has given me two-fold pleasure; first, because you say that you are always mindful of me in your prayers; and secondly, because you assure me of your entire conformity to the will of God in reference to the trial to which you are now subjected. As for myself, I wish you everything that is good, and that you may always advance in the service of God. I trust that you may remain steadfast in the good will by which you are ready, through obedience, and in the most perfect submission to your Superiors, to live only for the accomplishment of the divine will. I think of you in my poor prayers to our Lord and the Blessed Virgin Mary, that the strength may be given you which is necessary to make you in all things conformable to the will of God, and to fulfil the pious wishes which you entertain."

Similar affectionate consolations on the part of men might not have had much effect on the severely tried soul of the saintly brother, if God, on His part, had not come to his assistance with an abundance of consolation. But this He did; and while He afflicted Gerard with the greatest trials, He bestowed upon him new favors.

"The subjects of his meditations were at that time," as Father Tannoja observed, "the attributes of God. In this ocean he quenched in some measure the violent thirst which he had for the reception of Holy Communion. Upon being asked one day how he could exist without Jesus in the Blessed Sacrament, he replied: 'I recreate myself in the immensity of my good God.' Meditation on the divine attributes made him insensible to all earthly things, and he became wrapt in ecstasy."

Of such an ecstasy Father Cajone was one evening a witness. He was at that time discharging the duties of the office of Prefect of the sick, and as Gerard was sick in bed, he went to make the meditation with him, as is customary in the Congregation. "I had chosen," says Father Cajone, "for the subject of meditation, the love of God towards us, and His claim upon us for a return of this love. The mere mention of this subject was sufficient to make him entirely forgetful of himself. He lay quietly on his back, his head leaning against the wall and his eyes raised to heaven. His eyelids did not move during the whole time of meditation. At first I thought that there was nothing extraordinary in what I saw, but when the time of meditation had elapsed, and he continued in the same position, in spite of the noise which I made. I remarked that he had sunk into a supernatural recollectedness with God. To my astonishment he remained thus for a considerable time."

Another very wonderful occurrence during Gerard's illness is related by Father Landi: "Several of our brethren," he says, "have related it to me, and Father Rector Major (St. Alphonsus) can testify to the truth of it. The holy Founder was one day taking his dinner in the refectory, when all at once Gerard entered and stood before him half-dressed. St. Alphonsus reproved the brother for this impropriety, and wished to know why he had dared to come before him in such an attire. 'I came immediately,' answered Gerard modestly, 'because your Reverence called me.' It was true. Gerard hereby proved that the desire which his Superior expressed in his mind to see him, had been communicated to him in a supernatural manner."

The continual, inviolable silence, observed by the servant of God, furnished food for thought. Things looked rather doubtful; for although there were those who, knowing his spirit, were certain that there was question here of a base calumny, and who desired only an open defence of his innocence from the lips of Gerard, yet there were others who believed that the accusation was not without foundation. Gerard, they said, was undoubtedly acquainted and on a familiar footing with all who were in the house when the crime was committed, and the question must be asked whether his conscience was not tarnished in the foulest manner, and whether he did not need the services of an influential friend to rescue him from his sad error, and induce him, to make an humble acknowledgment of his guilt.

St. Alphonsus therefore sent the brother to Ciorani, where the Novitiate was conducted at that time, in order that he might here reflect in solitude and with greater liberty upon the affairs of his conscience. Letters to the Rector of the house, Father Xavier Rossi, and the Master of Novices, Father Tannoja instructed them to keep a sharp eye upon the servant of God and to observe his conduct minutely and carefully. That they faithfully responded to this charge cannot be doubted, in view of the spirit which animated these two zealous Fathers. "There was, however," as Father Tannoja himself confesses, "nothing that could be censured in his conduct; he was always cheerful, serene and humble towards all, and ready to fulfil every command. What most astonished them was the fact that he never uttered a word about the misfortune that had come upon him. What leisure time he had after his work was spent in church before the Blessed Sacrament, or in his cell.

The simplicity of his obedience he also displayed during the few days he passed at Ciorani to the great admiration of his Superior. One day the latter sent him, for some reason or other, to the neighboring town of Castellamare. The Rector, mindful no doubt of the bodily weakness of the brother who was scarcely convalescent, wished that he should ride; he simply said: "Take the donkey with you." Gerard took the animal out of the stable, but did not mount it, and led it by the bridle to the town and back again. He arrived home bathed in perspiration and covered with dust.

Father Rossi remarking the exhausted condition of Gerard, and greatly annoyed on this account called him to task, and asked him why he had not used the animal, since it had been placed at his service. "Your Reverence," said Gerard in reply, "commanded me to take the donkey with me, but not that I should ride it."

Gerard had spent ten or twelve days at Ciorani, during which time opinions about the delicate affair began to take a more hopeful turn for the brother.

The exemplary conduct of the servant of God, in which the most experienced eye could detect nothing that could furnish the least reason for condemning him, threw a heavy weight into the balance for those who hitherto were in doubt about Gerard's innocence. Even though the affair was not yet decided, the scales pointed undeniably to the purity of the brother, as well as to the horrible conspiracy that had been formed against him.

As Father Giovenale had just then to set out for Caposele in order to replace Father Mazzzini, who, since Father Cafaro's death, had discharged the office of Superior, and who was now sick, St. Alphonsus told him to take with him Brother Gerard, to whom he granted permission again to receive Holy Communion every Sunday. The brother was still to remain separated from the outside world, and Father Giovenale was charged with the duty that had before been assigned to Father Rossi and Father Tannoja in regard to Gerard, namely, that he should watch carefully over him, and should test his spirit by means of humiliation and mortification.

CHAPTER XIX.
A Rule Of Life.

Toward the end of June — on a Friday — the servant of God came with Father Giovenale to Caposele. He again breathed freely, since he could approach the holy table and was infinitely delighted when the hour arrived in which he could receive our Lord in the Blessed Sacrament.

Just at this time our Lord glorified His humbled servant by a miracle, which according to the testimony of witnesses, had occurred several times at Iliceto. We will relate it according to the account given by Father Landi.

On Saturday evening, after recreation, Gerard came to Father Giovenale, and asked permission to spend in strict seclusion the time that would elapse till the moment when, on the following morning he was to receive Holy Communion. Permission was granted. On Sunday morning the Superior having need of his services, sent for him. A brother called for him in his cell, but did not find him there. He sought him in the church, in the choir; but all in vain. Others searched the whole house, but it was impossible to discover him. Every one was asked where he was. Again they looked for him in his cell; even under the bed. Everything was carefully examined; nowhere was there a vestige of the brother. In the meantime the physician, Nicholas Santorelli, a frequent guest of the house, who was quite acquainted with Gerard, had arrived, and met Father Giovenale. "Do you know," he said, "that we have lost Brother Gerard? We can find him nowhere."

"How? he is lost? Why do you not look for him?" "We have already looked for him, but all in vain." "I wager he has concealed himself under his bed." "I had a thorough examination made of his cell," said the Superior; "he is not there." "Very well," the doctor answered, "I shall go to look for him," and then he went away with Brother Nicholas di Sapia. The search was as unsuccessful as the others. "Oh! it does not matter," said Santorelli, who did not wish to acknowledge himself vanquished, "it does not matter; when the time for Holy Communion arrives you will see him come from his hiding-place."

And so it was. When the time had arrived Gerard moved through the corridor in the happiest of moods. He was called, and conducted to Father Giovenale, who was walking in the garden with Santorelli. The Rector rebuked him severely for his disappearance, and wished to know where he had been in the morning. "In my cell" answered Gerard. "What, in your cell? Ah! but did I not have others look for you there? Make ten crosses on the ground with your tongue, immediately." Gerard knelt down at once and made the crosses, but as the ground round the cistern was covered with mud his tongue was very much soiled. "You really deserve to be deprived of Holy Communion, and to fast on bread and water for a month." "My Father," said Gerard, "you need only to impose it on me for the love of Jesus Christ, and I will obey." Father Landi relates: "But when he was urged to explain the matter, Gerard answered with all simplicity: 'Since I feared that I would be disturbed in my seclusion, I prayed to the Lord to make me invisible.' 'Why did you do that?' said Father Giovenale; 'I forgive you this time, but take care never again to make such a request.'"

On his way to Church, Gerard met Dr. Santorelli. "Do you know," he said, "that I am again to receive Holy

Communion?" They then both entered the sacristy, and the doctor asked him: "Gerard tell me the truth, where were you? How can you maintain that you were in the cell, when Brother Nicholas and myself examined every corner of it, without finding you?" Gerard took the doctor by the arm, led him to the cell, and showed him the place near the entrance where he had been sitting on a small chair. "But we looked for you everywhere and did not find you." "Yes," he replied smiling, "I sometimes make myself very small."

"This event," says the nephew of the doctor, "was so impressed on the memories of us children, that when we wished to play that game usually called accovarella (hide-and-seek), we generally said, 'Let us play Brother Gerard!'"

Scarcely had Gerard arrived at Caposele when the affair was fully explained and his innocence gloriously vindicated. The calumniator of the saintly religious, Neria Caggiano, had been seized with an illness which placed her in a very critical condition. Tormented by remorse of conscience, she thought seriously of making amends for the wrong she had done the servant of God, told her confessor all about it, and asked him to write a letter to St. Alphonsus, in which she recanted her former declaration against the lay-brother as untrue, and as a calumny, acknowledging with deep contrition that she was inspired by the evil spirit to ascribe to the servant of God a crime of which he was wholly innocent.

What joy the holy Founder experienced when he received these written declarations, what a burden was taken from his heart, it is needless to describe. Nothing could have afforded him greater consolation. He observed the servant of God's self-denial, submission and obedience, and would gladly have regarded it as the result of solid virtue, if calumny had not covered

St. Alphonsus discovers the innocence
of Blessed Gerard.

When the calumny, that had been circulated about the Blessed Brother, came to light, St. Alphonsus said to him: "My Son, why did you not utter a single word in defence of your innocence?"—"My Father," answered Gerard, "how could I? Does not the Rule tell me never to justify myself, but to suffer in silence the mortifications, that come to me from my Superior?" St. Alphonsus, edified at the virtue of the saintly Brother replied: "Well done! Well done, my Son! May God's blessing be with you."

all with a dark, mysterious veil, putting him in the perplexing situation of questioning the virtue which he wished to believe above suspicion, and forcing him at the same time to question whether that virtue might be a successful mask of dissimulation. Now, when all things had been explained, he rejoiced as Jacob did when he found his lost son in high honor.

There was universal rejoicing when the brother's innocence was proved. Perhaps Gerard was the only one who did not take pleasure in the vindication. "As the calumny had failed to cast him down," says Father Tannoja, "so the vindication of his innocence did not elate him."

St. Alphonsus sent for him immediately to come to Nocera, where he received him in a most fatherly manner, regretting exceedingly, that during the past weeks the kindly feelings which he had entertained towards him were embittered by doubts and fears. "But, my son," said the saint to Gerard among other things, "why did you not say a word in defence of your innocence?" "How could I do this, my Father," replied Gerard, "since the Rule forbids us to excuse ourselves, and tells us to bear all mortifications in silence." Greatly touched by so exact an observance of the Rule, St. Alphonsus responded: "Well! Well! my son, go now, and may God bless you!"

On another occasion Gerard was asked by the saint: "You certainly must have been very dejected when you were not allowed to receive Holy Communion." "Never, my Father," answered the servant of God, "if our Lord did not chose to come to me, what right could I have to complain?"

Such rare virtue greatly pleased St. Alphonsus. Up to the present time he was not fully aware of the greatness of Gerard's sanctity, as the saintly brother had generally been living at Iliceto; he now esteemed him most highly. "Gerard," he said one day to Father Cimini, "is a miracle of regular observance. He has given me remarkable **testimony, and I was** greatly edified when I perceived the high degree of perfection to which he had already attained."

St. Alphonsus spoke in the same way to Father Margotta. For when Father Margotta, who was convinced of Gerards sanctity, praised his virtues, spoke of his gift of miracles, his zeal, his wonderful innocence, and his indefatigable striving after perfection, and remarked the saintly conduct of the servant of God, St. Alphonsus said: "Even if **he** had exhibited his virtues in **no other way, I should be satisfied with his** behavior during the late trial."

The exalted opinion which the holy Founder had for the humble brother, and which was confirmed on the occasion of the trial, was continually on the increase; even at the hour of death, St. Alphonsus thought of his faithful son, who was at that time already a glorified inhabitant of heaven, and specially invoked his intercession.

Let us follow the servant of God to Caposele. Although his stay there was only for a few weeks, from the end of June till the end of July, it made a lasting impression. We have already stated how the children were affected.

Of Gerard's most wonderful knowledge of secret events Father Tannoja tells the following example: "**One day Father Giovenale sat** in the confessional and was hearing a **man's** confession, when Gerard passed **by and cast a** threatening look upon the confessional. As soon as he met the Father, he said: "The confession of this man was not valid; do try to regain this soul for God." The Father called the man back, and really found him guilty of sacrilege and other sins. He induced him to make a good confession, that he might again be restored to grace.

Father Giovenale experienced the same supernatural prophetic look on another occasion. One day he was troubled as to whether he was in the state of grace, when Gerard came to make his confession. After confession he said: "My Father, be at peace. You are in the state of grace. It is the devil who causes you this anxiety." Father Giovenale was surprised at this disclosure, although he reprimanded the brother rather harshly: "You are a fool," said he, "and do not know, what you say." Then he imposed a penance upon him and bade him go. Gerard had penetrated his interior.

Canon Rossi, to whom we have previously referred, at the same time experienced Gerard's prophetic look into the future. Rossi was at our house to spend a few days in retirement when a message was sent to him from Melfi, his native city, which obliged him to send a messenger there at once. The messenger did not return for a long time, which circumstance caused the Canon great confusion. No one in the house knew of his state of mind; the Canon was not even in the house at the time, but in the garden. Suddenly, he saw the servant of God coming toward him, smilingly accosting him: "Lord Canon, be at ease, everything is well at Melfi." When the messenger returned, Rossi was convinced of the truth of Gerard's words from the report he received.

The recollection of an event, not similarly supernatural, yet an acknowledgment, characteristic of the spirit of the brother, relative to his stay in Caposele at that time, has been preserved by the family of Santorelli. Nicholas Santorelli, the doctor, joked with Gerard one day: "Brother" said he, "it is growing hot, and the insects are increasing in number. How will you spend the night with so many fleas?" "Oh,"

Gerard replied, "I am greatly indebted to these little creatures; they do not let me sleep, and so I can think of God continually."

There is another circumstance on record, during his stay at Caposele, namely his notes, which reveal the interior of the servant of God. The notes are authentic.

Under the pretense of subjecting the interior of the brother to a more exact test, Father Giovenale demanded that he note down, as well as he could, his desires, sentiments and resolutions. Gerard did so with the simplicity and sincerity of a child.

Gerard begins with his customary wish, as follows: "May the grace of God be always in our hearts, and may the Blessed Virgin Mary preserve it for us! Amen.

"My dear Father:

"Your Reverence wishes to know all the mortifications which I usually practise; you likewise ask that I should communicate to you in writing, the pious desires, sentiments and resolutions which I cherish, and lastly, explain to you the vow which I have made always to do what is most perfect."

After this introduction he puts before us the following list of the mortifications practised by him.

"Mortifications for every day. I take the discipline once. — I wear a chain nine inches broad and eighteen long, as a cincture. Morning and evening, that is when rising and going to bed, I make nine crosses on the floor with my tongue. — With one portion of my dinner and supper I mix bitter herbs or wormwood (nascenzo). — I wear on my breast a heart furnished with iron points. — At least three times a day I chew bitter herbs or wormwood. — I say in the morning and evening, six Hail Marys, with my face on the ground.

"Wednesdays, Fridays and Saturdays, and on all vigils, I eat my meals kneeling. — Moreover, at dinner as well as at supper I make nine crosses with my tongue on the floor; and on all these days I leave untouched the fruit that is served.

"On Fridays at noon, I partake of two courses, and at supper, of one.

"On Saturdays I fast on bread and water.

"On Wednesdays, Fridays and Saturdays during sleep, I girdle my forehead with a little chain, I put another about my waist; I lie upon a chain nine inches broad and eighteen inches long, which also serves me as a cincture during the day; I always wear a chain around my arm.

"Once a week, I scourge myself to blood.

"During all the novenas which precede the festivals of our Lord, of our Blessed Mother, and of other saints, besides the aforesaid penances, I scourge myself to blood once during the novena and every ordinary day therein. To these must be added other extraordinary exercises, for which I shall specially ask your Reverence's permission."

To this list Gerard adds those "desires" with which he felt his soul specially filled, as also a few of those thoughts which stirred his soul very powerfully, and to which he gave the title of "the most ardent sentiments of my heart."

"Desires. — To love God very much; always to be united with God; to do every thing for God; to love every thing for God; to conform myself entirely to His holy will; to suffer much for God.

"The most ardent sentiments of my heart: I have a favorable opportunity of sanctifying myself; if I allow it to pass unemployed, I shall lose it forever. If once I have the opportunity to become a saint, what is wanting to accomplish it? Yes! I will become a saint. But alas! what is it to become a saint? O Lord! how great is my folly! I must sanctify myself. Others procure for me the means thereto, and should I complain?

"Brother Gerard! resolve to give thyself entirely to God! Henceforth be firmly convinced and remember that, by prayer and meditation alone, thou wilt not yet become a saint. The best prayer consists in being just what pleases the Lord, in acting fearlessly according to God's will, and in exerting himself continually for God. This is what God requires of thee. Neither the world nor thyself shouldst thou serve. It is sufficient to have God always present and to be always united with Him. Truly, what ever we do, provided it is done for God, may be called prayer. Some follow this business, others that; but my business is to do God's will. Every exertion ceases to be an exertion as soon as we exert ourselves for God.

"On the 21st. of September, 1752, I became better aquainted with the following truths: If I had died ten years sooner, I would seek nothing more, desire nothing more. To suffer and not to suffer for God, is an infinite torment. To suffer every thing and to suffer it for God, is nothing. I will live and work in this world as if only God and myself were therein. Many say that I am deceiving the world; O God! what would it be to deceive the world! far more astonishing were it if I endeavored to deceive God!"

These thoughts move him to a serious "reflection" to which he subjoins a few "resolutions," mingled with prayers; also a list of "resolutions" which enter into particulars.

"Reflection: If I am lost, I shall lose God, and what remains to me after the loss of God? O Lord! grant me the grace to have a specially firm belief in the mystery of the Most Blessed Sacrament.

"Resolutions: My Lord Jesus Christ, see me here with paper and ink, ready to write the resolutions which I have already made before Thy Majesty, and which I now renew as obedience requires me to do.

Mayest Thou, O my Lord, assist me, that I may faithfully carry out what I promise! Alas! I cannot depend on myself, and am incapable of acting according to my promises; I confide entirely in Thee, Who art infinite goodness and mercy, and canst not allow Thy promise to remain unfulfilled. O supreme Goodness! if before, I have so often erred, these errors proceeded from my wish to do every thing by myself; now I desire that Thou shouldst be the One Who should labor in me. Help me, O Lord, that I may do all things with the greatest exactness! I hope firmly in Thee, Thou inexhaustible Treasure!

"I chose the Holy Ghost to be my only Consoler and Protector in all things. Let Him be my Defender and the Conqueror of all my faults. Amen!

"And thou, my only treasure! Immaculate Virgin Mary; be thou in all the accidents of life, my particular guardian, ever intercede speedily for me with God, so that I may put in execution all my resolutions.

"To you also, blessed spirits, do I address myself, and beg you in the name of our common Creator, the Creator of all things, to aid me as true advocates. In your presence I am writing these things; may you read them from the heavens above, and read them well, and exert yourselves in my behalf with the divine Majesty, so that I may faithfully observe all things. May your prayers be heard! Thus also, in your company, do I make my promises to the Most High, and to the Blessed Virgin Mary. Assist me specially and constantly St. Teresa, St. Mary Magdalene of Pazzi, St. Catharine of Sienna, and St. Agnes!

"Every two weeks I will examine my conscience, in order to see whether I have failed against the resolutions which I here record.

"O Gerard! — what art thou doing? Dost thou not know that one day what thou hast written will be held up before thee? — Think therefore, seriously, that thou must observe all things! But who art thou who dost reproach me in this way? Thou speakest well, **thou tellest the truth,** but thou dost not know that I never dared confide in myself, and that I do not dare do so now; nor shall I ever dare do so; for, after having learned my own misery, I fear greatly to trust myself, and if I did so, truly, I should have lost my senses. In God only I trust and hope; into His hands I have entirely commended my life, so that He may do with me what He may please. And though I am in life, yet I am, strictly speaking, **without life, for** my life is my God. In Him only do I find my rest and of Him only do I hope to receive help in order truly to fulfil every thing what I am now promising to fulfil. Live Jesus and Mary!

"Resolutions. 1. O my dearest and only Love, True God! to-day and forever I commend myself to Thy holy will. In all temptations and trials of this world I will say: 'Fiat voluntas tua!' (Thy will be done!) Every thing that Thou ordainest I will accept with my whole heart, and while continually raising my eyes to heaven, will revere Thy divine hands, which scatter upon me these precious jewels of the divine will.

"2. My Lord Jesus Christ! I will do whatever the Catholic Church, my holy Mother, tells me to do.

"3. My God! for the love of Thee, I will render obedience to my Superiors, as if I saw Thy divine Person before me, and would obey Thee personally. I will live just as if I were no longer myself, by making myself conformable to the judgment and will of those who command me, being convinced that I shall find Thee in them.

"4. I wish to be poor, very poor in pleasure, and in the delights of self-will; and, on the contrary, **very** rich in every kind of discomfort.

"5. Among all the virtues which please Thee, O my God, are especially holy purity and innocence. O infinite Purity! I trust in Thee that Thou wilt preserve me from every even the least impure thought which I, a miserable being of this world, may conceive.

"6. Only in three cases will I speak: 1. When it is for the greater honor of God; 2. When it is for the good of my neighbor; 3. When my own necessities require me to do so.

"7. In recreation I will speak only when I am spoken to, or when the previously mentioned cases occur.

"8. For every word which I shall be tempted to say against the greater pleasure of God, I shall render compensation by the ejaculatory prayer: 'O my Jesus, I love Thee with all my heart.'

"9. I shall speak neither what is good, nor what is evil about myself, but act in such a way as if I were not in the world.

"10. I will never excuse myself, not even when I have good reason to do so; provided there is no offence against God, or injury to my neighbor.

"11. I will allways be an enemy of singularity.

"12. When reprimanded, I will make no reply unless required to do so.

"13. I will never accuse, nor speak ill of any one, even in jest.

"14. I will always endeavor to excuse my neighbors by seeing in them the person of Jesus Christ Whom the Jews unjustly accused; I will do this especially in the absence of the accused.

"15. Should any one — even if it were the Rector Major — speak ill of his neighbor, I will draw his attention to his error.

"16. I will always carefully avoid doing any thing likely to make my neighbor impatient.

"17. Should I notice a fault committed, I will avoid reproving the deliquent before others; I will do so privately, charitably, yet inaudibly.

"18. **When a Father or a Brother** appears to need assistance, I will lay aside every thing to help him, unless otherwise instructed.

"19. **If I am allowed,** I will visit the sick several times a day.

"20. **I will not interfere** with the affairs of others, nor will I say: 'That man does his work badly,' or the like.

"21. In all work where I assist another, I will quietly render him the most exact obedience; if told to do anything I will not say: 'This is not right,' or, 'that does not please me.' But if I know from experience that a certain way of doing a thing is not good, I will say so modestly.

"22. In all duties, important or unimportant, such as house-cleaning, etc., where I work with others, I will never choose the best place, the most convenient position, the best tools; but I will give to others what is most convenient, and be satisfied with what God allows me to have. In this way all will be contented.

"23. I shall never seek any office or other duty, unless ordered by others.

"24. During meals I will not look about me, unless to serve others, or through duty.

"25. I will take from the board (on which the food is carried to the refectory) the portion that is nearest to me, without looking at the other portions.

"26. "I shall ignore all unreasonable interior motions. Thus, when any one reproves or accuses me, I will allow the bitterness of feeling to pass away and await the return of peace.

"27. The sum of my resolution is this: to give myself entirely to God. Therefore the three words, deaf, blind and dumb, will always be before my mind.

"28. "The words, 'I will and I will not,' shall always be unknown to me. I wish nothing but that 'in me sint Deus vota tua et non vota mea.' (Thy wishes, O my God, and not mine may be fulfilled in me.)

"29. In order to be able to do the will of God, I must renounce my own will. Yes! I wish nothing but God; if I wish God only it is right that I should separate myself from everything that is not God.

"30. It shall be my endeavor never to seek my own advantage in anything.

"31. During the whole time of silence, I will strive to be mindful of the sufferings and death of Jesus Christ, and of the trials of the blessed Virgin.

"32. All my prayers, communions, etc., shall be for the benefit of poor sinners, for whom I will offer them up to God in union with the precious blood of Jesus Christ.

"33. If any one who is not able to bear the sufferings which God has sent him calls upon me for help, or if I hear others speak of such a one, I will pray to God for him, and offer up all the good works which I perform during three days, that God may give him the grace of conformity to His will.

"34. When I receive the Superior's blessing, I will think that I am receiving it from our Lord, Jesus Christ Himself.

"35. When unnecessary, I will not ask permission the evening before to receive Holy Communion, but will do so in the morning, so that I may communicate with better preparation. But if Holy Communion is refused me, I will communicate spiritually, at the Communion of the priest.

"36. My thanksgiving after Holy Communion is to

last from the time I communicate till noon; my preparation for the next day, from noon till evening."

To these resolutions given here in detail the conscientious brother adds a few acts which he was accustomed to make when visiting the Blessed Sacrament, as also when wishing to express his love for God.

"Acts when visiting the Blessed Sacrament: O my Lord! I believe that Thou art present in the Most Blessed Sacrament; I adore Thee with my whole heart, and intend by this visit to adore Thee in all those places where Thou art present in the Blessed Sacrament. I offer Thee Thy most precious blood for all poor sinners; at the same time I wish to receive Thee spiritually wherever Thou art sacramentally present.

"Acts of love of God: O my God! I should wish to make as many acts of love for Thee as were made by the Blessed Virgin Mary, by all the blessed spirits from the beginning of their existence, as also by all the faithful on earth. I wish to love Thee with the love with which Jesus Christ loves Thee, and with which the elect love Thee; and I wish to repeat these acts of love every moment. I will also make similar acts of love in regard to my dear Mother, the Blessed Virgin."

These acts which Gerard resolves to make, he concludes with a resolution which exhibits the liveliness of his faith in a beautiful light. It is as follows:

"From this day forward I will treat priests with the greatest possible respect, with a respect that is due to Jesus Christ Himself. I will never lose sight of their great dignity."

Then follows an explanation of the vow always to do what is most perfect. The servant of God continues:

"Explanation of my vow: I have imposed upon myself the duty always to do what is most perfect. This shall extend to all my works, even the most trivial; and I bind myself to perform them with the greatest self denial and perfection. I shall presuppose in all these things the general permission of your Reverence, in order that I may act safely.

"Restrictions of this vow: 1. All the actions which I perform distractedly, without reflecting that they are against this vow, are not included.

"2. Outside of the house, I may ask a dispensation from this vow. Such dispensation is not contrary to it. I make this reservation in order to prevent confusion and scruples arising from lack of liberty in action. I also reserve the liberty to ask of my Confessor a release from this vow, who may then free me from it as often as he deems proper."

Finally, the servant of God records a series of remarks concerning devotion, permitting us to cast a glance at his heart which was so zealous for salvation of souls. He concludes his notes with a resolution which has as its object something quite ordinary, but which beautifully shows his fidelity in small things:

"Devotion to the Most Blessed Trinity: Whenever I see a cross or picture representing one of the three Divine Persons, or hear the Adorable Persons mentioned, and whenever I begin or end any work, I will recite a 'Gloria Patri,' and will say this little prayer with devotion.

"In honor of the Most Blessed Virgin Mary: I will do the same thing in regard to the Blessed Virgin Mary; I will recite an 'Ave Maria' in honor of her purity every time I happen to see a woman.

"In honor of holy Patrons: As such I regard the Archangel St. Michael and all the blessed spirits; St. Joachim and St. Anne, St. Joseph, St. John the Baptist, St. Elizabeth, St. John the Evangelist, the saint of the day, the patron saint of the year, the patron saint of the month, the saint of the day on which I was born, as well as the saint of the day on which I shall die.

Moreover, St. Francis Xavier, St. Teresa, St. Mary Magdalene of Pazzi, St. Philip Neri, St. Nicholas of Bari, St. Vincent Ferrer, St. Bernard, St. Bonaventure, St. Thomas of Aquin, St. Francis of Assisi, St. Francis of Sales, St. Francis of Paula, St. Felix the Capuchin, St. Pascal, St. Vitus, St. Aloysius Gonzaga, St. Mary Magdalene, St. Catharine of Sienna, St. Agnes, Saints Peter and Paul, St. James, and the Venerable Sister Mary Crucifixa.

"Before and after meals: Three 'Gloria Patri' in honor of the Most Blessed Trinity, and three 'Ave Maria,' in honor of the Blessed Virgin. Every time I cut the loaf of bread, one 'Gloria Patri,' likewise every time I drink wine; when drinking water, one 'Ave;' also when the clock strikes the hours.

"Affections: O my Lord! could I but save as many souls as there are grains of sand in the ocean and on the land, leaves on the trees, blades of grass in the field, atoms in the air; as many as there are rays of light in the sun and moon, and as there are creatures in the whole world!

"When rising and going to bed, I will say the usual community prayers of thanksgiving; in the evening and in the morning the acts for Holy Communion; and lastly, I shall examine my conscience at noon and in the evening, and then make an act of contrition.

"Live Jesus and Mary, Michael, Teresa, Magdalene of Pazzi and Aloysius!"

These were the rules which the servant of God laid down for his conduct in life. In the simplicity with which they are composed, there appears true greatness of mind; and in spite of many gaps which Gerard has left, by omitting the connecting links in the construction of his sentences, we can still recognize the harmony of desires, aims and affections which controlled his heart.

CHAPTER XX.
At Naples.

Toward the end of July, 1754, Gerard was obliged to leave the solitude of Caposele, to repair to Pagani. Father Margotta, the Procurator of the Congregation, who spent the greater part of the year at Naples, was in need of a ley-brother, and accordingly Gerard had to replace Brother Francesco Tartaglione whose services were required elsewhere. Father Margotta highly esteemed Gerard and appealed to St. Alphonsus that the servant of God might be his assistant.

The saintly Founder, appreciating the holy friendship that existed between Father Margotta and the brother, availed himself of the opportunity to recompense, in some measure, the severely tried brother, by a special mark of confidence. Hence he appointed the servant of God to the office.

This arrangement afforded the greatest consolation to Father Margotta, and it was not less pleasing to Brother Gerard. He felt himself amply recompensed for the humiliations and trials which he had suffered, in being permitted to spend some time in the company of this most exemplary priest.

Father Margotta was Gerard's equal in virtue. In many things he bore great resemblance to St. Alphonsus. His early career was like that of the holy Founder. Born February 10th., 1699, at Calitri, of respectable parents, he was reared a devout Christian by his mother, having lost his father at a very early age. When a child, he plainly exhibited his inclination to piety, and gave all those marks of future sanctity about which we are accustomed to read in the lives of great Saints. He studied at the capital of the kingdom with so much success that at the age of sixteen he finished his course in philosophy. He had suffered nothing from the seductive charms of the city; he remained innocent and free from the vices to which students are usually addicted, and was an ardent lover of our Lord in the Blessed Sacrament. In his demeanor he was modest, and his whole conduct made him a model for the youth of Naples.

After the examinations, which he passed most brilliantly, and after having through dispensation on account of age received the degree of doctor, he returned to his native place.

Talented as he was, the world offered him honors and earthly joys. Had he so desired he might have tasted abundantly of that which the world calls happiness. But his mind was already turned from what is earthly, and was directed to higher things. A daughter of the Capucci family in Lacedogna had been offered him in marriage, but he promptly refused. His earnest inclination became so manifest that as soon as he had been appointed governor of Andretta, a position of great importance, one of his officers jokingly remarked: "Let us hope for good things, since now we have a Capuchin for our governor."

Indeed, Margotta's life as governor was not very different from that of a religious. Justice, charity and piety were virtues which the inhabitants of Andretta could daily witness for their edification. On the other hand, his relatives painfully noticed that his own affairs were failing, and his financial condition began to create just alarm. His mother, therefore, persuaded him to resign his office at Andretta, and return to Calitri, to which he agreed.

Marriage was again suggested, but Francis positively declined, declaring that he wished to have nothing to do with the world.

An excursion to Bisaccia, where he visited some relatives, brought him nearer to his vocation and enlightened him thereon.

About this time, there lived at this place a certain Don Cajetan Guiliani, a saintly priest a disciple of the venerable Father Anthony de Torres. He had spent a great portion of his life in giving missions, and had now retired into solitude where he wished to spend the last years of his life in attending to the affairs of his own soul, without however ceasing to give spiritual aid to a number of chosen penitents.

The acquaintance which Margotta made at Bisaccia with this holy priest opened a new field of knowledge for him. Attracted by the sublimity of the service of God, he resolved to become a priest and was ordained, after due preparation, by the Archbishop of Conza, in 1731. It was his sole aim to save souls and to work as much as possible in the vineyard of the Lord. In order to labor with greater blessing in the confessional and in the pulpit, he joined the Congregation of missionaries of Father Pavone, in which he devoted himself to his vocation as a "holy priest, holy confessor, and holy missionary."

When the foundation at Caposele was established by the Congregation, he donated a considerable sum of money out of his patrimony. He joined the Congregation in 1747.

As a Redemptorist, he labored successfully in the missions as well as at home in the capacity of a director of souls. He was for all a shining light of virtue, especially in obedience and humility. The word of the Superior was for him God's word. He even joyfully rendered obedience to the lay-brothers. His obedience did not outdo his humility. He sought humiliations wherever he believed he could find them. His love for the Blessed Sacrament and the Blessed Mother of God justly entitled him to a place next to St. Alphonsus.

Father Margotta labored indefatigably at his own perfection, and while Father Cafaro was alive he followed with great devotedness the guidance of this highly spiritual man.

At the first General Chapter of the Congregation held in 1749, Father Margotta was chosen General Procurator of the Institute; this office he filled till his death, which occurred on the 11th. of August, 1764, at Naples.

As Procurator, he lived in the house of Don Hercules de Liguori, the brother of St. Alphonsus, a part of whose home was arranged as lodgings for the Founder's spiritual sons. It was here that Gerard, accompanied by Father Francis Margotta resided, upon his arrival in Naples.

It was the first time that Gerard had ever visited the famous city. Yet it did not distract his recollectedness and his tranquillity of mind. He continued to live the life he had led at Iliceto, and though he could no longer wander through the fields and the little towns of Apulia, being obliged to pass by grand palaces, and through the thickly populated streets of a noisy capital, this outward change produced no alteration in his interior. "Among the curiosities of the capital," says Father Tannoja, "his mind did not become dissipated; on the contrary, it is safe to admit that he became even more absorbed in God."

The palace in which he and Father Margotta were quartered was for him a continual reminder that in the great city he should not forget that which, amid the noise of human cares, is too often cast aside. Everything in this house reminded him of the virtues, the first combats, the ardent prayers, the penances and the acts of charity of his revered Father, St. Alphonsus. These two holy souls so vied with each other in acquiring virtue that it was highly pleasing to God. The zeal of the one inflamed that of the other; neither wished to be outdone.

As business was not very pressing, it was possible for them to devote considerable time to the exercise of prayer. For Father Margotta and for Gerard this was certainly a happy contingency of which they made the best use.

The former was frequently seen before the altar. He usually performed his devotions in the church of the Oratorians. He celebrated Holy Mass there, and was often on his knees absorbed in prayer for hours; sometimes he spent part of the night in meditation, and in visiting our Lord in the Blessed Sacrament.

That in these things the saintly brother could be, and wished to become his rival, can easily be imagined. We know his intense love for prayer, meditation and the Blessed Sacrament. After having attended to necessary affairs in the city, and having finished his work in the kitchen, he spent the rest of the time in works of piety, and visited the different sacred shrines and monuments of the churches in the city. Often, he remained in one church for half days, hidden in a corner, or stretched out on the floor. The usual witnesses of these long interviews with our Lord were the church of the Holy Ghost and that of the Oratorians.

The fact that the devotion of the Forty Hours continued without interruption in the different churches of Naples during the year, each one in its turn, was a cause of great joy to him. This gave him an opportunity daily to visit our Lord exposed in the Blessed Sacrament, and to find material and strength for his meditations. Frequently, Father Margotta and Gerard would go to the church where this devotion was in progress, and would sometimes become so wrapt in a certain ecstatic condition that the time for returning home was greatly protracted. They usually visited those places where indulgences could be gained. Stimulated by the fervor and zeal of Father Margotta, Gerard led a life which, as Father Tannoja says, appeared to him "paradise." What he wrote at this time to Ripacandida perfectly evinces such a frame of mind: "I am staying here at Naples," he says, "in the company of Father Margotta, and can now more than ever recreate my heart in intercourse with God." (Ora piu che mai me la scialo col caro mio Dio).

Not only in the love of God and in His service, but also in practices of penance and self-denial, did these holy men vie with each other. According to Father Tannoja's account, Father Margotta clad in a hair-shirt and wearing little iron chains went to Naples like one crucified; frequently he slept on the bare floor, scourged himself most severely, and was so little concerned about the nourishment of his body that he very often forgot all about it."

But in all these things, Gerard imitated him in the most perfect manner. He also tortured his body with hair-shirts, scourged himself unmercifully, used the hard floor as his couch, and cared very little for necessary food. It often happened that because the Superior had forgotten to arrange a bill of fare, both had to remain hungry. When one day Father Margotta came home about dinner-time and asked his companion what he had prepared for dinner, the latter answered in his usual good humor: "My dear Father, just what you yourself have prepared." He wished to say that nothing was ready.

In view of such a Superior and such a lay-brother, a biographer of Gerard is quite correct in stating: "The life led by Father Margotta and Brother Gerard was an uninterrupted fast; they satisfied only their hunger for God."

As regards self-denial, Father Margotta went so far that he not only had the greatest regard for poverty, so that every new garment had to be forced upon him, but he often went like a beggar to the convent gates and there asked for alms, without noticing the ridicule to which he was thereby exposed.

In this the servant of God also faithfully followed his example. The lazzaroni of Naples are well known as not belonging to the class of well-dressed people. They could nevertheless laugh at him and joke about his cassock when he happened to pass by them, so wretched an appearance did it present. To beg at the convent door was likewise entirely according to his taste, and thus he appeared sometimes alone, sometimes accompanied by Father Margotta, at the door of the convent of the Oratorians, to obtain some bread, with the rest of the beggars. And he would gladly have continued this manner of life if it had not been forbidden by his Superior, who heard of what he was doing.

Even after this prohibition, occasions for the practice of self-denial were not wanting. One day he chanced to be in the workshop of a carver, a friend of his, when there entered one of those odd beings in whom are combined good nature, rascality and rudenes commonly known as lazzaroni. The man immediatly began to annoy the good brother. He went up to him, overwhelmed him with all kinds of rude familiarities, put his fingers over his eyes and nose, and accompanied this buffoonery with the words: "Ah! indeed how beautiful you are!" Gerard remained quite indifferent, but those who were present felt themselves grossly insulted by the behavior of this wicked fellow, and would have handled him roughly, had not the servant of God interceded for him and retained them from giving expression to their outraged feelings, at least until the man was able to escape. "Oh," said Gerard, "it does not matter; I am a sinner; I am a wretch. The man wished to have a little sport with me."

The workshop in which this scene was enacted was a place in which Gerard spent many an hour, and spent it we might say, with great devotion. He had one day come to this place, where he saw how crucifixes and images of 'Ecce homo' were made of 'papier maché.' He immediately experienced a lively desire to acquire the art of carving; and as the master, who, as we have said, was a friend of the Congregation, showed his willingness to teach him this kind of work. The servant of God took a few lessons, in which he was so successful that in a short time he learned the art fully. Ever after, and until his death, he made images of our Lord which he used to distribute.

The life of the servant of God at Naples was not altogether a quiet one. He could not have remained a long time without some external occupation. Wherever there is fire, light and warmth issue, latent though they be.

As Father Margotta had already found in a short time a small sphere of apostolic activity, so did Gerard find one that was suited to him without being obliged to seek for one very long. In the city there were many poor people and also many sinners.

The former Father Margotta cared for chiefly; he was so full of compassion that he not unfrequently gave away his own most necessary articles of clothing. While walking through the city one day he met an unfortunate man who was the picture of misery. As he could not offer the assistance which the man's needs required, he took off his shoes, gave them to him, and walked home bare-foot.

How Gerard competed with his master in this respect, the following incident will show. Brother Francis Tartaglione, who, after the arrival of the two Redemptorists had left his quarters, again returned to stay for a longer time. As Father Margotta was absent, he gave his companions some money with which to buy some provisions and to prepare dinner. Gerard therefore went to the city to make the purchases, but on the way met a man miserably clad, a vender of flint stones and tinder, which in later days are substituted by matches. The look of sympathy cast on him by Gerard might have encouraged the man to address the lay-brother and to ask him to have compassion on him, as he was well nigh dying of starvation. The pitiable sight made Gerard forget to buy bread and fish, and instead to purchase the poor vender's whole stock. Brother Francis had in the meantime attended to some business in the city. When he came home, he asked Gerard about the food which he supposed was prepared. Instead therefore of answering the question, he embraced the brother and said joyfully: "Ah! why so many cares? God alone, and nothing else!" "Very well," said Tartaglione, "but we should now think about getting something to eat." He noticed the flint stones and tinder that were lying on the table. "What is that?" he asked. "My dear brother," answered Gerard, "all this can be of no use to us. But I must tell you plainly what happened. When I went out to buy the eatables, a poor man met me. He had these things for sale, and was nearly dying of hunger. I could not help it; I had to buy the things with the money which you gave me." This answer was certainly not adapted to satisfy the hungry brother, who was asking for his dinner. He, however, concealed his displeasure, and could do so very easily since the great charity of the servant of God elicited his admiration. Meantime Father Margotta had also returned home, and Gerard of course hastened to inform him of what had happened. Especially had he to communicate to him that he presupposed his permission to give those alms. The Superior smiled. "But, what shall we have for dinner?" "God will provide," answered Gerard. And in fact, while they were conversing and the time for dinner had arrived, the door-bell rang. "That's the help for which we are waiting," cried out Gerard, overjoyed, and hastened to the door, accompanied by Father Margotta. Here they found a servant-girl with a basket full of eatables, which a woman, who was not even known to the two Redemptorists, had sent. One may imagine with what gratitude and astonishment this gift was accepted, as it appeared to be a manifest reward for the charity of the servant of God shown to the poor and a divine approval of his good work.

Not only upon the poor, but also upon the sick, did the holy brother bestow special care. A glimpse which he had occasion to get of the interior of the hospital for incurables at Naples enkindled his sympathy. He believed he could not devote too much time to consoling these suffering members of Christ. He often visited these poor incurables, went from bed to bed, spoke of patience, of the merit of sufferings, of resignation to the will of God, or of the joys of heaven. To the dying he exhibited a greater measure of charity, and with most wonderful skill, prepared them for death and for their journey into eternity. To the spiritual works of mercy he always joined various kind attentions. He made up the beds of the sick, helped to wash and bind up their wounds, and offered them food and drink. He would have been delighted to make these visits every day, if the regulations of the hospital permitted him; at least he never failed to avail himself of the days on which he was allowed to visit these suffering people.

Besides the incurables, the compassionate brother displayed special charity and care in behalf of that class of sick persons who are the least attractive, most despised and neglected, and who very often create disgust and fear. These were the insane. We do not know how the servant of God procured admission into the large insane asylum of the city. His biographers merely tell us that he often visited it, and that his visits frequently resulted in wonderful success. It was a touching sight to witness how Gerard treated these unfortunate people, how he conversed with them according to their powers of comprehension, and endeavored to work upon their disturbed minds in a salutary way, by quietly cheering and gently encouraging them. Sometimes he gathered them around himself, instructed them as far as it was possible, taught them how to invoke God and the Saints, and labored to awaken in them docility and obedience towards their overseers and nurses. Such charity exercised the most favorable influence over the insane. In a short time Gerard was the most welcome visitor, and the insane gathered around him as children gather around their mother. Those whose minds where less affected gave expression to their pleasure by the flattering words: "Dear Father, you give us much consolation; we should very much like to be with you always; do not leave us!" "We do not wish you to go away," they often cried out when he was leaving them, "for the things which you tell us no one else tells us. Your mouth is a heavenly mouth; we wish to hear you speak always." Sometimes Gerard carried with him sweets or fruit which he distributed among them in order to make them more docile and obedient.

Still, the attachment of these lunatics might once have proved fatal. After an interview with them, during which it appears he had greatly pleased them, he wished to depart, when two of them rushed forward, and, each one seizing one of Gerard's arms, held it so fast that the latter could not move a step. "No, no, no! we do not wish you to go away; no, no, no!" the crazy men shouted, and embraced him still more closely. Their affection became yet stronger,—their joy, the joy of crazy people, knew no bounds; and **thus the brother was exposed to the danger of being crushed or strangled. Fortunately, another** crazy man came to the **rescue.** Striking his two companions a few vigorous blows with his fist, he exclaimed in a voice of authority: "Stop, that! you are too familiar with the confessor of the crazy people." This had the desired effect. A few kind words of advice given by Gerard made a good impression, and thus enabled him to go away without **being further annoyed.**

At Naples, as indeed everywhere, the favorite business of the servant of God was to go in search of sinners and convert them. This kind of work he performed with great zeal, particularly since Father Margotta preceded him as a shining example. The latter, though intending to remain at the capital but a short time was very soon actively engaged in behalf of souls and used every effort to bring sinners back to the path of virtue. That he was a most exellent instrument in God's hands is proved from the following occurrence, related of him while staying at the capital. Walking by a palace, he one day heard an interior voice saying to him: "Go into the palace and tell its owner that he should amend his life; if he will not do so, God's anger will visit him." Filled with supernatural courage, **Father Margotta** entered the magificently furnished house, and did as he had been told. His appearance as well as his threat, uttered by a higher command, had the desired effect. The sinner became greatly agitated, yielded to the inspiration of grace, and showed himself ready to begin a life worthy of a Christian.

Father Margotta was as zealous as Gerard. He threw out his net wherever it was possible, and "scarcely a day passed," says Father Tannoja, "on which he did not see his labors rewarded." He frequently entered the shops on his way, especially those of booksellers and printers, who were friends of the Fathers, and endeavored to win by his kindness, and to inflame with virtue, the young people whom he met there, especially those of the working classes. If he found any young man whose soul was ailing, he would never lose sight of him, and kindly importuned him until the latter had become reconciled with God. Those who had been gained over and converted usually entered his service as apostles, and strove to lead to the servant of God their own relatives and acquaintances, as they wished them to experience the happiness which they themselves enjoyed. This caused one of Gerard's biographers to remark that our house at Naples during Gerard's stay was an "anticamera della penitenza," (an anti-chamber of penance) and that Father Margotta had often the great pleasure to receive from the hands of the brother, repentant souls whom he led into the arms of our Lord.

Gerard's look into the interior of consciences was the first lever which divine grace applied to remove the stone of guilt from the heart of man. One day the servant of God was in a shop in which rosaries, medals, and other articles of devotion were sold. At the same time there was an ecclesiastic named Francis Colella in the shop. When the vender saw the two ecclesiastics before him, he began an edifying and pious discourse, for it was peculiar to him to wish to dispose of his piety rather than of his rosaries. As to his piety however, things were in a bad state, and his life was very unlike that which he so much praised. After the servant of God had listened for some time to the shopkeeper, he made a sign to him as if he had something to tell him in private, and led him aside. Here he rebuked him severely on account of his hypocritical behavior and made known to him a very grievous sin which burdened his conscience, and of which no one had any knowledge except God and himself. Gerard then withdrew, leaving the poor sinner in a condition of salutary fear. The latter however, after having somewhat recovered from his fright, turned to Colella and said: "This Father must be a great servant of God." "What did he say to you?" asked Colella. "Alas!" answered the shopkeeper, "I am almost beside myself; he revealed to me a sin of which only God and I have had any knowledge." It need scarcely be mentioned that this man's conversion was effected.

While the servant of God was distributing with a liberal hand the gifts of his charity, he was also mindful of rendering his charitable aid in a most desirable manner to him who had the best claim thereto, to Father Margotta.

This saintly priest again suffered most keenly under the pressure of interior trials. Several months had already elapsed during which his soul was immersed in darkness. His heart was without consolation or joy; his will was without energy, and his heart full of sadnes. Gerard felt great compassion for the Father, expecially since his trials where not unknown to him. He therefore consoled and encouraged him in every possible way. And, according to what Father Margotta himself acknowledged to Father de Rubertis, the brother was admirably successfull.

With absolute help naturally, he could not furnish him, as he expressly told him. One day when Father Margotta was more than usually depressed in spirits, he addressed these words to Gerard: "Come, let us go to St. George's to see Brother Cosimo, and beseech him to obtain for me some consolation from our Lady of Power" (della Potenza). (He referred to the greatly venerated miraculous picture in the church of the "Pii operarii.") "Yes," answered Gerard, "let us go, but you will not receive this grace." They visited St. George's, the venerable Brother Cosimo was seen and his prayers asked, but after Father Margotta had returned home, he was sadder and his spirits more depressed than before. We shall, however, see that the servant of God was still able to complete this work of consolation in behalf of Father Margotta.

As Gerard in this case displayed his knowledge of the future, so he also proved about this time that things at a distance were not wholly kept from his sight. We may still remember the Archpriest Felix Coccicone, who had baptized our saintly brother. He had a brother named Frank who had followed him in the dignity of Archpriest, and who was greatly esteemed at Muro. This good Man was one day murdered in the public street. On the same day Gerard mentioned this sad occurrence to three of his countrymen. "Gerard," one of them related, "used to come to me towards evening to say the beads with me. One evening he appeared to be very much downcast. I asked him what was the matter, and he said: 'My dear Pascal, our good Archpriest Coccicone was murdered at Muro.' 'That is not possible,' I said, 'since by yesterday's mail I received a letter from Muro, and there is not a word in it about such an occurrence.' Gerard said: 'There is not the least doubt, my dear friend, it is so.' In fact the subsequent mail brought me the sad information. To my greatest astonishment I found that Gerard knew of it the very same day on which it happened."

Two or three days previous (the murder at Muro occurred on the 14th. of October 1754) on the 11th. or 12th., the servant of God was at recreation when he cried out suddenly: "Our Father Latessa has just entered paradise." Father Angelo Latessa, a very worthy son of St. Alphonsus departed this life at Caposele on the 5th. of October. Eight days after his death, Gerard saw his soul translated to heaven.

Though he desired to remain unknown in the city, yet he failed in his efforts to conceal himself. His virtues, his charity towards his neighbor, his natural as well as his supernatural qualities attracted the attention of men everywhere. and won for him friends and admirers.

Father Margotta visited the different convents at Naples very often; he generally took Gerard with him. A word from the servant of God was sufficient to make every one entertain the greatest respect for him. Thus it happened with the "Pious Workmen," the Oratorians, and the Jesuit Fathers.

About this time there was a member of the Society of Jesus at Naples as famous for his learning and sanctity of life, as for his zeal in guiding souls. This was Father Francis Pepe. He became specially attached to the servant of God, and after he had become acquainted with his extraordinary gifts, he frequently conversed with him for hours about spiritual things. Father Pepe received from the Pope, Benedict XIV., the most extensive powers in regard to the application of indulgences, and as he was anxious to apply them in the best manner, and for the good of truly worthy souls, he desired that Gerard should take upon himself a part of this good work, and transferred to him the power to distribute a certain number of these indulgences according to his own judgment. Consequently Gerard could, at his own pleasure, grant indulgences

to all those who frequently received Holy Communion
or who daily visited the Blessed Sacrament, as also to
those who specially venerated the Blessed Virgin by
visiting her image, or who fasted on Saturdays. By
virtue of this power he could likewise procure for
priests the indulgences of "a privileged altar."

What astonished priests and religious, and filled all
with the greatest respect for Gerard was his wonderful
knowledge. To hear the simple lay-brother speaking
with the intelligence of an experienced teacher about
the most sublime mysteries of our religion, made the
deepest impression. After the fame of this gift had
spread among the priests of the city, he was often tested
severely; the result, however, was always in his favor,
and not unfrequently discomfited those who urged by
charitable motives had begun to dispute with him.
Cœlestine de Rubertis says: "I happened to be at Naples
one day when there came to us an ecclesiastic who
was just then engaged in the study of the treatise on
the Blessed Trinity, and who began a conversation
with the brother on this subject. He brought forward
one difficult point after another — for instance, the
generation of the Word, the co-eternity of the Word
with the Father, the Procession of the Holy Ghost
from both. Brother Gerard answered all these questions as accurately as a thoroughly trained theologian.
I was astonished at his successful treatment of every
objection, as well as at the ease and clearness with
which he expressed himself. Nothing could disconcert
the brother; on the contrary, the good priest found it
difficult not to become entrapped in his own snares."

In the course of time Gerard became the talk of the
city, and ere long our house was visited by persons of
all ranks. While some were desirous of having an interview with the brother only through curiosity, others
wished to procure from him advice and consolation, or

to manifest to him their interior, and to ask his assistance to make a good confession.

Gerard was held in high esteem and greatly venerated by Don Paul di Majo, who was living at Naples at that time, was distinguished for his artistic skill.

Noble women and ladies of the highest rank did not hesitate to seek the advice of the poor lay-brother, in affairs of conscience. Donna Eleonora Sanfelice, duchess of Ascoli, who had known him in Apulia, became everywhere the panegyrist of his virtues. Her zeal and enthusiasm however, brought upon the brother only troubles and caused his humility innumerable annoyances. Servants of different places came to ask the permission of Father Margotta to allow the brother to visit the palace of their masters, where he was honored as a saint, and consulted as a confessor. Even though the servant of God may have refused many of these requests and frequently excused himself, yet there were reasons which he had to consider and in view of which he had to bow his head and quietly accept what was so unpleasant to him.

One day he was alone at home, when a knock was heard at the door. The messenger was a servant in rich livery, who informed him that his mistress, the dutchess de Maddaloni, requested that Brother Gerard should visit her. Gerard at once noticed that the servant did not know him, and believed therefore that he could escape so unpleasant an affair. He contracted his lips to a very contemptuous smile and said: "I cannot understand why people should always want to see this brother, for he, I must acknowledge, is a blockhead and a half-witted fellow." With this answer he dismissed the servant, who delivered the remark faithfully to her ladyship, adding that he had received it from the lips of the porter himself. From the circumstances narrated, the duchess could easily discover that the very uncivil porter was the servant of God himself, whose humility was offended and who had spoken so disparagingly of himself. But as she had excellent reasons for seeing the brother, and wished to recommend to him her little daughter who was seriously ill, she went next morning to the church of the Holy Ghost, which Gerard usually visited. She was already in the church when Gerard entered it, and she hastened towards him, for her maternal solicitude would not allow any delay. She at once implored him to ask of God the restoration of her child's health. Gerard turned his eyes towards the tabernacle, and pointing to it said: "There is One who distributes favors!" "Yes, through Him, but also through you shall I be able to obtain this favor," answered the distressed mother, full of confidence. Gerard, however, honored this confidence by promising that he would pray for the welfare of the child. The duchess remained in the church for a short time, engaged in prayer. Shortly after her maid came, and in great joy informed her that the sickness of her daughter had suddenly taken a change for the better; that she had risen from bed; in fact that she appeared to be quite well. The time of this change coincided exactly with the moment when Gerard promised the duchess that he would pray for her child. We may imagine with what joy the happy mother hastened home in order to embrace her child that had been so wonderfully cured, and we shall be able to understand that she thenceforward esteemed the sanctity of the brother more highly than before.

Though occurrences of this kind produced a great sensation in many places, the miracle performed by the servant of God in the presence of a great crowd of people, by which the lives of several persons were saved created still greater sensation and joyous excitement in all Naples.

On a very stormy day in autumn, Gerard, while attending to some business, came near the sea-shore, and noticed at a distance a great crowd of people, who were shouting and making violent gestures expressive of terror and anguish. Soon there was presented to his sight a truly deplorable spectacle. On the waves, lashed by a storm, was a boat in imminent danger of capsizing and being lost. Although it was within sight of land, the boat could not be brought to the shore on account of the breakers. The cries of distress of those in the boat as well as the shouts of the spectators on the land, who could furnish no help, excited the greatest compassion in Brother Gerard. But what could he do? He reflected for a few moments, threw his cloak back over his shoulders, signed himself with the sign of the Cross, and rushed into the water in the direction of the boat. The waves which threw the boat about like a ball did not seem to hinder him. "In the name of the Most Blessed Trinity, stop!" he cried out to the boat, while he stretched out his hands towards it, and, behold! it stood still so that Gerard could take hold of it. As if it were a piece of light wood, he drew it after him, and thus brought it safely to shore. The imminent danger of the persons on board, the unheard-of and hazardous undertaking of the brother, who all at once was seen struggling in the midst of the waves, had at first attracted the attention of all the spectators. But as soon as the anxiety and fright had given way to reflection, and the people began to realize what a wonderful deed had been accomplished, there came from the multitude a storm of applause and an outburst of admiration. "A miracle, a miracle! He is a saint! —where is the saint? O God! what a miracle." Whilst, however, all were moving towards the servant of God, and in doing so were hindering and crowding one another, he managed to escape. Before they were able to seize him, he had slipped into the workshop of a man with whom he was acquainted, in order to avoid the demonstrations of the people. The noise made by the latter, the search for the performer of miracles and the manifestations of joy continued for a long time, compelling him to remain in hiding till evening.

Upon returning home, he was asked by Father Margotta how it had been possible for him to draw the boat to the shore. He answered in his simplicity: "O my Father, if God wishes He can do every thing!" In answer to the same question, he said to Father Cajone in the presence of Doctor Santorelli: "I seized the boat with two of my fingers and drew it to the shore." "No doubt you must have been very warm," said the Doctor, "to take so cold a bath." Gerard answered, hinting at his ecstatic condition: "In the condition in which I then found myself, I could also have arisen into the air."

The day after this event, Canon Bozzio arrived at the capital and naturally paid a visit to his saintly friend. Both then took a walk through the city. While walking together, they noticed an ecclesiastic, who, pointing to the lay-brother, said to those around him: "Oh! there is the one who plunged into the sea yesterday!" Gerard felt very much annoyed at these words; he thought in spite of what had occurred on the seashore he was yet unknown; he was disappointed.

He hastened his steps. Bozzio, unable to keep pace with him cried out: "Why do you not wait for me? stop!" But Gerard walked faster. Several lazzaroni who had noticed him also recognized him, and began to shout: "There, there is the saint! See! there is the saint!" The Canon, who did not know what these enthusiastic outcries signified, made inquiries and learned from the lips of these people the history of the wonderful saving of the boat. Meanwhile Gerard had escaped.

The excitement which was elicited by this last miracle of the servant of God was so great that it could not but cause considerable disturbance in Gerards quiet home at Naples. The number of visitors who wished to see the worker of miracles increased day by day. Gerard was inconsolable on this account, for his humility was painfully wounded thereby. He anxiously wished to be in a secluded house of the Congregation, in order to be free from the looks, questions and honors of the **Neapolitans**, although in regard to this matter he was resignation personified. "My will," he wrote, "is entirely in the hands of the Superiors; they may do with me what they please; I shall always be satisfied."

Though **Father Margotta** believed that a great part of his interior peace and quiet was owing to the presence of this holy **friend** and brother yet he saw that the stay of Gerard at the capital would draw to a close. He scrupled to permit him to be exposed in no uncommon a degree to a continual temptation to vanity, and therefore begged St. Alphonsus to recall the holy brother from Naples. The Rector Major complied with his request, and designated Caposele as the further dwelling-place of Gerard.

This removal was a most joyful event for the servant of God. In his humility he believed that he was doing good nowhere and sighed for solitude. "O my God," he wrote to Ripacandida before his departure from the capital, "I am loosing my time. O what a misfortune! I permit so many moments, hours and days to pass uselessly, and do not understand how to derive profit therefrom. Alas! what a loss! may God forgive me!.... But now I shall retire to please my God, and I shall ask Him to restrain me that I may not be able to leave the house. I hope that He will hear my prayer."

This hope was not fully realized. In the early part of November Gerard left Naples where he had spent more than three months, and repaired to his place of destination, Caposele.

CHAPTER XXI.
THE PORTER.

The servant of God was near the close of his career. Only ten months more, and this beautiful star, which shone more brilliantly the higher it arose above the horizon, was, according to God's decree, to finish its course and disappear from the sight of the pilgrims of earth. On his way to Caposele the brother had a presentiment of his approaching end. He therefore redoubled his zeal in the practice of every virtue during his stay at the convent of that town.

The happiness to be subject to a Superior who was not only an able man in the office which he filled, but who was capable of exercising the most salutary influence over him, — accompanied him also to Caposele.

It is true, here he no longer found his paternal guide, Father Giovenale, who had been his Superior at the time of his trial. His place, was, however, supplied by a man who was not inferior to him in virtue and ability. He, like Father Cafaro and Father Fiocchi, was an ornament and pillar of the Congregation.

Father Caspar Cajone was born on the 4th. of August 1722, at Troy, an episcopal see in the kingdom of Naples. Originally, his plan of life was to devote himself to the service of the State, but this plan was entirely changed when he was only twenty-four years old. The change was brought about by a mission which was given at Troy by St. Alphonsus, whose name was held in high esteem at Naples at that time. In the process of beatification of St. Alphonsus, he testified as follows: "I attended the sermons of St. Alphonsus without having had the pleasure of enjoying closer acquaintance with him, and

I conceived a high idea of his sanctity. The poverty of his dress, his modesty, his uninterrupted interior recollection, the true apostolic zeal with which he preached the word of God, — all this filled me with the desire to bid farewell to the world." This desire, however, was not realized till long after. In the year 1751, the young priest happened to read a little book entitled "Vocation to the Religious State," which had just been published by the saint. He read it, and while reading the former holy inspirations were not only renewed, but grace operated more efficaciously, and rent asunthe bond which still kept Cajone's heart tied to the world. A year after he began his novitiate, and entered upon the religious life with a manliness corresponding to his age and character, so that two years after his profession he appeared to be well fitted to exercise the office of Rector of Caposele, and in this capacity he rendered services to the Congregation for many years. At the General Chapter which St. Alphonsus held at Nocera in 1764, he was General Consultor, which office he filled till his death. He founded the house at Benevento in 1779, and was its first Rector. An indefatigable laborer in the vineyard of the Lord, a wise counseller and a holy religious, strict, exact and prudent, he attained an advanced age and appeared at the process of beatification of his spiritual Father, Alphonsus. He died on the 30th. of October, 1809.

It was this man who was to direct our saintly brother and to assist him in accomplishing the last part of his task.

"The life which Gerard led at Caposele," says Father Tannoja, "was the same as at Iliceto. Always humble and patient, he was a friend of work, of recollection and of union with God. Every kind of office was agreeable to him; whether he was employed in the kitchen, at baking bread, or attending to the door, he discharged every duty with holy indifference. "One can" he used to say, "please God and do His holy will in every office." Father Cajone testified that Gerard almost snatched the work from the hands of others. No matter how he felt, whether he was in good health or ailing, he was always at work.

His principal occupation during the early part of his stay at Caposele was that of porter.

How well-fitted he was to discharge this important office we know from what he said in regard to the keys that had been intrusted to him. "These keys," he said, "must open for me the gates of paradise."

What pleased him particularly was the duty connected with this office, to be the right hand of the Superior in dispensing alms, and to have the care of the beggars and other needy persons who usually appeared at the door.

"Gerard," his biographer says, "was greatly pleased with the office which had been intrusted to him, because the care of the poor was connected with it. Our house was besieged by beggars every day and no mother could have shown more tender solicitude for her little ones than Gerard bestowed upon these poor people. He understood how to satisfy everyone; the abuse and insolence which he had to suffer neither made him angry, nor robbed him of his usual affable manner. There were some poor persons who after having received their share of alms came back a second time. Gerard noticed this, but he rejoiced that these people were calling forth his charity by their deceit. "Yes," he said, "they are thieves, but their deeds are the means of procuring pleasure to our Lord Jesus Christ."

In order to excuse them he once said: "Our Lord Jesus Christ also steals — hearts!" (Anche Gesu Christo ruba i cuori.) He generally called them "my poor," or the "poor of Christ." Santorelli one day found fault with his great liberality, which appeared to him excessive, and said: "But you should make a distinction and be satisfied with giving alms only to those who are really in want." "Not at all!" answered Gerard, "all must receive something, for all ask me in the name of Jesus Christ."

That Gerard, however, knew how to discriminate according to the actual needs of the person is proved by the special interest he took in those poor persons who, being sick, could not come themselves, but sent their children or relatives to procure some food.

Being sick, he considered them worthy of greater charity. He often went to the kitchen and selected better food than was usually given, that they might relish it, and did not hesitate to deprive himself of the necessary food to procure something more palatable for them. If he found nothing better for these poor sick persons, he obtained at least a piece of white bread and some cheese. Sometimes Gerard was also permitted to search the pantry and was delighted when he found some sweetmeats or raisins. He often said with great tenderness and delicay: "We must sacrifice everything for the poor; the poor person is a true likeness of Jesus Christ." He once expressed the same thought more beautifully when he said: "The Most Blessed Sacrament is Christ made invisible; the poor sick person is Christ again made visible."

When he received permission, he also carried provisions to the houses of the sick poor; then not only supplied them with abundant alms, but he also distributed medicine gratuitously and soothed their mental sufferings by words of charity and of heavenly consolation.

"What he gave at the door," says Father Tannoja, speaking of the visits which Gerard paid to the dwellings of the poor, "was comparatively little. There were many families that he supported, though they were unable to visit him; widows who had recourse to him, he relieved. He made most zealous efforts, and employed all attainable means, to obtain good situations for poor girls, to protect them against danger, or to help them effect a suitable marriage."

When there was question of the poor, he felt that he had a commission from divine Providence to supply them with every thing necessarry for their relief. Besides, we cannot deny that the Lord Himself only confirmed him in this confidence and belief.

One day dinner had already been prepared, when Gerard entered the kitchen with the vessels which he wished to replenish for the poor. The cook was, humanly speaking, no friend of the kindhearted father of the poor; for the latter's liberality was of no benefit to him, and frequently caused him a great deal of embarrassment. He therefore watched him very closely. The servant of God carefully scrutinized the dishes that had been prepared, and began to take what he thought he needed for the poor, till the cook losing all patience, said to him: "What are you doing? There will be nothing left for the community." Gerard answered: "God will provide;" and kept on taking what he needed. "Now we shall see how this will end," said the cook petulantly, believing that what was left would not be sufficient to furnish the brethren with a dinner. When the time for dinner came, however, nothing was wanting; on the contrary, there was a superabundance, so that a considerable quantity was left for the poor.

A porter so amiable, and so wonderfully sustained by Providence was just then a necessity at Caposele. Not only was the winter which Gerard spent there in the discharge of the duties of his office extremely cold, but as the harvest of the year 1754 had been very unsatisfactory, famine ensued in December among the poorer class. The inhabitants of Caposele suffered much; consequently there was a large increase of beggars at the door of the convent. Every morning there appeared about two hundred, men, women, children and old men, in the most needy circumstances. Father Cajone, who witnessed this great misery with heartfelt compassion recommended these poor people to the porter, that he should take care of them, and said to him: "Brother, now you must think of everything. If these people are not liberally assisted they will die. I shall not restrict you, but I give permission for everything that we have in the house."

Such an order needed no repetition; such a permission was not given in vain. The brother was soon engaged in relieving the large number of poor persons.

These good people wretchedly clad, often half-naked, suffered greatly from the inclemency of the unusual weather. This evil Gerard sought above all to remedy according to his ability. By reason of the very general permission that had been granted, it was not a difficult matter for his inventive charity. He searched the whole house, especially the clothes-room; examined the old garments, had them mended and altered, if necessary. With these he clothed a considerable number of the poor. As for his own apparel, he restricted himself to what was most necessary, in order to assist others.

On account of the severe cold, it was no slight hardship for the poor to stand and wait in the vestibule of the convent. Thither Gerard often carried some wood, and made a fire at which the people could warm themselves.

The sight of delicate children who sometimes gathered around him trembling and crying, moved him to tears. "Alas! we have sinned," he said, "and these innocent little ones must suffer for our sins." He then took their little hands and warmed them in his own, while he represented to himself that he saw in these little children our Lord, Who Himself, though innocent, was obliged to suffer for our sins.

The more the misery increased, the greater was his confidence in divine Providence. God's assistance was equal to Gerard's confidence. It happened more than once that sums of money of which no one had any knowledge, were found in the house, thus affording relief to the poor at the right time. "Three or four times," says Father Cajone, "Gerard himself brought me a considerable sum which he had found wrapped in paper, sticking in the key-hole of the large front door. Whence the money had come, who had brought it, was known only to God and Gerard."

How much bread and other victuals the servant of God distributed at the door is incredible. "It was," says Father Tannoja, "the common opinion at Caposcle, that bread was multiplied in his hands, and our own brethren have often experienced the fact. One of our students, Francis Siniscalchi, testified that he saw the baskets from which Gerard had just taken some bread, and which he had entirely emptied, suddenly filled again with bread. Another student related that on opening a basket the contents of which had been distributed, he found to his great astonishment that it was completely filled."

One day the brother who had been entrusted with the care of providing bread for the community, discovered that Gerard had given all the bread that was on hand to the poor, and that there was not a crumb left for supper. The brother being very much displeased, he hurried to Father Rector's room, a few hours before supper-time and accused the servant of God of having given to the poor all the bread, so that nothing was left for the community, although on the same day a whole oven of bread had been baked. Father Cajone immediately sent for the culprit and called him to account in the presence of the accuser, remarking how imprudently he had acted, since at the advanced hour a purchase of bread was impossible. Gerard modestly listened to the Rector and then said: "Your Reverence need not be afraid; God will provide!" and turning to the lay-brother he continued: "My dear Brother, let us look more carefully to see whether any bread is left." "Not the least bit is here," the brother answered in an angry tone of voice, "and as you insist so much in asserting the contrary, come with me and I will prove what I say." Gerard followed the brother with the greatest humility, the latter walking rapidly towards the cupboard. While opening it, he said: "Now look whether there is any bread left." The cupboard was opened, and it was found entirely filled with loaves of bread. "O may God always be praised!" exclaimed Gerard, when he saw this, and immediately hurried to the church to give thanks to God. Meanwhile, the brother who had reproached the servant of God on account of his liberality, stood speechless with astonishment. In this state he was found by the Rector who had followed to see what he could do to remedy the want. Wondering at such an abundance of bread, he turned to the brother for an explanation: "O my Father," the latter answered, greatly moved, "Gerard is truly a saint. I wished to have him punished. When I went to see your Reverence there was not a loaf of bread in the cupboard, I assure you. After returning with brother Gerard, I found it quite full. My dear Father, no one could have done this except Almighty God. Certainly it was God who did this." "Yes" answered the Rector, "it was God who did this. Let us therefore allow

Gerard to act as he pleases, for truly the Lord is playing a wonderful game with him."

On another occasion, Gerard wished the poor to have a feast. He therefore called to his assistance some lay-brothers, and prepared macaroni for them, the favorite dish of the Italians. In a most cheerful frame of mind Gerard carried the food to them. The poor, however, were at this time more numerous than he had supposed, and the quantity contained in the vessel was not in proportion to the number of the invited. Yet the brother did not allow his happiness to be disturbed. He courageously distributed the food, filled one plate after the other; none was left unfilled; and he put no restriction on his liberality. Nevertheless, what had been prepared was not only sufficient, but there was some left, to the astonishment of all the lay-brothers who had assisted Gerard, and knew how much macaroni had been cooked. It was evident that it had been increased in the hands of the holy man.

The frequent distribution of bread had, however, greatly diminished the supply of grain. Father Cajone was of opinion, that one should not tempt God, and wished therefore to limit Gerard's liberality. Hence he said to him one day: "Brother, you may give away all you wish, but the community should not suffer for what is necessary." Gerard answered: "Your Reverence need not be troubled. God, I confidently hope, will provide." "But, Brother," answered the Superior, "you seem to wish that miracles should always be performed." He then went to the grain-loft, but found it so full that there was no necessity of anticipating want. Filled with wonder, and inwardly thanking God, he withdrew.

"My dear Doctor," he said to Santorelli, who had just entered the house, "I am overwhelmed with astonishment. Our supply of grain was nearly exhausted.

To the complaints which I made on this account to Gerard he answered in his usual manner, so full of confidence, 'God will provide!' I then went to inspect the loft, and I found it abundantly supplied with grain. O Lord! I am ashamed at the sight of this power of miracles and of the virtues of our holy brother!"

Not only did the necessaries of life which Gerard so charitably distributed among the poor appear to multiply in his hands, but there were cases in which it seemed as if they had been brought to him by invisible hands, or had actually been created in his own. The following is an example: Lorenzo Miniello of Caposele had two daughters whom he believed he could not support during the time of famine and whom he therefore recommended to the charity of the servant of God. Gerard took special care of the girls; for the thought that poverty might bring these poor creatures nearer to the death of the soul than of the body, was to his mind of the highest importance. One day the two girls arrived later than usual to obtain alms, after Gerard had distributed everything among the rest of the poor. Greatly grieved thereat, he began to reflect. Suddenly, going into the house and returning after a few moments, he carried in his hands two loaves of bread which looked as if they had just been taken from the oven. These he gave to the girls, who accepted them with the greatest amazement. They could not understand how things had happened. Having watched him when he entered the house, they did not remark that he procured the bread anywhere; besides, the loaves had also a form different from that of the bread which was used in the convent. Convinced that a miracle had been wrought, and full of gratitude to God and His servant, they related the occurrence to their father, who made it everywhere known, to the greater honor of God.

Something similar happpened in the case of a respectable woman, who having become very poor, thought to have recourse to the charitable porter. Restrained by shame, she did not, however, dare to mingle with the poor when Gerard was distributing food among them; she remained in the vestibule, and was not observed by the servant of God. When the poor people left, he perceived her, but thought that she had not come as a person who was in want, and therefore took no further notice of her, for it was no extraordinary thing that persons who did not desire alms, and who wished only to see their distribution, should be standing near the door. It even happened that respectable and wealthy persons would send their children to mingle with the beggars, in order to receive from the hands of the saintly brother some bread, which was then preserved at home as a relic. A man, Theodore Cleffi, however, who was present and who was acquainted with the sad condition of this woman, noticing that Gerard would pass her by, drew his attention to her and explained what she wanted. "O God! why did she not tell me?" Gerard cried out in a tone of great compassion. After a few moments of reflection, he hurried into the house, and returning in a short time, drew forth from his breast-pocket a small loaf of fine white bread, still warm, and as if it had been just baked, and most kindly handed it to the distressed woman. This loaf of bread was also of a peculiar form, and when he brought it the house oven was empty and cold.

In this manner, actuated by heroic charity and wonderfully sustained by divine Providence, the servant of God alleviated the miseries of many hundred poor persons during the famine, which lasted during January and February of 1755.

While engaged in this charitable work he was always

very cheerful. His heart was so full of gratitude to God that often very little was wanting to make it overflow in rapturous delight.

Philip Falcone was the most skillful flute-player and singer at Caposele. As a poor blind man he was one of the best friends of the porter at the convent of "Mater Domini," and was very often seen at its door. One day, when Falcone had again come for his alms, Gerard said to him in an unusually joyful manner: "Play something." "What shall I play?" asked the blind man. "Play the hymn: 'Il tuo gusto e non il mio — Voglio solo in te mio Dio,' etc. ("Not my pleasure, but Thine only — do I seek in Thee, O my God," etc.) The blind man had scarcely begun to play the air, when entirely abandoning himself to the emotions which it expressed, Gerard became excessively joyful. Quite inebriated with delight, he began to dance, and continually repeated the words: "Not my pleasure, but Thine only!" Suddenly, all external movements ceased, the eyes assumed the fixed but mild look towards heaven, which they usually assumed during an ecstasy, and in the presence of all who were present, among whom was Santorelli, he was raised in the air a few feet from the ground.

In imitation of our divine Saviour, Gerard was solicitous to aid the poor not only in their bodily wants, but he was anxious to exert the fullest possible salutary influence on their souls. For this purpose, he usually taught catechism before the distribution of bread. After he had arranged his poor in groups, placing the little boys and girls in front, he spoke to them of their duties as Christians, and of matters of religion as his faith and charity inspired him, and the capacity of his hearers demanded. In order to urge them to the practice of patience, and to the resigned endurance of their suffering condition, he frequently pointed out to them our dear Lord, Who spent His life in great trials. Above all did he exhort his poor people to pray, to receive the sacraments, and endeavored to awaken in their hearts sentiments of contrition, and of detachment from sin.

The instructions of Gerard served as a healing balm to the souls of the poor, and proved to be of great benefit to many others who were not mendicants.

As soon as it became known that instructions were given by the brother, other inhabitants of Caposele came at the time of the distribution of bread for the purpose of hearing the sermons of the holy brother. Not a few learnt from them what they never knew, or they felt themselves moved as they had never been before.

"It was consoling to see," says Father Tannoja, "that many, immediately after hearing him, hastened to the church, where in deep contrition they cast themselves at the feet of the priests and made their confession. Several of them, whose wicked lives were well known, and who had not received the sacraments for a long time, went away from Gerard's instructions filled with the necessary strength to approach the sacred tribunal of penance."

One of these conversions, brought about by the servant of God at the door, was that of a young woman who though regarded as very pious had for a long time been committing sacrileges, and was the slave of very wicked habits. The unfortunate person deceived herself and her spiritual director. One day she was met by Gerard at the gate of the convent. He knew the condition of her interior by inspiration. Having dismissed the poor, he represented to her in most vivid colors the terrible condition of her soul. She could not resist such an admonition from the lips of a saint, and therefore no longer disregarded the call of grace, begging the servant of God to point out to her the path in which she should walk. Gerard sent her to Iliceto, to Father Fiocchi, for the purpose of making her confession to him, which was done amid floods of tears. Her subsequent life proved that these tears were sincere, springing from true contrition. With great humility she made her past irregularities known to all, and told how Gerard had saved her; she afterwards became the mirror of virtue for the whole town of Caposele.

In an account written by Father Cajone some time afterwards, he praised her perseverance. "She continues," he said, "to edify every one, but cannot think of Brother Gerard without bursting into tears."

Those, who had once met the servant of God at the door of the house at Caposele, and had received bread or consolation from him, held in grateful remembrance these benefits and frequently mentioned them under tears. Gerard was ever remembered by the poor; they continued to speak of him as their "Father," and honored him as they would honor a saint.

That this great charity towards the poor, exhibited by the saintly porter of Caposele, was only a branch of the great tree of his perfect charity toward his neighbor, is proved by his behavior towards those with whom he had to associate, especially his own brethren within the convent walls. Here he evinced the same pure, tender charity, the same friendliness, the same patience.

We may remember that at Naples the servant of God had been Father Margotta's consoler, but was not at that time able to assuage his interior trials, and was obliged to bid him hope for better days. That the suffering Father was out of sight did not cause him to escape Gerard's thoughts. The latter continually implored God to relieve Father Margotta of his sufferings, and not satisfied with praying, he finally offered himself to bear the burden, provided Father Margotta could find alleviation. And, behold! This offer of charity was not refused by our Lord. One day, Santorelli, on entering his cell, found him in the act of writing. "What are you doing there?" he asked the brother. "I am writing to Father Margotta," he said, "to inform him that henceforth he will be free from his interior sufferings, and to assure him of the joy I feel thereat." What Gerard had announced had really come to pass. Letters which were received from Father Margotta at Naples clearly indicated that at the time when Gerard wrote to him he was relieved of his sufferings. Strange to say, at that very time, there came over the servant of God such a depression of spirits, strangely contrasting with his former habitual cheerfulness. There was no fire in his eye, nor was there a smile on his face; he seemed to be very dejected, and to have lost all courage. As his Superior was not accustomed to see this, he asked him why he was sad. Gerard then explained: "Alas! I had not the courage to see Father Margotta suffering so long. I therefore offered myself to Jesus Christ to suffer torments instead of the good Father."

His genuine, well-grounded charity is shown by another incident. Although it reflects some dishonor on him who took part in it, we can relate the incident, especially since the guilty one did not conceal it, but made a public confession of it to the honor of the servant of God.

The art of making Crucifixes and 'Ecce Homo' images, which Gerard had learnt at Naples, he cultivated with great ardor at Caposele, with the permission of his Superior. For this kind of pious occupation the saintly brother needed, however, paint and glue, which he generally procured from the carpenter of the house, Stephen Sperduto. The continual requests made for these things soon became very offensive to Sperduto, and in order to be able to say that he had no more, he one day concealed them in his room. He was no doubt greatly astonished, when after telling the lie that he no longer had any, Gerard calmly mentioned the place where he had concealed them. This however did not convert him. A short while after, as he had to absent himself from the house for some time, he took the glue-pot in which there was some dry glue, as also the paint which he had placed on the top of it, and again concealed them so that Gerard should not be able to do anything. To find the concealed glue-pot was not, however, very difficult for him; only God permitted that he should now make a mistake, which he certainly wished to avoid, and could easily have avoided.

Gerard did not notice that the dry paint was lying on the top of the glue. Naturally, in a short time a strange mixture of paint and glue was formed whereby both were rendered useless. Upon his return, the carpenter perceiving what had been done became enraged. He did not doubt that Gerard was the cause of the damage, and became so incensed against him that he gave him a violent blow with a piece of wood which he happened to have in his hand. In an instant the humble lay-brother was on his knees. "Alas! strike, brother, strike; you are right in doing so!" It was, however, only the first emotion of passion which darkened Sperduto's understanding and betrayed him into such an act of injustice. Gerard's humility immediately calmed him. "Oh, my brother" he exclaimed, with great contrition, "you think that I am going to kill you. No, no! I will do you no harm. I was carried away by my anger." "And Gerard, — who would believe such a thing?" — as Stephen Sperduto himself afterwards related, "never complained to any one about my cruel behavior towards him, and always evinced his old friendship for me. But I learnt thenceforward how to value his sanctity which I had not hitherto appreciated."

This charity, meekness and humility procured friends for Gerard in the convent as well as out of it.

Among the latter may be mentioned Dr. Nicholas Santorelli, who was an uncommon man, and well-fitted to form a holy friendship with Gerard.

"He was," says Father Tannoja, "extremely pious and devout, and a fervent client of the Most Blessed Virgin. He loved Jesus Christ so intensely, that he received Holy Communion every day. Always recollected and united with God, he spent several hours in prayer every day. To this he added severe penances, was anxious to mortify himself in all thing, and in whatever he engaged always sought God's honor. After our house had been established at Caposele, he placed himself unter the direction of Father Sportelli, and later under that of Father Cafaro; and every morning, in all kinds of weather, he visited his director, and performed his devotions in church. At the sermon which was preached every Saturday, and during the novenas, as well as the exposition of the Blessed Sacrament, he was a regular attendant, and did not allow the long distance which he had to foot to prevent him from being present."

Scarcely had this man become acquainted with the servant of God, when he became attached to him as a friend, and used every opportunity to derive from his extraordinary gifts some special benefit for his own soul. As often as he came to the convent — this was every morning, — he paid Gerard a brief visit, if he was not otherwise engaged, and often conferred with the simple brother on most important matters.

Gerard justly esteemed Santorelli, delighted in making him a confidant, and tenderly helped him and his excellent family in many difficulties. We shall yet meet with several proofs of the intimate relation which existed between Santorelli and the servant of God.

As regards other admirers and friends of Gerard, who entertained a special affection for him, we will mention only one, the arch-priest Camillo Bozzio, whom we remember at Atella in close relationship with the saintly brother. The holy priest continued to maintain the friendship which he had formed at that time, and was delighted to have the brother near him, and to have frequent interviews with him. He often visited him, conversed with him about different subjects of piety, and studied the spirit and the life of the servant of God. He did this not only for his own benefit but for the edification of posterity; for Bozzio afterwards described in a long account of the man of God, what impressions the latter had made upon him.

We have already quoted several times from this account; but we here wish to give, word for word, its principal items, partly because in it is clearly expressed the high esteem with which Gerard's friends regarded him, partly also because it contains a splendid testimony of the saintly brother, given by a man who was able to observe, as well as to judge what he observed. The account will, moreover, conduct us in an appropriate manner to the subject of the next chapter.

"Since the beginning of our friendship," writes Bozzio in his account, "Gerard gave me numerous proofs of his well-grounded virtue. I entertained at that time the opinion (which I hold even at the present time) that the soul of the brother remained constantly in God's presence. By the practice of this, he attained to an intimate union with God. Distinguished as he was by his active union with God, which brings the human will into full harmony with the divine; speaking of it with deep emotion, and also living greatly detached from all earthly things, I do not doubt that God also raised him to a participative and receptive union with Himself. I was fully convinced of this, shortly before his last illness. We were conversing together quite alone, and he asked me the meaning of some verses of the 17th. Psalm that begins with the words: "Diligam te Domine fortitudo mea!" (I will love Thee, O Lord, my strength!) especially in regard to the meaning of the words: "Inclinavit cœlos et descendit et caligo sub pedibus ejus." (He bowed the heavens and came down; and darkness was under His feet.) His questions led me immediately to the belief that he wished to speak of the kind of prayer which mystics usually call "Contemplation in the negative way," and which when he participated in it, gave him the appearance of a man who is enveloped by a mysterious darkness. I gave him some information in reference to the questions proposed; he, however, who had had experience in this matter treated the matter much better than I did.

"In all that he did, the pleasure of God was the only end for which he strove with a most ardent desire. Yet, this striving of the heart was neither disturbed nor injured by the submission which he was accustomed to render to every one of his Superiors.

"His mind continued always the same; whether the 'Beloved of his soul' afflicted him or seemed to act as if he were going to forsake him; in spiritual dryness as well as in an abundance of light, he was the same. And if, at times, his interior sufferings manifested themselves, not the least sign of impatience or displeasure in them could be remarked.

"His intercourse with others was a mixture of the most charming modesty and the most agreeable cheerfulness. If many of his actions appeared strange and unseemly, they may be explained by his uninterrupted attention to God, partly also by his desire to be regarded and treated like a fool. He also had an extremely clear understanding and was of a very serene turn of mind.

"To express many things in few words, I repeat what Fathers of his Congregation — holy men, well experienced in matters concerning the spiritual life — have testified; namely, that Brother Gerard had wonderful ecstasies, possessed the virtue of obedience in a heroic degree; that he knew how to obey commands that were given only mentally; that as children of the world glory in false pleasures, Gerard gloried in his sufferings, by perfectly submitting to the dispensations of Providence, however painful they might be; and that without being indiscreet, he always hungered after sufferings. I also know for a certainty, what other persons worthy of belief have related of him: he was able to penetrate the hearts of men, and to recognize in them their actual temptations, their immortified inclinations, their aridities as well as their consolations; that he was able to indicate the best time for the purification of a soul, as well as the more or less distant periods of God's visitations; and that he possessed the light of prophecy and the gift of working miracles.

"Regarding his obedience, the Fathers of the Congregation may no doubt be able to give a more accurate account. I can, however, give the assurance that he always spoke of obedience with the highest respect, and entertained for it a burning love. One day I was standing in a field near the convent of 'Mater Domini,' during the time of recreation. The Superior, who had noticed me, said to Gerard that he should kiss my feet. He immediately hurried away to fulfil the command. When I saw him coming I wished to shun him and hastened my steps so that he could not overtake me; but he also hastened his steps. Not being able to overtake me, he cried out that I should wait for him. In order not to tire him and cause him anxiety I was compelled to stop; whereupon he kissed my feet.

"After all that has been mentioned, I say it is impossible to admit that Gerard's soul was guided by human or diabolical spirit, the Divine Spirit alone directed him. His heroism in obedience and in conformity to the divine will, as well as his heroic love of sufferings verify this assertion. The practice of these virtues clearly indicates and does not permit us to doubt, that Gerard's soul was moved entirely by the Spirit of God; for extraordinary things are free from all possible deception by the practice of these virtues. If to trials cheerfully borne for God's sake — as was the case with Gerard — is added the burning desire always to suffer more and more, then the highest point of love that can be reached on earth is attained. Then the soul is in that sublime condition of sanctity in which the Apostle St. Paul cried out: "Vivo ego, jam non ego, vivit vero in me Christus." (I live, now not I; but Christ liveth in me.)"

CHAPTER XXII.
Heavenly Gifts In Full Splendor.

"Gerard's sojourn at the house of Caposele," says Father Tannoja, "was nothing less than a chain of miracles and of the grandest virtues."

The earthly career of the servant of God was indeed drawing rapidly to a close. His bodily health was entirely destroyed. Nearly every morning he had a hemorrhage of the lungs, though he never complained or even mentioned the fact to any one. His austere life, his unremitting labors, had helped to destroy his naturally weak body. Entirely forgetful of self at Caposele as he had been at Iliceto, Gerard was always ready to serve and to help every one, without taking any rest.

His position at the door claimed his attention nearly all day. He also worked assiduously in the tailor-shop, or helped the other lay-brothers wherever he happened to be. And as he rigidly adhered to all his mortifications, his fasting, his scourging, his long vigils and similar bodily tortures, it was not astonishing that his weak, sickly body, was rapidly approaching dissolution.

But while physical strength was perceptibly deminishing, the supernatural gifts of the saintly brother shone forth more brilliantly.

Just as the sun sends its most resplendent rays over the earth, just before its setting and while sinking below the horizon attracts the attention of all by its brilliant gold and purple hues; so the highly privileged soul of the servant of God seemed to have reserved for the last period of life the most beautiful rays of its magnificence. All those heavenly gifts which we have so often found occasion to admire now show themselves according to a remark of Gerard's biographer, redoubled and refined. New forms of them appear; the perception of the infinite love which our Lord has exhibited and hidden in the mystery of the Altar; the tender, vehement devotion to the fountain of graces, **the Blessed Virgin Mary**; the knowledge of the truths of faith; the power over nature; the penetrating insight into men's hearts and into the future; that inconceivable vanquishing, annihilation of space, — all this we find in the servant of God in an increased measure during this last period of his life.

His love for the Most Blessed Sacrament, his desire to receive our Lord in the Sacrament of the Altar, increased every day. His visits to the tabernacle were now more frequent, his intercourse with our Lord became more intense and ardent. Gerard loved to spend the quiet hours of the night at the foot of the altar, while during the day he lost no time in order to gain moments to salute our Lord in the Most Blessed Sacrament. When he saw the Sacred Host he usually fell into an ecstasy; at least he would forget all his surroundings in such a way that he could not check his sighs and his loud expressions of interior joy.

As this demonstration of emotion disturbed others, Father Cajone one day called him to account about it. Gerard did not excuse himself, but seized the hand of the Rector and placed it on his breast, as if he wished to say: you see my dear Father, that I cannot do otherwise. Father Cajone felt that Gerard's heart was beating violently, and was astonished how he was able to bear such pulsations.

In referring to this, the servant of God said to Santorelli: "If I were on a high mountain, I would wish to set fire to the world with one breath;" and as he placed the doctor's hand on his heart, the latter remarked that it was beating as if it would burst his breast.

This phenomenon usually manifested itself when he assisted at the Holy Sacrifice of the Mass, and especially when engaged in making his thanksgiving, on his knees, hidden in some corner, after Holy Communion. As if spell-bound, he sighed and prayed: "O most sweet Jesus! never leave me! Thou callest me a fool. No, I am not a fool; I should rather call Thee a fool! Thou, an infinite God, remainest here, locked up day and night, and what canst Thou gain from so wretched a creature? But as for me, how much can I not gain by being in Thy company, O my Saviour?" If Gerard refers in such effusions of love to the fact that the Lord called him a fool, he refers to the immediate present; for the familiarity, — if we may so call it, of earlier years was renewed, and even now he frequently heard a voice saying to him from the altar that he was a little fool.

One morning as he was passing the tabernacle, Father Cajone, who was in the church, noticed that he burst out into a laugh. "Why are you laughing?" asked the Rector. "Ah!" said Gerard, "He told me that I was a fool, and I have told Him, He was much more so, since He so foolishly loves me."

This increased love towards our Lord in the Blessed Sacrament made it necessary to do violence to himself when it was time to leave the church; and often, he darted like an arrow past the altar in order not to yield to his desire to linger in the presence of God and be prevented from performing his ordinary duties.

"How can I do differently?" he said to Santorelli, who asked him why he walked so rapidly past the altar. "This good and noble Master has inflamed me more than once, so that I am always afraid that He is playing me another trick. (Piu d'una volta questo Galantuomo mi ha scottatto, e bisogna che fugga, temendo, mi faccia qualche corrivo.)"

Santorelli soon found occasion to convince himself of the truth and reasonableness of Gerard's fear. He had just paid his morning visit to the convent and to Gerard, and wished to go home through the sacristy and the church. The brother accompanied him, and wished to make a short visit to the Blessed Sacrament after he had left the doctor. Scarcely, however, had the servant of God knelt at the foot of the altar when Santorelli, who had passed through the church had just crossed the threshold, heard a piercing cry. Looking back to see why Gerard had screamed, he saw him stretched out senseless on the floor before the tabernacle. Some other persons, on hearing the cry, had approached and gathered around the brother out of curiosity. After Gerard had recovered, and noticed the people around him, he became greatly embarrassed, arose without saying a word and left the church with his head bowed down. The following day Doctor Santorelli met him in the corridor of the house and began to smile. Gerard immediately understood what the smile meant, and said: "Did I not tell you that there is no joking with my good Master? Do you see how many tricks He plays me?"

While Gerard's love of God became more exalted and refined towards the end of his life, his love and devotion to the Blessed Virgin was also increased. On one occasion Santorelli asked him whether he loved the Blessed Virgin; whereupon Gerard answered: "O my dear Doctor! You are tormenting me; you are tormenting me!" And in order to hide the ardor of the love which threatened to seize him at this moment, he hurried away.

On another occasion, during the time of recreation, Gerard was in the company of his brethren among whom chanced to be Father Andrew Strina, a man of great simplicity, and specially devoted to the Infant Jesus. There arose between him and the servant of God a friendly quarrel. In order to tease Father Strina Gerard said to him: "You do not love the Infant Jesus!" But Father Strina used the same weapon and replied: "And you, brother, do not love the Madonna!" Both were touched to the quick, and the brother more sensitive than Father Strina — barely reminded of his love for the Blessed Virgin, became quite inflamed. In his joy he clasped Father Strina in his arms; little was wanting for both to fall into ecstasy.

This intimate and animated intercourse with God increased the knowledge of the servant of God in regard to the truths of our holy religion in a most remarkable manner. These truths appeared to him clearer every day, so that he was able to penetrate the depths of their mysteries in a most astonishing manner.

"The wise men of the world," as Canon Camillo Bozzio expresses himself, "were silenced and put to shame in his presence. He was, it is true, unlearned; but he drew knowledge from the living fountain of the Redeemer, and not from the muddy streams of human wisdom; so it happened that distinguished theologians frequently became confused while speaking to him. No theologian, no scientific man, was able to follow his thoughts when he, inebriated with the love of God, began to sink into the mysteries of the Most High."

In the same manner did his friend Santorelli express himself about Gerard. "When Brother Gerard," he says, "began to speak of divine things, he, as it were, passed out of himself. The most difficult subjects were intelligible in his words. As often as I conversed with him, I was astonished when I considered that a poor lay-brother who had received no education could enter into deep mysteries and elucidate them."

Don Joseph de Lucia, who was studying at Caposele at that time and afterwards became Arch-priest of Santa Fede, made the same experience. "I entered into conversation with Brother Gerard," he relates, "about theological matters, and he enlightened me in regard the Incarnation and the Blessed Trinity in a manner that a St. Augustine and a St. Thomas could not have surpassed."

A young priest from Gerard's native place who was somewhat puffed up with his own acquirements mistook the first sensation for true strength, and did not wish to believe in the extraordinary knowledge of his countryman, and boasted of his own learning. A few questions about certain points of theology were sufficient, however, to puzzle him greatly; he was not able to say another word; he was silent. "My dear countryman," Gerard said most kindly to him, "you have indeed studied theology, but you are not on this account a theologian. O no! One does not acquire this science except by humility and prayer."

"But," says Father Tannoja, "it is not so wonderful that Gerard could become a theologian without study; greater astonishment was created that he could also make others theologians — that is, that he was able to communicate the gift which he himself possessed."

One of his friends, Don Donato Spicci, likewise a priest belonging to Muro, who had heard a profound exposition of the famous first verses of St. John's Gospel from Gerard's lips, experienced this personally. Being on a visit to the servant of God one day, he noticed a small book lying on Gerard's table. It was the life of the Venerable Mary Crucifixa, for whom Gerard entertained great devotion. Donato opened the book and found the chapter which treated of the "Solitude on Calvary." He read the title aloud. "Ah!" said Gerard to him, "these things are not for you. You are, it is true, a theologian," he added smiling, "but you will not understand the meaning of the words." In fact the good priest found the book rather obscure, but after a pause he said: "The book is written neither in French nor Hebrew; whoever has a little sense would be able to understand it." "Very well," replied the servant of God, "read some of it and tell me what the saint wishes to say. Donato read a passage; he read it several times, but when he wished to explain it, found that he could not. Santorelli, who was present and saw his predicament began to laugh. Donato already put to shame and therefore somewhat irritated, was displeased. Then Gerard said good humoredly: "My dear Donato, do not trouble yourself so much." He then signed the priest's forehead with the sign of the Cross and said: "Now read; you will understand and will be able to explain everything;" and Donato actually understood everything with the greatest ease.

The same wonderful communication of knowledge occurred to another priest. According to his testimony it had reference to several passages in a work of the Venerable Palafox. When he had mentioned his inability to understand them, the holy brother signed him with the sign of the Cross and said: "In the name of the Most Holy Trinity, read!" Immediately, he comprehended the text and was able to explain it easily and readily to others.

His superior knowledge of human hearts was in no way inferior to his supernatural knowledge of the divine mysteries. Hearts with their wishes, propensities and mysteries, were often lying open before his eyes, so that he appeared to read in a book. Thus, it was wonderful what a peculiar impression an impure soul made upon him.

Gerard used this gift of the knowledge of the human hearts at Caposele as he had done at Iliceto for the benefit of his fellow-men, especially of those poor sinners who were tempted to conceal the condition of their soul from God's representative.

A girl was about to leave the church where she had received the sacraments, when Gerard called her aside and said: "Why have you come here?" "To go to confession," she answered. "Of course," said Gerard, "but you did not make a good confession." The servant of God then mentioned to the frightened girl what she had concealed in confession through false shame. She became greatly agitated, sincerely repented, and made a good confession.

Once, several men came from Castelgrande to Caposele to make a retreat; among them was Francis Mugnone. While Francis was taking a walk in the garden during the retreat, he met Gerard, who looked at him seriously and said: "But, Francis have you made a good confession?" In reply to an affirmative answer Gerard said: "It is not true! your confession was not good. See whom you have behind you." Mugnone looked back and saw a diabolical appearance. His fright was very great, but it was salutary. He immediately returned to make a sincere confession, and received Holy Communion worthily.

An unfortunate woman had been indulging in the wretched pastime of deceiving several priests by pretending that she was possessed, in order to obtain pecuniary assistance from them. During six weeks or more some of them had been exerting themselves to expel a supposed devil. When Gerard had been informed of the matter he openly said that the person was not possessed; and when the hypocrite came to him he took her aside and said: "This business which you are carrying on, you are doing for one reason or another; but I tell you to give up these pretensions, or I will tear the mask from you and expose you." From this moment there was an end of the so-called possession, and the guilty woman, seeing the wrong which she had been doing amended her life.

That the servant God knew different places and their surroundings, the following incident will explain. Donna Candida Fongarelli was a rich lady who especially befriended him. He could therefore without fear of giving offence ask her for many little favors. Thus he asked her one day for some small pieces of white silk which he needed for a veil for a ciborium. The lady promised to give them to him, and accordingly examined her wardrobe to find a piece of silk such as the servant of God had asked for. Finding nothing suitable she thought to cut what she needed from her wedding dress which she did not intend to wear any more. On the following day she again met the brother who, without any introduction, as if there was question of a matter already communicated to him, said to her that she should not for the sake of two pieces spoil her dress, but should search again. "You will," he added, "surely find something that will answer." Donna Candida was surprised that Gerard knew what she intended to do, since she had not communicated her idea to any one.

Having reached home she again searched and found what she had before sought in vain. When Gerard showed the silk to his Superior the latter was erroneously impressed as to its size, and said that not only one but two veils might be made of it, and therefore told Gerard to make two. Obedient in all things, he at first calmly received the command but was soon convinced that the material was insufficient to make two veils. Having discovered this, he called upon the Rector. "Well, it must be done," said the Rector, "just try to do so." Gerard went to his workshop. Donato Spicci was there; he was, as has been said, a frequent visitor of the servant of God, and had received permission from Father Cajone to converse with him on pious subjects. The good religious immediately began the task the fulfilment of which only a miracle could render possible. Whatever way the pattern was fitted it was evident that only one veil could be made of the material. Gerard then turned to Spicci for counsel. The latter closed the book in which he was reading, and then tried to fit the pattern to the silk. He could not arrive at any conclusion different to the silk. He finally exclaimed: "Nobody is obliged to do what is impossible." The lay-brother however was not satisfied. "As far as I am concerned, I must obey, and obey at once. Since there is question about something that concerns our dear Lord, it rests with Him to do what I cannot do." After saying these words, he fell on his knees, raised his eyes to heaven and prayed. Then he took the scissors in one hand, the pattern in the other, and began to cut out the material. The result was, that Gerard effected in an inconceivable manner what was impossible, and obtained four equal parts, each of which had its own flower, and this as perfect as if it had been cut from the middle of a piece.

The gift of miracles which so singularly manifested itself in this case, was displayed more frequently and more strikingly during the latter part of his life.

From the many examples which could prove this, Gerard's biographers have selected only the following:

While passing through the town of Caposele, a stranger was seized with so violent an attack of gout of the hip (sciatica) that he was reduced to a most pitiable condition. The separation from his family distressed the poor man so much that he became very melancholy, and continually sighed and wept. Scarcely had Gerard heard this when he hastened to visit the sick man. He exhorted him to confide in the Blessed Virgin, and then signed him with the sign of the Cross. At the same moment his pains ceased. The man was overjoyed at the wonderful help he had received, and was so grateful to God and His servant, that every hour of the night seemed to him a century, and he could scarcely await the break of day in order to make the event known to the whole community.

Another cure which though not completed by Gerard, was at least begun by him: A workman of Muro, Alexander Fafilli, had a child called Anthony ten years of age, suffering from scrofula. All human aid had proved useless. The father, therefore, resolved to use the last means and to have recourse to Heaven. For this purpose he intended to make a pilgrimage with the child to the Madonna of Monte Vergine.

On his way thither he came to Caposele, where he visited the servant of God, and introduced his poor sick child. Gerard showed the most heartfelt compassion. After he had moistened his fingers with spittle, he applied them to the throat of the child and at once the scrofula began to heal. "Now go," said Gerard, "go and make your pilgrimage; the Madonna will grant the request which you will make." It was true. The child returned home quite well.

Gerard rendered a still more important service by his gift of miracles, to a certain Januarius Liguori. Being seriously ill, the latter had already lost consciousness, and seemed to be near death's door. Januarius had not received the sacraments for many years, in consequence of which the members of his family were much grieved. In their trouble they sent for Gerard and intimated that they wished him to pray that the sick man might recover consciousness so as to be able to make a good confession. The servant of

God readily complied with the request, and immediately went to the dying man. While praying, he leaned over him so that his face touched the face of Januarius, who was already in agony. Scarcely had this been done in the presence of the family and of the physician, Santorelli, when the dying man opened his eyes and became quite conscious. He made his confession, and amid signs of great contrition received the Holy Viaticum and Extreme Unction, and died a few days after, in sentiments of Christian resignation.

Still more remarkable is the following incident: Rose Marolda, a relative of the archpriest at Muro, had lost her sight through sickness. The remedies applied had no effect whatever. As the sick person had great confidence in her countryman, the saintly Brother Gerard, she asked Donato Spicci to bring her something from Gerard's hand, from Caposele, where he was about to go to make his retreat. The priest fulfilled this request when he took leave of the servant of God to return to Muro, and earnestly begged him to hear poor Rose. Gerard was at first reluctant. Seeking some pretext, he said that God wished to make her a saint, and that she should conform to His holy will. But Spicci was not satisfied with this refusal, and assailed the servant of God with new petitions. The latter, however, repeated what he had said, and concluded with the assertion that God did not wish that the sick woman should become well so soon, and that she had consolation enough in thinking of our Saviour on the Cross. "But I shall not leave the house before you have given me something for her," said Spicci; and he persisted. He finally prevailed upon Gerard, who then went to his cell, and having returned with a small bottle of water he gave it to the priest and said: "Give her this, but no one should know anything about it. Donato did as he had been charged. The blind woman, washed her eyes with the water, felt an improvement the very first time she applied it, and after the lapse of a week she was perfectly restored. The people who knew nothing about the remedy given by the saintly brother, were astonished; they ascribed the cure to the skill of the doctors.

But Rose, knowing very well who had cured her, was filled with gratitude and cried out: "May the honor be God's Who has granted me this great favor."

The miracle of vicarious labor by heavenly spirits, of which we read in the lives of many saints similar in character to Brother Gerard, also occurred at Caposele.

The servant of God had been appointed cook for one day. In the morning, after Communion, he retired to his thanksgiving in the oratory, where there was a large crucifix before which he loved to pray. Sunk in meditation, the good brother forgot all about the kitchen and the preparation of dinner. What was transacted during the entire forenoon between himself and his dear Lord, no one knew. When, however, the time for dinner was approaching and the door of the kitchen remained locked, search was made for Brother Gerard. Brother Carmine Santagniello, who was attending to this matter, found him the moment in which he was leaving the oratory. His eyes were radiant with joy; his face was all aglow. "But, Brother Gerard," Carmine said to him, "what have you been doing? In the refectory the cloth is already laid, and the kitchen is locked." "You have too little faith, dear Brother," answered Gerard, "are there no angels, and what have they to do?"

Immediately after, the Community came to the refectory; in the kitchen there was no delay; everything seemed to be in the best of order and well prepared.

Yet more wonderful than the service of the angels, is

another favor from heaven which the servant of God enjoyed several times during the latter part of his life; we mean the mysterious annihilation of space and of that law to which bodies are naturally subject, and in consequence of which they cannot be present in several places at the same time. On many occasions Gerard appeared in different and distant places at the same time as is proved by undeniable evidence.

To the special friends of the holy brother belonged among others the family Di Gregorio, at Lacedogna. Here, with the sign of the Cross which he made over a barrel of wine that began to turn into vinegar, he prevented threatening damage and gained the thanks and the highest confidence of all. Now it happened that a servant of the house became very ill. To his violent sufferings were added continual anxieties, so that the poor man suffered excruciating tortures. One evening amid his sufferings he thought of the wonderful lay-brother, and in the confidence which he placed in him exclaimed: "O my dear Brother Gerard, where are you? Why do you not come to help me?" Immediately a knock was heard at the door. It was opened, and the servant of God stood before it. He straightway went to the sick man. "You called for me, and I am here!" he said, "I have come to assist you. Have you a lively faith in God? Make a whole-souled act of faith, and you will become well." While he was thus exhorting the sick man, he signed the patient's forehead with the sign of the Cross and left the room. The pains of the sick man had, in the meantime, vanished, and he could now rise from his bed without difficulty. His first impulse was to express his most heartfelt thanks to his benefactor. He imagined that he would find him with the family, but was greatly astonished in being unable to find him in any part of the house! With the exception of himself and the family of Di Gregorio, no one at Lacedogna had seen the servant of God.

A confidant of Gerard's, and his right hand in the distribution of alms among different poor persons living at a distance, was Theodore Cleffi. One day he had a long interview with the servant of God, who dismissed him with the request to obtain for him an accurate list of the neediest poor of Caposele. Leaving Brother Gerard, Cleffi called at the house of a sick man whose sad circumstances he well knew, and asked him what he most needed. "I need nothing at present," he answered, "for Brother Gerard, who just now visited me, provided me with all that I wanted." Cleffi was startled at this answer. Since he had come straight from Brother Gerard, after speaking a long time with him, and the latter could not possibly have been there a short time before, he regarded the assertion of the sick man as a falsehood, and expressed great displeasure on this account. The man however, showed him what he had received, and maintained most emphatically that Gerard had just left him. Cleffi could not doubt any longer that here there was question of another miracle, and that the servant of God had received from the Lord, as a reward for his charity, the grace to be in different places at the same time.

Another fact of this kind is mentioned by Father Tannoja. "One day Gerard was waiting to hear from Muro about some pressing business that concerned the honor of God. No intelligence being received, he said: "It is necessary that I should go there myself to-morrow." On the following day, according to the testimony of Lorenzo di Majo, he was actually seen at Muro, while he was staying at our house at Caposele."

Father Margotta could also tell of this wonderful power possessed by the brother. "Just imagine," he once said to Santorelli: "this 'little fool,' Brother

Gerard was in his room last night, and yet he was seen in an ecstasy before the Blessed Sacrament in the choir of the Franciscans."

Sometimes the presence of the servant of God in another place was of a purely spiritual, though very noticeable nature. As he was able to see and know things at a distance, — whether or not people were keeping their promises, — he frequently in a most wonderful manner made his co-operation sensible, as well as his participation and his spiritual presence in behalf of those living or acting at a distance. In such a case the impression made on the minds of those whom he visited, guided, or supported, became as vivid and as strong as if he had stood at their side visibly and bodily.

The sick at Caposele were not unfrequently visited by the saintly brother in this mysterious manner; and Dr. Santorelli relates from his own experience as follows: "One day while I was visiting my patients I felt that Brother Gerard was continually at my side as distinctly as if I had seen him with my own eyes. When I afterwards came to 'Mater Domini' and met him I told him of the experience which I had had. 'What did you mean,' I asked, 'by following me continually on my walk?' 'Do you not know,' he answered,[1] 'that I must go away to-morrrow? I therefore did not wish to leave this place without again visiting my poor sick people.'"

On another occasion Gerard was with the members of the doctor's family, conversing with them in an edifying manner, as was his wont. When going away he promised to return in the evening. It was known that the Rule forbade him to go out after the "Angelus;" whereupon Santorelli began to smile. Gerard, however,

---

[1] He referred to his journey to Naples, which we shall soon have occasion to mention.

reproved him. "I am not joking," he said, "I will come, not bodily but spiritually." But, when evening came, the doctor's sister saw before her the servant of God who cast a piercing glance at her. Of the reality of this apparition she was so convinced that she declared she was ready to take an oath to confirm her assertion.

A similarly wonderful occurrence was experienced in regard to Gerard by the archpriest of Teora, Don Nicholas Fiore. As he had heard of the extraordinary gifts of the brother, he felt a very strong desire to become acquainted with him. He expressed his wish to Santorelli, and the latter would gladly have introduced him to Gerard, but the brother was not at Caposele; he promised however, that on the servant of God's return, he would speak to him about his desire. When Gerard came home, Santorelli did as he had promised. "Well, then I shall try to find him," Gerard answered briefly. Santorelli did not imagine how speedily and wonderfully the servant of God would act on this resolution. A few days afterwards, the Archbishop of Conza came to Caposele, and the arch-priest of Teora made use of this opportunity to wait on his Grace. "Now is the best time," said Santorelli when he met Fiore, "to make the acquaintance of Gerard, as you so much desire to do so." "But I have already made his acquaintance," the archpriest answered; "a few evenings ago he was with me at Teora." Fiore then related that on that evening at a certain hour — it was on the same evening and at the same hour in which Santorelli had communicated to the servant of God the desire of the archpriest — he saw in his room a Redemptorist lay-brother. He did not see him with his bodily eyes but perceived him clearly and distinctly by means of a certain higher, indescribable sight, so that the outlines of the brother were still in his memory. "You desire to see me," said the lay-brother; "Well I have come in order that you may understand that I am nothing but a poor man, more wretched than all others." Santorelli was greatly astonished when he heard this. He, however, wished to convince himself of the truth of what had occurred, and for this purpose led the archpriest to a room of the house where were assembled several Redemptorists, among whom was Gerard. "Now," said he, "which of these is Gerard?" Fiore pointed him out without hesitation, and quite correctly.

In the midst of these heavenly gifts and miracles, the holy brother continued to remain the humblest and simplest of souls. The lowly opinion which he formerly expressed about his abilities and virtues had experienced no change amid the multiplication of divine favors and the innumerable demonstrations of veneration, love and respect on the part of the people; and while heaven's gifts were a continual source of confusion to him, the honors bestowed upon him by men only frightened and tortured him. Whenever he perceived the shadow of such marks of respect he fled and disappeared as far as he was able.

The noble lords, De Fillippis, living at Serino, were very desirous of making Gerard's aquaintance, having heard so much about his miracles. Gerard knew this, and when one day they came to Serino, he purposely avoided meeting them, and repaired immediately to a public inn. As friends of the Congregation, they sent for him as soon as they heard that a lay-brother had gone to the inn, and thus they met him whom they were so anxious to see. Gerard, however, did not betray himself, and acted in so reserved a manner that this time he remained unknown, and the Lords De Fillippis became acquainted with the man of God without recognizing him.

In his humility the servant of God often envied the

poor who are despised by the world and treated with scorn, because they seemed to him to be nearer to Jesus Christ. One day on seeing a poor man at the convent who acted as messenger, and was drenched with rain and bespattered with mud, he exclaimed: "Oh how satisfied I would be, if everything were wanting to me, like this poor man! This man for the sake of a piece of bread, must be satisfied with the neglect and want of the world and I — and I. . . ." He could not finish the sentence, and began to weep bitterly.

He desired most earnestly to escape the honors and distinctions heaped upon him by men, and to live in obscurity. His brethren frequently heard him give expression to this wish in loud exclamations. Thus he once said: "O my Lord! Thou dost such great things in me and allowest everything to be immediately known. Why dost Thou not conceal them?" "O my Lord," he cried out on another occasion, "who am I that Thou shouldst reveal Thyself so wonderfully in me? In all things Thy will is enough for me." "O will of God," he added, "how happy is he, who knows nothing except the will of God!"

CHAPTER XXIII.

OTHER APOSTOLIC LABORS.

Father Margotta regretted that Gerard should be obliged to leave Naples, and looked forward for an opportunity to ask the Superior's consent to his return. The time for this seemed to have come after three months, and it was presumed that the excitement which Gerard had caused at Naples had subsided, and that the difficulties which his stay had caused were removed.

St. Alphonsus, who had only called the brother away in consequence of these difficulties, complied with Father Margotta's wish to have the servant of God under his immediate direction, and therefore sent him to the Capital again towards the end of February, 1755. Father Margotta came to Caposele himself to bring Gerard to Naples; he had some business to transact in Calitri, his native town, and therefore took Gerard there with him before returning to Naples.

Gerard did not hesitate to make this journey for he was comparatively little known at Calitri and could therefore devote himself quietly to his pious exercises and other good works.

For a few days everything passed off as Gerard desired. While Father Margotta was attending to his affairs the lay-brother spent his time in praying in the church before the tabernacle. While his spirit of recollectedness and piety edified all who saw him, nothing remarkable was noticed, and he remained at rest. However, one morning, a woman came from Bisaccia where Gerard was well known, and interrupted his peace. She had heard of his arrival at Calitri. As one of her relatives was very ill she hastened to ask the assistance of the miracle-worker. Both Redemptorists were then living at the house of the Archpriest Berilli. She came and asked for the brother. When told that he was not at home she waited for his return. Gerard did not remain away very long. As soon as the woman saw him she cast herself at his feet, told him her trouble, and begged him most earnestly to cure the sick person. The servant of God listened to her with his usual kindness, consoled her, and dismissed her with the assurance that her relative would be restored to health. The people of the house who witnessed this scene were naturally very much astonished; the prayer of the woman, said with the greatest confidence, as well as the behavior of the brother, seemed to them incomprehensible; they spoke of it to Father Margotta, and while doing so could not refrain from laughing. This annoyed Father Margotta. "You are laughing," he said, "because you do not know the gifts which this brother possesses." He then divulged the secret, and told these people about the virtues, miracles and career of Brother Gerard. This narration went through the whole of Calitri like wild-fire. Gerard could no longer remain in seclusion. The poor, those full of doubt or in need of advice and consolation, as also those attracted by curiosity called on the brother, giving him an opportunity to exchange the role of the hermit for that of a missionary. As he recognized the will of God in this change, he did not hesitate to do at Calitri what he had done in other cities. From morning till night he practiced the corporal and spiritual works of mercy.

Don John Cioglia, an eminent surgeon and a man beloved by all was taken seriously ill. He was the first who experienced Gerard's charity, as well as his wonderful power. As the physicians had given up his case as hopeless, his friends had recourse to Gerard, and Father Margotta commanded him not to refuse the petition. He therefore called on the sick man, and made the sign of the Cross on his forehead. At that very moment consciousness returned, and Cioglia felt that he was well. Those who were present were astonished at the change. They all acknowledged it to be a miracle. "Yes," said Gerard in his simplicity, "you see what obedience can do."

In the same manner, he healed another man. Father Margotta, who had been softened by the tears of the man's sister, sent him to Gerard. The consequence of his visit was not only immediate improvement, but also the resolution which the sick man made to approach the Sacraments worthily, and to become reconciled with God.

A noble lady, Donna Arcangela Rinaldi, happened to be at Berilli's house, when she was seized with a very violent headache. She saw Gerard's hat lying in the corner of the room and thought within herself, half in earnest, half in jest: "Let me see whether this man is really a saint." She then put the hat on her head; scarcely had she done so, when all pain left her. This incident induced the members of the Berilli family to procure something which Gerard generally used. It was remarked that his shoes were very much worn. They therefore had new ones made, and kept the old ones. These shoes, like the hat, proved to be a holy relic. A boy of the same house who was suffering from the severest pains that no medicine could alleviate became well as soon as he had been touched with Gerard's shoes. When subsequently during the night these pains returned, the boy exclaimed: "Bring me the shoes of Brother Gerard quickly," and they again produced an immediate cure. According to the testimony of Don Joseph Berilli, these shoes became quite renowned at Calitri; they were regarded as a universal remedy; they went the rounds among the sick and the suffering, and by their touch many wonderful cures were effected.

Gerard's greatest desire however was the cure of souls in which he manifested the greatest ardor blended with charity and kindness. Hence he acted in the capacity of an awakener of consciences, an exhorter, an inciter to good works, and according to circumstances, a stern monitor.

A very pious lady, Maria Candida Strace, who had heard of Gerard's sanctity, wished to converse with him about the matters of conscience. Something weighed heavily on her mind, and she hesitated to ask advice of anyone. Even when she stood before Gerard she lost courage and could not express herself. The servant of God, however, when he saw her hesitating, interrupted her and said compassionately: "Now as you do not speak I will speak in your stead." He then told her everything that troubled her, and gave her the necessary counsel. She afterwards acknowledged that no one but God could have known what Gerard communicated to her.

An affectionate monitor, but, alas! in vain, was the servant of God, in behalf of a prominent man, Nicholas Xavier Berilli, who, unconcerned about eternal things, wasted his time in earthly pleasure. Good friends who were anxious about his soul directed the brother's attention to him. Gerard understood the hint and immediately paid him a visit. He tried to infuse into the worldly-minded man more serious thoughts than those which he had hitherto entertained; he endeavored to persuade him to make a retreat at Caposele. The man listened quietly to the exhortations and proposals of Gerard, but maintained that, for many reasons, it would be impossible for him to make a retreat. Finally, hard pressed by the arguments of the servant of

God, he said: "I will come during the month of October." "Alas!" answered Gerard in a sorrowful tone of voice, "you wish to come in October. Oh! you will never see the month of October." And so it happened. Though enjoying the best of health at this time, the nobleman was seized with a violent fever during the month of August 1755, and before he realized the seriousness of his condition, passed into eternity.

Naturally, the convent of the Benedictine nuns which **was** situated at Calitri, was not left unnoticed by Gerard. The nuns desired to become acquainted with the servant of God, and offered him an opportunity to visit them, while Father Margotta also urged him to visit them.

Here, too, he produced incredible **results.** It appeared as if an extraordinary director had come among them. His reputation inspired them, with unusual confidence which impelled them to speak to him in all sincerity, and to submit their spiritual wants and shortcommings to his judgment. His sanctity and wisdom lent his exhortations, reproofs and counsels that **flavor which made them** palatable even to the weakest or the most stubborn minds. The opinion of the nuns was unanimous that every one of Gerard's words penetrated their hearts like a dart and inflamed them with love for Jesus Christ and the Blessed Virgin.

At that time there was in the convent a novice to whom the life of the cloister appeared altogether too severe, and who thought of returning to the world. Gerard called for her and spoke to her about the advantages of the religious state; but he spoke with such warmth and power that she who had been tempted against her vocation, henceforth thought of nothing more than of how to become a holy religious.

Another Sister was very much tormented by scruples; no one could quiet her conscience satisfactorily. One interview with Gerard, who himself told her what was troubling her, proved most successful. The servant of God also gave her advice how she should act in such temptations, so that she might rid herself of mental sufferings.

Whenever Gerard had a favorable opportunity he labored with redoubled zeal to renew the fervor of the religious. As often as he had an interview with them, he exhorted them to observe the Rules most faithfully; he recommended to them the worthy, frequent and devout reception of the sacraments. He attacked abuses without mercy. In doing this he exhibited the greatest prudence and forbearance, and also convinced all of the importance of abiding by his counsel; his efforts were generally crowned with success. Only in one point did the otherwise tractable and docile nuns show a little stubbornness.

The parlor of the Sisters was in an unusual place; the grate faced the vestibule of the church. This circumstance, besides other evils, could easily be the occasion of faults against the respect due to the holy place. Gerard was greatly displeased with this arrangement. He spoke of it to the Abbess, and informed her that it was her duty to remedy the evil. The Abbess however remarked that in this matter she could not act herself, but was obliged to consult the community. Her interview with the Sisters was however fruitless; they could not agree. This petty stubbornness of the religious displeased Gerard greatly; he complained of it to Father Margotta and said he could not understand how so wretched a little matter, a sacrifice of which would please our Lord, could create so much difficulty. Father Margotta advised him to address a few earnest words to the community at his afternoon visit. The servant of God spoke accordingly. The result of his discourse was that all the nuns declared that the evil should be remedied. Gerard wished that the matter **be attended to** at once; but they pleaded that the day was too far advanced to do any thing; on the following morning, they said, the work was to begin at once. In **the meantime,** the minds of these fickle women changed and when they spoke about the work during the evening recreation, so many objections were raised against it that the resolution that had been made was given up and it was decided that the execution of the **plan be postponed.** While the nuns were coming to this decision, Gerard saw their wavering and their desertion from their former resolution. A noticeable **sadness** immediately came over him, and as Father Margotta asked why he was so sad, Gerard answered: "I am troubled about those nuns." On the following **morning he went to** the convent, called for the Abbess and asked whether they still abided by the resolution which had been made. The Abbess answered in a general way, and betrayed the greatest embarrassment; nothing positive, she said, had been urged against the matter, and there was no difficulty in the way. "What! no difficulty in the way!" interposed Gerard. "But let it pass; we shall not speak of the matter. Yesterday you did not wish to change; and now it shall not take place." Then he left the convent. His last words, however, were not spoken without knowledge of the future.

In fact, although the nuns often thought of putting the grate elsewhere, the change was never accomplished. Only after **the** death **of** the nuns who did not wish **to act** according to Gerard's words, was the change **effected.**

In the meantime, Father Margotta had finished the business which he had to settle in his native place, and now prepared to return to Naples. The servant of God also received orders to accompany him. Toward the end of February, or the beginning of March, 1755, the two Redemptorists arrived at the Capital.

As the first sojourn of the saintly brother at Naples had been a chain of miracles and of works of charity, so was also this second visit.

In order not to be the subject of everybody's **conversation**, as this would **cause** him many annoyances, he now more than ever shunned the more **frequented** places of the city and generally walked through quiet and secluded little streets.

If this mode of proceeding on his part had for him some advantage, it also had its annoyances, for Gerard was once placed in a position which was most undesirable, as he was obliged to threaten parties with God's anger and to see the threat immediately fulfilled, in a terrible manner.

One of the **narrow little streets** through which he used to pass was that between the **Queen's Convent**, (Monastero di D. Regina) and "**S. Guiseppe dei Ruffi**." During his first stay in the city, two lewd women had the boldness to ridicule and to scoff at **him as he was** modestly walking along the street. Neither his patience nor the influence of time was able to moderate the insolence of these wretched women. When **Gerard made his** appearance at Naples **again they behaved** worse than before. They waited for him in **the above-mentioned street, and when he was about to enter it** they prevented it by placing **themselves before him** and uttering cries of derision. One **of them held a** tambourine in her hand, while the other had another instrument suspended from her neck. They **then began a kind of dance which was improper**, and which they accompanied by gestures which were an outrage **to decency. At this** spectacle, holy anger flashed from the countenance of the saintly brother; he stood still, **and in an earnest** tone of voice exclaimed: "You will not put an end to your wicked conduct? Well, then, do you wish to see how terribly God can punish?" This threat had scarcely come from the lips of Gerard when one of the women, as if struck by a thunderbolt, fell to the ground, exclaiming: "O Madonna, I am dying!" Quite unconscious, she was carried home by some men who had been attracted by her cry.

This holy anger of Gerard, unfollowed by any sad consequences, was experienced by a certain vagrant and imposter who, relying upon the compassion of the people pretended to be a cripple in order to obtain alms. Daily was he seen near our house creeping along on crutches, with one foot wrapped in rags, as if suffering from a severe wound. Those who passed by were deceived and gave him abundant alms. The imposter was for a long time a subject of displeasure to Gerard, as his love for truth made him intolerant of every kind of dissimulation. Several times he exhorted him to give up this mode of life, and to engage in some honest kind of labor. The rogue cared very little for such **advice and continued** his nefarious business. The good lay-brother then lost all patience; having one day again met him begging in the street not only reprimanded him in the severest terms but tore away the rags from his foot. "You vile wretch," he cried out, "if you do not wish to be damned, cease mocking God **and your** neighbor!" The imposter, much frightened, let his crutches fall and ran away as fast as he could.

Though the servant of God, during his second appearance at Naples, took great care not to attract attention, he secured this in a particular manner when he **applied his miraculous** gift. **This** gift could not remain **idle in him, for** it was an instrument of his glowing charity that was always ready to assist others. But he endeavored to conceal it as much as possible. Thus, one day while conversing with a friend named Don

Philip Rossi, from Caposele, near the church of the Holy Ghost, two ladies approached him. "O my dear Brother Gerard," exclaimed one of them, with tears in her eyes, "do come and cure my poor little daughter." However much Gerard felt inclined to oppose what the lady desired, he had not the heart absolutely to refuse her petition. Still, in order to keep himself in the background as much as possible he did not wish to appear at the bedside of the sick child except as a messenger sent by another. He therefore said: "Yes, I will visit your daughter, but I must first get permission." Only after he had done this did he hasten to where he had been called. From this time forward he always acted in this manner. The success of his efforts he would then ascribe to the power of obedience, hoping thereby to divert all admiration from himself.

The number of visitors was not less than during his first visit at the Capital. Persons of every condition in life, priests and laymen, even very learned men and eminent directors of souls, came to consult him.

There is a letter extant, written at this time by Gerard, which enables us to realize how much he was respected even by his own brethren, and by aged Fathers of the Congregation. It is addressed to Father Francis Garzilli, who was distinguished by his learning, as well as by his piety. Himself a spiritual man, before his entrance into the Congregation a Canon at Foggia, and now a venerable man of seventy, he was in his old age troubled by many scruples and had therefore applied to the servant of God for counsel, help and consolation. The beautiful answer which he received is as follows:—

"May divine grace fill the heart of your Reverence, and may the Blessed Virgin preserve it for you!

"Oh my dear Father, I am filled with joy and consolation on account of the game which the Divine Majesty is playing with you. I confidently hope that our Lord will grant you a complete victory. Well then! do not fear, but be of good cheer, for the Lord is with you, and will not abandon **you.**

"Your Reverence has doubts about your confessions. Ah! the fears which God permits to come over you in this respect, should serve you as a slight mortification. You say that you have been the cause of these troubles. Certainly, you must be convinced of this; for if you believed the contrary to be true, you **would** not be so uneasy. But this is the way the Divine Majesty treats His favorites; He allows them to think that all their trials are a consequence of their **negligence. If your** Reverence could conceive the thought that all this comes from God, where would there be trials and sufferings? Everything would be changed for you into a paradise on earth!

"Besides, though we commit many little faults, and often stumble, let us remember that even the saints on earth were not pure angels. Confide and hope in God, my dear Father, and **recommend me -- oh, I beg you** for the love you bear me! — recommend me to Jesus Christ and to Mary, the Blessed Virgin, who, I hope, may abundantly bless us both!"

Gerard's friendship for Father Pepe during his first stay at Naples suffered no diminution during his absence, and now the servant of God is frequently associated **with this** noble-minded man. They needed, each **others services, as** it were, in order to promote the **honor of God and the salvation of** souls. Gerard again **drew largely** from Father Pepe's treasures.

A letter written by the servant of God on the 8th. of **March, 1755, to** the venerable Sister Mary Cœlestis Costarosa in Foggia confirms this. In this letter he informed her that he had applied in behalf of the convent, to Father Pepe and obtained a considerable number of indulgences which the Sisters could gain on the different feasts of the year. What he asked as a remuneration for this favor he indicates at the end of his letter in the following words: "Preserve this memorandum, I beg of you, so that those coming after you may avail themselves of these favors. At the same time I would remind you all of your obligation to pray for me, and also to apply to my soul these indulgences when I am dead. This I recommend to all the Superiors that come after you with the additional request to offer for my soul one or the other Holy Communion. I must also earnestly beg the Superior who will preside over the community at the time of my death to have offered up for my benefit all the communions the Sisters will receive during eight days as also the indulgences that they will be able to gain for me during the same time. I shall not forget to recommend you to the Lord, that He may make you saints. Amen."

These words of the servant of God were regarded by the religious as a last will and testament. Gerard was remembered after his death as he had desired, and the memorandum written by him was preserved with great veneration. It was used even among the sick after the manner of a relic, and not unsuccessfully. In 1840, God glorified His servant by means of it, for in this year, Sister Raphaela Pitasse, who was suffering from a disease of the eyes took the manuscript of the holy brother, touched her diseased eyes with it, and was immediately freed from pain.

Gerard's second visit to Naples was not less fruitful than the first in results. Neither was it to be of longer duration. After the feast of Pentecost, May 18th., 1755, Gerard was commissioned to leave Naples and return to Caposele; he was to accompany the Fathers on a mission given in Calitri, probably from the 25th. of May till the 8th. of June. Accordingly, during the week of

Pentecost the servant of God left the Capital, which he was never to see again, and hastened to Calitri to the mission.

"During this mission," says Father Tannoja, "he again performed things that were incredible. Prophecies, conversions, and reading of peoples' consciences daily occurred; the chief task of the Fathers was to absolve sinners whom the good brother had moved to contrition."

The missionaries lived, as formerly Father Margotta did, at the house of the Berilli family. Here it one day happened that the servant of God who was occupied in the kitchen, let a large jar containing oil fall so that it broke into pieces, and all the oil was poured out on the floor. On seeing this accident, the little daughter of the family began to scream and uttered some coarse, abusive words against the brother. In order to find out the cause of the angry outcry of the child her mother hurried to the kitchen and rebuked her for her conduct; but when she saw what had happened, she ran quickly to procure some cotton with which to catch up the oil which had been spilt. In the meantime, Gerard picked up the pieces of the broken jar as if he wished to put them away. When, however, the woman returned to secure the oil she perceived that the jar that had been broken was entire and filled with oil, and that it contained a larger quantity than before. The astonishment of both mother and daughter was very great, and Gerard withdrew to give thanks to the Lord Who had so happily helped him out of his perplexity. When, after a short time a search was made for Gerard he was found in his room, immovable on his knees, his eyes raised towards heaven. This fact was attested by the girl who had been present and who subsequently took the veil in the convent at Calitri; also by several inhabitants of the city.

At the close of the mission, probably on the 9th. of June, Gerard returned to Caposele, not to take rest as seemed necessary, but to make new efforts, and to take upon himself new cares for the honor of God and the salvation of souls. Soon after his return he found an opportunity to display his zeal. On the 19th. of June, Monsignor Joseph Nicolai, Archbishop of Conza, a great patron of our house at Caposele, came to spend a few days there. He was accompanied by his secretary, a layman, a Roman by birth, a man specially endeared to the Archbishop on account of his great skill in transacting business, and greatly beloved by all because of his social deportment. Wherever he happened to be, all sadness was banished, his sparkling wit and his unfailing playful humor enlivened every social entertainment, while his courteous and refined manners attracted general admiration. In a short time this Roman was regarded by the inmates of the house at Caposele as their most favorite guest. Even Gerard from the very beginning showed him great affection, which he always exhibited, as far as modesty allowed. He treated him most kindly, indulged in many an unrestrained easy talk with him, laughed at his jokes and answered them in like humorous manner. But the reason of this friendliness on the part of Gerard was by no means to be found, as was also the case with others, in the man's attractive manners. His supernaturally enlightened glance had quickly informed him that he who exhibited so joyous a disposition allowed his conscience to remain in a most lamentable condition. If, therefore, Gerard treated him with exceptional kindness it was only because he hoped to win his confidence in this manner. In order to pave the way to his conversion, he deemed an exhibition of kindness an essential condition.

In fact, this "hunter of souls," as Father Tannoja

calls the servant of God, was not disappointed in his hope. Fortunately for him, the sinner was caught in a net which Gerard's charity had spread.

One day when Gerard again saw the secretary very cheerful he most cordially embraced him, and pressed him to his bosom. This mark of affection produced a mysterious effect upon the sinner. As if a clear light had flowed from the heart of the brother to his own he instantly felt in his interior unusual disquiet and remorse of conscience. He was at the same time attracted to the servant of God by special confidence and now sought his society and conversation more frequently.

When Geard noticed that grace had opened the first furrows and that seed could now be profitably sown, he resolved to take a more decided step. He called the secretary to the oratory of the house and cast himself, weeping, at his feet. The man knew not the meaning of this, but soon understood. In plain words the brother made a disclosure to him that was as unexpected as it was startling. "O my friend!" said he, with emotion: "I do not understand how you can be so constantly cheerful, for you are living at enmity with God. You cannot deny that you are married, and have left your wife at Rome. How can you pretend that you are single; how can you dare to deceive an unfortunate woman?" Gerard continued in this way, to scourge the secretary for his wicked life, and pointed out to him the exact time in which his wickedness and neglect of his soul's salvation originated.

The poor sinner stood dumbfounded! He then fell on his knees and acknowledged that what Gerard said was true; that he really had led such a wicked life, and had committed such crimes. He finally begged the servant of God to advise him how he should again walk in the path of duty.

Gerard rejoiced at the work of grace; exhorted the

penitent man to have confidence in the divine mercy; counselled him to correct the disordered state of his soul immediately, and to communicate with Father Fiocchi who was just then at Caposele waiting on the Archbishop.

Pale with fear and dejection, the secretary called upon the Father, and related in detail what had happened to him through Brother Gerard; and how the latter had converted him.

"Only God or the devil," he concluded, "could have made my condition known to him; but it could not have been the devil, as I was truly moved to sorrow and contrition."

Father Fiocchi, who knew Gerard very well, had no difficulty in admitting that the repentant secretary was right in his conclusion. He heard his confession, instructed him how to repair the great wrong which he had committed, and above all advised him to carry out, as soon as possible, his resolution to return to his wife.

When, after his confession, the secretary was going to the Church to receive Holy Communion, he again experienced the wonderful help and care of the servant of God. At the entrance of the church Gerard met him and asked where he was going. "I am going to Holy Communion," answered the secretary. "But," said the brother, "you forgot to confess a certain sin. Go and confess it, and then you may receive our Lord in peace." The converted man was obedient also in this point, went back to his confessor, and had the consolation of approaching the holy banquet with the conviction that here again he was fully the recipient of God's mercy.

Necessarily, the interior change had to exercise its influence over the exterior. The sentiments of compunction, of deep contrition, and of holy sadness which controlled his heart were very soon noticeable in his whole behavior. The man who had formerly been in a continually cheerful humor, from whose lips jocose words escaped every moment, became at once serious, quiet and reserved. He was often seen with moistened eyes and heard to sob aloud. Every one was astonished at this, and the Archbishop, who did not suspect what had happened to his secretary, sent for him and asked him about this new phenomenon. His answer was a flood of tears, and the words which in the Gospel are put in the mouth of the Samaritan woman to whom our Lord manifested all her secret sins: "Venite et **videte hominem,** qui dixit mihi omnia, quæcumque feci!" (Come and see the man who has told me all things whatsoever I have done!) Hereupon he acknowledged to the Archbishop in all sincerity what his spiritual condition had been, that Gerard had drawn him out of darkness and shadow of death, and had awakened in his soul thoughts and desires of which he **formerly had no notion.**

This sanctity of the servant of God was not unknown to Monsignor Nicolai; this event, however, greatly increased his esteem for the holy brother. He requested some one to tell him all the particulars of Gerard's miracles, and did not neglect to draw profit for himself from the holy brother's heavenly wisdom. In the interviews which he usually held with him, he often found such consolation that, filled with pleasant emotions, he would shed tears; and although he was of a very reserved disposition, at his departure he gave Gerard the most lively proofs of his attachment and respect, and recommended himself to his prayers. "O **Monsignor,"** answered Gerard, quite confused by so much kindness, "I need God's entire mercy to save myself, and I ask your Grace rather to remember me **at the altar."**

The secretary's good resolves never wavered, his sentiments never changed after he had lost sight of Gerard. Having returned to St. Andrea where the Archbishop usually resided, the change that had taken place in him created general comment. "What is the matter?" he was asked one day by the director of the seminary, Don Jacob Bozzio. "I no longer notice your former cheerfulness; I cannot understand the change." "Very naturally," he answered, "for you do not know what happened to me at Caposele. Alas! my dear friend, I am not a single man, as I pretended to be, but am married, and brother Gerard showed me most clearly the sad condition of my soul." The good man was now so filled with contrition for his past irregularities that it was not difficult for him to tell everyone how things had formerly been, and how brother Gerard had led him back to a correct path.

Monsignor Nicolai no longer kept him in his service, but sent him to Rome as soon as possible, with a letter of recommendation addressed to Monsignor Casone, his relative.

There too the converted man narrated everything that happened to him while he was at the house of the Redemptorists at Caposele, and what brought him back to Rome. Thus, in the Capital of the Catholic world he procured for the servant of God friends and admirers. Moreover, according to the testimony of Father Cajone, he kept up with the servant of God till the latter's death, a pious correspondence, of which, unfortunately, nothing is in existence.

While Monsignor Casone was one day conversing with a Roman Cardinal, he related among other things what had occurred to the secretary of the Archbishop of Conza. The Cardinal was not only astonished at what he heard, but was seized with a great desire to become acquainted with Gerard. He therefore wrote specially to the Archbishop, and asked him to send the brother to Rome. When the letter reached its destination, **the servant** of God was no longer among the living.

CHAPTER XXIV.
Last Undertaking And Last Journeyings.

The remaining time of Gerard's life was to be dedicated to a work of obedience and fraternal charity. It was a work which, being in total contradiction to Gerards quiet and reserved disposition and to his ever increasing desire for solitude, became the last and glorious proof of his religious spirit.

The house at Caposele was a new foundation, therefore small and inconvenient. In a short time they felt the necessity of building several additions. This was done as soon as their means permitted.

When Gerard returned from Naples to Caposele, he found the house full of workmen, masons and carpenters; building material of all kinds was lying about, and during the whole day the noise of the work and the cries of the workmen were heard. If the servant of God in returning home from a thickly populated and noisy city rejoiced at the prospect of the solitude and quiet he was to enjoy, he found his pleasure spoilt, and recognized an opportunity to make a great sacrifice to the Lord.

But the annoyances and distractions occasioned by the erection of the building itself was not the greatest sacrifice the Lord demanded of him.

Father Cajone thought it well to appoint the servant of God as the superintendent of the building, and to assign to him the charge of the workmen employed, the procuring of the necessary conveyances, the proper awarding of wages, and such things. This very distracting office was not in harmony with the disposition of Gerard's soul; much less was it suited to his bodily strength. The obedient brother, however, trusted in God, willingly accepted the task and was very soon acquainted to the new duties which he fulfilled with wonderful ardor and zeal. His simple faith permitted him to see in this charge nothing else than the will of God, and his confidence prompted him to pass unnoticed whatever objections human prudence might offer.

Gerard was not satisfied with merely doing what was easy, such as the ordinary superintendence of the work and a few general instructions: he took an active part in the work, and gave orders and advice wherever needed. He was the first at work, giving all an example of diligence and activity. Now he was at the sand-pit there helping to dig, again at the brick-kiln, then about the little town hiring men to carry building materials. Day and night we might say, he was on his feet. Amid these labors he forgot his bodily wants, and what was still more important, suppressed the longing for quiet prayers before the tabernacle.

That this activity in a man of miracles could not pass by without apparent supernatural help is easily understood.

One day the Rector was in great distress about the wages due the workmen and said to Gerard: "How shall we be able to pay these people? In a few days, Saturday comes and payment must be made." "O!" answered the confident builder, "send in a petition to our Lord in the Blessed Sacrament." His advice met with approval, the petition was drawn up and given to its originator that he might present it. "Brother Gerard," said Father Cajone to him, "you must now help us in our trouble." Forthwith Gerard hastened to the church with the petition and laid it on the altar. He then rapped in childlike simplicity at the tabernacle and said: "Thou seest, dear Lord, here is our petition; answer it!" In order to obtain a favorable answer, he remained on his knees before the altar the whole night, from Friday till Saturday, and implored his Master for help in behalf of the house.

At daybreak he repeated the knocking at the tabernacle door, which was the outward expression of his most earnest prayer to the Father of the poor. A short time after he heard the door-bell ring; hastening, he found two little bags filled with money. The perplexity of the Superior was now removed. Donato Spicci, who was in the convent when this miracle was wrought asked for a few of the coins that had been sent from heaven and took them with him to Muro.

Even the elements seemed at times to heed and respect the zeal and obedience of the servant of God. Gerard was one day obliged to go to town on business. As he was preparing to leave the house a thunderstorm which threatened broke forth with great violence when he had barely crossed the treshold. Rain fell in torrents, accompanied by lightning and thunder. But this did not prevent the servant of God from attending to his errand, though Father Cajone did not wish that Gerard should get wet, and sent to call him back. The messenger found that he was already on the public street, but noticed that he was walking along quietly. How great was his astonishment when he saw that not even a thread of Gerard's garments had become wet. The servant of God, however, returned immediately when told that the Superior wished him to come back.

This wonderful exemption, as several other incidents proved at that time, applied not only to inanimate but even more so to animate creatures.

On a certain occasion while Gerard was staying at the house of the Illario family, he was standing on the veranda, when he saw a rooster proudly strutting up the street. Flowers, birds or any other creatures of

God reminded the servant of God of his Creator. Thus **also** did the rooster in the street remind him of the omnipotence of God, and he joyfully called out to **the fowl:** "**Come here!** come here! little creature of God!" and behold! as if the rooster understood his words, he stretched out his wings, and beating the air, he came to Gerard, in two or three bounds and lay down as chickens do when they are resting. The brother fondled the fowl which remained with him a long time without fear.

It frequently happened that the birds responded to his call. They would fly towards him, and sit fearlessly **on his hand.**

A cry uttered by him was at times sufficient to control the most furious animals. Gerard was once standing with his former good master, Vitus Mennona at a window of the college when there came dashing along a frightened horse whose rider could no longer check **the** animal that was rushing on towards the precipice down which he would certainly have been hurled. "He **is lost!" every** one exclaimed. The servant of God, however, stretching forth his hands towards the rider cried out: "O holy Virgin, help!" He then turned to **the** bystanders and said: "He will fall, but will not be **hurt.**" And this really happened. The infuriated animal had scarcely heard the voice of the servant of God when it stopped short at the precipice, throwing the rider off, but without injury.

While Gerard was actively engaged in the building of the house, the Archbishop of Conza, of whom we spoke in the last chapter, arrived to pay the Fathers a **visit.** In order to furnish the latter with some aid for the benefit of their house, he made them a present of three hundred ducats himself and issued a circular in which he asked his priests and people to contribute something towards the building of the convent at Caposele, which had already proved so beneficial to all the people in his diocese. He desired the Rector to send some of his religious to collect in the various parishes. However much Gerard was needed at home, and however successfully the building was going on under his direction, the famous gatherer of alms of Iliceto naturally attracted the attention of Father Cajone, when the latter in obedience to the wish of the Archbishop was to send some one to collect the subscriptions to the building fund. The saintly brother had already found an opportunity to prove his fitness for so delicate a business.

Yet, it was Gerard's health that made the Superior waver in the resolution to burden him again with this office. It was in the middle of the summer; the heat was excessive; many places that he was obliged to visit were unhealthy during this season; and it was feared that the weak lay-brother, who never spared himself, would not be able to bear up against the exertion.

In his perplexity, Father Cajone finally sent for Gerard, asked him how he felt, and unfolded to him his half-formed plan. The servant of God told him with all sincerity how matters stood in regard to his health, but declared that he was ready to devote all his strength to the undertaking.

Then Father Cajone, as if he wished to express his satisfaction at Gerard's willingness, put his hand on the latter's head without uttering a word. Inwardly he, however, spoke as follows: "In the name of the Most Blessed Trinity I wish you to be well and to go on this collecting tour." Gerard at once smiled and looked at the Rector. "Why are you laughing?" said the Superior. "Your Reverence," answered Gerard, "is not saying anything, and yet you speak; you wish that I should be well and go out collecting. Well, I will be in good health and will undertake the office of collector. Yes, my Father, yes; I will be obedient; I will be well!"

This wonderful knowledge appeared to Father Cajone as a pledge of the divine will that Gerard should be appointed to collect the contributions; he therefore commanded him to do so.

The good brother at once prepared to set out, and began his journey in the latter part of July, 1755.

Senerchia was the first place he visited. Here the building of a church had just been begun. A neighboring forest was to furnish the necessary timber, and immense chestnut trees had already been cut down and were ready for transportation. The requisite means for shipping were wanting. The inhabitants had endeavored to move these large trees, but they were ponderous and immovable. When the servant of God had heard of their perplexity, he said: "Take courage; it is God's church, and God will take care that it is finished." He was conducted to the forest, fell on his knees, and asked God to help these people. He then asked for a rope, selected the largest of the trees, and tied the rope to it. "Well, now, creature of God," he exclaimed, "in the name of the Most Blessed Trinity, I command you to follow me." He then began to pull, and to the astonishment of those present he dragged the immense tree to the place where they were to build the church, and did this as easily as if he had been dragging after him a wisp of straw. He exhorted the people to imitate him, and to set to work, and, behold! the wonderful strength of the servant of God seemed to have passed into all of them; for with the greatest ease they dragged the trees to their destined places.

Besides this miracle, mention is made by biographers of the cure of a woman, at Senerchia; she was near death in consequence of childbirth. We are also informed of an ecstasy with which he was seized in the church before all the people, and which released him so far from physical laws that he remained suspended several feet above the earth, just as if he were held in the air by an invisible power.

"But," adds Father Tannoja in the narration of these facts, "this was not the only wonder; he performed many other works of charity, which for brevity's sake I shall pass over."

The inhabitants of Senerchia were always gratefully devoted to the servant of God. They acknowledged him to be a great saint, and after his death they invoked him as their patron in heaven.

A certain woman relates: "There is no one at Senerchia who has not chosen the venerable brother to be his special patron. We add one 'Pater' and one 'Ave' to our morning prayers to thank the Most Blessed Trinity for the gifts which we have received through the servant of God. Every body recommends himself to him in difficulties; and as our family has the happiness to possess a tooth of the servant of God, people are constantly calling upon us for this relic."

From Senerchia, Gerard's journey took him to Oliveto where he was to lodge at the house of Archpriest Don Angelo Salvatore. Gerard had written to him announcing his arrival. The letter concluded with these words: "Your Reverence desired to become acquainted with me, a sinful man. Well! the Lord has fulfilled your wish."

When Salvatore read these words he was very much astonished, for he had entertained the desire to know this wonderful man, but had never communicated this wish to any one.

Don Salvatore received Gerard with the greatest reverence and cordiality. As Gerard was embracing him he whispered into his ear: "Did you read the last words of my letter?" Salvatore feigned ignorance of what Gerard meant. "Yes," he said, "I noticed the words, 'Your very unworthy servant' and was astonished at your humility." "Not those words, not those words!" "I also read the words: 'Your brother in Jesus Christ.'" "Neither do I mean that expression." "But what then?" "Ah!" Gerard now answered with sincerity: "I meant the words: 'You have been wishing to see me. Now the Lord has sent me to you.'"

This first proof of miraculous power, which the happy archpriest witnessed was confirmed and increased by other and greater ones.

The hour for dinner had arrived and Gerard did not appear. Don Angelo therefore went to the room of his guest, but instead of entering it, he remained standing before the door, and only looked through the key-hole. He then saw the servant God in an exstasy, about three feet above the floor. He was deeply moved by this spectacle and retired in silence. After a little while he went to the brother's room again and found him in the same state. No one thought any more about dinner. Don Salvatore related what he had seen to the members of the household who were all deeply moved. When Gerard had returned to consciousness he was quite inflamed, and as if nothing had happened said to the priest: "Pray do not let me be a burden to your household."

The archpriest, in order to perpetuate the memory of this incident had a mark put into the wall of the room which the servant of God sanctified by his presence, testifying that Gerard was raised to such a height by an ecstasy.

The archpriest was convinced of Gerard's sanctity as the brother confessed to him daily while at Oliveto. The servant of God confessed daily in order to receive Holy Communion with greater purity. Salvatore therefore had opportunity to become acquainted with an angel of innocence, in his most profound humility and self-abasement; and through the confessions of this brother he was himself stimulated to the practice of virtue.

The first of the ecstasies noticed by Don Angelo had greatly excited the pious curiosity of all the inmates of the house. The life of the holy brother became the object of special study. Only in this manner was it possible to discover what Gerard endeavored so assiduously to conceal. At Don Salvatore's house people could speak in detail of the fasting of the servant of God for he allowed himself only two ounces of food; of his vigils, taking only two hours sleep, and of the bloody flagellations and other tortures with which he afflicted his body. Yet everything that curiosity could observe only served to edify them, and Gerard's presence at the house served as a mission and was equivalent to an impressive sermon.

The servant of God found opportunity for his zeal outside of the house and influenced men's minds in his own peculiar way.

Father Tannoja and others relate, by way of illustration, two occurrences which created a profound sensation. One day Gerard noticed a great crowd gathered around an unfortunate man who, acting like a maniac, inflicted blows right and left allowing no one to come near him. Approaching him, Gerard at once discovered the real cause of the frightful condition of the man. He went up to him and said without fear: "who are you?" The answer was: "I am the devil." "In the name of the Most Blessed Trinity, I command you to leave this creature," said the servant of God; and with the words: "Yes, I will go, but I shall pay you off for this," the demon ceased controlling the body of the unfortunate man.

On another occasion the brother saw standing before

the house a little child, the son of Philip Inelli, and seemed terrified at the sight of him. "O!" he cried out, "what a monster is growing up in Oliveto!" These words created some excitement, but no one understood their meaning. The future, however, proved but too plainly the reason of Gerard's cry of terror, for Michael Angelo, the child, had scarcely grown to boyhood when he seemed filled with a malignant spirit that made him appear rather as a devil then a human being. When only fifteen years of age he wished to outrage his own sister, and having been sharply reprimanded by his father, on this account he attempted to take his **father's** life. He seized a gun and was on the point of committing the awful crime, when his father, seeing himself threatened and in extreme danger, undertook to defend himself. Being quicker than his son, he killed the monster, a term which Gerard had applied to him **years before.**

Towards the end of July Gerard was in Auletta, where he remained only one day, but his stay was no **less** rich in miracles. While walking through **the** public square he met a man who was a stranger to him and said: "My friend, how can you live in peace? On a certain occasion you committed a certain grievous sin which you have not yet confessed. Go quickly and confess it, and be concerned about the grace of our Lord Jesus Christ." The poor man was very much confused by the reprimand of the brother whom he had never before seen. Casting himself at his feet, he promised to amend his life, and immediately went to a priest in order to make his **confession.** He changed his life and persevered in his good resolutions till his **death.**

The little daughter of Don Joseph Mari was subject **to convulsions.** Gerard happened to be at her father's house when she had a very severe attack. Yielding to the importunity of her parents he made the sign of the Cross over her, whereupon the spasms ceased and — what was more astonishing — never troubled her again.

At Auletta, in the house of very poor people, his attention was called to a girl who had been lame and deformed from her birth, and could not move. Besides this evil, the poor creature was in extreme poverty and want. When, however, Gerard had been asked to recommend her to the Lord, he said: "There is nothing the matter with her; she is well." Gerard called the girl to come to him, and behold! she arose from her bed, and hastened to the servant of God to kiss his hand.

This miracle again occasioned an excitement that was very annoying to the saintly brother. Those persons who could not restrain their astonishment cried out in the street: "Miracle! miracle!" and pointed him out as the "saint!" There was prospect of a great concourse of people. As soon as Gerard observed what was going to happen, he fled to the house of a priest, Don Raphael Abbondati, who afterwards related the occurrence. The people, however, who had discovered his retreat followed him and cried out: "The saint! where is the saint?"

As the tumult did not subside, Gerard began to think of flight. Through a door in the rear of the house he escaped unseen, and hurried through the street towards a neighboring place, called Vietri da Potenza, where he arrived quite tired, since he had to travel the whole way at the quickest pace.

In Vietri he was accosted by a young woman of bad character. Jokingly she asked the religious for a picture of the Madonna. He gave her one, but added: "Think of putting your affairs in order, and earnestly recommend yourself to the Blessed Virgin, for you have only a few days to live." And Gerard had spoken the truth. This woman who was apparently in good health, had scarcely reached her home when she was seized with a violent fever. Luckily, she immediately recalled the words of the brother, sent for a priest at once, made her confession, repented of her past wicked life, and breathed her last, three days after her meeting with the servant of God.

From Vietri the servant of God proceeded to San Gregorio, to the house of the Archpriest Robertazzi, to whom he was a stranger. Here he hoped to spend at least a few days in obscurity, and perhaps to merit the contempt and ridicule of others. "O my dear Lord Jesus," he exclaimed after being ushered to his room on the floor of which he prostrated himself, "I thank Thee with all my heart that Thou hast released me from so great a torture. Here no one knows me. Oh! I thank Thee!" But this release was not to last long. He whom God wishes to put on a candle-stick cannot hide himself; at least he cannot remain long in seclusion. As the rays of the sun pass through the smallest crevice, so were the supernatural powers of the servant of God evident on the slightest occasion, and thus he became popular against his will. This was the case at San Gregorio.

Even the loud sigh of joy to which he gave went in his little room and which he thought was unobserved, had been heard by his host who was led to the thought that he was giving shelter to a very pious, humble soul.

He was fully convinced of this the following day. While he was familiarly conversing with Brother Gerard a gentleman accidentally arrived and without interrupting the conversation, listened and afterwards took part in it. Suddenly Gerard turned the conversation intentionally to a case of moral theology by addressing the following words to Robertazzi: "Your

Reverence, if any one who inwardly has made the resolution to commit adultery, but moved by the grace of God does not carry the resolution into effect, is he obliged to mention in confession the resolution he made, although he did not commit the sin in act?" The archpriest was surprised at this question, since it did not seem to pertain to what had just been discussed; he however answered him in the manner in which theologians usually answer such a case. Soon after, the visitor prepared to go away. Before he took leave he seized the hand of the priest, drew him aside, and said to him in a tone of the greatest surprise: „You have a saint in your house. Every thing that this Brother Gerard proposed to you in the form of a question happened to me a short time ago. Blinded by the evil spirit, I had resolved to commit the crime, but did not accomplish it. I acknowledge this to my own shame, and to the honor of this holy man." Then it became clear to the archpriest why Gerard had put the strange question; and his respect for him greatly increased.

Till now the holy brother had been able to perform the arduous duties of his vocation in a very active manner. His health, though never strong, had not failed him. It was at the house of the Archpriest of San Gregorio that it began to decline. His hemorrhages afflicted him to an alarming extent; to this was added so violent a fever that he had to give up all thought of continuing his journey and a physician had to be summoned. The latter did not regard his condition as dangerous and was satisfied with merely bleeding him. Gerard, however, knew that this attack was nothing else than death's first knock at his door.

Several months before he had spoken of the near approach of his death. It was Santorelli with whom he confidentially spoke on this subject. "My dear Doctor," he said to him in a cheerful tone of voice, "you do not know perhaps that I shall die this year, and that consumption will carry me off." "How do you know, dear brother?" asked Santorelli. "I have asked our Lord for this grace," answered Gerard, "and He has promised to grant me the favor." "But why do you wish to die of consumption?" continued the doctor. "Because I shall then be able to die more forsaken," answered Gerard. "You see that although in our community the greatest charity is exercised towards the sick, yet I know if I die of so tedious a disease the brethren will take less care of me."

Even previous to this time he had foretold his approaching death to Brother Januarius Rendina, and had also remarked that he had asked the Lord for the grace to die of consumption, and to die quite forsaken. The time was really fast approaching when his prayer would be fully granted. After the declaration of the physician of San Gregorio that his condition was not serious Gerard did not hesitate to continue his journey. On Friday, the 22nd. of August, he journeyed to Buccino. On the evening of this day he again spat blood, and two physicians who had been hastily summoned again bled him.

The following day he returned to Oliveto where the air was less keen, and was more suited to his condition. In spite of the short distance of Oliveto from Buccino the brother became exceedingly tired particularly since he had lost so much blood by having been bled. In order not to be disobedient to the physicians who had required a change of air he had voluntarily undertaken the distressing walk.

In the evening he arrived at the house of his friend, Don Angelo Salvatore, where he immediately sat down and wrote a report to his Superior about the mishap that had befallen him.

The letter — a masterpiece of simplicity, peace and conformity to the will of God — is dated August 23rd., and reads as follows:

"I must inform your Reverence that at the time in which I was kneeling in the church of San Gregorio I was surprised by a violent hemorrhage. A physician who had been called examined me and after having asserted that I had neither fever nor headache, several times declared that the blood came rather from the throat than from the lungs, and assured me that the trouble was not serious. He then bled me, and this caused no inconvenience. Last evening I arrived at Buccino; there, just as I was going to bed, and was coughing as usual, the same thing happened to me as at San Gregorio. Two physicians who had been hastily called prescribed some remedies and again bled me. This time a vein of my foot was cut. The second hemorrhage was accompanied by no greater pain than the first. These physicians also declared that the blood did not come from the lungs; they nevertheless told me to return immediately to Oliveto. This I did the following morning, that is, to-day, partly to be able to breathe pure air, partly to consult Dr. Joseph Salvatore, who is an eminent physician. I did not find him on my arrival, but his brother, the archpriest, told me that he would be at home this evening.

"I beg your Reverence to tell me what I shall do. If you wish that I should come home at once, I will do so without delay. If you wish that I should continue on my collecting tour, I will do so most willingly. I seem to be in a better condition than when I was at Caposele; nor do I cough so much.

"To conclude: Send me a very emphatic command, and all will be well. It gives me pain to distress you, my dear Father; but do not be anxious about me. This trouble amounts to nothing. Recommend me to

God that He may always grant me the grace to fulfil His holy will and to deserve His favor."

This letter, which a special messenger delivered late in the evening in Caposele, gave considerable pain to Father Cajone. He immediately sent the bearer with a message to the servant of God, telling him to remain at Don Salvatore's house for the present, and earnestly recommended him to the charity of this pious family until he could be brought to Caposele. It was Saturday when the people usually came for the evening Benediction, so he requested their prayers for the sick brother. The Salvatore family were indeed happy to have this brother with them for a few days, he was so amiable and modest. Gerard however employed these days less for recreation than for the honor of God, and did not fail to manifest His gifts in a most extraordinary manner.

On account of some business, Gerard sent a messenger to Caposele to a certain Lorenzo di Masi. When the messenger arrived, the father of this man, named Stefano, was seized with a violent fever which made his son fear the worst. Lorenzo then wrote to the servant of God, begging him to recommend his sick father to the Blessed Virgin. And, behold! While Gerard was reading Lorenzo's letter at Oliveto, the sick man visibly gained his health at Caposele, though all hope of his recovery had been abandoned.

Brother Francis Fiore had been appointed to join the servant of God at Oliveto; he arrived there, but so shattered was he by fever, that on his entrance into Don Salvatore's house he could not stand, much less ascend to the upper story where Gerard was. He was obliged to lie down in a room on the first floor; and Don Joseph Salvatore, who was a physician immediately paid a visit to the sick new-comer went up to tell Gerard of his arrival and of his condition. The news of the illness of Brother Francis made the servant of God somewhat thoughtful; but he soon made up his mind. "You would do me a favor," he said, turning to Don Joseph, "if you would inform Brother Francis in my name that out of obedience he should drive away his fever, should arise and come to me, for our occupations have been assigned us and I have no time to nurse a sick man." Don Joseph smiled on receiving this message, (who would not be astonished at such a thing?) and objected to deliver it. "Do what I tell you," said Gerard. In order not to oppose him, Don Joseph went to the sick lay-brother and gave him Gerard's order which seemed altogether impracticable to him, but as soon as brother Francis had received the command he felt so well that he could without difficulty go up-stairs to Gerard. The latter received him with a reprimand. "How is this?" said he, "we have come here to gather alms, and you allow yourself to be seized with a fever! Well now! out of obedience, do not allow it to attack you." "I will obey," answered Fiore. "Doctor, will you please feel his pulse?" said Gerard, turning to Don Joseph. The latter did so and found that the high fever had entirely left him. He, as well as the archpriest, was astonished, but Gerard endeavored to moderate their surprise by saying: "Perhaps you wonder at this. You believe that this is a miracle; no, it is the effect of obedience."

At the same time the sister of Don Salvatore, Rosa by name, was lying sick of a fever. The servant of God visited her, and although he found her suffering greatly he said: "It is nothing, it is nothing." These were his usual words when he healed the sick. She also recovered, as the examination by her brother immediately proved.

After such experiences Don Salvatore could venture to recommend to the wonderful and saintly brother a sick person about whose cure he was very much concerned, since the poor man's condition was a very sad one and worthy of great compassion.

This sick man was Don Dominic Sassi, a priest, who was greatly troubled at first by scruples afterwards fell into deep melancholy till finally, overpowered, he led a wretched life. He usually remained locked up in his room where he howled and cried, and sometimes, without reason, broke out into imprecations, though his previous life had been blameless and pure.

His mind had thus been enveloped in darkness for seven years during which time the unfortunate man could neither celebrate Mass nor receive Holy Communion. His family did everything to restore his health. All medical help having been exhausted, recourse was had to supernatural means. The sick man was taken several times to visit the famous shrine of the Blessed Virgin where earnest prayers were offered up for him to the "Comforter of the Afflicted."

Application was then made to the saintly Father Cafaro, and the sufferer was sent to Caposele with the hope that this holy missionary might obtain for him a release from the dreadful malady. He too prayed over him for several days, without success, and Dominic was obliged to return to Oliveto, wretched as ever.

God reserved the cure of the good priest for His humble servant Gerard, and inspired the brothers Salvatore to intercede with him most earnestly in behalf of the sick man. "But what can I do?" modestly asked the saintly brother.

The latter, however, without the knowledge of the archpriest, immediately went to the sick man. The first impression which the servant of God made upon him was very unfavorable. Dominic, as usual, broke out into violent cries and imprecations. This produced very little effect upon the servant of God, he made the sign of the Cross upon the unruly man, and quieted him. There was a piano in the room. Gerard told him to sit down and play, and both sang the Litany of the Blessed Virgin. A great commotion was created in the house when the voice of the priest was heard; all rejoiced that he had again become cheerful, and Don Angelo Salvatore could not refrain from shedding tears when he was informed of what had happened.

Dominic was fully restored and could have gone to the altar the following morning, but Gerard desired him to abstain from the celebration of Mass for two days.

In the evening of the day on which the cure had taken place the saintly brother said to the members of the Salvatore family and to the other persons of the house who had taken an interest in the sick man: "The day after to-morrow, Don Dominic will say Mass; I should be glad if all of you would receive Holy Communion." This proposal was received with great joy. Every one was desirous of seeing the good priest at the altar celebrating Mass after the lapse of seven years, and to receive our Lord from the hand into which the servant of God had, as it were, again put Him.

The 28th. of August was the day appointed for this celebration. On this occasion Dominic's friends and relatives assembled to conduct him to the church. The saintly brother was to lead, and to be the first to receive Holy Communion at his hands.

All had come to the festival, but Gerard had not yet arrived. They waited for him for some time, but as he did not make his appearance, some one went to his room and rapped at the door. Receiving no answer from Gerard, they opened the door. Then they saw Gerard kneeling rapt in a most profound ecstasy; in one hand he held a crucifix, the other was resting on his breast as if in protestation; his countenance was pale; his eyes half open; his breathing scarcely noticeable. The archpriest, his brother and several others, who had hastened thither, observed him without daring to disturb the holy man in so sublime a seclusion, and silently withdrew. Some time afterwards, when they again looked after him, they saw him recovering from his ecstasy and ready to attend the solemnity. "I slept very little last night, and toward morning I was overcome by sleep," said he in excuse for his delay, to those who, he thought, had seen him in an ecstatic condition.

Meanwhile, a large concourse of people had gathered in the church, since all wished to attend the Mass of the priest who had been so wonderfully cured. Mass was celebrated by Dominic, assisted by Archpriest Salvatore, to the edification of all, and with such devotion and with so exact an observance of the rubrics that no one could have suspected that he had not said Mass for a long time. Brother Gerard and the entire Salvatore family went to Holy Communion.

From this day forward Don Dominic Sassi said Mass regularly. When the bell was rung for this purpose people would say: "Come, let us see the miracle of Brother Gerard." This cure was also made known in distant places, and created no little excitement.

In order to prevent the evil from returning, the servant of God transmitted to Archpriest Salvatore — and this was as marvelous as the cure itself — the power to see to it that Don Dominic would celebrate Mass. As often therefore as it afterwards occurred that the priest objected to celebrate the holy mysteries, the archpriest needed only to command him in the name of the servant of God, to drive away all hesitation.

Don Salvatore's house was, moreover, the scene of many other miraculous occurrences during Gerard's stay.

Thus – to mention only a few of them – the innkeeper's brother, Don Philip came to Gerard's room to consult him about something. He found him in prayer before the crucifix, his eyes fixed on heaven and his body raised considerably above the floor. Astonished, he quietly closed the door and withdrew. Scarcely had he done so when he heard Gerard's voice calling out to him. "Don Philip," said he to him as he entered, "I know why you have come. Do not be scrupulous about that affair; trust in Divine Providence." These words, which intimated a supernatural knowledge of men's thoughts, did not of course miss the effect that was intended.

John, Don Salvatore's little nephew, also occasioned a very wonderful incident. One day the boy received a pretty bird of which he was very fond. The servant of God took the bird, played with it, fondled it, and finally set it free, without reflecting that this might give great pain to the boy. The boy broke out into lamentations and cried aloud for his little favorite. In order to pacify him and to restore his happiness Gerard went to the window by which the little bird had escaped and exclaimed: "Little bird! do you hear? come back! come! the boy is crying and is angry because you are free. Come, my little bird!" And like an escaped prisoner whom contrition had induced to return the little bird came flying to the servant of God, who was thus enabled to restore it to the boy.

The respect entertained by the Salvatore family increased day by day. They revered him as a saint. Don Philip had conceived so high an idea of him that he did not hesitate to compare him to St. Vincent Ferrer. Don Joseph, the physician, called him "a model of every virtue, especially of obedience, and a miracle of penance."

The love, respect and confidence which the Archpriest Don Angelo cherished in his heart, had become so great that he was accustomed to praise the servant of God not only as an "angel in the flesh," and a man full of the love of God and of charity towards his neighbor, but he also endeavored to gain in a special manner his help and his holy affection. He proposed a compact according to which they should oblige themselves in life and after death to mutual support by prayer. The servant of God joyfully agreed to this.

The written compact is preserved as a testimony of Salvatore's esteem for Brother Gerard, and also of the love which the latter bore to this worthy priest and to his relatives. It reads as follows:

"In the name of the Most Blessed Trinity, of the Blessed Virgin Mary, and of the whole heavenly court.

Brother Gerard hereby binds himself:

1. To recommend me in all his prayers in an especial manner to the Lord, so that hereafter we may both enjoy the vision of God in paradise.

2. To come to my aid in all my spiritual and temporal necessities by vocal or interior prayers in whatever place he my be.

3. To obtain for me the grace to exercise my office in a holy manner, to sanctify all those who have been intrusted to me, to avoid every offence against the Lord, and to purify me from all my imperfections.

4. To pray to God above all for the spiritual and temporal welfare of the members of my household, as also for the general peace and quiet of Oliveto, which is my home.

5. To render me this spiritual aid as long as he lives, and after his entrance into eternity.

6. To procure for all my penitents perfect obedience.

I, Don Archangelo Salvatore, who am writing this, bind myself on my part to correspond faithfully to all the inspirations of the Lord; to pray and have prayers said to the divine Majesty for the above-mentioned Brother Gerard."

On the margin of this document is the following subscription: "I, Gerard Majella, of the Congregation of the Most Holy Redeemer, bind myself by what is contained in this document, by virtue of holy obedience, for the term of my natural life, and for the life after death."

In the mean time Gerard's health did not improve, in spite of the rest and care which he was taking. To the spitting of blood was added a violent fever which was regarded as an unmistakable forerunner of his approaching death.

As the saintly brother wished to die among his brethren, he took leave of the esteemed Salvatore family a week later, in order to return to Caposele.

However, before leaving for the latter place, he visited the members of another family to which he was much attached, the family of Angelo Pirofalo, in order to bid them farewell. He did this, and predicted his death. His last words to them were: "Look occasionally in the direction of Caposele. So long as you see a white cloth unfurled at a window, I shall still be alive. When you do not see it any more, you may know that I am dead."

Oliveto was several miles from our house at Caposele, so that with the naked eye one could not distinguish its windows, although the convent stood on an eminence. Nevertheless, what Gerard had said actually occurred.

The Pirofalo family perceived the mysterious sign which disappeared at Gerard's death and was never more seen.

Gerard left a keepsake to the family, which afterwards brought to mind most vividly his very great sanctity. When about to return home after having paid a visit to this house, he left his handkerchief on a chair on which he had been sitting. Pirofalo's daughter drew his attention to it, and wished to give it to him. "No matter," said the servant of God, "keep it; perhaps one day it may be useful to you." The prediction was verified. The girl was married, and was in danger of losing her life upon the birth of her first child. On finding no alleviation in her sufferings she invoked the intercession of all her patrons, one after the other; finally she remembered the relic of Gerard which she possessed. She had it brought to her immediately, and her confidence was rewarded, for no sooner had the handkerchief touched her than all pains ceased, and the child was happily born. With great respect and with special jealousy was this relic preserved ever afterwards, until later, her heirs cut it into very small pieces, in order to satisfy the wishes of the friends and admirers of the servant of God.

Brother Gerard left Oliveto on the 31. of August, on a Sunday morning, and arrived in Caposele at noon, "so feeble," says Father Tannoja, "that he no longer appeared to be a human being." "On first seeing him," says Father Cajone, "I had to do violence to myself not to shed tears." He had to retire immediately.

CHAPTER XXV.
THE CELL IN WHICH ONE DOES THE WILL OF GOD.

The cell of the sick man which we now enter to consider the saintly brother in his last labors and struggles can truly be called a school of Christian patience, of resignation and of charity. Gerard who was the joyful follower of Christ crucified, the enthusiastic friend of the will of God during his whole life, was faithful to the end.

His illness made rapid progress during the first few days. The hemorrhage became more and more violent, and constantly recurred. It was astonishing how he who was so emaciated could loose any more blood without dying. He was often bathed in perspiration, had one swoon after the other, while his heart beat violently; he was continually in an agony of death. He had a large crucifix and a picture of the Blessed Virgin put before his bed. At sight of these two sources of power and of consolation, he could not tire, nor become discouraged in his sufferings.

From the beginning it had been his passion to do the will of God. This passion was now more intense than the fever which was consuming him, and made sickness most desirable.

When the evil spirit appeared to him one day and made him an offer of health and of a longer life, Gerard cried out in a firm tone of voice: "Begone, miserable beast! I wish what God wills, and I command you to trouble me no longer."

The joy he experienced in fulfilling the will of God in every situation was so great that he wished to manifest it to everyone entering his cell. He therefore had a sheet of paper on which these words were written in large letters: "Here one does what God wills, as God wills, and as long as God wills," (Qui si sta facendo la volonta di Dio, come vuole Dio e per tutto quel tempo che piace a Dio,) fastened to the door of his cell.

On one occasion Father Cajone, who, like a father frequently visited him and sympathized with him in his sufferings, asked him whether in all things he conformed his will to the will of God. Gerard answered: "Yes, my Father; I represent to myself that this bed is for me the will of God, and that I am here nailed to the will of God. I am of opinion and hope that I and the will of God have already become one."

He expressed himself similarly to the brethren when they showed compassion for him. "I am fulfilling the will of God," he said, "I am satisfied to leave the world in order to unite myself to God." Several times he was heard to exclaim: "Oh my Redeemer, I have always desired, and I still desire to do Thy most holy will!"

The noblest attachment to the most adorable will of God is shown by the answer which the sufferer gave to Santorelli's questions whether he wished to live or die. "I wish neither to live nor to die," he said, "I wish only what God wishes. It is true it gives me pleasure to die, because I long for union with God; yet to die gives me displeasure, because I have not yet suffered anything for Jesus Christ."

How sincerely these last words were meant, how truly they came from his heart he proved more than once during his last sickness.

Once Father Rector found him in the agony of death; his face was deadly pale. Suddenly the eyes of the servant of God fell upon the crucifix; this seemed to revive him; his face became animated, his cheeks glowed. The Superior wished to know what interior emotion had effected such a change. Gerard sighed and answered with ardor: "O my Father, the desire to be united with God is so very great, it is so very great!"

How much he yearned for sufferings, and how he desired an opportunity of long suffering we find expressed by the prayer which he often said: "I suffer, O my God, because I do not suffer; to suffer, O my Jesus, to suffer and not to die!"

He received strength to devote himself to the will of the Lord and to a heroic desire for sufferings from his uninterrupted intercourse with Christ crucified.

Whenever it was possible, he arose from his bed and was placed in a chair before his crucifix, where he spent two or three hours in meditating on the sufferings of our divine Saviour. He then addressed his dear Lord in the sweetest language; and made declarations of loving heroism. Thus he often prayed: "I suffer very much, O my Jesus! but it is for Thee, Who for the love of me hast died on the Cross. To suffer is very little if one suffers for Thee." "O my Jesus," he exclaimed on another occasion, "Thou didst die for me, and I wish to die to please Thee!"

He found courage and perseverance in the wounds of the Saviour. All those who saw him left him edified and filled with veneration for such a sufferer.

Don Camillo Bozzio, who was one of the most zealous visitors of the sick man, said: "During his last very long and painful sickness I visited him nearly every day. I noticed that his mind wandered very often, and yet after he revived his soul was still in union with God.

"Never," he continues, "did I hear a complaint from his lips. I am convinced that his greatest desire was conformity with the Crucified. It also appears to me, that in consequence of the union of his soul with God, his body did not suffer in proportion to the violence of the fever that consumed him. One of his principles was: "that no prayer is more quickly heard than that which is addressed to God for sufferings. 'God,' he said, 'willingly grants all graces which serve for the salvation of our souls; but in order that these graces may be as highly valued as they deserve to be, He wishes us to pray for them for a long, a very long time. But this is not to be the case if we ask for sufferings. God gives us the grace at once, and perfectly.'"

Such knowledge as Bozzio had of the suffering servant of God was easily acquired by others; for scarcely was the news of the first illness of the saintly brother who was so much admired and loved spread among the people, when everyone wished to gain admission to his cell. "Not a day passed," says Tannoja, on which priests and prominent men of the vicinity did not come to pay him a visit. All were anxious to receive advice and instruction from him; the unalterable conformity which Gerard exhibited with God's will was truly marvelous.

Gerard, in spite of his weakness, counseled or exhorted each one as was necessary. To one he gave the assurance of his affection; to another he promised his prayers; and when he discovered a sinful heart, he punished it as it deserved.

This last happened to a young man who had visited him, no one knows for what special reason. He was a worthless fellow who had not only destroyed his own happiness but that of several families, to gratify his passions. As soon as Gerard saw him he addressed to him the following reproachful words: "How dare you come here, you, who are the cause of so many tears? And do you desire that Jesus Christ should bestow favors upon you?" It is not expressly stated that this sinner was converted; yet we can suppose that our Lord Who had inspired the servant of God with this reproach, also foresaw their effect.

Gerard not only devoted his loving attention to those who came to his sick-bed, but also to many others who could not approach him, and yet claimed and deserved his special care.

"Even in the feeble condition," says Father Tannoja, "when as it were, his soul was on the point of leaving his body, Gerard did not fail to console many of his friends by letter, and to exhort them to the practice of Christian virtues."

Of the letters which Gerard wrote on the threshold of eternity, only one is preserved. It is addressed to the niece of the Archpriest of Oliveto, Donna Isabella Salvatore, and is typical of the faithful, zealous and charitable heart of the servant of God. It reads thus:—

"Jesus! Mary! Blessed forever be the adorable Trinity, and our dearest and divine Mother Mary!

"My beloved Sister in Jesus Christ! God knows in what conditon I am, and yet He enables me to write to you with my own hand. From this you can see how much He loves you, and also how much more He will love you, if you do all that forms the subject of my prayers for you.

"My dear child, you cannot imagine how much I desire your eternal salvation. Our dear Lord wishes that I should cast a look of solicitude upon you.

"As I love all creatures that love God, so I love you. Yet you must know that if any creature were to love me outside of God, I would curse it in the name of our Lord; for our attachment must be entirely pure. We must love every creature only in God, and never outside of God.

"But now to what concerns us. I wish to say that if you do what I have so often asked you to do, then you will give God and myself the greatest pleasure.

"Everthing my child is worthless except the love of God. Therefore I beg of you to disengage yourself from all passions and worldly attachments, and to unite yourself most intimately to God. This, indeed, should be your principal endeavor: to belong entirely to God. Oh, how beautiful it is to belong entirely to God! Many happy souls have experienced this; you should also seek to experience it; and you will then be able to give me testimony of it. Of what benefit is it to love the world? Such a love produces only trials and bitterness.

"Well! nothing is wanting but that your heart should belong entirely to God. Henceforth, let nothing dwell therein except God. If, however, you should notice that a passion for whatever is not God wishes to penetrate your heart, say to yourself: my heart is given away, God has taken it for Himself, He lives therein; there is no room for another; therefore, begone all those things that are not God! The spouse must be jealous of the esteem of her divine bridegroom, and must therefore in all her actions guard against every shadow of vanity. She must watch over her heart that she may be justly called a temple of God, a palace of God. Yes, this is the name of a heart that has entirely consecrated itself to God.

"Pray for me; now I need your prayers more than ever. Your most unworthy servant and brother in Jesus Christ, Gerard Majella, of the Congregation of the Most Holy Redeemer."

Meanwhile, the illness of the servant of God was making notable progress; it was thought that the moment had come in which Holy Communion, which he had hitherto received daily, could be solemnly given him as viaticum. As the Superior, Father Cajone, was not at home, Father Buonamano, the minister of the house carried the Blessed Sacrament to the sick brother. The latter had raised himself in his bed and begged to be placed in a becoming posture to await the coming of our Lord with devotion and compunction. Holding the Sacred Host in his hand, Father Buonamano, turned to the servant of God and said: "Behold! here is our Lord, Who is your Father, and Who in a short time will be your judge. Make an act of faith, dear Brother, and openly profess it." In obedience to this invitation, Gerard said with great humility and confidence the following prayer: "O my God! Thou knowest that everything that I have done, everything that I have said, I have done and said to Thy honor. I die contented, because I trust that I have sought nothing else than Thy honor and Thy holy will."

How happy the soul that in so decisive a moment can pass such consoling judgment upon its past life!

After the servant of God had received Holy Communion he asked his brethren to leave the room, for he disired undisturbed intercourse with our Lord of which he did not wish to have witnesses.

On the following morning, the 6th. of September, his condition had become worse. To his other ailments, dysentery and constant perspiration had supervened, which very much exhausted him. He had taken no nourishment of any kind for several days. It was thought that it was time to administer Extreme Unction to him; but all at once things changed.

The same morning brought a note from his director, Father Fiocchi. In this note the Father gave him command to spit no more blood and to become well again. Gerard took the note, read it, and put it on his breast.

When Santorelli approached his bed he found Gerard quite recollected and holding a letter in his hand. He asked him: "What is that?" "A command," answered Gerard, "which Father Fiocchi has sent me; he wishes that I should no longer spit blood." "Very well," said the doctor, "and what do you think of doing?" The brother did not answer the question, but, turning to the infirmarian, said to him: "Brother, please take away this basin;" thereby indicating that he would obey. But when Santorelli perceived that the dysentery still continued, he said to the servant of God: "Of what benefit is it not to spit blood if the other complaint continues?" "I have received the command," said Gerard in his simplicity, "not to spit blood. As to the other ailment, I have received no order." Santorelli then went to Father Garzilli and begged him to convince the brother that the command which had been given was intended to bring about a complete cure. Father Garzilli hastened to the sick man. "Brother," said he, "is this the way in which you fulfil obedience? And have you no scruple on this account? Father Fiocchi wishes that you should not only stop spitting blood, but should rise from your bed in good health." "If this is the case," said Gerard, most humbly, "I will also obey in this point."

When Santorelli came again in the afternoon, Gerard received him with the words: "My dear Doctor, to-morrow I must leave my bed." The doctor smiled. "Yes, to-morrow I must rise," said Gerard. "If you wish to give me something to eat," he added, "I am ready to take it." Santorelli hesitated, but when he saw with what assurance the servant of God spoke, he resolved to give him permission. Just then a messenger arrived from Oliveto with a basket of peaches, sent by the Salvatore family; the infirmarian placed some of them on the table. While the doctor noticed them he said: "If you promise to do what Father Fiocchi commands, I will allow you to eat one of the peaches." "Yes," answered Gerard, "obedience must be rendered, God must be glorified." He then ate one of the peaches, then a second, and a third. The consequence was, he felt quite refreshed, and was changed in appearance. The spitting of blood troubled him no longer; the fever ceased, and there was every appearance that the sickness had vanished. Gerard arose, and would have been glad to resume all his usual occupations.

Not without anxiety did Santorelli come to the convent, the following day, to see his patient. On looking into the cell, he did not find him, and upon inquiring he was told that Gerard was walking in the garden supported by a cane. "This is a miracle of obedience!" the doctor exclaimed; and his astonishment was very great.

In fact, this recovery was nothing short of a miracle. Gerard had to acknowledge this himself, very well knowing, how near death he had been. "The day of the Nativity of the Blessed Virgin," he said confidentially to the doctor, "should have been the day of my death, and of my entrance into paradise. However, I begged our Lord to grant me the grace of dying on the following day, as on this festival so many pilgrims arrive here, and for this reason my death would have proved troublesome to the Community. But Father Fiocchi's command has delayed my death." And to one of his countrymen, Philip Galella, who was engaged at work at Caposele, he said the same in these words: "O my dear friend, I should have died on the feast of the Nativity of the Blessed Virgin, but the Lord has added a few more days to my life."

Instead, therefore, of reaching the much-desired end, he appeared in the refectory, to the great delight of the Community. All believed that he would recover.

A few days afterwards, a holy soul, that was very

dear to him, hastened to enter the celestial paradise. He did not begrudge her the privilege of going to God before him, for it was Sister Mary Cœlestis Costarosa, who died at Foggia on the 14th. (or 24th.) of September. Gerard had the consolation to see at the hour of her death the entrance of this holy soul into paradise; and was so affected by what he saw that he could not conceal his joy. A lay-brother noticing his special joy asked him the cause of it. "Do you know, my dear Brother," answered Gerard, "that to-day at Foggia the beautiful soul of Sister Mary Cœlestis entered heaven? She has gone to receive the reward of her love of Jesus Christ and of the Blessed Virgin." However much this ascension into heaven filled him with joy he still closed the narration of it with a deep sigh which was forced from him by his longing for this happiness. At first Gerard's assertion about Costarosa's death was not believed, but information was soon received from Foggia, confirming it.[1]

About this time another incident occurred which

---

[1] The sanctity of Mary Cœlestis Costarosa was proved in a marvelous way after her death. Among other things, her body remained for a long time incorrupt, so that whenever the Sisters opened the vault for the burial of a deceased nun, they were able to change Costarosa's garments Thirty years after her death, on the 1st. of January, 1785, when this was again to take place, the nun to whom this task had been assigned, found the garments adhering to her right foot, and tore it off with some violence. Thereby the skin was somewhat injured, and so much blood flowed from the wound that the hands of those who were dressing the corpse were entirely bespattered with it. Again, on the 18th. of October, 1788, on opening the coffin, the cloth which covered her face was quite saturated with the blood that had flowed from her mouth. Father Loyodice, C. SS. R. in his "Life of St. Alphonsus," published in Spain, mentions that he himself saw the body a hundred years after its burial, and that he found it incorrupt, with the exception of the feet and the point of the nose, which showed marks of decay.

shows the servant of God to have been endowed with the gift of seeing the death of distant friends.

Herbert Gaifi, a painter living at Oliveto, and a relative of the Salvatore family was obliged to start for the convent at Caposele, to do some work. Before he set out he called upon the archpriest and asked him whether he had any message for the convent. With the exception of cordial greetings he had nothing to confide to him. Early the following morning Gaifi arrived at the convent at Caposele and Gerard opened the door. He was on the point of delivering Salvatore's message when the brother interrupted him and said: "Our good archpriest is in deep sorrow; his father has just died." "It is not possible," said Gaifi, "for I left the old gentleman in good health. When I took leave of him last evening he was sitting with his family in quite a cheerful mood; it was he who cried to me in the loudest tone of voice not to forget kind regards for Coposele." Gerard however maintained his first assertion and added that the old gentlemen had suddenly died of apoplexy. "If this is the case," said Gaifi, "I will have to return to Oliveto, to pay him the last honors." "Yes, go," said the servant of God, "and tell the archpriest that he should rejoice, for his father has escaped purgatory. (Non ha neppure toccato il fuoco del purgatorio.)" On his return Gaifi found old Salvatore dead, and the whole house in mourning, but this mourning was considerably mitigated, nay, changed into joy, by the saintly brother's message.

Death, which had been put to flight by Gerard's obedience, had not however concluded peace, but only a truce, which was not of long duration. Scarcely had every one begun to rejoice that the holy brother had been restored to them when some symptoms created considerable anxiety. The improvement in Gerard's health was only the fruit of obedience; a further extension of the term of life lay not in God's plan. The servant of God expressly declared this when some of the brethren manifested their satisfaction at his being so well. "God did this," he said, "only for His own honor, and in order to show what obedience can do. I shall nevertheless die in a few days, and be in eternity."

The month of October had scarcely begun when his whole exterior began to change. His face was as pale as before; the fever also returned. The great emaciation of his body proved that the old disease had again taken hold.

His thirst for sufferings now reached its climax. The desire to become like his sorrowful Redeemer permeated his whole life, and impelled him to ask of God the grace of being thought worthy to feel the interior and exterior sufferings endured by our Most Holy Redeemer at the hour of death. This heroic petition was not refused: Gerard was now sunk in a sea of bitterness which often became so great that he could not refrain from giving expression to his sufferings.

One day Santorelli entered the cell, while Gerard was engaged in an interview with the Crucified, and heard the following words: "O Lord, help me in this purgatory! (Adjutami in questo purgatorio!)" The doctor asked him why he spoke thus. "My dear doctor," Gerard answered, "I have asked Jesus Christ to make it possible to satisfy for all my debts here below, by suffering for the love of Him; and He has heard my prayer. I am suffering purgatory; but the thought that thereby I am pleasing Jesus Christ consoles me." "I suffer true martyrdom," he said on another occasion; "I am in such a condition that I have scarcely strength to speak."

In the same way did he express himself to a priest, Don Gerard Gisone, who later became a Redemptorist, and Master of Novices and who had come to speak to the servant of God in regard to matters of conscience. On taking leave, he said to Gerard: "Pray for me, for I suffer much." "But I am also full of suffering," remarked the sick brother. "Oh! it must be; I must suffer!" As he did not give the reason, the priest made inquiries and said: "But what do you suffer?" "I am," answered Gerard, "constantly in the wounds of Jesus, and the wounds of Jesus are in me. I suffer incessantly all the torments and pains that Jesus Christ had to endure during His bitter Passion."

In the meantime he showed no impatience, no weariness, and when reference was made to his sufferings he made light of them.

In fact it seemed to him he was not suffering enough. "I suffer very much, it is true, O my Jesus!" he was heard to say, "but I suffer for Thee Who didst die for me on the Cross. Oh! it is not enough. Indeed it is not enough." He often exclaimed: "I wish to suffer, O Lord! I wish to suffer." This was one of his usual ejaculatory prayers, and so was the following: "Oh! how I do suffer, because I do not suffer!" and this ejaculation he pronounced with the fullest conviction, though he was sunk in a sea of sorrow. "Brother Gerard," the doctor used to say, when he made his morning visit to the sick man, "did you suffer during the night?" Gerard always answered with great confusion and embarrassment: "But I am not suffering anything!" or: "yes, I am suffering because I am not suffering."

The inconvenience and trouble which his sickness created for his brethren was painful to his sensitive nature.

Santorelli had ordered that a brother should watch with him at night for the purpose of regularly giving him a certain kind of medicine. When Gerard heard of this order, he said, with tears in his eyes: "O my dear Doctor, this gives me great pain!" and he repeated these words with every sign of dissatisfaction.

That the members of the Community offered up for him special prayers was very annoying to his humility. "I am only a useless creature," he said, "and do not deserve such charity."

The expenses incurred for medicines weighed very heavily on his heart. One day Santorelli found him very much depressed. Gerard begged him to state what would be the amount so far expended. For he thought of writing to his relatives, so that the expenses which the house had to bear might, in some measure, be defrayed. "Do not think of this," said Santorelli, and he endeavored to quiet him. Gerard, however, said: "My dear Doctor, of what use have I been to the Congregation, and why should the Congregation bear such a burden?" This delicacy on his part caused his heart to overflow with gratitude; for any service that was rendered him he was grateful with touching humility.

Astonishment was created by his indifference in regard to medicine, and his wonderful obedience to the doctor and to the brother infirmarian. Very much weakened as he was, he could not take the medicine himself; but whenever the brother wished to give him some of it he always took it without the slightest objection. Several times he felt great disgust, and became nauseated, but with great effort he suppressed it. "My God," he said, "help me, for I have no strength." A single word that referred to obedience would induce him to perform what was apparently impossible, and to act against his natural repugnances; and all this he did, well knowing the uselessness of all medicines.

As he was already very weak and found it difficult to speak, he frequently asked Stephen Sperduto to say aloud acts of resignation, of love and of contrition, which Gerard said after him in a low tone of voice. This brother one day asked him whether he had any fear or temptations. Gerard answered: "I have done everything for the love of God; I have never lost sight of Him. I have always endeavored to walk in His presence, and because I have desired nothing else than His holy will, I die in peace."

On his death-bed he was most edifying to all those who approached him. Those who visited him could imagine, according to the words of Santorelli, the physician, that he was in Paradise, so holy, so celestial were the words proceeding from the lips of the dying brother.

The favors bestowed on him by heaven and which had given his life so peculiar a character, did not now cease. He who entered his cell could at once notice that he was in the vicinity of a wonderful man. An exceedingly balmly fragrance filled the cell; and this could not be accounted for in a natural way.

Probably on the 14th. of October a very learned priest, Prosper d'Aquila, of San Andrea, came to pay him a visit, and Dr. Joseph Salvatore of Oliveto introduced him to Gerard. The priest was accompanied by a very simple, ignorant peasant boy, to whom he had promised that he would show him a saint. The boy came to the cell of the servant of God in all the excitement which such an expectation is apt to produce. In spite of his curiosity he did not dare to enter the room and remained behind the door so that Gerard could not see him. The latter, however, knew that he had hidden himself, and sent word that he should come in. Very much abashed and frightened the youth entered the room and viewed the "saint" with an embarrassed look. Mustering courage he allowed his eyes to wander about the cell and noticed a piano in the corner of the room, and was soon absorbed in regarding the instrument. He had never before seen one. Gerard, who saw everything invited him to sit down and play. The embarrassment of the young man was naturally very great; the by-standers laughed, and he excused himself, saying that he was ignorant of the art. But Gerard urged him. Then the young peasant, having looked at his patron, Don Prosper, who laughingly nodded to him that he should obey, finally sat down at the instrument, and placed his heavy fingers on the key-board so as accidentally to strike some of the keys. It was of course expected that the attempt would result in a harsh discord. Yet the very first touch of the keys woke the most charming chords, and the illiterate youth played a soft, soothing symphony, to which those present listened with emotion and amazement. When later on the player was asked how he felt when at the piano, he said that he did not himself know what was going on; for scarcely had he put his fingers on the keys when he felt a marvellous power which moved his fingers over the key-board. The instrument used in this miraculous manner was afterwards purchased by the Santorelli family, and preserved with such veneration that it was still in existence in 1843.

On the 15th. of October, the feast of his very dear patroness, St. Teresa, Gerard's strength was exhausted.

"O Doctor," he said to Santorelli in the morning, "recommend me to St. Teresa, and receive Holy Communion for me." He himself received it as Viaticum with such great devotion, fervor, joy, calmness and dignity, that according to the testimony of a witness, he was like an angel, a seraph who is absorbed in God. After Communion the servant of God asked for the corporal on which the sacred species had just been laid, having received it, he placed it on his breast, where it remained till his last breath, as a token of his love for the Most Blessed Sacrament.

In the evening, Gerard asked what time it was. He was told that it was six o'clock.[1] "Then we have six hours more," answered Gerard. Soon afterwards Santorelli arrived. He found him very much exhausted, but did not suspect that the end was as near as it actually was; on the contrary, the sick man appeared better than in the morning. When Gerard, contrary to his practice, had begged him to stay with him, he excused himself on the plea that some of his other patients needed him. He very much regretted this, when, upon his arrival next morning, he heard that the servant of God had already expired. He understood, but too late, that Gerard wished to detain him the previous evening to have him at his side when he was dying.

About seven o'clock in the evening a messenger arrived from Oliveto with a letter from the archpriest, begging the saintly brother to recommend to the Lord a matter, the happy issue of which was of the highest importance to him. He had undertaken to build a chapel of our Lady of Consolation, and the lime-kiln which he had prepared for this purpose had proved, as soon as fire was kindled in it, to be so weak that there was danger of a colapse. In this difficulty Salvator thought of the compact made with Gerard, and therefore sent the messenger to entreat him to recommend the unfortunate affair to Almighty God. The Father Minister who received the letter, read it in the cell of the sick man without informing the latter of its contents. But Gerard had received knowledge of the matter in an extraordinary manner, and said to the messenger: "Do not be afraid, the lime-kiln will not be

---

[1] Literally told, twenty-four o'clock; according to our calculations of time, 5.45 P. M.

injured." After the letter had been read to him he nodded assent, promising he would recite the desired prayer. He then had some dust from the grave of St. Teresa brought to him, and gave it to the messenger, telling him to scatter it over the kiln; he asserted again that the kiln would remain uninjured. The event showed that he had foretold the truth.

The nearer the hour of his dissolution approached, the more careful he was to prepare himself properly for the comming of his divine Redeemer. In spite of his baptismal innocence, which he had the great happiness to preserve untarnished, he considered himself before God as a very great debtor, who with many sighs would have to implore the mercies of the Lord. "O help me prepare myself," he said to the infirmarian; "I shall die to-night, and wish to say the Office for my soul."

A few hours before his death he sat up in bed and began to recite the Miserere, every word of which he pronounced with the most touching devotion. To each verse he added an act of contrition, and each time repeated the words: "Tibi soli peccavi et malum coram te feci; a peccato meo munda me! (To Thee only have I sinned, and have done evil before Thee; blot out my iniquity!)" While thus praying, he was filled with so much contrition that he shed tears.

It was eight o'clock when he was repeatedly heard to say: "O my God! where art Thou? let me see Thee!" Thereupon he turned to those present and begged them to help him to become united with God. Brother Carmine Santagniello noticing the disquiet that seemed to come over him, asked him whether he was disturbed in conscience. "Why talk to me about being disturbed?" answered the dying man. Soon after Carmine said to him: "My dear brother, we have always loved each other; I beg of you to remember me when you are with God." "Oh, how could I forget you?" answered Gerard.

The doctor, as has been said, did not think that death was very near; hence no one remained with him after night prayers except Brother Xavier d'Auria, who was always near him.

Between ten and eleven o'clock it appeared as if Gerard were going to faint. Having recovered, he became restless, timid, and cried out with animation: "Quick, Brother, drive away that miserable creature! what do you want here?" These may have been the last terrors of the devil that disturbed him in this manner.

Soon afterwards, his countenance brightened, and becoming more and more cheerful, he repeated these words: "See the Madonna! Oh, let us honor her, let us honor her!" And kneeling on his bed he became rapt in ecstasy. A few hours before, he seems to have been favored with an apparition of the Mother of God. His face then flushed, and, pointing with his hand to a corner of his cell, he said to the brother who was with him: "See, Brother, oh see, how many scapulars!" He had always been very zealous in spreading the devotion of the holy scapular; it is possible that on this account he was favored with a consoling vision of the Queen whose habit he had given to very many persons.

Like St. Teresa, Gerard had a great devotion to the Forty Martyrs, and some time before he said that they had promised to visit him at the hour of death, just as they had done to St. Teresa; there is no doubt that the saints kept their promise; though from the behavior of the servant of God on his death-bed, nothing of this could be noticed.

The last two hours of his life were spent in continual intercourse with Heaven. Gerard's eyes were steadfastly fixed on the crucifix, or on a picture of the Blessed Virgin, and his lips constantly uttered the most ardent ejaculations. "O my God," he said, "grant me pardon! pardon! I am sorry!" and again: "My God, I wish to die to please Thee; I wish to die in order to do Thy most holy will!" After his voice had entirely failed him, the movement of his lips showed that he was continuing his protestations and his acts of love.

About a half an hour before his death he asked for a little water. The brother who was watching by his bedside went away to procure some, but delayed in returning as the refectory was locked and he had first to obtain the key to unlock it. When he returned with the water he found the servant of God facing the wall, and believed that he had fallen asleep. A few minutes afterward he noticed that he came to himself. Gerard heaved a deep sigh. The brother at once saw that he was dying, and ran out of the room to awake the Father Minister. The latter hastened to come, but arrived just in time to see Gerard breathing his last; and while he was giving him the final absolution, the holy soul winged its flight to its Creator.

Gerard had prayed to God to die forsaken. His wish was gratified as far as this is possible in a place where holy charity watches to make such a thing impossible.

His death occured at 1.15 A.M. the 16th. of October. Gerard was thirty years old, and had spent six years in the religious life.

Immediately after his death, Gerard appeared to a pious person who had been very much devoted to him. He was clothed in the habit of his order; shortly after he appeared a second time in still richer garments and radiant with glory. He encouraged her to suffer cheerfully for Jesus Christ, and said: "Oh how generously God rewards the slight sufferings which we endure on earth for His sake!"

Immediately after his death he also appeared to Father Peter Paul Petrella,[1] with whom he had been living at Iliceto, and permitted him to see a ray of the glory which he was enjoying in heaven.

When Father Buonamano had assured himself of the death of the brother, he awakened the members of the Community and desired that all should immediately perform an act of penance in thanksgiving to God and the Blessed Virgin for all the favors bestowed upon the deceased. After this thanksgiving they all repaired to the corpse of the holy brother, whom they intended to bleed. Father Buonamano took Gerard's arm, and said: "Brother Gerard, you have always been very obedient. Now I command you in the name of the Most Blessed Trinity and of the Blessed Virgin Mary not to neglect to give us a proof of your sanctity." After a vein had been cut, the blood flowed as abundantly as from a living person. It was caught up in basins, and afterwards some handkerchiefs were saturated with it, and distributed among the friends and admirers of the servant of God.

The fragrance which had hitherto filled Gerard's cell did not pass away with his death; it now issued from his body in a remarkable manner, and could be perceived in the whole house.

The following morning Brother Carmine Santagniello wished to give the usual sign by tolling the bell. Strange to say, he began to ring it as merrily as was customary on festivals; and when a Father noticing his mistake, hastened to draw his attention to what he was doing, the brother excused himself by saying that he knew not how it happened, but that he yielded to an inward impulse when he began to ring the bell in a festive manner, instead of ringing it as is done on the death of

---

[1] He died a holy death in 1771, aged 45 years.

a brother. For the inhabitants of Caposele, this ringing, the meaning of which they surmised, was the sign for a general move towards the convent.

There, at an early hour, the body of the servant of God had been placed in the church, where crowds of people came to view and venerate it.

"The coffin," says Father Tannoja, "was surrounded by the rich and the poor, by seculars and ecclesiastics. One mentioned a prophecy of the servant of God which had been wonderfully verified; another told how Gerard had penetrated into the secrets of his heart; another spoke of the way in which the saintly brother had led him to Jesus Christ, and had put his soul into a better state. The poor especially, who had lost in him a true father, filled the house and the church with their lamentations. Not satisfied with these demonstrations of veneration and love, and impelled by their devotion, the people began to cut his religious habit into pieces and to cut off his hair; and lest the body might be entirely stripped of its garments, guards had to be stationed near the coffin, in order to check the impetuosity of the people."

On the morning of the 16th. of October the Office of the Dead was chanted in presence of the clergy and people of Caposele. Father Garzilli sang the Mass and Father Buonamano delivered a discourse which moved all to tears. The corpse was exposed in the church and during this time visitors were innumerable, for the news of the death of the wonderful lay-brother had rapidly spread all over the country, and clients, friends, and admirers of Gerard came from far and near to pay him their last respects. Such a crowd of people had not been seen at Caposele for a long time. With unspeakable joy and devotion these good people, with their handkerchiefs dried the perspiration which constantly covered the face of the deceased in a miraculous manner. Every one wished to obtain some souvenir.

Among others, there also came to the bier a pious woman named Rose Sturchio, who had always highly esteemed the servant of God, and who for her own benefit had frequently asked his advice in many difficulties. Bathed in tears, she was kneeling near the body, and in her heart begged the glorified brother to procure for her some relic by which she might remember him. While she was thus praying there suddenly rolled to her feet a tooth which had fallen from the mouth of the servant of God. The possession of so marvelous a gift no one seemed inclined to dispute; she took the tooth and preserved it as a treasure. After her death this relic came into the possession of her daughter, who wore it around her neck constantly. It was afterwards divided among several of Gerard's friends.

It was quite natural that the people should be anxious to preserve the portrait of the holy brother for posterity. In the absence of a competent painter, there was fortunately a person who was engaged in the work of casting small statues, and who understood how to take wax impressions of corpses. Two of these casts of Gerard's face were taken, one of which was for the house; the other was destined for the Salvatore family. Only afterwards it was thought expedient to have Gerard's portrait painted, and one of the casts was given to an artist. Yet in spite of every effort, the painter did not succeed in giving an approximately true likeness of Gerard: there was not question of similarity. Then Father Cajone again had recourse to the frequently tested mysterious obedience of the blessed brother, the obedience on which he believed he might depend, so that even now Gerard would pay special regard to his command. "My dear Brother Gerard," he prayed, "you see that your portrait is a failure. See that it is a success." After the painter had again done the work the portrait gave general satisfaction. It represents the servant of God in the attitude in which he was seen at the house of the archpriest at Oliveto when he fell into an ecstasy; he is holding a crucifix in one hand, while the other is on his breast, as if in protestation.

In external appearance, Gerard was quite tall in stature and of very slight build. Sickness and austerity of life had so reduced him, that he resembled a living skeleton. His face was long and pale, having color only when in ecstasy, and then often glowing; his forehead was high and broad, his head remarkably large, so that it became a subject of merriment to his companions in his youth. His temperament was animated and choleric; mildness and tranquility, so characteristic of him, were the fruits of his virtue. The physical strength and endurance amid all his labors exhibited by Gerard, especially in the convent, were in open contradiction to the weakness and delicacy of his body, and ultimately appeared to be the effects of a higher gift. Over his whole exterior was diffused that indescribable higher splendor which lends to the saints, in spite of the abjectness of their bodily appearance, that amiability, dignity and majesty, which so powerfully attract some, while they fill others with veneration and awe.

Friday the 17th. of October, thirty hours after his death, the funeral services took place. Previous to the burial of the body, Father Buonamano again wished to extract blood from it, and gave the same order that he had given before. The result was the same; the blood was still fresh and red. His lips were flexible, and the wonderful perspiration on his forehead, which people had continually wiped off with handkerchiefs, did not cease.

A special place was assigned for the reception of his remains, and his grave was prepared just in front of the door of the sacristy.

Justly presuming that the deceased would one day receive the honors of the Church, Father Buonamano on the very day of the funeral, had a verbal process drawn up by Joseph Fungaroli, a notary, in regard to the miracles which had already been wrought by the servant of God since his death. Besides the Fathers and ten lay-brothers, who at that time formed the Community at Caposele, ten inhabitants of the place submitted their testimony upon solemn oath, and this the notary embodied in the act which is found in the process of beatification.

CHAPTER XXVI.
Honors Shown To Gerard After Death.

The high opinion which was entertained of the sanctity of the servant of God during his mortal life, as well as the confidence reposed in the power of his intercession with God in the greatest difficulties, did not suffer any diminution after his death. On the contrary, his beautiful end, corresponding perfectly to his whole life, and the splendor of the first miracles at his bier quickened the confidence that had heretofore been reposed in him. No one doubted that the poor lay-brother, whose mortal remains were resting near the door of the "Mater Domini," was now their friend and intercessor before the throne of God.

In the Congregation to which he belonged he was unanimously praised. They looked upon him as a glorified saint in heaven, whom they might invoke with confidence.

The holy Founder St. Alphonsus gave his subjects a brilliant example of reverence. He regarded the sainted brother as a second Pasqual Baylon. He was filled with respect for his son, and was so convinced of the solidity of his virtue that he himself wished to begin the work of transmitting to posterity the memory of the saintly brother. He gathered material for the publication of the life of the holy religious, but a multiplicity of duties, sickness and various other things prevented him from executing his plan. Among the unpublished letters of the holy Doctor, one is preserved in which he informs a religious that he forwarded to him some relics of Brother Gerard. Even on his death-bed, St. Alphonsus manifested his veneration towards the holy brother, for when his picture was shown him, he seized it with an air of confidence, pressed it respectfully to his bosom, kissed it, and recommended himself to the intercession of the servant of God. The thought of having the process of his beatification introduced was uppermost in his mind; but various cares and obstacles prevented him from beginning the work.

His spiritual sons most zealously imitated their holy Founder in this respect, and took great interest in spreading the veneration of the servant of God. They considered Gerard a model of virtue and regularity; as a bright example, especially for the younger brothers who had just entered upon their career in the religious life.

Pictures of the servant of God were distributed during our missions, and the people were encouraged to invoke his intercession.

Forty years after his death, the room in which Gerard died was converted into a chapel, in honor of St. Stanislaus, and near the entrance was placed the following inscription, indicating its former as well as its present use:

CUBICULUM
QUOD EXIMIA INNOCENTIA AC PIETATE VIR
FRATER GERARDUS MAJELLA, MURANUS,
CONGREGATIONIS SANCTISSIMI REDEMPTORIS,
PRÆSENTIA QUONDAM USUQUE COHONESTANS,
SANCTORUM TANDEM MORTE DECORAVIT;
ADOLESCENTULORUM INNOCENTISSIMO,
ANGELICARUM PULCHRITUDINE ET ODORE VIRTUTUM
PULCHERRIMI INSTAR FLORIS INTER CŒLITES NITENTI,
BEATO STANISLAO KOSTKA,
IN SACELLI FORMAM REDACTUM,
PATRES EJUSDEM CONGREGATIONIS DOMUM HANC INCOLENTES
TERTIO IDUS JULII A. D. MDCCXCVI. [1]

---

[1] See next page.

Not less great was the honor paid to the saintly brother by persons not belonging to the Congregation. During his life-time they had regarded him with enthusiasm, honored him as a messenger from heaven; after death they venerated him as a powerful intercessor before the throne of God.

The convents of Muro, Foggia, Ripacandida and others, in which the servant of God specially labored, honored and invoked the deceased as their patron in heaven, and their invocations frequently met with marvellous success.

Among the clergy and laity of the diocese in which Gerard had become known, the veneration towards him was general; they called upon him in all their trials and difficulties.

"Real emulation has arisen between Gerard and his friends," Don Angelo Salvatore wrote, some time after the death of the servant of God, "they honor and invoke Gerard as a saint of heaven; while Gerard distributes without intermission the most marvellous gifts. Who could enumerate all the miracles which occur almost daily in our archdiocese, and in the neighborhood where his intercession is invoked."

In fact, the servant of God continued working miracles after his death, and proved himself a faithful friend to

THIS IS THE CELL
WHICH BROTHER GERARD MAJELLA OF MURO,
RELIGIOUS OF THE CONGREGATION OF THE MOST HOLY REDEEMER,
A MODEL OF INNOCENCE AND OF PIETY,
CONSECRATED BY HIS PRESENCE
AND MADE ILLUSTRIOUS BY A HOLY DEATH.
HIS BRETHREN CHANGED IT INTO A **CHAPEL**
AND DEDICATED IT ON THE **13TH. OF JULY,** 1796,
TO THE **FLOWER** OF YOUTH,
TO HIM WHOM THE RENOWN & PERFUME OF HIS ANGELIC VIRTUES
CAUSE TO BLOOM IN HEAVEN AS **A** MAGNIFICENT LILY,
SAINT STANISLAUS KOSTKA.

all those who called upon him with confidence; so that the miracles, and the requests granted, are exceedingly numerous.

A biography of the holy brother, published in 1875, mentions seventy of these wonderful events. These are the most important and the most stricking, while a countless number have been entirely forgotten.

"I cannot help," thus complains Father Tannoja, "charging our people with neglect, since they took so little interest in recording the most important miracles wrought by Gerard. The narration of them would fill volumes."

We will mention a few of the more recent miracles by which God proved to all men the sanctity of His servant; especially those in which he manifested his brotherly love and most tender solicitude in regard to the members of his Congregation, even after death.

His last Superior, Father Cajone, was one day assailed by great melancholy. In this state he remembered Brother Gerard, and called upon him for help. The holy brother, who during life was always obedient to the slightest sign, did not seem to have lost this good quality after death. At the same moment he appeared to the Rector, radiant with glory, and said to him in a most cheerful manner: "Courage! it is all over!" (Statevi allegro, che tutto è finito.) And as he had said, so it was. Joy again took possession of Father Cajone's soul, and all his sadness vanished.

He rendered similar service to another of his brethren at Caposele. It was Brother Nicholas Sapio, who was afflicted with troubles of conscience. He manifested his condition to the Rector of the house, who encouraged him to have recourse to Brother Gerard, and to visit his grave, there to thank God for the graces which He bestowed upon this holy man. Nicholas did this, and "scarcely," so he testified, "had

I uttered my prayer, when I found myself free from temptation, and more cheerful than before."

It was Gerard's wonderful power that made Father Tannoja his biographer. The latter writes as follows, in the preface of his "Life of the Servant of God:" "If I now publish this little work, it is Gerard himself, who, by a miracle wrought in me, has induced me to do so. I happened to be at "San Angelo dei Lombardi," when on the 26th. of August, 1786, I was attacked by a dangerous illness. When I returned to the house at Caposele, my disease increased rather than diminished. On the evening of the 9th. of September, one of the brethrern, Father Januarius Orlando, seeing me in a very deplorable state, said to me: 'Promise Brother Gerard to write his life, and he will obtain for you a restoration of your health.' As I had not the faith that was needed, I did not follow Father Orlando's advice. On the morning of the 10th., however, I found myself in extreme danger. I was seized with convulsions, and the chill of death came upon me. I then remembered the counsel that had been given me, and as all other help seemed to be fruitless, I turned to the blessed brother with confidence and exclaimed: 'O Gerard, help me!' I experienced the efficacy of his intercession immediately, for at the same moment I was freed from all sufferings. I acknowledged the favor, and in gratitude promised to write the life of the servant of God. And if I am late in fulfilling it, I hope that in his goodness he will pardon me."

Of the miracles which the privileged brother performed from his place in heaven, in favor of his other friends and admirers, we mention those by which he proved his affection for his friend Canon Camillo Bozzio.

The latter had a nephew named de Rogatis, who was suffering from a lingering fever, accompanied by dysentary. One morning he was found in his bed apparently dead, and his uncle, who himself examined him, and vainly searched for a sign of life, was convinced that his nephew was dead. By the members of the family, Gerard's intercession was highly esteemed. They were in possession of a tooth that had belonged to the servant of God, and this the disconsolate mother placed upon the deceased and said: "O my dear Gerard! do not forsake me in my misery; restore my son's life!" and lo! after this prayer, the young man opened his eyes and arose from his bed perfectly well.

In no less charitable a manner did the servant of God come to the assistance of another of Bozzio's nephews, Dominic Anthony Bozzio. He had been seized with a mortal illness during the month of July, 1789. The physicians declared that they were unable to save the life of the sick man. This created great consternation in the family, for Anthony was the father of many children. The uncle, however, remarked to the sick man that Gerard had promised to be a special intercessor for them in heaven. "If that is the case," said the sick man, "let us remind him of his promise." In union with his family he then addressed a few prayers to Gerard, asking his assistance. On the seventh day, when the crisis was feared, the sufferer fell into a very quiet slumber. While asleep, in a dream, he saw the holy brother who seated himself at his bedside and said: "We have gained everything" (Abbiamo fatto tutto). When the sick man awoke he called the members of his family and related to them what he had seen. It was not a freak of his imagination; the fever had really left him.

That Gerard continued to remain consoler, helper and monitor, of the inhabitants of Caposele is proved by a long series of miraculous events of which we will mention only a few.

The spiritual condition of a certain young man of

Caposele was very sad. A charitable friend much interested in him, recommended him to the prayers of Father Petrella. The latter said: "Very well; I will command Brother Gerard to find him, and to convert him." The following night, Gerard appeared to the sinner and by an earnest exhortation induced him to repent and to go to confession. Very early on the following morning he came to the church where he carried out his resolution, and made known the cause of his conversion.

In 1785, the notary, John Baptist Fungaroli of Caposele, was also miraculously helped by Gerard. Being already in the agony of death, he sent for Father Nicholas Mansione to assist him. The latter came at once, and while he was with the sick man, Pascal Stila called to pay him a visit. When Stila remarked the condition in which Fungaroli was, he cried out: "O Brother Gerard, I hear of miracles performed by you; if you do not cure my friend, I will not believe what others say of you." He then placed the picture of the servant of God on Fungaroli's breast, and at the same moment, so Father Mansione testifies — the groans of the sick man ceased, the fever disappeared, and he was well.

Donna Michele Giordano of Corbara came to Caposele to enjoy its pure country air. While there she heard so many things about the saintly lay-brother that she conceived a great devotion towards him, and began to invoke his help in many necessities. One day while she was leaving the house to go to church, Gerard stood before her and said: "Prepare yourself for great trials but do not become discouraged; God will sustain you." The woman was surprised at the language of the unknown lay-brother, and when she met Father d'Agostino, who was then Rector, at Caposele, she related the incident to him. "Which of our lay-brothers was it?" he asked. "None of this house," was the answer. The Rector, who suspected a mystery, asked her to come into the parlor, where Gerard's portrait was hanging. As soon as Donna Giordano had cast a glance at it she cried out: "Ah! that is the one who met me!" Soon afterwards, heavy trials afflicted her, just as the servant of God had foretold.

The miraculous help of the servant of God was also bestowed upon all who invoked him with confidence, at the place of his death as well as elsewhere. Ignatius Cozza, a canon of the cathedral of Trevico, had been suffering from a bodily injury several years. It caused him great pain and was pronounced incurable. One day — it was the 5th. of August, 1766 — as he was in the greatest distress, he had recourse to Gerard with whom he had been very familiar during life, and while applying a piece of one of the saintly brother's garments to the wound he prayed as follows: "O my dear Brother Gerard, if it be for the greater honor of God and for the benefit of my soul, free me, I beg you, from these sufferings." The conclusion of the prayer was also the end of his sufferings. The Canon was no longer afflicted with the ailment, and in spite of the great exertions to which he subjected himself by preaching he no longer felt any inconvenience.

A Benedictine nun in a convent in Sicily had a diseased arm which was regarded as incurable. A Father of the Congregation gave her a picture of the servant of God, and told her that she should recommend herself to him with lively faith. She did so, and, behold! when the surgeon came to dress the wound, he did not even find the mark nor a trace of where it had been.

In April, 1776, a lady of Benevento, named Antonia del Vallo, was suffering great pain, and her life despaired of. One of her relatives, a priest, seeing the sick woman in so precarious a state, put a few relics of the servant of God under her pillow, and at the same time invoked his aid. During the night of the 23rd., Gerard appeared to her, signed her with the sign of the Cross, and said: "You are healed." Then he disappeared. When her relative again asked her how she felt, she answered: "I have been well ever since that unknown religious was with me and signed my forehead with the sign of the Cross." When she was shown the various pictures of saints which had been placed under her pillow she recognized in none of them the countenance of him whom she had seen during that night. But when a picture of our servant of God was shown her, she immediately cried out: "This one, yes, this one it was who healed me."

Another woman, Leonarda Miocore, had been troubled with a membrane growing over her left eye, which prevented her from seeing. As the other eye was half covered with a similar membrane, the unfortunate woman was nearly blind. In her misery she had recourse to Gerard, of whose miracles she had heard, and the faith and confidence with which she did this where worthy of consideration and deserved a miraculous cure. In a short time she was entirely well. When she afterwards met the oculist, she said in a joyous tone of voice: "You could not cure me; I applied to another, and he has undertaken to cure me." "You are joking," said the doctor. But she showed him her eyes, and said: "See whether I am not cured," and triumphantly exhibiting a picture of the saintly brother, which she usually wore around her neck, she added: "This was the doctor!" The examination which the astonished doctor now made proved that both eyes were perfectly well, and in a better condition than at any previous time.

"One day," thus relates Brother Anthony de Cosimo, a great admirer of the servant of God, "I was in the

Commune of Spechia-Gallone, at the house of the Marchioness Granafè, who asked me to relate something of the life of the saintly Brother Gerard. I tried to comply with her request; I desired particularly to extol his obedience and simplicity, and therefore I described how, taking the words of the Superior in their literal sense, he had crept into the oven. 'Oh!' cried out the Marchioness, 'that is enough for me: I see that he was a very stupid saint.' 'God forbid that you should ever be forced to have recourse to this stupid saint!' was my reply. But how wonderful is the Lord in His saints! Two months afterwards I received a letter from this lady which informed me that she had been attacked with a dangerous illness, and had been given up by the doctors. She then addressed herself to Gerard, and said: 'If you are really a saint, let me be convinced of it. I will then contribute my share to your beatification.' She had scarcely said the words when she found herself free from all pain. Three days after she wrote to me. In the letter was inclosed a present of a hundred ducats to defray part of the process of the beatification. She now in a very contrite manner asked Gerard's forgiveness for having him called a stupid saint."

It is noteworthy how often the servant of God helped in a marvelous way not only mothers who at the birth of their children were exposed to the danger of death, but also those children whose vital spark came near being extinguished, from weakness, before receiving Baptism. Among the few miracles enumerated by Father Tannoja, we find as many as nine cases of the kind, and many an infant at Baptism received Gerard's name in gratitude for such preservation.

Caterina di Viggiano was attacked by a dangerous fever when she was about to give birth to her child. The malady had already continued for two weeks, and her death was momentarily expected. At this critical time, her friends gave her a picture of the **servant of God.** The sick woman pressed it to her lips and said in **a broken voice:** "Not for myself do I wish the favor, but for my child." After this prayer, Caterina, to the astonishment of all, became well, and the girl that was born was called Gerarda, out of gratitude to the holy brother.

The glorified brother obtained a still greater favor for the wife of Thomas Ronco. She had given premature birth to a child that died immediately after Baptism. The distressed parents had recourse to the servant of God, placed a relic upon the cold body of the little child, and behold! on examination it was found to be alive **and quite healthy.**

Among the many miracles wrought by the servant of God after his death we shall only mention four which deserve special attention since they **have been subjected** to ecclesiastical investigation and have been approved. The first was wrought in favor of Joseph Santorelli, the grandson of a great friend of the servant of God, Nicolas Santorelli, during the octave of the Immaculate Conception, in 1823 or 1824. Joseph Santorelli **was seized with a serious** attack of typhoid, and everyone doubted his recovery. Death seemed inevitable. His relatives thought it necessary to make preparations for the funeral. He received Extreme Unction and the priest stood at his bed-side to say the prayers for the dying. In this hopeless condition they placed a picture of Blessed Gerard in the **cap** of the dying man, and his brother hastened to the church of "Mater Domini" to implore the assistance of the servant of God. **Mass was said** for him in honor of Blessed Alphonsus, that he might command Gerard to procure the grace of recovery for the grandson of his friend. Meanwhile there **was** no change in the condition of the dying man; all day he struggled with death, and no one doubted but that death would gain the victory. But, in the evening, to the great astonishment of his relatives, the sick man sat up in his bed and breaking forth into a torrent of tears, kissed the picture of the servant of God, put it into his mouth, and swallowed it. When asked why he did this, he answered: "I was completely oppressed by a fatal sleep which lasted all day, during which time I constantly saw a lay-brother from 'Mater Domini.' As he drew nearer to me, I repeated in a loud voice: 'Brother, hear me!' (Those who stood around him had really heard these words several times from the dying man). The brother had a crutch in his hand, and his hat under his arm. When the clock was on the stroke of one, he granted my wish and came to my bed. 'Rejoice' said he, 'you have received the grace.' At that moment I noticed my deceased grandfather at his side. Overcome by emotion I wished to apply to my grandfather but he said: 'Apply to him!' 'Who is he?' I asked. 'It is brother Gerard,' answered my grandfather. Brother Gerard made the sign of the Cross on my forehead, whereupon both disappeared." This narration of the sick man surprised the by-standers so much the more, as his strength now revived and he seemed to have escaped the danger of death. When his physician, Don Andrea Cleffi, was informed of what had happened, he came and told the patient to make an attempt to rise from his bed. The sick man, who previously could hardly be lifted by four men, was now able to rise without any assistance, and without the slightest difficulty. To convince them of the miraculous recovery of his health, he ate macaroni, omelet and cheese, like a person in health, while his relatives were amazed and rejoicing.

On September 15th., 1849, Teresa Deheneffe, of the archdiocese of Malines, in Belgium, received a deep wound from the thrust of a dagger, in the hand of a **wicked person.** Teresa did not wish to betray her assailent, and therefore said nothing about her wound to which she applied linen bandages, hoping thereby to heal it without the assistance of a physician. However, she was deceived. Slowly, and in consequence proving the more dangerous, a fistula developed in her wound, and after two years and ten months, when the sufferer was obliged to make her condition known, it was declared that an operation was necessary. This verdict **was the source** of much distress to Teresa; in her necessity she sought refuge from the servant of God who, however, did not seem to heed her prayer at first. On the 18th. of July 1852, the **painful** operation was performed, but it soon proved to be unsuccessful, and the physician was obliged to declare that the wound had every symptom of being incurable. Her confessor now ordered Teresa, who was very much surprised at **this,** again to have recourse to the servant of God. She obeyed, and on the 27th. of July began a second Novena in his honor, at the beginning and end of which she had the Holy Sacrifice offered. This time it was not without the desired effect. During the night of the 3rd. to the 4th. of August, the poultices and bandages fell from the wound of themselves. Teresa, on awakening in the morning and examining the wound, found it not only entirely closed but that not the least scar remained. Beside herself with joy, Teresa hastened to the surgeon and wished to have a testimonial of her cure written. **She** then told him the particulars. The physician replied that to accept the affair as a miracle, no scar should be found. "Very well," replied Teresa smil**ing, "find** one if you can." He then made a most careful examination and convinced himself of the truth of his patient's statement. He did not hesitate to acknowledge this as **the** work of God. "This instantaneous cure," he wrote in the testimony concerning it, "must indeed be considered a miracle."

In March, 1850, Ursula Solito of Francavilla Fontana, in the diocese of Oria, had a swelling on her forehead, in consequence of which her eye and her whole face became inflamed; as it became cancerous and was continually spreading, it caused her great pain in her head and back. The patient called her sufferings — "the very pains of hell." — The remedies of the physician as well as the advice of a professor who had been consulted had proved useless, and they both agreed that no operation could possibly be performed without accelerating the patient's death. Nothing further could be done, save that a few applications could be made to relieve the sufferer. It was thought necessary to have the last sacraments administered. The affliction of the family at Ursula's disconsolate condition may easily be imagined. The daughter of the sick woman inquired of the physician as to what hopes there were of her mother's recovery. He answered that she could live but a few hours. There happened to be in the room at that time a certain Anna Maria Giancola, who encouraged them to have recourse to heaven alone. She then went to procure a picture of Blessed Gerard, and placed it between the bandages around the head. Then all knelt down and recited the Litany of Our Blessed Lady, and some other prayers. A few minutes later Ursula trembled violently and sat up in bed. She told them she had received a great shock, and had experienced an acute and unusual pain. She then lay down and slept well that night. The following morning, the physicians, upon their arrival, found her in good spirits without any pain and free from fever. The bandages were removed from the forehead, and lo! the terrible cancer had disappeared, leaving no other trace than a very faint red mark. Undoubtedly this cure amazed the physicians. But Ursula said: "I am cured," **not by your** skill, but by the favor of Blessed Gerard. **Both** physicians reserved the honor of this remarkable cure to the servant of God, and considered it of a **supernatural order.**

In April 1867, Lorenzo Riola, a boy ten years old, of S. Giorgio la Montagna, in the archdiocese of Benevento, was ill of incipient dropsy which resisted all the remedies of science and was bringing the child to an early grave. Distinguished professors of Naples were as much at a loss to give advice as the physicians of Benevento. A surgeon of Naples feared the child was not even strong enough to undergo the operation of **tapping.** The child pined away unaided, burning of thirst, and filled with disgust for food and medicine. The boy was in this sad condition when the life of Brother Gerard was given him to read. He immediately conceived a great devotion to him, asked for a relic of his, and received one. He applied this relic to the afflicted part of his body several times, and recited three "Gloria Patris" in honor of the most Blessed Trinity, to obtain a cure through Blessed Gerard's intercession. During the afternoon of one of the last days of August the invalid fell asleep, and in his dreams saw a golden ladder reaching to heaven and leaning against his body. A religious very like Blessed Majella descended the ladder holding a crucifix in his left hand. When he reached the sick boy he stooped with his face turned toward little Lorenzo's body; after some time he disappeared without having uttered a word. From this instant there was a change in the condition of the sick boy; the symptoms of suppuration vanished, **the fever and thirst left** him, the abdomen returned to its normal condition, and every other symptom of the disease vanished. From that time until the 18th. of **June 1879,** when Lorenzo gave testimony of this miracle, he had not experienced the least trace of his former trouble, and had always enjoyed excellent health.

The numerous miracles which the servant of God performed without interruption after his death, spread his reputation, so that he became known not only throughout Italy but in other parts of Europe. On all sides voices were raised, expressing the wish that the Church might pass her decisive judgment on the life and miracles of the wonderful lay-brother.

Father Camillo Ripoli, Superior General of the Congregation, was able to give noble testimony of the great renown of Gerard's sanctity. We quote his words:

"All those," so says this witness, "who knew the great servant of God during his lifetime and saw the splendor of his virtues did not for a moment doubt that immediately after his death he was admitted to the beatific vision. People began to visit his humble grave in our church in Caposele, and day after day the concourse of the faithful augmented, and has not yet ceased. Moved by special devotion towards the servant of God, I too have visited this grave, and his Eminence Philip Caracciolo del Giudice, Cardinal of Naples, assured me in his last illness that he had resolved if he ever was restored to health, to undertake a pious pilgrimage to the same place. It was the opinion which I entertained of the sanctity of Gerard that induced me to enter the Congregation; every day of my life I have endeavored to prove myself grateful to this holy brother.... At the present time the reputation of his sanctity has spread very far; and not only from Rome, the Papal States, and the rest of Italy, but also from Austria and other lands there came petitions for biographies and pictures of the servant of God. This universal reputation of his sanctity finally induced me to take measures to have the process of beatification begun at Rome, for God's greater glory."

Not until the present century was quite advanced was it possible to think seriously of introducing this process. It appears that divine Providence wished **the honors of the Church** to be bestowed upon the father, before his highly favored son should receive them, however, after St. Alphonsus had been enrolled in 1839 in the calendar of saints, active steps were taken to submit the virtues and miracles of the humble lay-brother to the judgement of the Church. In the year 1843 the so-called process of information was begun at Muro, as well as at Conza. There it was opened by Monsignor Gigli, in April of the same year, and was continued during the following two years; **during this time sixty witnesses were** permitted to give their testimony. At Conza, to which Caposele belongs, a similar process was opened on the 13th. of December, 1843, and closed on the 24th. of February, 1845, after ninety-four witnesses had testified. According to custom, **the acts** of the processes were forwarded to the Holy Father at Rome, with a petition to begin the **process of beatification.** Numerous letters from most prominent persons supported this petition to the Pope.

Among these advocates we find the then reigning **King of Naples, Ferdinand II**, who, in his letter, dated the 5th. of September, 1846, calls our servant of God "a Christian hero, of whose virtues and miracles, he heard most astonishing things from trustworthy persons." The Cardinal, Archbishop of Naples, Riario Sforza, also raised his suppliant voice in Gerard's cause; he wished to see the process of beatification **introduced "in order that,"** as he expressed himself, "the admirable example of the servant of God might **be proposed to the imitation** of all, and his incomparable piety might shine as a new star in the firmament **of the Church."**

Similar petitions, with like proofs, were addressed to

the Holy Father by forty-six other bishops of the kingdom of Naples, as well as by many prominent persons of every walk in life.

These requests did not remain without notice. On the 11th. of September, 1847, the introduction of the apostolic process was proposed; and on the 17th. of the same month, Pope Pius IX signed the decree by which Gerard Majella received the honorable title of "Venerable Servant of God."

Again the process regarding the life and virtue of the servant of God was undertaken in Muro and Conza, this time by order of the Holy Father; at Muro from 1850 till 1856. In Muro there were thirty-six persons who testified; in Conza twenty-four. Before the conclusion of this process, the legal examination of the bones of Blessed Gerard was made, at which the miraculous character of the servant of God became evident in the most consoling manner. "We found," relates the present bishop of Nusco, Monsignor Joseph Consenti, C. SS. R. an eye-witness of the fact, "the bones of Blessed Gerard white and dry. Every eye was upon them. At first the head was raised (from the urn) then the physicians approached to count and examine the other bones.

"But what happened at this moment in the presence of all? From the forehead, and later from the entire skull, clear drops similar to lymph were oozing, which flowed quite freely and uniting, ran into the vase (in which bones were lying.) Imagine the emotion of the by-standers at so evident a miracle! Involuntarily, they sank on their knees, burst into tears, prayed, or expressed their surprise in loud exclamations. To the great surprise of all, it was seen that one of the physicians who was supposed to be an infidel, was moved to tears. When the officials were somewhat calmed, they proceeded with the examination of the remaining bones.

These in turn presented the same spectacle as the skull. Hardly had they been laid in the vase, when this liquid oozed from them also, and filled the entire vase with this wonderful liquid, and flowed upon the table and floor." It can easily be imagined what a happy impression it made on all present. It may here be remarked, that the same miracle occurred again at the second examination of the bones of the servant of God, on the 11th. of October 1892.

Though the researches in regard to the virtues and miracles of Gerard had been concluded most successfully, a considerable time passed before the decree was published concerning the heroic degree of the virtues of the servant of God. Sessions were held to this effect March 12th., 1872; March 4th., 1873; and April 21st. 1874, and on the 8th. of June of the same year, the feast of the Sacred Heart. During the feast of his twenty-fifth anniversary as bishop, Pius IX could solemnly declare the virtues of brother Gerard, heroic.

It has been reserved for our present glorious sovereign Pontiff to issue a similar decree regarding the miracles of Blessed Gerard. The difficult examination of the four miracles submitted for that purpose covered more than a decade of years. It was only on the 20th. of November 1888, that the *Congregation of Rites* was in session for the first time; the second council was convened on March 10th., 1891; and the third on January 26th. 1892; which last was conducted most solemnly under the direct supervision of the Holy Father. The decree which recognizes the four miracles was issued on March 25th. of the same year, and one month later, April 25th., 1892, the question of Beatification was proposed and ratified. The decree was published by his Holiness, on the Feast of Our Lady's Nativity, September, 8th., 1892.

Finally, on the 29th. of January 1893, at the time of

the celebration of the fiftieth anniversary of Leo XIII's consecration, the papal brief which admitted Gerard Majella among the number of the Blessed was read in the elaborately decorated hall of St. Peter's. The picture of the servant of was unveiled, and on the afternoon of the same day the Sovereign Pontiff venerated it publicly for the first time.

It is to be hoped that this solemnity has not put an end to the honors which God has destined for the blessed brother, in the eyes of the Church.

We dare to entertain the expectation that she will soon enroll the humble Gerard Majella among the number of her privileged friends and intercessors, and that we may soon be permitted, to approach the blessed Brother with the petition: "Saint Gerard pray for us!"

And now, after having meditated at length on Gerard's strivings, struggles, labors and sufferings, we take leave of him with the sentiments which filled the noble Peter de Blois on having had an opportunity to meditate on the life and labors of a namesake of our servant of God, a quiet monk who so much resembled the latter. These sentiments he beautifully expresses in the following manner:

"A short time ago I saw a brother, named Gerard, who in his last years had no other wish then to die, while he always said with the royal prophet: 'Educ Domine de carcere animam meam' (Bring my soul out of prison.) His desire was to be dissolved and to be with Christ. While we slept, he spent the night in prayer and weeping, longing for eternity, and although a layman and unlettered, he yet had the science of life written in his heart by the finger of God Himself. As to the articles of our faith, he answered with as much caution as if he had spent a large part of his life in the schools of Paris. He was indeed of the schools of the

Apostles; a disciple of Him Who said: 'De excelso misit Dominus ignem in ossibus meis et erudivit me.' (From above He hath sent fire into my bones and instructed me.) Ah! how truly learned and wise he was! What good has the windy loquacity of worldly philosophy done for its votaries? Puffed up with worldly science, they did not know the God of hosts!

"*May therefore my wisdom and philosophy be the philosophy of Brother Gerard, who had in his mouth and heart only Jesus Christ; May my philosophy be that of St. Paul, who declared that he knew nothing except Jesus Christ? and him crucified.*" (*Com. in Job. c.* 5.)

INDEX

CHAPTER. PAGE.

    Approbations.........................II. III.
    Preface to the First German Edition........V.
    Preface to the Second German Edition......X.
    Preface to the Present English Edition...XII.
    Letters Apostolic in Reference to the
    Beatification of Bl. Bro. Gerard..........XIII.
    I. The Highly Favored Child...............21
   II. The Apprentice..........................32
  III. At the House of the Bishop of Lacedogna..40
  IV. Gerard Becomes Foolish for the Love of God.50
   V. On the Road to the Convent..............64
  VI. The Lay-brother........................80
 VII. The Celestial Life of the Novice..........103
VIII. Austere Life and Charity Towards Others..118
  IX. First Public Appearance.
      Religious Profession....................139
   X. The Gatherer of Alms....................159
  XI. Labors at Muro and Corato..............178
 XII. The Angel of Peace at Castelgrande......201
XIII. Sojourn at Melfi. Death of Father Cafaro..214
XIV. Pilgrimage to Mount Gargano............220
 XV. Labors at Melfi and Lacedogna...........235
XVI. Apostolate Among Virgins Consecrated
     to God...............................252
XVII. Spiritual Counsels......................276
XVIII. Stormy Days...........................286
XIX. A Rule of Life..........................306
 XX. At Naples..............................323
XXI. The Porter.............................346
XXII. Heavenly Gifts in Full Splendor..........367
XXIII. Other Apostolic Labors..................386
XXIV. Last Undertakings and Last Journeying...405
XXV. The Cell in which one does the Will of God.429
XXVI. Honors Shown to Gerard After Death.....454

www.ingramcontent.com/pod-product-compliance
Lightning Source LLC
Chambersburg PA
CBHW051854300426
44117CB00006B/385